Every1's Guide® to Electronic Contracts

Contract Law on How to Create Electronic Signatures and Contracts

Charles H. Martin, J.D., M.B.A.

Copyright and Trademark

Copyright © 2013 by Charles H. Martin

First Print Edition: October, 2014

EVERY1'S GUIDE PRESS

ISBN 978-0-9896488-2-0

Additional Online Resources

www.every1sguide.com

www.charleshmartin.com

Dedication

For H.B.M., teacher and librarian, and for A.B.J., English
teacher and literary advisor -- The Encouragers

About the Author

Charles H. Martin is an attorney with more than twenty
years of experience practicing law for private, government
and corporate clients. Mr. Martin has been a full-time
professor, teaching contracts, sales law and international law
at U.S. and foreign law schools and universities. After
graduating cum laude from Harvard College, Mr. Martin
received his Juris Doctor degree from the University of
California (Boalt Hall) School of Law, and his M.B.A. from
Columbia Business School. He lives in Washington, D.C.

Disclaimer

The author and publisher are not engaged in rendering legal or other professional advice, and this publication is not a substitute for the advice of an attorney. If you require legal or other expert advice, you should seek the services of a competent attorney or other professional.

This publication is designed to provide competent and reliable information regarding the subject matter covered. However, it is sold with the understanding that the author and publisher are not engaged in rendering legal, financial, or other professional advice. Laws and practices often vary from state to state and if legal, financial, or other expert assistance is required, the services of a professional should be sought. The author and publisher specifically disclaim any liability that is incurred from the use or application of the contents of this book.

How To Use This Book

This book is written for consumers, professionals and business people, and for students and lawyers. It is intended for those with little or no knowledge of contract law, and for those with a great deal of contract law knowledge. It can be read from start to finish. It can also be read by skipping to specific topics.

In various chapters, I cross-reference other chapters, and sub-chapters, that mention the same subjects. The Table of Contents for the e-book version is interactive. It permits readers to skip to and from a listed item directly. This is useful for quickly navigating to cross-referenced chapters and sub-chapters.

Some e-book devices permit searches of the body of the book for words or phrases, and some permit jumps between the text and referenced endnotes. The Notes section provides the detailed sources for various legal rules, principles and judicial decisions discussed. The Index provides a quick reference to where specific topics are repeatedly mentioned. Although page numbers are not included in the Tables and Index at the end of the e-book version, many e- book formats allow searches for the locations in the text of the listed cases, statutes, treaties, authorities and topics.

This book is intended to increase the knowledge of readers regarding web site and other electronic contracts, which are frequently encountered by anyone using a computer for personal or business purposes. Appendix A and Appendix B present examples of a printed service contract and an electronic sales contract. These examples can be read before the main text to see how the legal concepts described in the main text apply in practice. The examples include cross- referenced links to parts of the book where applicable legal concepts are discussed. These discussions might be understood better by some readers with this practical framework in mind.

This book is also intended to help readers resolve their

print and electronic contract related disputes in a faster, more efficient and less stressful manner. Appendix C presents rules for negotiating contracts (when negotiation is possible) based on my thirteen years of negotiating contracts for a large corporation. Appendix D presents brief descriptions of some dispute resolution problems, and possible paths to solutions. Like Appendices A and B, it can be read before the main text to see how the legal concepts described there apply in practice. Appendix D also includes cross-referenced links to the parts of the book where applicable concepts are discussed.

Whether read from beginning to end, or read in only parts relevant to specific concerns about contract law and electronic transactions, I intend that your time spent reading this book will be useful and practical. To provide context, I have inserted in the text scattered epigraphs from literature, court cases and other sources relevant to contract law, and some "data points" about the expansion of internet and electronic commerce.

Part A and Part B use many brief descriptions of actual litigation, or of facts based on actual cases, as examples of how different rules of contract law are applied in practice. Some of these cases are amusing, and some are interesting for other reasons. The descriptions show how contract law affects real lives and businesses. I believe that contract law is the most interesting and far-reaching of all the categories of law. I hope these descriptions will show how this has been true for many years, and will continue to be true for many years to come.

Part C has fewer case descriptions, because most applications of international contract treaty law are not made in common law courts. They are usually made in arbitration decisions, which do not disclose the details of the facts of legal disputes to the same extent as do common law court decisions. Readers of Part C might want to think about their own actual or potential international contracts to give context to how these rules might affect them.

The information in this book has many sources. I am particularly grateful for the research and analysis of the members of the American Bar Association, Section of International Law, and Section of Business Law, Committee on Cyberspace Law, Subcommittee on International Trade. I have also benefited from the legal discussions of the U.S. Department of State Advisory Committee on Private International Law, and the symposia of the Center for Transnational Business and the Law of the Georgetown University Law Center.

Prologue: The "Cloudy" Trade-off --When You Buy an E-Book, What Do You Own?

<u>Answer</u>: The buyer of an e-book has a very weak property law right called a "license". Like many licenses (think of a spectator's license to watch a baseball game at a ballpark), the e-book license can be revoked by the licensor for many reasons.

The e-book buyer also, however, has contract law rights. These rights may be more useful than some property law rights. This book describes and explains the contract law rights of the buyer of an e-book and of other parties who enter into electronic contracts.

<u>Explanation</u>: In computer jargon, "the cloud" has become a popular buzzword (or buzzphrase). It refers to computer applications, data, files and services that are provided, through the internet, and stored remotely in the computer servers of their providers, rather than in the computer terminals or devices that a customer uses to access them.

Early e-mail services stored their messages in the computers of the service customers. For more than a decade, however, customers have used e-mail services in which messages are stored remotely on the e-mail service providers' computer servers. These messages can only be accessed through the internet. Information processing applications, such as word processing, spreadsheets, and presentation software, are also being shifted from customer devices to remote servers accessible only through the internet.

E-books are a combination of software, through which the e-books are accessed and read, and digital files, which contain the e-book content. E-book sellers refer to their customers' transactions as "buying" e-books. However, a closer review of the actual contract terms governing those transactions, usually referred to as "Terms of Use", reveals some details that are different from printed book purchase contracts.

For example, a recent description of e-book buyer and seller rights states

> Subject to your compliance with these Conditions of Use and your payment of any applicable fees, _____ or its content providers grant you *a limited, non-exclusive, non-transferable, non-sublicensable license to access and make personal and non-commercial use of the Services....*(emphasis added)

> The licenses granted by _____ terminate if you do not comply with these Conditions of Use or any Service Terms ...

> Use of the Software. You may use _____ Software solely for purposes of enabling you to use and enjoy the Services as provided by _____, and as permitted by the Conditions of Use, these Software Terms and any Service Terms....

> *We may cease providing any Software and we may terminate your right to use any Software at any time.* Your rights to use the Software will automatically terminate without notice from us if you fail to comply with any of these Software Terms, the Conditions of Use or any other Service Terms....(emphasis added)

> All software used in any Service is the property of _____ or its software suppliers and protected by United States and international copyright laws....

> In order to keep the Software up-to-date, we may offer automatic or manual updates at any time and without notice to you.

These are typical contract terms that apply to e-book "purchases". What a purchaser owns, under this contract, however, is not a property right to keep or transfer an e-book, as they might keep or transfer a printed book. What the purchaser receives, in return for their money, is a "limited...license to access and make personal and non-commercial use of" the e-book services, software and digital files provided by the e-book seller, which it may terminate "if you do not comply with these Conditions of Use or any Service terms", or which it may terminate "at any time".

Whether, why, and how these types of contract terms may be enforceable against buyers of various on-line computer services and digital goods is one of the subjects of this book. In the recent U.S. Supreme Court case of *Kirtsaeng v. John Wiley & Sons, Inc.*1, a student from Thailand was studying in the United States. He observed that the prices for textbooks printed and sold in Thailand by a U.S. publisher were much lower than the prices for the same books printed in the U.S. He asked his friends and family to buy the textbooks in Thailand, and to send them to him in the U.S., where he sold them for a profit. The books contained statements that they could only be sold in specific regions outside of the U.S. The publisher sued the student for violating its exclusive right, under U.S. copyright law, to distribute its copyrighted work, including its right to restrict importation of such works printed outside the U.S.

A majority of the Supreme Court disagreed with the publisher's argument, deciding that the "first sale doctrine" of U.S. copyright law overcame the copyright owner's exclusive distribution right. The first sale doctrine allows an owner of a lawfully made copyrighted work to sell it without the permission of the copyright owner. The Court majority's decision was justified, in part, by concerns that allowing book publishers to prevent importation of legally made and copyrighted books could lead to serious, and unforeseeable problems for booksellers, libraries, museums, retailers and other importers of foreign-made machines and goods with embedded copyrighted software.

The extensive rights of a printed book owner, under U.S. copyright law, might seem to be equally available to an e-book owner. Thus far they are not. In the case of *Vernor v. Autodesk, Inc.*2, a U.S. purchaser of used copies of computer-assisted design (CAD) software sold them on e-Bay. When threatened with legal action by the software maker, the purchaser sued for a declaratory judgment that his sales were legal under the copyright first sale doctrine. Because Autodesk sold the software pursuant to a limited license agreement, which did not transfer ownership of the software to a buyer, the federal appeals court decided that Vernor could not claim the defense of the copyright first sale doctrine. In 2011, the U.S. Supreme Court denied a petition to review this decision.3

Congress has the constitutional power to amend the Copyright Act, which it enacted, and which it has amended numerous times. The U.S. Supreme Court might someday interpret contracts for the sale of e-book licenses as giving buyers the same copyright first sale doctrine rights that the buyers of printed books enjoy. If, and when the Court makes that judgment, practical considerations might be as important to that decision as they were to the *Kirtsaeng* decision. Some of these considerations are the trade-offs involved in buying an e-book.

E-books cost less than printed books, because they are (much) less expensive to physically produce and distribute. Multiple e-books are much easier to carry and to store than printed books (at least if the user accesses them through a small device like an e-book reader or smartphone). Multiple copies of e-books could also be much easier for a first buyer to make and to distribute than printed books. The substitution of a limited license for use of the e-book, in place of an absolute sale of ownership of the e-book, has been imposed by e-book sellers in exchange for these conveniences.4   It might also be imposed as part of the business strategy of the sellers, in order to capture the future business of customers through the incompatibility of the buyers' already purchased software library with the technical requirements of competing software license sellers. (Do you remember VHS versus Betamax video recorders?)

Until the U.S. Congress, or the U.S. Supreme Court, provides to e-book owners, and other digital software goods buyers, greater copyright ownership rights, they must seek refuge in contract law from any unfair or oppressive terms of exchange imposed by software sellers. This book describes the rules of U.S. contract law, which protect parties to consumer and commercial contracts. These rules include federal and state statutory requirements for "clear and conspicuous" disclosure of sale terms in online advertising, requirements of notice of terms, objective evidence of agreement to terms, and requirements of good faith in contract performance and enforcement. European Union law protecting online consumers is also described.

The protections and rights of parties in national and state contract law, in most cases, extend to businesses, as well as to consumers. International contract law applies only to contracts between businesses. It will also be discussed in detail.

SUMMARY OF CONTENTS

TABLE OF CONTENTS

| Table of Contents

Preface

When I sat in a large lecture hall for my first class in law school, Contracts taught by Friedrich Kessler, I had already made many contracts, whether I knew it or not. The U.S. legal system of judicial decisions, common law cases, statutes, codes, treatises, treaties and Restatements that I learned in that class was often bewildering. One purpose of this book is to make that legal system less confusing for you.

Another purpose is to make the process of obtaining information about contract law and electronic contracts less expensive for you. The internet is a (mostly) free and always available source of information about law and other subjects. The internet links page near the end of this book offers some suggested sources of free information about U.S. law, including contract law.

The e-book format provides new opportunities for the sharing and explanation of information in electronic devices. Its portability is valuable for readers living in parts of the world that are remote from the centers of printed book publishing and distribution. I recall the difficult process of getting printed law books to my students outside of the U.S. I hope that their access to this and other e-books on law, business and other subjects will improve their understanding of United States and international law, and of government and business practices.

I will define and explain the procedural law of U.S. litigation, as and where necessary in the context of describing U.S. contract law. A very brief description is appropriate here for the benefit of non-lawyers and non-U.S. lawyers, because in the U.S. "common law" system, appeals court rulings regarding trial judge decisions, and the reasons for those rulings, can be a non-statutory source of law. When relevant statutes exist, they have priority over conflicting court rulings on the same legal issue.

In the "civil law" legal systems of most non-English speaking nations5, by contrast, statutes and codes (collections of statutes) enacted by legislatures are the dominant sources of law. Judicial decisions are sources of law independent from statutes usually only in appellate court applications of national constitutional rules.

U.S. trials are called "adversary proceedings", because the determination of guilt or non-guilt in criminal trials, and liability or non-liability in civil trials, must be the result of a type of contest between the lawyers for each side. The judge acts only as a neutral referee, rather than as an active participant in the trial, as is true in many civil law systems. A U.S. judge issues rulings on whether evidence or argument presented by lawyers is permitted. In U.S. civil litigation, before arguments are made to a judge or jury, and before evidence is presented, lawyers can make "motions" to the judge to stop the litigation because the "pleadings" (written allegations of facts and legal arguments) made to begin the litigation are insufficient to state a case upon which the plaintiff (the party initiating civil litigation) can succeed. Before evidence is presented, these motions are often called a "motion for a judgment on the pleadings" or a "motion for dismissal for failure to state a claim upon which relief may be granted" or a "motion for summary judgment". If such a motion is granted by the judge, the litigation ends, and the moving party wins.

Many appeals court rulings are made during a review of the granting of such motions by trial judges. The appellate courts review a trial judge's decision usually only for legal errors, and not for errors in evaluation of facts by the trial judge, or by a jury. This is because trial judges and juries are in a much better position than appellate judges to evaluate evidence presented to prove facts. Trial judges see and hear witnesses, see physical evidence, and read documentary evidence. Appellate judges do not see or hear witnesses, and do not see physical evidence. They decide appeals based only on a written transcript of the trial proceedings, the written arguments of the parties, and a brief oral argument by the parties' lawyers.

The opinions that appellate judges write in support of their decisions are the basis for the "common law" of contracts, and of other areas of U.S. law. Only the highest appellate court within any state or federal system is authorized to overturn ("overrule") common law derived from prior appellate decisions. Lower trial courts can only apply prior common law decisions, and cannot overrule them. Lower appellate courts may, however, establish new common law. Most of the cases referred to in this book are decisions of federal or state appeals courts. Some are the decisions of federal trial courts.

In some areas of U.S. law, such as criminal law, statutes and codes are more important than common law. Regarding contracts for the sale of goods, every state, except Louisiana, has enacted a similar version of Article 2 of the Uniform Commercial Code (UCC), a model code drafted by an advisory organization of government experts, and promoted as a vehicle to facilitate interstate commerce through the harmonization of different state laws on contracts for transactions in (primarily sales of) goods. The UCC, and the Florida statutes enacting the UCC (which are similar to most state versions of the UCC) will be referred to frequently in this book.

Finally, state and federal appellate court decisions sometimes refer to scholarly writings for support, particularly where the legal issue has not been clearly addressed by a prior judicial decision or statute. The most popular scholarly resource for judicial decisions on contract law is one of a series of "Restatements of the Law" written and published by a private organization, the American Law Institute. The purpose of the Restatement of the Law (Second) of Contracts (the "Restatement 2d") is to summarize the common law of contracts, as applied by the majority of U.S. state appellate courts. Contract law is primarily state law in the U.S., not federal law. The Restatement 2d will be frequently referred to in this book in support of a description of a common law rule of contract law. The Restatements are private publications that can be purchased in various longer or shorter versions.

They are also often available in the law libraries of U.S. state and municipal trial courts that are open to the public.

Other scholarly sources used by appellate courts to support their decisions on contract law are the treatises of law professors who have taught and written about contract law. The three most important U.S. contract law treatise authors to date have been Samuel Williston in the late 19th and early 20th century, Arthur Corbin in the early and mid-20th century, and E. Allan Farnsworth in the middle to late 20th century.

Datapoint #1

U.S. e-commerce retail sales for the 4th quarter of 2012 were $59 billion, up 15% from the 4th quarter of 2011. Total 2012 e-commerce retail sales were $225.5 billion, up 15.8% from 2011. E-commerce sales in 2012 accounted for 5.2%of total retail sales.

--U.S. Census Bureau News

February 15, 2013

Introduction

If you are reading this e-book on a portable electronic device or computer, you were probably required to make what is called a "click-wrap" contract by clicking on an "Accept" or "I Agree" screen "button". Nearby text might have warned you that by clicking you agreed to certain Terms and Conditions. It might have even warned you that it was your duty to read those terms before agreeing to them.

Before you used your electronic device for the first time, its packaging might have contained an Important Product Information sheet, which included a reference to a License Agreement or Terms of Use that were available at the device maker's web site. The sheet might have contained a statement that "by using the [named] device you agree to be bound by the terms of this [referenced] Agreement". You might then have been informed that if you did not accept the terms of what is called a "shrink-wrap" contract, with its web site terms "incorporated by reference", you could return the device within 30 days for a full refund.

Have you ever wondered what was in these agreements, or terms and conditions? They have proliferated with the growth of electronic computing and electronic reading devices and services. Consumer and business purchasers rarely read these long agreements that could bore even a contract lawyer! Have you wondered what you are committing yourself to by clicking the "Accept" or "I Agree" button, or by keeping a shipped product beyond the time period that a sheet of paper in its packaging states is the limit of your time to return it for a full refund? If you wanted to know the answers to these questions, you have come to the right book.

This book will explain in simple language the legal rules that apply to click-wrap web site contracts, and to shrink-wrap contract product packaging sheets referring to web site contract terms. It will also explain "browse-wrap" contracts formed merely by reading a web page and then using its content or downloading a software application from it, if a notice of terms of use is displayed on that web site. It will also explain the rules for contracts formed through electronic communications like e-mails and text messages.

This book does not cover contracts for transferable property rights that are governed by special commercial laws outside of contract law, such as negotiable promissory notes, chattel paper and documents of title. Neither does it cover many government regulations that mandate specific information disclosures for some consumer transactions.

This book does not address internet user privacy rights and related issues of "cookie"-tracking, information-sharing, and privacy policy disclosures. This is an important and quickly changing area of the law that deserves its own book.

An agreement will be enforceable in court by the parties making it as a "contract" if it meets some basic requirements, and, for some types of contracts, if it satisfies certain formalities.

When I teach the law school course on contracts, my students are often surprised (as you might be) when I tell them that they probably enter into four or five separate contracts every day. When you buy something, like a bus or rail pass, a newspaper or a magazine, or a meal at school or work, you enter into a contract with the company or person who sells that item to you. If you purchase a service, like parking your car in a parking lot, you enter into a contract with the parking lot owner or operator.

Before the internet became a popular method of commerce (sales of goods and services to consumers and businesses), most commercial contracts like these were represented by a printed writing. That writing might be the fine print on the back of a bus or rail pass, or the sales receipt for a newspaper, magazine, meal or parking space. Once the internet became a common method to buy, sell and rent information, entertainment, food, clothes and services, printed proof of the sales contracts that you make through the internet were often not delivered at the time of the purchase, if at all. If you printed a receipt at a later time, it did not have your handwritten signature.

You already know why many of these e-mail and internet electronic contracts are not printed, except on a computer printer at some later time, and are not signed by hand when they are made. It would reduce the advantages of doing business quickly and at a distance through computers if you were required to wait for both parties to exchange printed, signed writings in order for an internet contract to become final and legal. It would make mobile computing a lot less mobile if you needed to wait for a seller of a smartphone "app" to send you a physical receipt in order for your app purchase to be completed.

This book is not written to show you why electronic contracts are necessary and useful to help electronic commerce grow and flourish. By buying an e-book, you have already shown your familiarity with these benefits. It is written to explain to you the laws and practices of the various states and territories, and the federal laws, of the United States, international treaties and model national laws proposed by the United Nations, and the accepted business practices of internet users and service providers, all of which have adapted the traditional requirements for formation of a contract to the digital age.

It is written to show you how these laws and practices

have worked to permit contract formation through methods undreamed of only a few years ago, while maintaining many long-established essential protections for contract parties, and encouraging buyers and sellers to exchange valuable goods and services for their mutual benefit.

PART A – GENERAL CONTRACT LAW IN THE UNITED STATES

Epigraph #1

I began to think it was high time to settle with myself at what terms I would be willing to engage for the voyage. I was already aware that in the whaling business they paid no wages; but all hands, including the captain, received certain shares of the profits called lays, and that these lays were proportioned to the degree of importance pertaining to the respective duties of the ship's company...I made no doubt from all I had heard I should be offered at least the 275th lay – that is, the 275th part of the clear nett proceeds of the voyage, whatever that might eventually amount to...

"Well, Captain Bildad," interrupted Peleg, "what d'ye say, what lay shall we give this young man?"

"Thou knowest best," was the sepulchral reply, "the seven hundred and seventy-seventh wouldn't be too much, would it?"

"Why, blast your eyes, Bildad," cried Peleg, "thou dost not want to swindle this young man! He must have more than that."...

"That's he; thank ye, Bildad. Now then, my young man, Ishmael's thy name, didn't ye say? Well then, down ye go here, Ishmael, for the three hundredth lay."

"Captain Peleg," said I, "I have a friend with me who wants to ship too-- shall I bring him down to-morrow?"... And, after signing the papers, off I went; nothing doubting but that I had done a good morning's work, and that the Pequod was the identical ship that Yojo had provided to carry Queequeg and me round the Cape.

-- from Moby Dick by Herman Melville

Summary of Part A

The Requirements for a Contract and its Enforcement

A contract is a legally enforceable promise, or set of promises. Its legal requirements can be stated as first, a promise to perform (or not perform) some act, which indicates the intention of its maker that the promise be enforceable by law, and second, the absence of any defense against enforceability. The remedies for a breach of contract require the maker of the promise (the "promisor") to either fulfill the contract expectation of the recipient of the promise (the "promisee"), or to compensate them for their reliance on the promise, or to restore them to the position they were in before the contract was breached. While the requirements of a contract can be stated simply, their application to the numerous and various circumstances of commercial, consumer and personal disputes presents a never-ending parade of difficult questions for business people, consumers, individuals, lawyers and, ultimately, judges to resolve.

The Application of Contract Requirements to Various Circumstances

Most contracts are performed to their parties' satisfaction, and are never heard of again. The contracts described in this book are here because they were either not completely performed, or were performed in a way that disappointed one or more of the parties, to the extent that they were willing to spend their time in court, and their money on lawyers, to try to achieve satisfaction. In addition, because most of the contracts described here were the subject of appellate court decisions, the disputes presented by them involved novel issues of contract law, which justified their handling by an appeals court, to which the U.S. legal system assigns responsibility for resolving questions of law.

Besides establishing the requirements for all contracts, Part A introduces you to the writing and signature formalities required for certain types of contracts. These required formalities necessitated the enactment of federal and state statutes making electronic contracts legally equivalent to printed contracts.

Part A describes how contract law might require a contract to include certain unwritten (or unspoken) terms in addition to their written (or spoken) terms. It describes how certain actions, or inaction, might create a legal right to treat a contract as "breached" (broken), which allows the non-breaching party to stop its own performance and to get compensation from the breaching party for certain types of harm (damages) caused by the breach. Part A describes the typical defenses that can be used against a claim of contract breach, and the typical types of compensation that are awarded under contract law for breached contracts for which a defense is either not available, or is not proved.

CHAPTER 1 - What is a Contract?

In the excerpt from Moby Dick that begins Part A, the captains in charge of hiring the crew of the Pequod engage in a brief negotiation of employment with Ishmael. They also engage in what seems to be a sham argument over Ishmael's profit share, which succeeds in making Ishmael happy with receiving a smaller share than he originally believed he deserved. Ishmael "signed the papers" and went away satisfied. Did Ishmael enter a contract?

Every contract begins with a promise. If the promise is enforceable by law, we call it a contract. Lots of promises are not enforceable by law. For example, if a husband promises to take his wife to dinner on Saturday, is that a contract? No, it's a promise that the law will not enforce. If Jane promises to take her best friend Karen to lunch next Tuesday, is that a contract that Karen can take to court (maybe small claims) and enforce through the law? If there are no other relevant facts, it's not a contract.

What if Jane owed $50 to her friend, Karen, and, instead of paying the $50, Jane promised to repay Karen by taking her to a $50 lunch, which Karen agreed to? If at the time for lunch, at the restaurant where they agreed to meet, Jane fails to show up without any excuse, can Karen sue Jane for breaching a contract? Yes, she probably can. Should she take Jane to court? Probably not. People often have legal rights that are not worth enforcing, because it would take more effort and money to enforce those rights than it is worth. If the amount of money at stake were $500, however, rather than $50, it might be worth it to Karen to take Jane to small claims court.

What makes a promise to do something, like paying money or buying lunch, an enforceable contract in some situations, but not other situations? As we will see in more detail in Chapter 4, the law of the state where the contract is made requires certain "elements" of a contract to exist in order for a promise to be enforceable by law. These elements are generally: 1) the "capacity" to enter a contract (age and mental ability), 2) evidence of the intention of the "promisor" (promise maker) to be legally bound to perform his/her promise, through a) either something of value received by the promisor in return for his/her promise ("consideration"), or b) some significant detriment suffered by the "promisee" (promise receiver) that was reasonably and foreseeably suffered because of his reliance on the promise ("detrimental reliance"), 3) a written and signed promise, in some situations, and 4) the absence of any of several defenses to enforcement of the promise.

Exceptions – Firm Offer by Merchant to Buy or Sell Goods; Modification of Sale of Goods Contract

Although most promises for the sale of goods (moveable physical things not including money) require either "consideration" (an exchanged value) or "detrimental reliance" (the foreseeable and reasonable detriment suffered in reliance on a promise) to become enforceable contracts, one type of promise of this kind, a "firm offer" by a merchant to buy or sell goods in a signed writing stating it will not be withdrawn/revoked, is enforceable in most U.S. states for up to three months without either of these usual requirements.6 The position of the merchant as a business person, plus the formality of the written and signed firm offer by the merchant, replace consideration or detrimental reliance as evidence of the intention of the merchant to be legally bound to perform his promise.

Another type of sale of goods promise that does not require consideration or detrimental reliance to be legally binding as a contract is an agreement modifying a contract for the sale of goods.7 For example, if a seller of goods agrees to change the price for the goods before the sale is complete, the buyer is not required to provide any new value to the seller in return for the change, or to suffer any detriment in reliance on the change, in order to enforce the promised change in price. Perhaps, because bargaining is predictable even after an initial sale agreement is formed, no consideration or detrimental reliance is required in this situation. In order to avoid unfair post-sale bargaining, however, Uniform Commercial Code (UCC) §2-209 requires that such modifications must be requested and given in "good faith" and with a legitimate commercial reason.8

CHAPTER 2 - Laws Governing Contracts – Common Law and Commercial Code Law of U.S. States; Federal Diversity Jurisdiction Applicable Law; Federal Law on Contracts for the International Sale of Goods

Epigraph #2

The life of the law has not been logic; it has been experience...The law embodies the story of a nation's development through many centuries, and it cannot be dealt with as if it contained only the axioms and corollaries of a book of mathematics. In order to know what it is, we must know what it has been, and what it tends to become.

-- from The Common Law by Oliver Wendell Holmes, Jr.

a) Common Law and Commercial Code Law of U.S. States

Most of the rules for contracts in the United States come from decisions by state court judges in appeals of trial judgments. When these decisions, and the reasons given for them ("opinions"), are followed in future decisions they are called "precedents". The sum of these precedents on specific legal subjects in a State (or territory) of the United States is called the "common law" of that State. Most contracts are governed by state common law.

The Restatement (Second) of Contracts ("Restatement 2d") is a summary of the common law rules of contract, as applied by a majority of the U.S. states. Like any summary of complex and changing laws, it can never be definitive. Because each state is, in this area, sovereign, it may make different rules for contract law, and any attempted summary will not describe all the variations in common law rules that arise among the states. Nevertheless, the rules stated in the Restatement 2d are a useful general guide to the common law of contracts in the majority of U.S. states.

Contracts for the sale of goods between sellers and buyers in U.S. states are governed not by state common law, however, but by state statutes, collectively called "commercial codes". In the mid-20th century, state legislatures were persuaded, by examples of European commercial codes, to enact more or less uniform versions of the Uniform Commercial Code in order to streamline the formation and enforcement of contracts for the sale of goods, for which legal issues, terms and procedures were routine, repetitive and predictable.

For example, assume Jason goes to his local retailer to purchase soap. He sees the soap that he wants to buy on a shelf, with a posted price that he agrees to pay. He takes the soap to the store clerk (or the automated check-out register). He pays for the soap. He receives a receipt for his payment. He leaves the store with his purchase. Who made the enforceable promise in this situation that was previously stated as necessary for a contract? Was the purchase by Jason a contract? Yes, it was. If the soap turns out to not be what Jason reasonably expected it to be, Jason can enforce the contract by getting his money back.

Because the type of purchase that Jason made is very routine (and numerous) in a modern economy, the Uniform Commercial Code of each U.S. state provides standard rules for this transaction. It might seem that the retailer promises to sell Jason the soap in "offering" it to him at a posted price on its store shelves, and that Jason "accepts" the store's offer by taking the soap to the cash register and paying the posted price. The money paid is the consideration exchanged for the goods that Jason purchases. Under the rules of contract law that we will see hereafter, however, the retailer is considered to only invite an offer to buy from Jason by putting its goods on its shelves with a posted price. By taking the soap from the shelf and presenting it at the cash register with his money, under these rules, Jason offers to buy the soap on the terms of the retailer's invitation. The retailer accepts Jason's offer by taking his payment.

As stated in Chapter 1, many contracts are governed by the law of the state where the contract is made, unless the contract provides otherwise. When the terms of a contract are negotiated, it is possible for the parties to choose a law to govern their contract other than the law of the state where the contract is made. (Part C, Section I, Chapter 1 discusses choice-of-law clauses in contracts.) A contract for the sale of goods is governed by the commercial code law of the state where the contract is made, unless a different law is dictated by one party alone, or is chosen by both parties through a contract negotiation.

b) Federal Diversity Jurisdiction Applicable Law

In federal court litigation, it is possible for law developed through federal appellate judicial opinions, rather than through state appellate judicial opinions, to apply to a breach of contract dispute. When a dispute arises between parties who are citizens (permanent residents) of different states, if the money at stake in the dispute exceeds a required statutory amount ($75,000 in 2012), either party has the right, under the U.S. Constitution9, and under a federal "diversity jurisdiction" statute implementing this constitutional right10, to "remove" the dispute to a federal court in a federal district where one of them is a citizen.

The federal judge deciding a diversity case, however, applies to the case the same law (state common law or code law or other chosen law) that would have been applied by a state judge in the state where the case was removed from. If the state law on the question in dispute is unclear, the federal judge must predict how the state law would apply to the facts. Until a state appellate court says the applicable law is otherwise, other federal trial judges in the same state must then follow the opinion of the federal appellate court on the applicable state law in future diversity cases. Diversity jurisdiction is designed to provide parties with neutral judges, but not to create different law for those judges to apply to their cases.11

c) Federal Law on Contracts for the International Sale of Goods

Another situation in which a federal court will apply its own view of the applicable law to a contract involves federal law in any case governed by a treaty called the Convention on Contracts for the International Sale of Goods (CISG).12 The CISG was proposed by the United Nations in 1980 and ratified (approved) by the United States in 1986. If a contract comes within the jurisdictional scope of the CISG (generally business-to-business contracts between parties with places of business in different nations that have ratified the CISG, and the contract parties have not effectively opted out of the CISG applying to their contract), the CISG will automatically apply to the contract as the "supreme Law of the Land" under the U.S. Constitution.13

The language of the CISG leaves open a lot of questions about how it should apply to a specific contract dispute. More questions have arisen as time has passed since the CISG became effective U.S. law in 1988. (For example, we will look at the question of whether a contract can be made electronically under the CISG in Part C, Section II, Chapter 1.) Federal trial judges are required to answer these open questions when a breach of contract dispute comes to their court by "interpreting" and "construing" the language of the CISG in order to apply it to the dispute before them. These federal judicial interpretations of the CISG, after explicit or implicit approval by federal appellate judges, become a type of federal international contract law of the CISG.

CHAPTER 3 - Legal Rights Similar to Contracts – Restitution (Unjust Enrichment) and Equity

Epigraph #3

BLMIS was operated as if it were the family piggy bank. Each of the Family and Spouse Defendants received, directly or indirectly, huge sums of Customer Property from BLMIS to fund personal business ventures and personal expenses such as homes, cars, and boats. The Family and Spouse Defendants' misappropriation of BLMIS Customer Property ranged from the extraordinary (the use of BLMIS Customer Property to pay for multi-million dollar vacation homes) to the routine (the use of BLMIS Customer Property to pay their monthly credit card charges for restaurants, vacations, and clothing). The means of diverting Customer Property ranged from the simple (merely transferring money to the Family and Spouse Defendants' own personal bank accounts) to the complex (fabricating the purchases of securities on the Family Defendants' personal BLMIS investment advisory account statements and then cashing out those positions). These transfers necessitate a judgment in favor of the Trustee for the benefit of BLMIS and its defrauded customers.

–from Amended Complaint of Bankruptcy Trustee Irving H. Picard against daughters-in-law of convicted Ponzi schemer Bernie Madoff for $54.5 million in unjust enrichment in U.S. Bankruptcy Court, Southern District of New York (May 4, 2012)

United States law is often described as either criminal law or civil law. Criminal law is law that involves offenses against society in general. Criminal "offenses" are always prosecuted in court by government lawyers in cases with headings that indicate the societal interest being vindicated, such as "The People versus Smith" or "The State versus Jones".

Civil law involves all of the other types of laws that govern the relationships of, and interactions among, private parties. When those interactions begin with a promise by one party, or an exchange of promises between parties, we have seen in Chapter 1, a contract might be involved. Some situations that might resemble a contract do not in fact involve a contract, because no promise or exchange of promises exists. Nevertheless, the common law of English-speaking nations (and the civil code law of many non-English speaking nations) provides money damages as a remedy in some of those situations, if an injustice would occur if no remedy were provided. This type of law, and its related remedies, is called the law of restitution or unjust enrichment.

A restitution situation begins with the giving of a benefit, rather than the making of a promise. For example, Dr. Smith finds a stranger, Mr. Jones, lying unconscious on a city street. Mr. Jones does not appear to be inebriated or sleeping. Dr. Smith sees a bruise on Mr. Jones's face and a small trickle of blood coming from his mouth. Dr. Smith immediately gives Mr. Jones emergency first aid and then calls an ambulance that takes Mr. Jones to the closest hospital.

After Mr. Jones is admitted to the hospital, it is discovered that the first aid given by Dr. Smith almost certainly prevented Mr. Jones from dying from a heart attack that caused him to collapse and to hit his head on the sidewalk. It is also discovered that Mr. Jones is the richest man in town. Dr. Smith is a young doctor who only serves the poorest patients in town. He is having difficulty keeping his clinic in business because of a lack of money.

If Dr. Smith later tries to get Mr. Jones to pay him the reasonable value of the emergency medical services he provided, can he recover money from Mr. Jones in a court case for breach of contract? No, because Mr. Jones never promised in any way to pay Dr. Smith for his services. How could he? He was unconscious the entire time that Dr. Smith was helping him.

Dr. Smith might recover the value of his services from Mr. Jones, however, under the common law of "restitution". Restitution law provides that a person who performs professional services reasonably necessary for the protection of another person's life or health may recover a reasonable charge for the services provided, if an injustice would otherwise occur under the circumstances.14

Restitution law is not contract law. It exists to prevent the occurrence of an injustice to one person who provides a benefit to another person, even though the recipient of the benefit never promised to pay for it. Another type of civil law, tort law, exists to compensate people for unjustified harm that is done to them by another person, usually in the form of an injury to their body, to their property or to their reputation. Restitution law exists somewhere between tort law, which compensates for unjustified harm caused to another person, and contract law, which compensates for the unjustified breaking of a promise to another person. Restitution or unjust enrichment compensates for the value of a benefit provided to another person, if an injustice would occur to the person providing the benefit if they were not compensated for it.15

CHAPTER 4 - Requirements, Formalities and Parties

Epigraph #4

"Quick, Bildad," said Peleg, his partner, who, aghast, at the close vicinity of the flying harpoon, had retreated towards the cabin gangway. "Quick, I say you Bildad, and get the ship's papers. We must have Hedgehog there, I mean Quohog, in one of our boats. Look ye, Quohog, we'll give ye the ninetieth lay, and that's more than ever was given a harpooner yet out of Nantucket."…

When all preliminaries were over and Peleg had got everything ready for signing, he turned to me and said, "I guess, Quohog there don't know how to write, does he? I say, Quohog, blast ye! Dost thou sign thy name or make thy mark?" But at this question, Queequeg, who had twice or thrice before taken part in similar ceremonies, looked noways abashed; but taking the offered pen, copied upon the paper, in the proper place, an exact counterpart of the queer round figure which was tattooed upon his arm; so that through Captain Peleg's obstinate mistake touching his appellative, it stood something like this: --

Quohog. His X mark.

- from Moby Dick by Herman Melville

a) The Requirement of a Promise/Offer – Express or Implied

As stated in Chapter 1, all contracts begin with a promise. In contract law, the promise that begins a contract is called an offer. Once the offer is accepted, and either the requested consideration for the promise is provided, or reasonable and foreseeable detrimental reliance by the offeree occurs, a contract is formed.

An offer is an indication of an intention to enter a contract.16 Usually, it is a spoken or a written promise, and it is unambiguously a commitment to do something. In that case it is called an "express" promise, to indicate that the commitment has been expressed in spoken or written language. For example, if John tells Bob "I will pay you $50 for washing and detailing my car today at 3 p.m.", this is an express promise.

Some promises are made impliedly, however, by the words or the actions of the offeror/promisor. For example, if Bob tells John "I will wash and detail your car at 3 p.m. today at my house, if you pay me $50", and then John brings his car to Bob's house at 3 p.m. and leaves it without saying anything, then John has probably made an implied promise to pay Bob $50 for washing and detailing his car.

Both kinds of promises must be commitments. For example, if John tells Bob "I will pay you $50 for washing and detailing my car the next time I need it", this is not a clear commitment because it will never be clear exactly when the next time will be that John's car needs washing and detailing. Similarly, if, in response to Bob's offer to wash and detail John's car for $50 at 3 p.m., John merely says "Sounds like a nice idea", this is not a clear commitment, because John is not clearly and presently indicating that he wants Bob to wash and detail his car at 3 p.m.17

How can you tell whether or not a clear commitment to do something has been made, expressly or impliedly, which amounts to a promise? U.S. common law provides that the meaning of a spoken or written expression or an action is tested by how an average "reasonable person" would understand its meaning.18 In the examples of the previous paragraph, it is likely that most average, reasonable people would not believe that John had clearly committed to paying Bob $50 for washing and detailing his car by saying only "Sounds like a nice idea". This test is called the "objective test" of whether or not a promise is made. A "subjective test" would, in contrast, test the existence of a promise by determining whether or not the speaker herself believed that her statement was a clear commitment to do something. Although the subjective test was used before the 20th century in U.S. law, it eventually became too difficult to use accurately to determine what an alleged promisor really believed (if anything) about the legal effects of her statements or actions. The easier-to-use objective test was, therefore, substituted for the less practical subjective test.19

b) The Requirement of Acceptance of an Offer

The promise that begins the process of contract formation is called an "offer". As described in Chapter 4, a), it is sometimes difficult to determine who is making an offer in a sale of goods situation. A person might think that an advertisement of goods for sale or the placement of goods for sale on a store shelf would be an offer to sell those goods. U.S. law, however, says that an advertisement of goods or services, or a placement of goods on shelves, without other language permitting the reader to legally bind the advertiser, is not a contract offer.20 It is instead an invitation for a buyer to make an offer to buy the goods or services from the seller.

i) Exceptions to revocability of offers – "Option contracts" and "Firm offers"

Why is it important to determine which of several statements or actions is a contract offer? It is important because most offers do not remain open forever. The offeree, the person to whom the offer is made, cannot take all the time that they want to think about the offer, and whether or not to accept it. Usually, this would be unfair to the offeror. Consequently, the offeror may usually revoke his offer at any time before it is accepted by the offeree.21

U.S. common law requires that, in order for an offer to remain open beyond the normal time reasonably necessary to accept it, the offeree must provide something of value to the offeror in return for this "option" to delay accepting the offer for an agreed period of time.22 The Uniform Commercial Code rule about such "irrevocable offers", called the "firm offer" rule, however, provides that

An offer by a merchant to buy or sell goods in a signed writing which by its terms gives assurance that it will be held open is not revocable, for lack of consideration, during the time stated or if no time is stated for a reasonable time, but in no event may such period of irrevocability exceed 3 months; but any such term of assurance on a form supplied by the offeree must be separately signed by the offeror."23

ii) Methods of Acceptance – Bilateral and Unilateral Contracts

Methods of acceptance of offers usually are dictated by the offeror's indication that she wants the offeree to accept either by making a promise to do something, or by actually doing something required by the offeror.24 For example, if John tells Bob "I will pay you $50 if you promise to wash and detail my car at 3 p.m.", John wants Bob to both promise to perform this work, and to actually do the job. This promise-for-a-promise bargain is called a "bilateral" contract.

On the other hand, if John offers $50 to Bob for washing and detailing his car at 3 p.m. at his home, but he does not ask or expect Bob to promise anything to him (for example, if John said "If you come by my house and wash and detail my car at 3 p.m., I will pay you $50"), this would be a promise-for-a-performance bargain called a "unilateral" contract. John does not want Bob to accept his offer by promising to do anything. John asks Bob to accept his offer by actually washing and detailing his car at a specified time and place. The offeror is the "master of the offer" and controls how the offer must be accepted.

c) The Requirement of Either Consideration or Detrimental Reliance

i) Requested Consideration

The requirement that either consideration or detrimental reliance must exist in order to form a contract is related to the requirement of acceptance of an offer. An offer must be accepted in order to bind the offeror to fulfill her promise and to prevent her from revoking her offer. The purpose of the consideration or detrimental reliance requirement is to separate agreements formed by acceptances through promises (for bilateral contracts), and through non-promise performances (for unilateral contracts), that merit legal enforcement from those that do not merit such enforcement. The existence of consideration, or detrimental reliance, is treated by contract law as evidence that the parties (or at least one of them) intended their bargain to be legally enforceable.

An early test for determining the existence of consideration was whether a benefit to the promisor, or a detriment to the promisee, would occur through the promisee's acceptance of the offer and performance of the terms of the acceptance. For example, an uncle tells his nephew that he will give him his coat to keep as his own if the nephew takes the uncle's payment for the dry cleaning of his coat to the cleaners, where the nephew was going anyway. If the nephew agrees, but the uncle changes his mind and refuses to give his coat to the nephew, does the nephew have a contract that he can enforce against his uncle? Most lawyers and judges would say no. It is not because a nephew cannot sue his uncle for breach of contract. For better or worse, family members sue each other in court frequently.

The reason that many lawyers and judges say that the nephew cannot sue his uncle to enforce a contract on these facts is that neither consideration nor detrimental reliance exists. There is no consideration, because there appears to be no significant benefit to the promisor-uncle from the promisee-nephew picking up the cleaning. (Judges will not measure the value of a requested benefit, so let's assume there is none here, because the uncle could get the coat as easily as the nephew; and let's assume there is no detriment to the nephew from picking up the coat, since he was going to the cleaners anyway.) It is said that, based on these facts, the uncle merely promised a gift to his nephew with a condition that the nephew had to pick up the gift. Gift promises are not enforceable if they are broken.

How might consideration or detrimental reliance have been created in this situation? If the uncle had requested his nephew to rearrange his plans to pick up the coat from the cleaners, and he did so, this would be a specific detriment to the nephew (and benefit to the uncle) that would amount to consideration.25

This example shows, however, that the benefit/detriment search made enforceability of a contract turn on the existence of very small differences. In order to avoid a hair-splitting search for consideration through benefits or detriments, the modern test of consideration requires only a mutual exchange of promises that is "bargained for".26 This does not mean that each party has actual bargaining power, but that each party understands that their promise is necessary in order to receive the other party's promise. The act that is promised must not be a pre-existing legal obligation.27

The modern criticism of the consideration requirement does not mean that U.S. state courts have eliminated it from their checklist of contract requirements. It only means that most judges will not try to determine if a promised performance is an actual benefit or detriment. For example, marriage is sometimes described as the required consideration for a pre-nuptial agreement dividing assets upon death or divorce.28

Even with such evidence of consideration, contrary evidence of the circumstances of a promise can show that it was not intended by the promisor to be legally enforceable, and that it should not be so perceived by reasonable third parties. For example, promises made to family members and promises made as jokes are often not intended to be legally enforceable. The impossibility of a judicial evaluation of the subjective worth of a promise to another person, and the formalistic character of consideration, has caused it to be eliminated as a contract requirement in international commercial law.29 Civil law nations require some contracts to be notarized in order to be enforced.

This history of formalism in U.S. contract formation rules often leads to a formalism in contract drafting (writing) through the recitation of the existence of consideration in a signed, written contract. Written contracts often recite that "In exchange for one dollar hereby given and other good and valuable consideration, the parties hereby agree that…". This is totemic language for assuring the enforceability of a promise. If the promise is important enough to enforce through legal procedures, U.S. contract law will evaluate any evidence created by contract parties, prior to their dispute, of their intention to make a legally enforceable agreement, such as through compliance with contract formalities. Such language does no harm, and it may become useful for this purpose.

ii) Foreseeable and Reasonable Detrimental Reliance

In the early 20th century, a contract situation arose for which, many lawyers and judges believed, the U.S. legal requirement of consideration created an injustice. For example, a lender promises a borrower that, if he completely pays off his loan on a certain date before it is otherwise due to be completely paid, then the lender will allow the borrower to pay less interest on the loan. The lender thereby makes an offer for a unilateral contract to the borrower that can only be accepted by paying off the loan on a certain date. When the date arrives and the borrower comes to pay off the loan, however, the lender refuses to accept the payment. The borrower sues the lender for breach of contract, but the lender defends by saying that he had requested acceptance of the unilateral contract offer by the performance of paying off the loan. Since the borrower did not pay off the loan before the lender revoked his offer (by refusing the payment), there was no consideration and no contract.30

Section b) i) above stated that a promisee, such as the borrower, might protect himself against revocation of an offer by paying a promisor, such as the lender, to keep his offer open for a certain period of time as an "option contract". Promisees will not, however, always foresee that promisors might revoke their unilateral contract offers. If a promisee suffers a loss or detriment, because she reasonably and foreseeably relies on a promise inviting an acceptance by performance, lawyers and judges gradually came to believe that an injustice would occur. To remedy this type of injustice, a new common law rule was proposed and gradually accepted, whereby an option contract/irrevocable offer could be created not only by payment of consideration, but also by the beginning, or the tendered beginning, of the performance required for acceptance of the unilateral contract.31

The substitution of "detrimental reliance" for consideration in contract formation requirements eventually spread from option contracts to contracts in general, with certain safeguards required to prevent enforcement of promises that should not have been expected to be enforced by law. The common law rules that were eventually developed required that 1) a promise be made that the promisor should reasonably expect to induce (cause) 2) action or forbearance (inaction) 3) by the promisee or a third person 4) which action or inaction actually occurs, and 5) injustice can only be avoided by enforcement of the promise. The rules also required that the remedy granted for breach of a "detrimental reliance" contract "may be limited as justice requires".32 This remedy limitation does not exist for contracts with consideration, and its importance will be described in Chapter 8 below.

For example, if our lender in the situation described above 1) should have reasonably (according to an objective "reasonable person" test, rather than a subjective "actually expected" test) expected that his promise would cause 2) the borrower to 3) sell his property to raise the money to pay off his debt on the requested day ahead of schedule, and 4) the borrower did in fact sell such property, then 5) an injustice would occur if the borrower sold the property at an unusually cheap ("fire sale") price to pay off the debt, at which he would have not have otherwise sold. Because the borrower now has neither the property he sold, nor the benefit of saving money on a loan paid off early, a judge could determine that a contract was breached by the promisor/lender, even though the requested consideration by performance was not provided by the promisee/borrower.

Allowing contracts to be created through detrimental reliance, as a substitute for consideration, became more acceptable through the 20th century in U.S. law. Once accepted as a new way to form a contract, however, detrimental reliance contracts remained an exception to the normal method of contract formation. Most U.S. contracts today continue to be created through the exchange of requested promises.33

d) Required Formalities of Writing and Signature ("Statute of Frauds")

Most contracts do not require specific formalities in order to be enforceable. The typical daily contracts that we make are very informal, especially our contracts to buy goods or services. Money is exchanged for goods or services and the transaction is documented by a receipt or a ticket. Most contracts can be formed by oral statements of offer and acceptance, or even non-verbal actions that indicate to a reasonable person the existence of an offer and an acceptance. The terms of a contract are documented by posted prices, and by other terms disclosed in and on the packaging of goods, or on the reverse side of a ticket for services. For example, if a shopper takes a product from a store shelf to a cashier, offers money for payment, and the cashier subtracts the payment from the money offered and returns the difference to the buyer with a receipt, a contract has been formed even without any words being said.

In U.S. law, however, certain types of contracts do require specific formalities. These formalities are the requirements that the contract be documented "in writing", and be "signed" by the party against whom the contract is to be enforced. Part B discusses how these requirements are satisfied by electronic contracts.

Origins of the Statute of Frauds in Jury Trials

U.S. common law has its roots in English common law. One unusual aspect of both legal systems is the jury trial. The trial by jury was not invented in England. The philosopher Socrates was tried for treason by vote of a jury of five hundred Athenian citizens.34 Its reinvention in England, however, made it a hallmark of the "adversarial" character of common law trials in most English-speaking nations, in contrast to the "inquisitorial" character of trials in many non-English speaking, civil law nations, where fact determinations are not made by juries. In civil law systems, a judge both investigates the facts and applies the law without the participation of a "jury of peers".

The Fifth Amendment to the U.S. Constitution provides

In suits at common law, where the value in controversy shall exceed twenty dollars, the right of trial by jury shall be preserved, and no fact tried by a jury, shall be otherwise reexamined in any Court of the United States, than according to the rules of the common law.

Similar rights to jury trials in civil cases are provided in U.S. state constitutions.35

Oral testimony is the primary method of introduction of evidence of relevant facts into the official record of a common law trial. The unreliability, or possible bias, of trial witnesses regarding their memory of relevant facts was apparent very early in the evolution of the modern English jury trial. The fear that minimally educated jurors might be misled by the faulty recollections of biased witnesses led the English Parliament in 1677 to enact the so-called "Statute of Frauds". This statute required certain types of contracts to be documented in writing, and signed by the party against whom the contract was to be enforced, in order to be enforceable in court. The idea was that a few types of contracts were so infrequently made, and/or were so important in their impact on wealth or well-being, that the imposition of a requirement that they be written and signed was a small burden to require for the benefit of their enforceability by law.

Types of Contracts that Must be Written and Signed

Although it has been severely reduced in importance in England, most U.S. states maintain statutory requirements for written and signed contracts concerning specific subjects. In practice, the most frequent types of contracts that must be written and signed are 1) a contract for the sale of an interest in land, 2) a contract that is to be performed later than one year from its making, and 3) a contract to pay the debt of another person.36 In addition, under the UCC §2-201(1), a written and signed contract is required for 1) a contract for the sale of goods for the price of $500 or more37, 2) a contract for the sale of personal property (not otherwise covered by the sale of goods statute) enforceable for more than $5,000 in amount of value of remedy38, and 3) a contract creating a security interest in personal property or fixtures not in the possession of the secured party.39

In the epigraph at the beginning of this Chapter, the Pequod captains had Ishmael and Queequeg "sign the papers" to join the crew for their whaling voyage. Whaling voyages from Nantucket, Massachusetts to the Pacific Ocean and back in the early 19th century often took more than a year to complete. A signed contract might have been required under the Statute of Frauds rule for "a contract that is to be performed later than one year from its making".

For example, Pat orally promises to pay Alex $100 a month to clean her yard and watch her house while Pat makes three business trips. Alex orally agrees. Pat doesn't know when she will make the business trips. Because it is possible that Pat will make business trips later than one year from the date of their agreement, the contract is covered by the second rule stated above, namely "a promise in a contract that is not to be performed within one year from its making". However, if Pat completes all three trips and Alex completes his work, Pat cannot escape her contract obligation, because an exception to the signed writing requirement makes a contract enforceable "[W]hen one party to a contract has completed his performance".40

Statutes of Frauds commonly provide that a sufficient "writing" must a) reasonably identify the subject matter of the contract, b) identify the parties to the contract, and c) state with reasonable certainty the essential terms of the promises in the contract.41 Statutes of Frauds commonly provide that a "signature" may be any symbol made or adopted with an intention to authenticate the writing as that of the signer.42 Other rules might provide exceptions to these basic requirements.43 As noted above in Chapter 4, c) i), regarding consideration, even though a contract might not be required to be written and signed, these formalities can later become very useful in proving the validity of the contract, or its required duties of performance.

e) Contract Parties

i) Assignment of Rights and Delegation of Duties

Most contracts are made between only two parties. Sometimes those contract parties might be corporations doing business through many officers and other employees. A contract party might be a married couple jointly buying or selling a house. More complicated contracts can have multiple parties responsible for multiple duties of performance.

Contract rights are treated like other personal property rights under U.S. law. Contract rights can be transferred from the original holder of the rights to a new party who was not originally a party to the contract. State contract law typically permits an "assignment" (complete transfer) of contract rights from their original holder to a new party, unless this transfer a) would materially change the duty of the other party to perform the contract, b) would materially increase the burden or risk imposed on the performing party by the contract, c) would materially impair the performing party's chance of receiving its promised return performance, or d) would materially reduce the value of the return performance.44 Thus, the law generally favors the assignability of contract rights, although in limited circumstances assignments may be validly prohibited by the contract itself.45

For example, Jackie hires Shannon as a lawyer to represent her in a negligence lawsuit against Brenda for a personal injury. Jackie later is treated by Dr. Casey for her injury. Because she has no money to pay Dr. Casey, Jackie sends Shannon a letter asking Shannon to subtract from any money that Jackie wins, in the lawsuit against Brenda, an amount equal to the medical bill that Jackie owes Dr. Casey. Shannon and Dr. Casey agree with this method of payment. If, after she wins her lawsuit against Brenda, Jackie changes her mind and asks Shannon to pay all the money to her and none to Dr. Casey, Shannon must ignore this second request and pay Dr. Casey according to Jackie's letter. Jackie's letter was a valid assignment of her rights in the legal judgment to Dr. Casey, to the extent of her medical bill. It did not materially change Shannon's duty as a lawyer to represent Jackie, nor did it materially increase any risk to or burden upon Shannon.46

State contract law might prohibit assignments of certain types of contracts for public policy reasons.47 A contract itself can also prohibit the assignment of rights derived from it, if the prohibition is written clearly and unambiguously.48

Like an assignment of rights, a contract party can delegate its duty of performance under a contract to a substituted party, unless this delegation a) is prohibited by the contract terms, b) is contrary to state public policy, or c) is contrary to the substantial interest of the party receiving the performance in having the original party perform or control the acts promised. An assignment of rights eliminates those rights in the assigning party. Unless otherwise agreed by the party to whom the performance is owed, however, a delegation of duties does not eliminate the duty of the delegating party until the performance is actually completed.49

For example, Marion signs a contract with the famous

portrait painter Orlando to paint Marion's portrait. Before the portrait is painted, however, Orlando tells Marion that he has assigned his duty to paint Marion's portrait to his assistant Oliver, a younger and less experienced portrait painter. The price of the portrait has not changed. Even if the contract says nothing about assignability of contract rights or delegation of duties, the assigned duty will not be valid, because it is contrary to Marion's substantial interest in having his portrait painted by a well-established painter, rather than by a lesser-known artist.

ii) Third Party Beneficiary Contracts

Certain types of contracts are intended to provide a benefit to a person or entity that is not a direct party to the contract. Such a third party might thereby have enforceable contract rights. Contract rights are enforceable by a "third party beneficiary" if a) the contract parties have not otherwise prohibited such enforcement by a third party, and b) i) the circumstances of the contract indicate to the contract parties that one of them intended to give the third party the benefit of his promised performance, or ii) performance of their promise will satisfy an obligation of the contract party to pay money to the third party beneficiary.50

For example, Ted and Alice agree with First Bank to use a construction loan from the bank to build their new house. The loan proceeds are disbursed by First Bank according to the stages of completion of the house. First Bank hires Accurate Appraisers to monitor the stages of completion of the house and to recommend payments of the construction budget according to the percentage of building completion. On November 1, Accurate Appraisers certifies to First Bank that the building of the house is 100% complete and that 100% of the loan funds should be disbursed to the builder. In fact, only 25% of the building has been completed. First Bank pays the builder 100% of the loan funds and tells Ted and Alice that they must reimburse First Bank for the 100% of the loan amount it paid to the builder, because the disbursements were approved by Accurate Appraisers. Even though Ted and Alice did not enter into a contract directly with Accurate Appraisers (AA), they can sue AA for breach of its contract with First Bank, as third party beneficiaries of First Bank's contract with AA. AA knew that it was First Bank's intention that AA's appraisals of the percentage of building completion would be done to benefit Ted and Alice by protecting them from owing more to the bank for its construction loan for the building of their new home than was justified by the percentage of building completion.51

A third party beneficiary, with enforceable contract rights, has the additional advantage of not being subject to certain contract defenses that the contract promisor might have against the contract promisee, nor to certain defenses that the contract promisee might have against its duty to deliver its contract performance to the third party.52

CHAPTER 5 - What Are The Terms of a Contract?

a) Interpretation of Contract Language and Parol Evidence Rule

The terms of a contract are the rules for its performance. They might be written in a printed (or electronic) contract, or be spoken or shown by actions in an oral contract.

Complications arise, however, if the terms of a contract are both written and orally stated, or if a contract is based on one or more unwritten and unstated assumptions, such as that a separate group of terms will be automatically added to the contract, because the contract is of a type for which such "outside" terms are usually included. In addition, the words of every language, including English, can be ambiguous and susceptible to more than one meaning.53 It is the job of contract lawyers to argue, and of a judge and jury in contract litigation to decide, what intended meaning and what final and legally binding results are created by the language of a contract, if a disagreement arises regarding it. It is even more important, however, for good contract lawyers to avoid such expensive disputes by making the terms of their contracts as clear as possible when they are negotiated and written.

The process of determination of the intended meaning and legal result of contract language is called "interpretation". The determination of the intended meaning of enacted legislation is called "statutory construction". As described above in Chapter 4 on contract formation, modern U.S. contract law generally determines the meaning and legal result of contract words and actions by an "objective" or reasonable person standard, regardless of the meaning intended by one of the parties. The meaning is given to words and actions that a reasonable third person would give to them, rather than any unique "subjective" or personal meaning that the offeror or offeree might give such words or actions.54

For example, Wilma agrees to pay Betty for Betty to feed and walk her dog, Boomer, while Wilma is at work. Wilma suspects that Betty is not taking Boomer outside for walks.

She sets up a surveillance camera that shows that Betty is not walking her dog. If, when confronted by Wilma, Betty argues that she met her obligation by walking the dog inside the house, a reasonable person would not believe that a contract, which requires "walking the dog", is satisfied by walking a dog inside a house.

In order to prepare parties for their contract duties, and in order to make the interpretation of contract language as consistent and predictable as possible, courts and legislatures have developed some rules for interpretation of contract language. Some of the rules follow "common sense", such as the rule that words and other conduct are interpreted in the light of all of the circumstances, and the rule that if the principal purpose of the parties is ascertainable it is given great weight.55 Other common sense rules are that a writing will be interpreted as a whole, and that all writings that are part of the same transaction are interpreted together.56 Similar rules are that, unless a different intention is made clear, the general meaning of language used in a contract applies57, technical terms are given their technical meaning when used in a transaction within that same technical field58, and terms with special meaning in a particular trade are given that special meaning.59

Other rules of interpretation derive not from a "wisdom of the crowd" or "common sense" source, but rather from the experience of judges in many contract cases regarding the most reliably accurate interpretations of contract language. For example, a judge can give a term the meaning that the parties by their practices acknowledge through their "course of performance" of the contract.60 Similarly, if the parties' words or actions in the process of forming a contract show that they intended a contract term to have a particular meaning, a judge can give the term that meaning shown by the parties' "course of dealing".61

Sometimes, however, the parties will disagree on the meaning intended to apply to contract language. They might even dispute that all of the terms that they agreed upon are written in the contract that they signed. Because of the frequency of these types of disputes, U.S. judges and legislatures developed a number of rules, collectively referred to as the "Parol Evidence Rule", to determine how contracts must be written in order to allow or disallow the later addition of terms that were not part of the original written and signed agreement.62

The most commonly used, and usually successful, technique for defeating an argument that later terms should be added to an already written and signed contract is the use of a so-called "merger clause". A merger clause states that the written terms of a contract are the only terms of the contract, and that no other statements or writings can be included in the terms of the contract, if they were not included in the written contract.

b) Implied Contract Terms

Contract parties are required to agree on the contract's essential terms. This is necessary in order to know how the contract should be enforced by a court. The consideration to be exchanged, the timing of the exchange, and how the contract is generally to be performed are examples of essential terms. There are enforceable aspects of contract performance, however, that the parties can reasonably expect, without being specified in detail in the contract.

For example, Lucy, a fashion designer, hires Otis, a licensing agent, to obtain licensing agreements with manufacturers for Lucy's designs, for which Otis will be paid a percentage of each license's value. The employment contract gives Otis the exclusive right to represent Lucy in all her licensing deals. Lucy later signs a licensing deal with a manufacturer without Otis's knowledge or participation. Otis sues Lucy for breach of the exclusive representation provision of the contract. Lucy argues that no enforceable contract existed because, although Lucy committed herself to refrain from licensing deals without Otis's representation, Otis did not commit to take any specific action and therefore provided no consideration.

In "exclusive representation" contracts, like the one described above, common law court decisions, and statutes, have determined that a promise to represent someone as an exclusive agent for business purposes is a contract in which the law implies a good faith "duty of reasonable efforts" to actually try to obtain business for the represented party.63

The basic reason for this implied duty, like many other implied duties, is that, without it, one party could take unfair advantage of the other by using the formalities of contract law to defeat the other party's reasonable expectations. Another example is a contract in which one party commits to buy all of its "requirements" of a certain product from one source. The source, the other contract party, benefits from an implied contract term that imposes on the first party a duty to conduct reasonable business activities that would require the product, which must then be obtained from the single source.64

UCC §2-207 was developed to make routine sales of goods easier by allowing them to be made pursuant to informal contracts, such as purchase orders and invoices. These routine documents, combined with the statements and actions of a buyer and a seller, can create a contract, even if they do not describe every action required for performance of that contract. The exchanged documents might even contradict each other regarding the terms of the contract that they form, because business parties usually include standard terms of sale or purchase that are written to favor themselves. UCC §2-207 attempts to reconcile this "battle of the forms" by establishing detailed rules by which the parties (or their lawyers) will understand which standard form terms are included in the final contract, and which terms are not included.

Unless otherwise agreed by the parties, the UCC will imply, into a contract, terms for the place of delivery of goods65, time of payment66, party bearing risk of loss of goods in transit67, and a buyer's right to inspect   goods delivered.68   The UCC has created these "missing terms" based on the collective trade practices and customs of many industries. The purposes of the Uniform Commercial Code are stated as:

(a) To simplify, clarify and modernize the law governing commercial transactions.

(b) To permit the continued expansion of commercial practices through custom, usage and agreement of the parties.

(c) To make uniform the law among the various jurisdictions.69

Besides implementing the UCC's purpose to promote efficiency in the sale of goods by implying reasonable missing terms, implied-by-law terms are also intended to fulfill the parties' demonstrated intentions to form a binding contract and to avoid unfairness through the manipulation of contract form over substance.70

It is impossible, however, for contract law, as applied by judges or as enacted by legislators, to anticipate every situation in which a missing contract term should be implied. Therefore, a general "duty of good faith" has been imposed by the UCC on both parties during the performance and enforcement stages of a contract for the sale of goods71, and has been imposed by common law judicial decisions, at least in the stages of performance and enforcement of all other contracts.72 A duty of good faith has even been imposed by common law judicial decisions in some cases during the formation stage of a contract, either directly or by providing negative legal consequences for bad faith behavior in contract formation.

"Good faith" is defined by UCC §1-201(19) as "honesty-in-fact" for all types of parties, which at least excludes behavior like lying or deception.73 In addition to the more subjective "honesty-in-fact" standard, UCC §2-103(1)(b) imposes on "merchants" (generally persons who sell goods for a living) a more objective standard of the observance of reasonable commercial standards for fair dealing in the trade.74

For example, Mario agrees to buy a used car from Richard for $2,000. They sign a written sale agreement on Monday. The car is agreed to be delivered to Mario in one week. When the contract is signed, the car has 80,000 miles on its odometer. Nothing is mentioned in the contract about the mileage of the car. Without telling Mario, Richard decides to take one last vacation in his car. He drives it to Florida and back during the week before it is to be delivered to Mario. This adds 4,000 miles to the car's odometer and substantial wear and tear. The next Monday, when he discovers this, Mario argues that he is not obligated to fulfill his contract promise to buy the car because of this unexpected use by Richard. Most judges and lawyers would agree with Mario that, unless Richard disclosed to Mario that he would take a substantial trip in the car between entering the contract for sale and delivering the car to Mario, Richard has violated the duty of good faith in performance of the contract implied into the contract terms by the UCC. Mario would not be obligated to complete his performance of the contract by paying the previously agreed price for the car. He could also refuse to buy the car at all.

c) Warranties

The American economy changed in the 19th century from an individual tradesman, "village blacksmith" model into a mass market model for the selling of goods. Under the old model, a "buyer beware" rule forced consumers and businesses to determine by personal inspection whether or not the goods they purchased were of the quality reasonably expected by a buyer. The separation of manufacturing from retailing in an industrial supply chain, however, prevents buyers from being able to personally determine the quality of the goods they purchase. Therefore, beginning in the late 19th century, judges began to impose "implied warranties" of quality into contracts for the sale of goods. A warranty is a guarantee. An express warranty is a guarantee stated orally or in writing. Many retailers are reluctant, however, to give an express warranty of quality for goods that they themselves have not manufactured.

As early as 1906, the Uniform Sales Act required sale of goods contracts to include implied warranties of general quality. These warranted that goods sold with a particular description would comply with that description, or that goods sold by sample would be representative of the sample. In the 1950s, the Uniform Commercial Code (UCC) expanded these statutory warranties.

UCC §2-313 added "express warranties" that were automatically created by a) any affirmation of fact or promise made by a seller to the buyer which relates to the goods and become part of the basis of the bargain, and which thereby creates (regardless of seller intent) an express warranty that the goods shall conform to the affirmation or promise; b) any description of the goods which is made part of the basis of the bargain, and which thereby creates (regardless of seller intent) an express warranty that the goods shall conform to the description; and c) any sample or model which is made part of the basis of the bargain, and which thereby creates (regardless of seller intent) an express warranty that the whole of the goods shall conform to the sample or model. In order to avoid the automatic creation of legal guarantees out of the inevitable sales practice of "puffing" (praising the general worthiness of the goods for sale), the UCC express warranty rules do not apply to an affirmation merely of the value of the goods or a statement purporting to be merely the seller's opinion or commendation of the goods.75 Buyers are expected to not rely on the positive opinion that sellers have of their own goods. Some tests of a warranty versus mere "puffing" are whether the substance of a statement can be proved to be true or false, and whether the seller's true opinion was misrepresented.76

For example, Alex signs a contract with Barry to buy a birchbark canoe. Alex tells Barry that she wants to use the canoe to paddle in it to her favorite fishing spot. When Alex asks Barry whether the canoe will be suitable to use to paddle on the river for fishing, Barry says "Sure, it will get you there." After Alex buys the canoe and takes it onto the river, the canoe leaks so badly that it sinks. An expert on canoes later tells Alex that she has purchased an antique reproduction canoe that is not designed for actual water use. Barry has made an express warranty to Alex under the UCC by his "affirmation" that the canoe was suitable for water use. This warranty was breached by the canoe's unsuitability for use on the river.

UCC §2-314 also creates two types of implied warranties. If the seller of goods is a "merchant" (a person who deals in goods of the kind sold, or otherwise by his occupation or through an intermediary represents himself as knowledgeable regarding the kind of goods sold), then every sale by the merchant of such goods includes a "warranty of merchantability" that a) the goods will "pass without objection" in the trade, as described in the contract, b) in the case of fungible goods (goods that are all alike), the goods are of "fair average quality" within the contract description, c) are "fit for the ordinary purposes for which such goods are used", d) are of the kind, quality and quantity described, e) are adequately contained, packaged, and labeled, and f) conform to the promises or affirmations of fact made on the container or label, if any. Other implied warranties of merchantability may be created from a course of dealing or usage of trade.77

Implied warranties of merchantability may, however, be negated, excluded or modified in a sale of goods contract by a contract statement that unambiguously and specifically mentions the word "merchantability" and is conspicuous.78 The language of many contracts for the sale of goods often includes such warranty "disclaimers". If a disclaimer uses common phrases such as "as is" or "with all faults", it need not specifically refer to "merchantability", because these phrases are assumed to be clear enough disclaimers of warranty.79 No warranty of merchantability is created if defects in the goods should have been seen by a buyer who was given an opportunity to inspect the goods.80 An implied warranty of merchantability can also be excluded or modified by a course of dealing or a course of performance or a usage of trade.81

For example, if Barry, a merchant of antique canoes, sells a birchbark canoe to Alex without any affirmation that it is suitable for water use, Barry's sale would include an implied warranty only that the canoe is fit for its ordinary purpose of display or collection as an antique. This warranty of merchantability would not have been breached by the unsuitability of the canoe for river fishing.

The second type of implied warranty created by the UCC is created where a seller of goods, whether or not a merchant, at the time of contracting has reason to know any particular purpose for which the goods are required, and that the buyer is relying on the seller's skill or judgment to select or furnish suitable goods. In this situation, the UCC creates an implied warranty that the goods sold will be suitable for that particular purpose.82 This type of implied warranty can also be excluded or modified in the sales contract, but it must be done so in writing, as well as unambiguously and conspicuously. It can also be excluded or modified by a course of dealing, a course of performance or a usage of trade.83

For example, Alex, a new angler, buys an antique birchbark canoe from Barry, while telling Barry that she intends to use it to paddle on the river to a fishing spot. Barry does not say anything about the canoe's suitability for use on water. Nevertheless, if Barry knows that Alex is relying on his judgment of the suitability of the canoe for fishing, then Barry's contract of sale includes an implied warranty of the fitness of the canoe for the particular purpose of fishing, because Barry knows that Alex intends to use it for that purpose and is relying on Barry's judgment.

Because they are viewed as unfair to consumers, who

neither understand legal disclaimers nor have the opportunity to bargain with merchants or to inspect consumer goods, some state UCC statutes make disclaimers of implied warranties of merchantability ineffective in sales to consumers.

CHAPTER 6 - How Are Contracts Broken/Breached?

When performance of a duty under a contract is due, any non-performance of that duty is a breach of contract.84 A contract duty is not due, however, if its non-performance is justified, such as because the time for performance, or another pre-condition to performance, has not occurred, or because the duty to perform has been discharged because of its impracticability.85

a) Conditions to Performance

i) Express Conditions

An express condition might be included in a contract in order to protect one party from the risk of having to perform its contract duty without getting the full benefit of the other party's performance. For example, a buyer of a house might make her purchase agreement conditional on a favorable home inspection. An express condition should be explicitly described as such to avoid later disagreements. Some courts have found that language prefacing contract requirements, such as "if" and "unless and until" will create express conditions. If the party who was intended under the contract to benefit from a condition wrongfully hinders or prevents it from occurring by not performing their own contract duty, the non-performance of the condition will usually be excused by a judge.86 This is an example of the duty of "good faith" as it applies to the performance stage of a contract.87

ii) Implied Constructive Conditions

Where the existence of an express condition is unclear, and the strict enforcement of the alleged express condition would cause a great hardship to the non-performing party, some state common law has interpreted the pre-requisite to the other party's contract duty as only an implied or "constructive" condition. If the constructive condition is only substantially performed, rather than exactly performed as promised, judges in those states will not excuse the party benefiting from that substantial performance from performing its own contract duty. Instead, the benefiting party will only be granted a remedy of damages equal to the difference between the value of the contract duty as exactly performed and its value as substantially performed.

For example, Jay, a homeowner, asks Sean, a builder, to construct a twenty million dollar house for him. One requirement of the construction is that the copper piping in the mansion must be manufactured by the Russell Company. Instead of Russell Company piping, Sean uses Campbell Company piping that is otherwise exactly the same. Jay refuses to make the final contract payment to Sean, because of Sean's failure to comply with the pipe manufacturer requirement. In this situation, unless Jay previously made it clear that final payment would depend on the manufacturer of the piping, some state judges will decide that this requirement is only an implied constructive condition, will determine the condition to have been substantially complied with, and will determine that Sean owes Jay only the difference in value, if any, between the two types of piping.[88]

b) Total, Partial and Material Breach

A party might have several different duties that it is obligated to perform under a contract. The non-performance of one of these duties, if such non-performance is a "total breach", will first, allow the other party to be discharged completely from its own contract duties, and second, will give the other party the right to a full contract "damages" remedy, rather than a lesser remedy provided for only a partial breach.[89]

Every total breach must first be a "material breach".[90] A material breach that is not a total breach is only a partial breach, and is very similar to the concept of substantial performance of a constructive condition.

Contracts may vary substantially in the duties they require. Several factors have often been used to determine whether or not a breach is material and total. Material breach factors include a) the extent to which the injured party will be deprived of the benefit he reasonably expected, b) the extent to which the injured party can be adequately compensated for the part of the benefit of which he will be deprived, c) the extent to which the party failing to perform will suffer a disproportionate loss from a breach, d) the likelihood that the non-performing party will later complete his performance, and e) the compliance of the non-performing party with standards of good faith and fair dealing.91

Two additional factors are often considered to determine whether or not a material breach is a total breach, namely a) the extent to which the injured party reasonably believes that delay in terminating its contract duties may prevent him from making reasonable substitute arrangements, and b) the extent to which the contract provided for the performance to have been done promptly, and the importance of this timing under the actual circumstances of the breach.92

For example, on January 1, Randolph agrees to buy a newspaper, the News, from its owner, Rupert, for $1 million, in installment payments of $250,000 each on April 1, July 1, October 1 and December 31. Randolph makes the first installment payment of $250,000 on April 1. Between January 1 and May 1, however, the circulation of the News declines from one million to 900,000 subscribers. When the second installment payment is due on July 1, Randolph believes that the News is now worth only $900,000. Randolph does not make his second installment payment until August 1. Between May 1 and September 1, the circulation of the News declines to 800,000 subscribers. Randolph does not make the third payment due on September 1. When Rupert inquires about the delay, Randolph tells Rupert that Randolph is working on his own finances and that he will complete the payments. By December 1, Randolph has not made paid the third installment, despite several requests by Rupert. Rupert is concerned that Randolph will not complete the purchase as agreed. Rupert tells Randolph that Randolph has breached their contract. Rupert then sells the News to Turner for $400,000, and sues Randolph for $100,000 damages for breach of contract.

In this example, the common law rules that determine whether a material breach occurred would look at the factors of: a) Rupert's reasonable contract expectation of a benefit of $1 million from the sale of the News, and his loss of $100,000 from that amount if Randolph does not pay contract damages; b) the unlikelihood that Rupert will get the $100,000 from any other source, if there is no buyer other than Turner who will pay more than $400,000 for the News; c) the disproportionate loss to Randolph of a total of $600,000 if he pays two installments plus contract damages, but does not get any ownership of the News; and d) the lateness of the third installment payment (three months late) compared to the second installment payment (one month late), making it less likely that Randolph will complete his performance on time, if at all. Factors a), b), and d) favor a determination of a material breach in this situation.

Looking at the remaining factors to determine whether a total breach occurred: a) a continuing decline in the number of subscribers to the News could have reasonably caused Rupert to believe that any further delay in selling the News would have prevented Rupert from receiving even as much as Turner offered for it, and b) the declining circulation circumstance would have made on-time installment payments important to avoid any further possible gap between the final per-subscriber sale price of the newspaper and the per-subscriber price agreed to be paid for it. Although many facts unique to a specific contract are used to determine whether a total breach occurs, judges in situations similar to these facts have determined that a total breach of contract occurred.93

State common law often requires the party threatened by a breach to take reasonable steps to communicate its concerns about an imminent breach to the other party in order to avoid a total breach. As we will see in the next section, such reasonable communications are also very useful to avoid a contract breach by the concerned party resulting from its non-performance of its own contract duties.

c) Anticipatory Repudiation and Demand for Adequate Assurances

If a contract party refuses to perform its duty when the performance is due, the biggest problem facing the other party is to determine whether or not a material and total breach has occurred. If a contract party indicates, however, that it will not perform its duty before its performance is due, the other party faces a different dilemma.

If the party owed the performance waits until the time the performance is due to declare a total breach, the breaching party might become unable to pay damages, and/or the damages that result from the breach might increase in amount. Alternatively, the party owed the performance might declare that the other party has totally breached its contract duty before it is due, and then terminate its own performance (or make it impossible by taking action like selling the subject of the contract as in the newspaper example above). In the latter situation, if that declaration proves later to have been unjustified, the party declaring a breach will itself have breached the contract, and will be liable for damages. This dilemma is made more difficult, because a party owed a performance might be faced not with an unambiguous advance repudiation of a contract duty, but rather with ambiguous circumstances that cause uncertainty and doubt regarding the probable performance of a future contract duty.

How can a contract party protect itself against this dilemma? State common law and the UCC each provide rules for a determination that an "anticipatory repudiation" of a future contract duty has occurred. Each requires a definite and unequivocal manifestation by words or actions of an intention to not perform the contract duty on the date of performance.94 Is a request to change or renegotiate contract terms by itself an anticipatory repudiation? Most judges would say it is not.95

If a party expresses its intention to not perform, but later, before its performance is due, retracts that statement or indication of intent, can it avoid a total breach? State common law and UCC §2-611(1) allow a retraction of an anticipatory repudiation unless a) the other party has materially relied upon the anticipatory repudiation, or b) the other party has told the repudiator that it considers the contract repudiation to be final.96 Retraction is permitted in order to recognize the inevitable friction that occurs in the course of performance of many contracts, and to avoid a premature termination of a contract (with resulting legal costs and difficulties) before the parties have exhausted reasonable possibilities for reconciliation of their differences.

The dilemma of an uncertain anticipatory repudiation is shown by the example above of the sale of the News. Did Randolph definitely and unequivocally manifest his intention to not complete the installment purchase payments? He did not do so by any words, but the lateness in payment of the third installment without any detailed excuse could be seen as a manifestation by conduct to not complete the purchase. The peril the party owed a performance faces is in either a) continuing to wait for a performance that they expect will not occur (with a possible increasing of eventual damages that might have been avoided), or in b) claiming a total breach (as in the News example) and/or an anticipatory repudiation (which Rupert in effect claimed occurred regarding the final installment payment by Randolph). Economic injury could be caused to the performing party if the party claiming anticipatory repudiation terminates its own performance or makes it impossible (such as by Rupert selling the News to Turner).

State common law and UCC §2-609(1) provide useful tools for the party owed a performance to use to avoid this dilemma. A party faced with reasonable grounds for insecurity with respect to the performance of a future contract duty owed to it may demand in writing the adequate assurance of due performance. Until he receives such assurance, he may, if commercially reasonable, suspend any performance for which he has not already received the agreed consideration in return.97 State common law gives a reasonable time to provide such adequate assurance.98 UCC §2-609(4) requires adequate assurances to be provided within no more than thirty days of a justified request.99 A failure to provide such adequate assurances within the appropriate time period may then safely be treated as an anticipatory repudiation of the contract by the requesting party.100

The circumstances creating reasonable grounds for insecurity will depend on the terms of each contract. State common law clearly requires that the circumstances that create uncertainty must have arisen after the contract was formed, rather existing prior to the contract. In the newspaper example above, Randolph's two late payments and the lack of specific explanation for them could be the "reasonable grounds for insecurity" basis for a demand by Rupert before December 31 for adequate assurances that the full remaining amounts due would be paid on time. If Randolph then failed to provide such assurances, Rupert could safely terminate the contract, even if the date for complete performance by Randolph had not yet arrived.

CHAPTER 7 - What Defenses Are Possible Against a Claim of Breach?

Epigraph #5

Nor is it difficult to see what is the tie between man and man which replaces by degrees those forms of reciprocity in rights and duties which have their origin in the Family. It is Contract. Starting, as from one terminus of history, from a condition of society in which all the relations of Persons are summed up in the relations of Family, we seem to have steadily moved towards a phase of social order in which all these relations arise from the free agreement of individuals. In Western Europe the progress achieved in this direction has been considerable...The apparent exceptions are exceptions of that stamp which illustrate the rule. The child before years of discretion, the orphan under guardianship, the adjudged lunatic, have all their capacities and incapacities regulated by the Law of Persons...on the single ground that they do not possess the faculty of forming a judgment on their own interests; in other words, that they are wanting in the first essential of an engagement by Contract...If then we employ Status...to signify these personal conditions only, and avoid applying the term to such conditions as are the immediate or remote result of agreement, we may say that the movement of the progressive societies has hitherto been a movement from Status to Contract.

--from Ancient Law-Its Connection to the History of Early Society by Henry Sumner Maine

a) Minority and Mental Incapacity

i) Minority

Common law has historically considered various classes of people to be incapable of obligating themselves to contract duties. The largest group that continues to be considered incapable today is "minors" or "infants", who are below a certain age level determined by state common law or statute. Eighteen years of age is a commonly chosen cutoff for legal capacity to make contracts.101 Like many legal rules, this "age of majority" might bear no exact relationship to the judgmental ability of a particular minor. It is an arbitrary rule that covers both the sophisticated and the unsophisticated. It has, however, the advantage of being easily applicable (being verifiable by a government-issued identification card) and well-known (in this case to would-be contract parties who might do business with minors).

Contracts made by minors are generally "voidable" by them. Their contract duties may be avoided, at the minor's option, even if the minor has received the full benefit of the other party's performance. Because socially important benefits to minors might be created through voidable contracts, exceptions have been created to make some types of contracts made by minors enforceable by their counter-parties. State common law often requires, through the law of restitution or unjust enrichment, a minor to pay for necessities, such as food, clothing and shelter that he receives under a voidable contract.102 Most courts apply the law of age incapacity even when a minor has actively misrepresented his age. Mere ignorance of a contract party's age is not an excuse for the other party. Contract parties deal with young counterparties at their peril. They are wise to seek proof of age in questionable or important circumstances.

Because their contracts are generally voidable, rather than completely void, after a minor reaches the age of majority they have the power to affirm or "ratify" a contract they made as a minor. If they want to disaffirm their contract, state laws may require that they take positive action to avoid a contract within a reasonable time after reaching their age of majority. Under such laws, without timely disaffirmation, they will be deemed to have ratified the contract by their inaction.

ii) Mental Incapacity

Like minors, persons with mental incapacities who enter contracts have voidable contract duties. Unlike minors, however, all adults are presumed to be mentally competent, and, as a defense to contract liability, must prove their mental incapacity as of the time they entered a contract.103 Mentally incompetent persons must generally restore to their counterparty any benefit they received from their disaffirmed contract.104 These differences can be justified, because the relative ease of proof of age, compared to mental capacity, makes it easier for counterparties to protect themselves against contracts with minors.

b) Duress and Undue Influence

i) Duress

U.S. common law has always recognized that some agreements should not be enforced because of unfair pressure applied to one of the parties in the process of formation of the agreement. Contract law presumes that promises are made pursuant to the freely exercised will of each party, as shown by their external actions. Therefore, when sufficient evidence is presented that a party was physically coerced by the other party into making an agreement, this evidence will make the contract void and unenforceable by either party.105

When duress or coercion of a non-physical type is proved, however, a contract will be only voidable; that is it may either be enforced or be avoided at the option of the coerced party. Such coercion may take the form of a wrongful or improper (but not necessarily illegal) threat, if the victim of the threat has no reasonable alternative but to comply with the threatening party's demands, and the compliance is actually caused by the threat.106 Most state common law also requires that, if a threat is of economic vulnerability, it must leave no reasonable alternative action, and the economic vulnerability must have been caused by the threatening party, rather than having existed prior to the threat. The remedy for a successful defense of duress is usually the rescission of the contract and the restitution to each side of any benefit they have received.

For example, a construction company hires a ship to

carry its construction equipment by sea to its distant construction site. Storms cause delays in arrival of the shipment. Halfway to the construction site, the company terminates the contract and orders the carrier to offload its cargo to the nearest port, which it does. When the carrier asks for payment for carrying the cargo to that port, the company refuses to pay the normal amount owed for a shipment of that distance. Several weeks pass before the company agrees to make any payment. During this delay, the carrier is pressed by its creditors and threatened with involuntary bankruptcy, which dilemma it communicates to the construction company. Finally, the company offers to make a final payment of only one third of the amount claimed by the carrier, without any explanation for the reduction. The carrier disputes this as the proper amount of money owed, but accepts it because of the financial difficulties created by the termination of its contract with the construction company. Although the construction company would probably argue that this was a legitimate settlement of a disputed amount owed (see accord and satisfaction in section g) below), the carrier could claim a defense of economic duress. Which party would prevail on these conflicting arguments would probably depend on what were the actual intentions of the construction company in disputing the amount owed. The legitimacy and good faith of their dispute of the amount owed would be a fact question to be resolved in a trial.107

ii) Undue Influence

State common law presumes that some non-family relationships create special legal duties. For example, a fiduciary relationship is created between a trustee and a beneficiary of a trust agreement, between an executor of a will and the will's beneficiary, and between a guardian and a minor subject to the guardianship. If the fiduciary (person who owes a fiduciary duty) enters into a contract with his beneficiary (person to whom the duty is owed), most state laws allow the beneficiary to avoid enforcement of the contract against him, unless the contract terms are fair, and unless the beneficiary at the time of contracting indicated his full understanding of his legal rights and the relevant facts.108

Without a fiduciary relationship, many state courts will allow a party to avoid enforcement of a contract if it was formed through an exercise of "undue influence" by the other party. The hallmarks of this defense are a) a relationship in which one party is dominant, or in which one party is justified in assuming that the other party will not act in a manner inconsistent with their welfare, and b) unfair persuasion by the dominant or trusted party.109

For example, a natural history museum discovers a dinosaur fossil near the land of a poor, uneducated rancher. A local lawyer and a local museum director visit the rancher at his house unexpectedly early in the morning, when the rancher is preparing to take his daughter to a doctor's appointment many miles away. The lawyer and museum director pressure the rancher to sign a contract immediately permitting the museum to excavate on his ranchland for $10,000 and to take ownership of any fossils they might find in their excavation. The museum director tells the rancher that, unless he signs the contract immediately, it might be his only chance to get a favorable deal. The rancher signs the contract permitting the excavation, which later uncovers a full dinosaur skeleton that is worth one million dollars. If the rancher later argues that the contract should be avoided because of undue influence, he might succeed under state common law, because the contract was discussed and made at an unusual place and time, the director pressured the rancher to finish the contract immediately, the director emphasized the risk of not finishing the contract immediately, several educated parties negotiated against an uneducated rancher, the rancher had no independent legal advice, and the director implied that there might not be any time to seek independent advice. These factors have been found by some state judges to add up to a successful defense of undue influence.110

c) Misrepresentation and Nondisclosure

U.S. common law permits a party induced into a contract by fraud or misrepresentation to rescind that contract. Rescission can be used affirmatively to undo a contract, or defensively to resist enforcement of contract duties. Rescission requires the fraud victim to return to the fraud perpetrator any benefits received under the contract. Actual intent to defraud is not a prerequisite to contract rescission, unlike a tort fraud action, so long as the misrepresentation was material.111

A misrepresentation is generally considered to be material if it would be likely to cause a reasonable person to indicate their agreement to the contract in question, or if the maker of the misrepresentation knows that it would be likely to make the other contract party agree to the particular contract they made.112 The victim of the fraud or misrepresentation must also have been justified in reasonably relying upon the fraudulent or misrepresented facts.113

Some state common law will include in the definition of a misrepresentation (rather than a mere opinion) a statement made by an expert on a subject, if it was made without knowledge or confidence whether it is true or false, and therefore made recklessly or negligently. Statements of opinion are also misrepresentations if they do not actually reflect the speaker's real opinion of the relevant facts.114

In the pre-industrial era of English and U.S. common law, the rule of "*caveat emptor*" (Latin for "buyer beware") warned all buyers that the goods they purchased were bought at their own risk for defects. (See Chapter 5, c) on warranties.) A buyer's only protection against defective goods was his own inspection before his purchase. As mass production and distribution of complex goods made buyer inspection less practical and effective, however, implied warranties were imposed by law for the protection of buyers. Since the implied warranties of the UCC apply only to sales of goods, however, state common law has often adjusted the requirements of the misrepresentation defense to contract enforcement, in order to recognize the injustice of non-disclosure of material facts by a seller of services or land. Some states will permit a contract to be rescinded by one party if the other fails to disclose a fact known to him, and its disclosure was necessary to prevent a previous statement by that party from being a material misrepresentation or fraudulent.115

For example, if a seller of land tells a buyer that the land is suitable for farming, but the seller knows that the land is annually visited by flocks of birds and other pests at harvest time that devour any mature crops, the buyer might successfully argue that the failure of the seller to disclose the fact of the annual bird and pest infestation was a material misrepresentation that should be a defense to enforcement of the contract, or a basis for contract rescission. If the written contract, however, includes a disclaimer of any warranties, and includes an agreement that the buyer is not entitled to rely on any oral statements or representations by the seller not written in the contract (a merger clause included for purposes of the Parol Evidence Rule discussed in Chapter 5, a)), then it will be more difficult for the buyer to argue that he reasonably relied on the seller's failure to disclose any material facts.116 The buyer will then probably be liable for contract duties and the old rule of "buyer beware" will apply.

In contracts between parties bound by a fiduciary relationship (a relationship automatically creating duties of trust and confidence), such as between a lawyer and client, many state judges will determine that not only does a duty exist to disclose all material facts, but also that the terms of the contract must be fair and fully explained to the beneficiary party.117

d) Unconscionability and Public Policy

i) Unconscionability

The path of the common law in English-speaking nations has diverged significantly from that of civil-code based legal systems. The role of judges in determining the shape of the law is one major difference. The use of juries to decide fact questions in trials is another. There have always been significant similarities between the two systems as well. For example, common law nations have long recognized that codes of statutory law are more appropriate than judicial precedents for criminal and commercial law, and therefore have used codes to establish and publicize specific rules of conduct to control anti-social or commercial behavior.

The Uniform Commercial Code (UCC), a model statute of U.S. commercial law, extended previous sales law statutes, under the leadership of Karl Llewellyn, other civil code-influenced American legal scholars, and European legal scholars, who immigrated to the United States in the mid-twentieth century.118 Another contracts concept brought to the United States from Europe was the defense to contract enforcement of unconscionability, which had existed for centuries in European civil law.

Common law equitable remedies had been limited or denied for unfair bargains. (See Chapter 8, f) and g) hereafter.) Lacking other tools, U.S. judges sometimes appeared to stretch rules regarding consideration, and offer and acceptance, in order to undo unfair contracts. As in the case of the rise in the 19th century of implied warranties, which replaced the rule of "caveat emptor", the law of unconscionability arose in 20th century U.S. law to mitigate the harshness of "take-it-or-leave-it" "contracts of adhesion" that imposed one-sided terms on parties lacking bargaining power in the marketplace for goods and services. My contracts professor, Friedrich Kessler, promoted the unconscionability defense as a method to stem a reversal of the progression "from status to contract" described in Epigraph #5. In his view, industrialization and mass marketing deprived individuals of negotiating power and imposed on them the status of objects of one-sided contracts.

UCC §2-302 introduced into U.S. law the rule that a judge could refuse to enforce an "unconscionable" contract, or could refuse to enforce or could limit the application of an "unconscionable" contract term or clause. The UCC rule did not define unconscionability. It described the principle's purpose as the prevention of oppression and unfair surprise, without disturbing the parties' allocation of risks reached through superior bargaining power.119

The UCC rule and its common law counterpart were widely adopted by U.S. states.120 The definition of unconscionability was left for judges to determine on a case-by-case basis for sale of goods contracts governed by the UCC, and for other contracts governed by the common law. Judges applied the contract defense of unconscionability to consumer and commercial contracts, to pure "take-it-or-leave-it" "adhesion" contracts, and to negotiated contracts.

Some courts separated the idea of "procedural unconscionability" from "substantive unconscionability". Procedural unconscionability existed if a contract formation process departed from an acceptable pattern, such as by a lack of any bargaining ("take-it-or-leave-it"). Substantive unconscionability existed if the actual terms of the contract were unfair. Some courts required only one of these types of unconscionability to exist in order to invalidate a contract or to invalidate a contract term. Other courts required both to exist in order to invalidate a contract or a contract term.

Some of the significance of unconscionability as a weapon against unfair consumer contracts has been supplanted by the development of U.S. consumer protection statutes, and their federal and state government enforcement agencies in the late 20th century. Nevertheless, it remains a significant weapon in the arsenal of legal arguments for consumers against "take-it-or-leave-it" adhesion contracts imposed on them by sellers. Cases in which unconscionability defenses have been successfully raised regarding web site electronic contracts are reviewed in Part B, Chapter 9, k).

One unconscionability argument, against the enforcement of arbitration clauses in consumer contract disputes, was recently invalidated by the U.S. Supreme Court. In *AT&T Mobility LLC v. Concepcion*121, the Court addressed a perceived conflict between California contract law, which invalidated, as unconscionable, arbitration clauses in consumer contracts that did not provide for resolution of disputes for similarly situated consumers as a class, and the requirements of the Federal Arbitration Act.122 Previously, the California Supreme Court's *Discover Bank v. Superior Court* decision had ruled that consumer contracts imposing non-class arbitration, as a method of dispute resolution, were unconscionable, if the disputed amount of damages was small and the consumer alleged a deliberate scheme by the seller to defraud.123

The Concepcions had purchased cell phone service from AT&T with a phone that was advertised as "free". After they were charged sales tax for the phone, the Concepcions joined a class action lawsuit against AT&T alleging false advertising and fraud. The federal trial court denied AT&T's motion to compel arbitration pursuant to the terms of the service contract, relying on *Discover Bank*, and the federal appeals court agreed.

The U.S. Supreme Court ruled that, if state contract law required class arbitration, as a substitute for class action litigation, in order to avoid unconscionability, this would "interfere with the fundamental attributes of arbitration" of informality, speed, and lower cost, while increasing the risk to defendants of non-reviewable, erroneous arbitration decisions. These fundamental attributes of arbitration are promoted by the Federal Arbitration Act (FAA). In the conflict between state contract law and the FAA presented by *Concepcion*, the Supreme Court ruled that the FAA prevailed. The unconscionability-based decisions of the federal trial and appellate courts in favor of the consumers were reversed.

In another recent case, *Compucredit Corp. v. Greenwood*124, the U.S. Supreme Court addressed the issue of whether the federal Credit Repair Organizations Act (CROA) permitted consumers to sue in court for violations of the CROA, despite agreeing to a mandatory arbitration clause in a contract with a credit repair business. The class action plaintiffs alleged that the defendants improperly added fees to their new accounts that deceptively reduced the advertised amount of their credit limit.

The CROA requires such businesses to give consumers a statement that "You have a right to sue a credit repair organization that violates the [Act]."125 Nevertheless, the Supreme Court decided that this part of the law did not clearly override the general rule of the FAA requiring enforcement of arbitration agreements, and despite another part of the CROA that prohibited any waiver by a consumer of any protection or right provided by the CROA. This type of narrow statutory construction applied in favor of the FAA requires federal statutes that provide consumer protections to explicitly state that mandatory arbitration contract clauses are prohibited in order to guarantee that result.

The Dodd-Frank Act126, among its many provisions, authorizes the new Consumer Financial Protection Bureau to issue rules to prohibit or impose restrictions on pre-dispute mandatory arbitration requirements in agreements between securities brokers, dealers, investment advisers and consumers, and in agreements in connection with "the offering or providing of consumer financial products or services"127"if the Bureau finds that such a prohibition or imposition of conditions or limitations is in the public interest and for the protection of consumers."128 It remains to be seen how the Bureau will exercise these new powers, and how the U.S. Supreme Court will view their exercise in light of its recent practice of statutory construction permitting mandatory consumer arbitration, unless explicitly prohibited.

ii) Public Policy and Covenants Not to Compete

Unconscionability defenses have been raised in some employment contracts. A similar, and more frequently successful, defense to a particular type of employment contract clause, however, has been the defense that a contract "covenant not to compete" with a former employer is unenforceable, because it is contrary to public policy. The policy at issue with this type of clause is the public policy in favor of free markets for labor. Pursuant to public policy, "naked" covenants to not compete between actual or potential business competitors (covenants not related to a legitimate transaction or relationship) are always unenforceable, because they violate the pro-competition and antitrust policies of American law.129

Post-employment covenants not to compete in an employment contract, post-sale covenants not to compete in a contract for a sale of a business, and similar "ancillary" (related to a legitimate purpose) covenants, might be enforceable. Most state courts have determined that: 1) the restraints in such covenants must not be greater than is needed to protect the legitimate interests of the beneficiary of the covenant, and 2) any benefit of the covenant must not be exceeded by any hardship caused to the restrained party or to the public.130

For example, an employment contract could restrict the right of an employee to work in a competing business after she leaves her job. This might be intended to serve the legitimate need of the employer to protect itself from unfair competition by an employee who works for a short time with the employer, learns trade secrets or customer information, and then uses that information to help her new employer compete against her previous employer. Even to protect a legitimate interest, however, most state contract law provides that, if the restriction is greater in its length of time, geographic scope, or scope of restricted activities than is necessary to serve its legitimate purpose, it will be unenforceable.

e) Mistake

Parties sometimes make mistakes in the negotiation and formation of their contracts. They might mistake the value of the consideration they exchange or the profit they expect to reap from contract performance. Only certain types of mistakes, however, will relieve a party from its duty of contract performance. Most judges no longer apply a subjective "meeting of the minds" requirement in order for a contract to be formed.

i) Mutual Mistake

If the objective indications of the parties' intentions show that both were mutually mistaken as to a basic assumption regarding the contract, and that the mutual mistake materially and adversely affects the contract benefit received by a party, then that party may avoid her contract duty, unless one of two exceptions applies. First, she may not use mutual mistake as a defense, if the contract has actually imposed the risk of such a mistake on her. Second, she cannot use mutual mistake as a defense, if she knowingly risked such a mistaken basic assumption in making the contract.131 Some state common law will also permit a judge to allocate the risk of a mistake to one party, if the judge considers this to be reasonable under the circumstances.132

For example, an apartment building is built with a defective septic sewage system. Later, the land where the building is located is subdivided into smaller parcels, with the effect that the septic system can never be fixed to comply with legal requirements, because the land the apartment is located upon has become too small to allow the system to be repaired. The apartment building is sold to a buyer who intends to rent the apartments. Soon after the sale, the property is condemned by the local government for non-compliance with building codes. If the buyer sues for rescission of the contract of sale and restitution of her purchase price, some state common law will permit the rescission if, at the time the contract was made, there was a mutual mistake by both parties as to the basic (income-producing) nature of the property that materially affects the purchase price, and there was neither an allocation of this risk in the contract nor a conscious assumption of the risk by the buyer.133

State common law is "split" (no majority rule exists for or against a particular rule) regarding whether the use in a contract of the term "as is" is sufficient to allocate to a buyer the risk that the subject of a contract will be worthless to the buyer. (Compare the effect of an "as is" clause in eliminating an implied warranty in Chapter 5, c).)

If the mutual mistake was made in transcribing (writing) the contract terms, the usual remedy given by a judge is the "reformation" of the writing to reflect the actual terms originally intended by both parties. If the mutual mistake is of another type that makes the contract voidable, the usual remedies given are first, the rescission of the contract, and second, the restitution to each party of any consideration they provided to the other that would be unjust for them to retain.

ii) Unilateral Mistake

Some state common law will permit the rescission of a contract for a unilateral mistake made by one party only. The mistake must have been made regarding a basic assumption that materially and adversely affects the benefit received by the party, and the risk of that mistake must not have been allocated to him by contract or judicial determination, nor assumed through knowing action despite limited knowledge of relevant facts. Additionally, either the other party's fault must have caused the mistake, or the other party must have had reason to know of it, or it would be "unconscionable" to enforce the contract because of the mistake (although unconscionable in this context seems to mean only very unfair, unlike the defense discussed in Chapter 7, d)).134

For example, a subcontractor bids to perform construction work for a city agency based on a mistaken assumption about the nature of the work caused by ambiguous language in the invitation for bid proposals. This assumption causes the subcontractor's bid to be 50% lower than any other bidder's proposal. After the prime contractor wins the contract because of the subcontractor's mistaken bid, the subcontractor discovers its mistake and asks for its subcontract to be rescinded, because it will lose so much money, if it performs, that it will be forced to close its business. The subcontractor has never made a similar mistake previously.

Some judges will allow the sub-contract to be rescinded, even though the mistake was "unilateral" (one-sided), if it was a mistake as to a basic term of the contract that materially and adversely affects the benefit received by the subcontractor. (Perhaps, someone should have suspected a mistake, because this bid was 50% lower than all others, and therefore looked "too good to be true"). If the subcontractor never made a similar mistake previously, it could be determined that it would be very unfair to enforce the contract if the result would be to destroy its business. If the city can be restored to the same position it was in before the contract was made, this might be a final factor that would help the subcontractor to rescind the contract for its unilateral mistake.135

f) Impossibility, Impracticability and Frustration

Each of these defenses usually involves changed circumstances that affect the ability to perform a contract after it has been created. Contract law generally requires a party either to perform its contract duties, regardless of how unprofitable or difficult that duty has become after the contract is made, or to pay to remedy the harm from its non-performance. In some extreme circumstances, however, contract law will excuse a party from its performance duties because of changed circumstances.

Three classic situations are generally recognized under state common law and the UCC as defenses to non-performance because of the objective impossibility or impracticability of performance: 1) the death or incapacity to perform of a person whose ability to perform was a basic contract assumption, 2) the destruction, deterioration, or failure to come into existence of a thing whose existence (or non-deterioration) was a basic contract assumption, and 3) the impossibility of legal performance of an action because of a new governmental regulation or order.136 Each of these situations involves objective impossibility (no one could perform as intended) rather than mere subjective impossibility (the contract party cannot perform as intended). Judges are reluctant to allow any of these defenses, if it appears in any way that the risk of occurrence of the supervening event was allocated by contract to one of the parties. Like the mistake defenses, if an impossibility/impracticability defense is successful, the remedies given will likely be the rescission of the contract and restitution to each side of any consideration exchanged.137

For example, a music hall owner contracts with a producer to rent the music hall for performances, but before they can occur, the music hall is destroyed by a fire. The owner can be excused from its contract duty to provide a music hall.138

A much less frequently available (or successful) defense is the so-called "frustration of purpose" defense in which performance is possible, but the value of the intended performance has been eliminated because of changed circumstances.139 For example, a party agrees to rent a room on a specific day to watch a parade, but because of an emergency the parade is cancelled. Some judges have determined that the duty to pay for the room is discharged, if the existence of the parade on the day of the rental was a basic contract assumption.140 Parties have tried to use this defense when the value of their contract benefits has unexpectedly and substantially declined. Successful defenses have been infrequent, however, because the defense conflicts with one of the basic purposes of a contract, which is to allocate through negotiated prices the risk of occurrence, or non-occurrence, of future events.

The third version of the changed circumstance defense is the reverse of the frustration defense, in which an unexpected and significant increase in the cost to perform a contract duty is argued as making the duty "impracticable" and unfair to require.141 The previous argument, that contracts are negotiated in order to allocate risks of future events, prevents the impracticability defense from having frequent success. Most courts refuse to allow either the frustration or impracticability defense, if the changed circumstance is only a shift in market values, or even if it is an extreme event like a natural disaster or war. Unfortunately, these types of events are all too predictable.

Besides allocating risk through contract prices, the risk of occurrence of unusual and devastating events may also be allocated between contract parties through the negotiation of a "force majeure" or "act of God" contract clause. This is a clause that excuses a required performance, so long as an event like a war, natural disaster or labor strike prevents the performance from occurring. Any party with a duty of performance (of an act other than mere payment of money) should consider including this type of clause in a contract in which its performance would likely occur over an extended period of time and involve a substantial expenditure of money.

g) Contract Modifications

Changed circumstances might not create a successful defense to liability for non-performance of a contract duty. Nevertheless, a party could seek to renegotiate its contract duty before its performance is due, if it expects that performance will be less profitable or more onerous than expected. If the other party initially resists this renegotiation, but eventually unwillingly accepts it, the issue arises of whether the unwilling party may later recover a remedy for the failure to perform as originally agreed.

Contract law has long promoted a rule that a party cannot enforce an agreement to change a "pre-existing duty" under an executory (not completely performed) contract, unless there is a change in the consideration provided for that performance. The rationale behind the rule is the protection of the party to whom the original duty is owed against unfair changes to the duty by the performing party. The first of the two most common methods of making an enforceable change in duty is the addition by the performing party, and the acceptance by the other, of a new, even if small, burden to the original duty, in order to add extra consideration to support the changed duty. The second method is the voluntary and mutual release and rescission of both parties' original duties, and the substitution of new duties.142

For example, in several cases courts have determined that an employer's agreement to pay more to workers for the same work previously agreed to be paid at a lower price is not enforceable when compelled under the threat of a strike.143 Other courts have circumvented this rule, however, by determining that an injustice would occur, if the promised contract change were not enforced, and if the performing party has relied on the other's promise to change the performer's contract duty.144 Those courts have enforced such modifications, if changed circumstances after creation of the contract justified the changed contract duty, and if the modifications are fair and equitable.145

UCC §2-209(1) has gone furthest to eliminate the pre-existing duty rule by making mutually-agreed modifications to performance duties in sale of goods contracts binding, even without any change to the original consideration promised.146 In order to provide some protection to a contract party from informal pressure to agree to changes through threats of non-performance, many state versions of the UCC allow "no oral modification" and "no oral waiver" clauses to be added to contracts, each of them requiring a signed, written agreement to the change of a party's original contract duties.147

Contract parties sometimes agree that one of them owes money to the other, but they disagree on the amount owed. In these circumstances, the parties can agree to fix the amount owed through a new agreement called an "accord and satisfaction".148 Under most state common law, an accord is a contract under which one party agrees to accept a new performance in satisfaction of the other party's existing contract duty. Once the new performance is completed, the original duty is discharged (satisfied). The accord and satisfaction is not an agreement that is contrary to the pre-existing duty rule, because both parties must agree that the nature of the original duty, such as the amount of the payment owed, is disputed in good faith.

For example, if two parties in good faith dispute the amount of a final payment owed under an existing contract, the party owing the money might send to the other a check with a (prominent) notation marked "payment in full". If the other party then cashes that check, the accord and satisfaction rule discharges the paying party from owing any further amount claimed to be owed. Sometimes, the recipient of such a payment will try to both cash the check, and to keep its rights to further payment, by sending a message to the payer that the check is cashed "under protest" or "with full reservation of rights". Under most state common law and UCC §1-207(2), this is an ineffective method of "trying to have your cake and eat it too".149 The original payment duty will still be discharged. If the payee wants to preserve his right to the full amount that he claims is owed, he must return the check for a lesser amount to the debtor with a message that it is insufficient, and it is not accepted as the actual amount owed.

CHAPTER 8 – How Are Contracts Enforced, or How Is Compensation Made for a Contract Breach?

Epigraph #6

But indeed, at the time, putting to death was a recipe much in vogue with all trades and professions, and not least of all with Tellson's [Bank]. Death is nature's remedy for all things, and why not legislation's? Accordingly, the forgerer was put to death; the utterer of a bad note was put to death; the unlawful opener of a letter was put to death; the purloiner of forty shillings and sixpence was put to death; the holder of a horse at Tellson's door, who made off with it, was put to death; the coiner of a bad shilling was put to death; the sounders of three-fourths of the notes in the whole gamut of crime, were put to death. Not that it did the least good in the way of prevention – it might almost have been worth remarking that the fact was exactly the reverse – but, it cleared off (as to this world) the trouble of each particular case and left nothing else connected with it to be looked after.

-- from A Tale of Two Cities by Charles Dickens

After a contract has been created, after one or more of its duties has been proved to have not been performed, and after any possible defenses to the non-performance have been disproved or disallowed, what does the party who is owed the performance get for their trouble of seeking a legal remedy? (A sentence of death is no longer a penalty for commercial crimes, as described by Dickens in the preceding epigraph!)

Most remedies in civil (non-criminal) legal cases have the purpose either of deterring future violations of the law, or of compensating the aggrieved party. Where a legal violation requires some type of blameworthy action, the remedies provided often tend towards the purpose of deterrence.

Contract law violations, unlike most tort (personal injury) law violations, require neither immoral nor socially blameworthy actions, such as negligence or intentional harmful acts. Thus, contract liability is sometimes called "strict liability". All that is required for a contract breach is the non-performance of a contract duty, without a defense. Contract liability is then automatically incurred. Consequently, contract remedies tend towards the compensation end of the remedies spectrum.

Among the three main types of contract remedies, however, the most deterrence-oriented remedy is the one most commonly awarded for a breach of contract. These three types of remedies correspond to the three types of contract "interests" commonly identified as being deserving of legal protection, namely 1) the "expectation interest" that a contract party has in receiving the "benefit of the bargain" that it struck with the party breaching the contract, which is protected by putting him in as good a position as he would have been in if the contract had been performed, 2) the "reliance interest" that a party has in being reimbursed for any loss caused to her by her reliance on the contract, which is protected by putting her in as good a position as if the contract had never been made, and 3) the "restitution interest" that a party has in recovering any benefit he has conferred on the breaching party.150

Although some legal scholars consider the restitution interest to be the most important interest to be protected, and the expectation interest to be the least important, remedies based on the expectation interest are the most common. This indicates the importance of deterrence of future contract breaches through the "warning" that expectation damages delivers.

a) Expectation Damages

"Damages", or "money damages" in the language of American civil remedies, refers to an award of money to a plaintiff at the end of a trial by a judge or jury. In contract cases, the damages are awarded as compensation for a breach of contract. The goal of expectation damages is to provide the plaintiff/non-breaching party with the gain that it would have received if the contract had been fully performed by both parties.

The formulation often used to determine the amount of money damages that should be awarded as "expectation" (or "benefit-of-the-bargain") damages is:

Expectation damages =

(A) loss in value caused by the failure or deficiency of the other party's performance, plus

(B) any other loss, including "incidental" or "consequential" loss caused by the breach, minus

(C) any cost of performance avoided by the non-breaching party, minus

(D) any loss avoided from not having to perform (reduction in expected benefit lost because of mitigating action taken by the non-breaching party).151

Expectation damages, including incidental and consequential loss damages, must always be a) reasonably foreseeable by the breaching party, and b) proved by the non-breaching party with reasonable certainty.152

For example, a local car dealer, Vinicius Autos reaches an agreement with an automobile maker, Nipponna Motors, to be its exclusive franchisee in Center City for its new Bossa car model. In order to meet all of Nipponna's franchise requirements, Vinicius Autos buys land to move to a new dealership location. Nipponna Motors later tells Vinicius Autos, however, that it made a mistake, and that Vinicius does not qualify to be its franchisee.

If Vinicius proves that Nipponna has breached a contract for an exclusive franchise dealership, Vinicius can recover expectation damages. These damages could include (A) its lost profits expected from the franchise relationship, if it can prove what profits it probably would have made from the contract. It is easier for an established business with a history of profits to prove lost profits damages, than it is for a completely new business to prove lost profits. In addition to "loss in value", such as lost profits, Vinicius can also recover (B) any extra costs it must pay related to relocating from its old dealership to its new location, if these costs were required only because of the contract breach, and if it proves that it was reasonable and foreseeable for it to have incurred these moving expenses because of the contract agreement. For example, if Vinicius will not need the new property after the breach, it might incur extra expenses of operating two dealership locations, until it can sell one of them.

Vinicius must subtract from its damages first (C) any "cost of performance" avoided by its not having to perform its own contract duties. This subtraction should be a part of its calculation of "loss in value" or lost profits in any event, because its lost profits should be calculated as its total revenue received from performing its duties under the contract minus its total expenses paid to perform its duties under the contract. Finally, Vinicius must subtract from its damages (D) any "loss avoided", such as by a reduction of its "incidental damages" relating to moving its dealership, if it can reasonably use the new location for another purpose.

Every non-breaching party has a duty to avoid loss by taking action to mitigate (reduce) damages, if possible.153 If the non-breaching party does not mitigate its damages, a judge will reduce the awarded damages by the amount that the breaching party proves should have been mitigated. The breaching party also has a duty to mitigate damages. In this situation, perhaps Niponna Motors could reduce Vinicius Autos incidental damages by purchasing the new dealership location from Vinicius.154

b) Reliance Damages

In the Vinicius Autos example above, the money that Vinicius might be awarded for its expense of an extra dealership   location could be called a type of "reliance damages", because that money was spent in reliance on a reasonable belief that the expense would be useful in performing the contract. Because the expense is minor, however, in relation to the total expectation value of the franchise contract, it is called an "incidental expense".

If Vinicius Autos had made a major expenditure in reliance on the breached franchise contract, however, it could not recover both this major expense "reliance damages" and "benefit-of-the-bargain" "expectation damages". It would be required to choose between these two types of damages, because the calculation of "expectation damages" subtracts from expected contract income the expected contract expense to produce that income, while "reliance damages" is itself the expense spent to produce the contract income. A recovery of both "expectation damages" and "reliance damages" would give the non-breaching party all of its expected income from performing the contract without any subtraction of the expected expenses it would have to pay to perform the contract. This would put the non-breaching party in a better position than if it had performed the contract, which contract law does not allow.

For example, assume that Vinicius Autos had a duty to build a new showroom and dealership in order to sell Bossa vehicles under its franchise contract. If Vinicius spent $1 million to buy the land for its new dealership in reliance on the contract agreement that was later breached by Nippona Motors, Vinicius could recover as reliance damages the $1 million it spent for the land, minus the market value price at which it could re-sell the land (in mitigation of its loss).155

Reliance damages is often awarded as damages for a promissory estoppel/detrimental reliance contract, for which the remedy for breach is not usually expectation damages. Instead, according to the well-known description of this "contract without consideration", the remedy "may be limited as justice requires."156

Reliance damages might also be easier for the injured party to prove with reasonable certainty than expectation damages. The burden of proof is on the breaching party to prove any loss that the injured party would have suffered had the contract been performed.157

For some breached contracts, such as one with a new business that has no history of profits upon which to predict future lost profits, it will be impossible to prove "loss in value" expectation damages. For other breached contracts, the amount provable as expectation damages might be less than the damages provable as reliance damages, and the non-breaching party will prefer to choose reliance damages as a better alternative to expectation damages.

Reliance damages are usually in the nature of money spent in preparation for performance of a contract. No reliance damages may be recovered, however, if the breaching party proves that the non-breaching party would have suffered a net monetary loss by performing the contract. In this way, the breaching party is allowed to avoid a guarantee of the success of a speculative venture.158

c) Examples of Types of Expectation Damages

Damages are generally easier to calculate if the party owing money breaches. If a party owing a non-money obligation breaches, the damage calculations are more difficult. For example, the contract expectation of a seller of real property is usually the price to be paid in money for the property, making damage calculations for a buyer's breach relatively easy. The contract sales price minus the fair market value of the property are the two basic elements of this formula for damages, which recognizes that the seller must mitigate its loss by selling the property to another buyer at its fair market value.

For a breach by a seller of real property, however, the calculation of a buyer's damages can be more difficult. For the breach of a contract for the sale of real property, the damages formula will often be the fair market value of the property minus the contract price. This provides the buyer with the benefit of its good bargain if the buyer had a contract to buy at a price below the fair market price. On the other hand, if the price was not below the fair market price, the buyer did not have a loss in value from the seller's breach. Some state common law, however, restricts the buyer to only receiving restitution from the breaching real property seller of any payments made, unless he has breached in bad faith.

In the case of either a property seller's or buyer's breach, the non-breaching party can recover incidental and consequential damages. These damages, however, must have been reasonably foreseeable by the breaching party at the time of the formation of the contract, must be proved (in amount) with reasonable certainty, and must be mitigated by the injured party.

When a non-breaching party is forced to enter the marketplace to obtain a replacement for the property or services that were not provided because of the other party's breach, this substitute transaction is called a "covering" transaction and its price is the "cover price". For example, if an employee breaches an employment contract to provide services for a period of time at a certain salary, and the employer is required to pay more than the contract price for the same services from a new employee, then the employee could be liable to pay to the employer the difference between the contract salary and the cover salary.159

Similarly, if a company breaches its contract duty to perform construction services after being paid for the work, the non-breaching party can recover the cost it must pay to another company to complete the work (at least if no other damages would better reflect its loss in value and if the cost to complete is not disproportionate).160 On the other hand, if a party breaches its duty to pay a building contractor in the middle of its work, the builder could recover its money already spent plus the profit it would have made if it had been able to complete its work.161

d) Restrictions on Incidental and Consequential Damages

As mentioned in section a), incidental and consequential

damages can also be recovered as expectation damages. Incidental damages are usually relatively minor costs paid by a non-breaching party that would not have been necessary if the contract had not been breached.

Consequential damages are expenses incurred by the non-breaching party as an indirect consequence of the breach of the contract, rather than expenses incurred directly to perform the contract. Examples of such indirect losses include: a) lost profits, not on the breached contract itself, but rather on a separate contract that is related to the breached contract, b) physical injuries to persons or property because of a contract breach, and c) "opportunity costs" of profit-making opportunities that were missed because of the breach.

Because these types of consequential damages are only indirectly related to the subject of the breached contract, state common law has developed several limitations on when they can be recovered for a contract breach. In the mid-19th century, English and U.S. common law first recognized that, in industrial economies, a geographically distant contract party might suffer economic injuries from contract breaches that were not of the type normally expected by the breaching party (and therefore not factored into the price of the breaching party's goods or services). In part to protect the breaching party from such unexpected liability, common law judges required that consequential damages, which were an indirect result of a contract breach, could only be recovered if they met a test of "reasonable foreseeability".

Reasonable foreseeability was proved if the indirect and injurious consequence of the breach was either a) "naturally arising" from, or "in the ordinary course of events" started by, a breach, or b) resulting from non-ordinary events caused by the breach, but which the breaching party had reason to foresee as a probable result of the breach at the time the contract was made.162

For example, a grain miller presented to a package carrier its broken mill shaft for shipment to a destination for its repair. The miller did not explain to the carrier that, unless its package was delivered within 24 hours, the miller could not grind any grain and would thereafter lose its expected profits for every day until the shaft was delivered, repaired and returned. Most common law judges have followed the rule that, in such a case, the carrier is not liable for the miller's lost profits, because the lost profits would not be a natural, direct consequence of the breach. The miller could only recover its lost profits if it proved that the carrier had reason to foresee that the miller would lose profits every day until the shaft was delivered, repaired and returned.163

In order to avoid an argument that a party, with a duty of contract performance involving more than the payment of money, should have foreseen the possibility of consequential damages from a contract breach, it is very common for a performing party to specifically exclude or to limit its liability for consequential damages. If the money-paying party desires the performing party to assume such indirect (and possibly unlimited) liability, it can negotiate a higher contract price in return for the higher liability assumed.

Incidental and consequential damages must also be proved with reasonable certainty. This is a requirement that the amount of indirect damages be actually proved by the non-breaching party, rather than, as in the case of direct damages, assumed from the circumstances of the contract. Such reasonably certain proof may often require the testimony of expert witnesses or the presentation of documentary proof.

Contract damages calculations are intended to fully compensate for the effects of a contract breach. Non-breaching parties who win lawsuits for contract breaches, however, are often left in a worse position than they would have been in, if the contract had been performed, for several reasons.

First, actual economic injury caused by a contract breach might not be compensated, because the injury was not reasonably foreseeable, or because the injury was not proved with reasonable certainty. Second, U.S. contract law does not usually permit the award of damages to compensate for a) the winning party's attorneys' fees and costs (unless provided forin the contract itself or in a contract-related statute or incurred in other litigation necessitated by the contract breach litigation), b) any mental distress caused to the non-breaching party by the breach that is not connected to a tortious type of physical injury directly caused by the breach,164 or c) "bad faith" or fault-related behavior by the breaching party that could be punished under tort law by the award of "punitive damages" (except in cases of failure to pay insurance claims where public policy considerations make bad faith failure to pay claims relevant to the amount of damages).165

e) Statutory Damages for Contracts for the Sale of Goods

i) Buyers' Remedies

A buyer of goods has five remedies to choose from in the case of a seller's failure to deliver goods in accordance with a contract. First, the buyer may recover any part of the purchase price already paid under UCC §2-711.166 Second, The buyer may get "cover" damages for the higher price of substitute goods under UCC §2-712 167(and the buyer might be required to buy substitute goods as a mitigation of damages under UCC §2-715(2)(a)).168 Third, the buyer may recover, under UCC §2-713, the difference between the market price of the goods at the time when the buyer learned of the breach and the contract price.169 Fourth, the buyer may recover under UCC §2-714(2), for accepted but non-conforming goods, the difference, at the time and place of acceptance, between the value of the goods as accepted and the value they would have had if they had been as warranted by the seller.170 Fifth, under UCC §2-716, if the goods are unique or a substitute is unavailable, the buyer may seek an order of specific performance, under the equity power of a court, for conforming goods to be delivered to him.171 Timely notice by the buyer to the seller of a breach of contract is required to preserve the buyer's right to any remedy.172

In addition to these five alternative remedies, which could satisfy a buyer's restitution, expectation, or reliance interests, the buyer can also recover incidental damages under UCC §2-715(1), such as "out-of-pocket" expenses paid to deal with the effects of the seller's breach.173 Consequential damages are also available under UCC §2-715(2), with economic injuries subject to the requirement of reasonable foreseeability, and to a duty of mitigation.174 Injuries to persons or property from a contract breach, however, are only subject to a requirement that they are "proximately resulting from any breach of warranty" (a tort-based standard of causation intended to avoid unforeseeable liability).175

ii) Sellers' Remedies

If a buyer has accepted a seller's goods without paying, the seller may recover the price under UCC §2-709(1)(a) for goods conforming to the contract, or for goods damaged after the risk of loss has passed to the buyer.176 If a seller tries, but fails, to resell conforming goods rejected by a buyer, she may also recover the purchase price from the buyer under UCC §2-709(1)(b).

If a buyer has rejected goods delivered in accordance with the contract of sale, the seller has a choice of three alternative recoveries. First, the seller may recover under UCC §2-706 the difference between the price at which the seller resells the rejected goods and the contract price. Prior notice of the resale must be given by the seller to the buyer.177 Second, the seller may recover under UCC §2-708(1) the difference between the market price at the time and place of delivery of the goods and the unpaid contract price.178 If the market price at the time and place of delivery is in fact less than the resale price, it is unclear whether or not the seller must recover the smaller difference between the contract and the resale price, rather than a larger difference between the contract and the market price. Third, a seller might recover its lost profits under a specific rule in UCC §2-708(2), if the UCC §2-708(1) contract price minus market price damages are "inadequate to put the seller in as good a position as performance would have done." Judicial decisions have divided, on the question of whether or not a non-breaching seller may choose, between §2-708(1) and (2), the remedy that would give it the highest monetary recovery.

In addition to one of these four remedies, a seller can recover incidental damages under UCC §2-710,179 and consequential damages under UCC §1-103(b), which preserves common law rules for contracts for the sale of goods, unless specifically displaced by other UCC rules.180

f) Restitution Contract Remedy

The restitution contract remedy is different than the restitution remedies provided in an unjust enrichment lawsuit under a judge's equity power described in Chapter 3. Modern state common law permits a non-breaching contract party to choose to recover, from a party that has committed a total breach of contract, any benefit that it has conferred on the other party through part performance or reliance, rather than the more common expectation or reliance damages remedy.181 This restitution remedy might be chosen because it provides a larger recovery than an expectation or reliance type of remedy would provide, such as where a party would have actually lost money by completing its contract performance duty.182 If the contract is rescinded by a judge and no longer exists, the non-breaching party's recovery might not be limited by its contract expectation. This remedy has not been provided, however, after the non- breaching party has in fact completed its performance duty, and the breaching party's duty has become limited only to payment of the contract price.183 The rationale offered for this exception, that the completed contract performance limits the non-breaching party's remedy to its expectation interest, could also apply to the fixing of its expectation by an unprofitable contract price.

Some state common law has even permitted a breaching party to recover, as a contract restitution remedy, any benefit provided by her in excess of the loss caused by her own breach, where the other party refuses to perform, because its duty has been discharged by a breach.184 This rule does not apply, however, if the parties have indicated that any such benefit provided can be retained as liquidated damages, and if it meets the rules for such damages as described in section h) hereafter.185 In addition, breaching parties should not recover through contract restitution more than their expectation damages.186

Finally, a right to restitution of benefits conferred on the other contract party may arise after avoidance or rescission of a contract by a party entitled to a contract defense. A party entitled to avoid a contract because of a defense of the Statute of Frauds, lack of capacity, mistake, fraud/misrepresentation, duress, undue influence, or abuse of a fiduciary relationship, may recover restitution of any benefit conferred on the other party through part performance or reliance.187 Similarly, a party whose duty of performance does not arise or is discharged (and whose contract is therefore rescinded), because of impossibility or impracticability of performance, frustration of purpose, or non- occurrence of a required condition, is entitled to restitution of any benefit that she has conferred on the other party through part performance or reliance.188

g) Specific Performance and Injunction Orders

Unlike the legal systems of many civil code nations, the U.S. common law and statutory law of contracts authorizes judges to order the actual performance of contract duties, other than a payment of money, only in extraordinary circumstances. Some reasons for this judicial reluctance to order contract performance include a desire to avoid the necessity of punishment of disobeyed orders through imprisonment or fines, and the discomfort of judges with oversight of the details of performance of business contracts, which is beyond their normal area of competence.

In order to avoid such difficulties and complexities, the remedy of a judicial order of specific performance, which compels a party breaching a contract to perform his contract duty, is available only after certain pre-conditions are satisfied.

First, the non-breaching party must prove that money damages are inadequate to protect its expectation interest.189 Factors affecting adequacy of money damages can include the difficulty of proving damages with reasonable certainty, the difficulty of buying a substitute performance with money damages, and the likelihood that an award of money damages could not be collected.190 Contracts for the sale of real property are often specifically enforced, if requested, because all land and buildings are considered to be unique; therefore money damages could never compensate for the loss of a property's unique future value.

Second, the terms of the breached contract must be specific enough to enable a judge to shape an appropriate order for performance.191 Third, because specific performance is an exercise of a judge's equity power, it must not create unfairness related to the contract formation or its terms, and the specific performance remedy must not cause unreasonable hardship or loss.192 Fourth, a performance will not be compelled if it would be contrary to established public policy.193 Fifth, a contract will not be specifically enforced, if it would burden the court with contract supervision duties that would be disproportionate to the benefit gained, or the loss avoided, by the injured party.194

Generally, contracts for personal services will not be specifically enforced, both because of the difficulties of assuring a satisfactory (and involuntary) performance, and because of the 13th Amendment to the U.S. Constitution, which prohibits involuntary servitude.195 Some courts will, however, order the "negative enforcement" of a breached exclusive personal services contract by an injunction against the breaching party providing the same services for another entity. This prevents the breaching party from working for someone other than the injured contract party during the remaining term of the contract. Usually such negative injunctions are used only against employees with unique abilities, such as artists, athletes or media personalities, in order to prevent them from working for competitors.196 This is similar to the enforcement by a judge of a covenant not to compete in a contract, described in Chapter 7, d), which meets the requirements of reasonableness regarding geographic, activity and time period scope.

h) Liquidated Damages

In order to avoid post-breach disputes between contract parties regarding evidence of economic harm, and to avoid legal arguments about damages, contract parties will often provide for a liquidated damages contract clause. This clause specifies how much a party must pay if it fails to perform its contract duties. Such clauses are often found in building construction contracts, and in employment contracts of unique employees, where the economic consequences of a breach by the performing party are difficult to measure.

In order to maintain the purpose of damages as compensation for a contract breach, rather than punishment, state common law usually imposes two requirements in order for a liquidated damages clause to be enforceable: 1) the actual damages resulting from a contract breach must be uncertain in amount, or difficult to prove, as of the time of contract formation; and 2) the liquidated damages amount specified must be reasonable in light of the loss anticipated by the parties to be caused by a breach, either as of the time of contract formation, or in light of the actual damages later shown to be caused by the breach.197 Many courts will place the burden of proof of the invalidity of a liquidated damages clause on the party that breaches the contract. The unavailability of specific performance for personal services, and limitations on negative injunctions preventing personal services for competitors, has increased the use of liquidated damages clauses in personal services contracts.

PART B - ELECTRONIC CONTRACTS

Datapoint #2

The [Denver] Broncos sought to renegotiate a middle ground. They offered to keep versus cut Dumervil but for a reduced salary amount of $8 million. According to various reports, that offer was only open until 1pm MDT [Mountain Daylight Time] on Friday, March 15th. The Broncos set that deadline because they faced a deadline of their own set by the NFL [National Football League]...The Broncos then renewed their $8 million offer but specified that Dumervil could accept only by faxing his acceptance to them prior to the NFL's 2pm deadline. When the Broncos did not receive a fax from Dumervil by that time, they cut him. Dumervil's agent has said that the fax was sent to the Broncos at 2:06pm [1:06 pm MDT] due to some delay in getting a fax from Dumervil.

--from "The Mystery of the Elvis Dumervil Contract Mix-up" by Heidi R. Anderson, March 19, 2013, Contracts Prof Blog

Summary of Part B

The Key Requirements for Electronic Contract Formation

The terms of an electronic contract may be offered in a variety of ways. Businesses often offer to consumers formal "take-it-or-leave-it" shrink-wrap, click-wrap or browse-wrap contracts. Between themselves, businesses or individuals might use formal contracts, or informal e-mail or text message agreements. If the contracts are subject to writing and signature requirements, such as under a state Statute of Frauds, U.S. federal and state laws permit electronic contracts to satisfy these requirements.

If Mr. Dumervil, the NFL and the Denver Broncos had agreed to do so, they could have completed his football contract, described in the preceding Datapoint, by e-mail. In fact, within weeks of the Dumervil contract fiasco, the NFL Players Association signed an agreement with an electronic-signature company that would allow NFL players "to sign anything, anywhere", including their million-dollar employment contracts. The company had already provided NFLPA union members with e-signature capability for marketing deals and agent verification forms.198

Electronic contracts in the U.S. must also satisfy the basic legal requirements of any contract, as described in Part A. These contract requirements, such as offer and acceptance, and consideration or detrimental reliance, are the most frequent reasons for legal challenges to the enforceability of electronic contracts. In addition, the defense of unconscionability has frequently been the basis for challenges to the enforceability of consumer electronic contracts. These legal arguments are often resolved through judicial analysis of the reasonableness of the methods of notice of the offered contract terms, and objective tests of whether the recipients of those offers assented to those terms.

The Typical Procedural Settings for Electronic Contract Judicial Decisions

Legal challenges to the enforceability of electronic consumer contracts (outside of arbitration or small claims court), which involve small dollar amounts relative to the cost of lawyers and litigation, should satisfy a cost-benefit analysis. That analysis often justifies the initiation of litigation only if it can be brought as a class action. A class action is a lawsuit on behalf of multiple plaintiffs who are similarly affected by the similar acts of a defendant, and whose interests would be effectively represented through a single lawsuit in which their common legal injuries could be proved and compensated.199

Many lawyers will not represent individual consumer plaintiffs to recover their individual damages, because of the disproportionate cost of litigation against well-funded corporate defendants. The same lawyers might be willing, or eager, however, to represent a class of similarly situated plaintiffs against the same corporate defendants, because the collective recovery of multiple individual damages in one lawsuit might far exceed the cost of litigation to prove that a common contract breach by a business defendant caused harm to numerous consumer plaintiffs. Consequently, electronic contract law is often made, and reported, in the context of judicial decisions regarding whether or not a web site or an e-mail contract term that prohibits the use of class actions for alleged contract breaches is enforceable. Another common context is a challenge to the enforceability of an electronic contract term that requires any lawsuit alleging a contract breach to be brought in a court at the location of the headquarters of the defendant business that offered the contract to a consumer.

The judicial decisions discussed in Part B are often limited to these procedural questions of whether or not a class action lawsuit may be litigated, and where any lawsuit may be litigated. Another threshold procedural issue that is the subject of many of these decisions is whether or not a defendant's motion for summary judgment, or a motion for dismissal for failure to state a claim, will be granted by a trial judge. These types of motions, if granted, terminate a case without the necessity for a trial, because no material facts are disputed by the parties, and the applicable law requires a judgment for one of the parties on the basis of those undisputed facts.

Whether or not these decisions ultimately decide that the electronic contracts in question are enforceable, they shape the law of electronic contracts through their statement and application of the relevant contract law. By knowing the shape and direction of contract law made through judicial decisions and through statutes and treaties, lawyers and their clients, and businesses, professionals and consumers, can protect themselves against unfair or unenforceable contracts, and can plan and execute their business and personal activities with confidence.

CHAPTER 1 - What is an Electronic Contract?

An electronic contract is a contract created through an exchange of electronic data, often through e-mails, or through interaction with a web site. Oral contracts have existed for many years. Before the internet, however, oral contracts occurred mainly in face-to-face retail or labor markets, where consumers could personally inspect the goods purchased or judge the services rendered. Dissatisfied consumers could often seek redress from sellers in the same geographic location.

Mail-order and telephone-order retail sales through catalog retailers became popular in the U.S. beginning in the 19th century. Internet retailing increases the efficiency of the catalog model through faster order processing and fulfillment, and through minimal physical "paperwork".

In the early 1990s, businesses began to commercialize the internet. In the fourth quarter of 2012, the value of electronic commerce retail sales in the U.S. alone grew to $59 billion, a 15% increase over 2011 fourth quarter e-commerce retail sales. Total 2012 e-commerce retail sales were $225.5 billion, up 15.8% from 2011. E-commerce sales in 2012 accounted for 5.2% of total U.S. retail sales.200

Electronic contracts might be negotiated between business parties. If Mr. Dumervil, the NFL and the Denver Broncos had agreed to do so, they could have completed his football contract, described in the preceding Datapoint, by e-mail. Like many printed consumer contracts, electronic contracts for consumer goods and services are often not negotiated, but are "take-it-or-leave-it" "adhesion contracts" (you are stuck with the terms) dictated by a seller. Where a "writing" and a "signature" are required by the Statute of Frauds rule described in Part A, Chapter 4, d), an electronic contract or signature might not satisfy these requirements, unless a statute specifically allows them to be the legal equivalents of a printed contract and a manual signature.

CHAPTER 2 – Laws Governing Electronic Contracts

Epigraph #7

No State shall...pass any...Law impairing the Obligation of Contracts...

-from Article I, Section 10 of the United States Constitution

Writings and signatures have been required for important contracts since the first English "Statute of Frauds" of 1677. The necessity to adjust traditional concepts of a "writing" or "signature" to their cyberspace counterparts of software data and codes prompted the enactment of new U.S. statutes permitting electronic contracts and signatures to comply with existing legal requirements for a writing or signature.

Utah, in 1994, was the first U.S. state to enact a statute validating electronic contracts as Statute of Frauds-compliant writings and signatures. In order to avoid confusing consumers and businesses with a mixture of divergent individual state laws, the Uniform Electronic Transactions Act (UETA) was developed in 1997 by the National Conference of Commissioners on Uniform State Laws (NCCUSL), the same organization that developed the Uniform Commercial Code. Its provisions are similar to those of the Model Law on Electronic Commerce (MLEC)201 developed by the United Nations in 1996, and it was promoted for enactment into law by state legislatures. The relatively slow pace of early UETA adoption (compared to the pace of internet commercialization) prompted the U.S. Congress, in 2000, to enact the Electronic Signatures in Global and National Commerce Act (E-SIGN).202

Like the UETA-based state statutes, the E-SIGN federal statute establishes rules that

...with respect to any transaction in or affecting interstate or foreign commerce --

(1) a signature, contract, or other record relating to such transaction may not be denied legal effect, validity,

or enforceability solely because it is in electronic form; and

(2) a contract relating to such transaction may not be denied legal effect, validity or enforceability solely because an electronic signature or electronic record was used in its formation.203

E-SIGN also authorizes consumer disclosures by businesses through electronic records, which otherwise are required by law to be in writing, if electronic disclosure is agreed to by a consumer, after a clear and conspicuous notice of the right to receive a printed disclosure, and after notice of how to access and retain the electronic record.204 E-SIGN's rules do not apply to writing and signature requirements related to estate and trust law, family law, UCC law unrelated to sales and leases, documents related to court proceedings, or other additional exceptions.205 E-SIGN provides other rules regarding the use of electronic records and signatures for mortgage-loan related transferable records subject to the commercial paper and negotiable instrument law of Article 3 of the Uniform Commercial Code.206 The following two judicial decisions show how E-SIGN works in real business deals.

In *Rafael "Rafa" Vergara Hermosilla v. Coca-Cola Co.*207, a lyricist was hired by Coca-Cola to adapt into Spanish the lyrics for the song "Wavin' Flag" for Coke's 2010 World Cup soccer marketing campaign. After the Spanish language version of the song was recorded, a dispute arose as to whether the lyricist was entitled to a songwriter's share of royalties (profits). When the dispute could not be resolved, the lyricist sued Coca-Cola for infringement of the copyright in his Spanish lyrics song version. Coca-Cola moved for a summary judgment in its favor.

The Florida federal trial judge reviewed an exchange of e-mails between the parties that occurred after Coca-Cola's refusal of the lyricist's request to share in songwriter copyright royalties. The lyricist had e-mailed the company's representative that he agreed that his work was a "work for hire" not requiring any compensation beyond that previously agreed to. The responding e-mail stated that "you can count on" the agreed terms, and that a formal contract would be sent.

When the formal contract was sent, it did not include some of the agreed terms. The lyricist e-mailed the Coca-Cola representative that "the proposal from which the contracts would supposedly derive is revoked as of now and without effect". The representative responded by e-mail that "I did not review the contracts. I will …make any necessary changes. I'm sorry." The lyricist subsequently sued for copyright infringement.

The judge noted that, under federal law, a copyright interest can be assigned to another party by a signed writing.208 E-SIGN was cited as a basis for treating e-mails as signed writings. No "magic words" of assignment are required. Only evidence of the parties' intent to transfer the copyright is necessary. The judge determined that the lyricist's e-mailed "proposal" for a work-for-hire, which does not retain copyright ownership, was accepted by the company representative's unequivocal "you can count on" e-mail language. At that point, a contract with all essential terms was formed. The later delivery of a formal contract without the agreed terms "only had the impact of an offer to modify an existing contract". When it was rejected, the original contract remained. Coca-Cola's motion for summary judgment was granted.

In *Metropolitan Regional Information Systems, Inc. v. American Home Realty Network, Inc.*209, Metropolitan Regional Information Systems (MRIS) provided a "multiple listing service" database of real estate for sale. Real estate agents and brokers had to execute a subscription agreement to use the service. Subscribers upload their listings to the service and agreed to assign their copyrights in all uploaded photographs to MRIS. Subscribers could use the database information and photographs on their own web sites pursuant to a Terms of Use agreement.

American Home Realty Network (AHRN) was a registered California real estate broker that operated the NeighborCity.com web site. This site provided a national real estate search engine, and ratings and rankings of real estate agents. NeighborCity.com displayed listings and photographs from the MRIS database without the permission of MRIS. After AHRN failed to comply with MRIS's request to cease its copyright infringements, MRIS sued AHRN, seeking an injunction.

In response to AHRN's motion to dismiss the lawsuit for failure to state a claim, a Maryland federal trial judge addressed AHRN's argument that the listings and photographs had not been assigned to MRIS in a signed writing by brokers and agents, as required by federal copyright law.210 The judge noted the applicability of E-SIGN to the MRIS Terms of Use. These Terms of Use provided that all images submitted to MRIS became its exclusive property through an irrevocable assignment by the submitter of all of its rights, including copyrights. The Terms of Use was sufficient evidence of the parties' intent to transfer ownership under the copyright law, and AHRN's use of the electronic submission process governed by the Terms of Use was a signed writing under E-SIGN. AHRN's motion to dismiss was denied, and MRIS was granted a preliminary injunction.

Because of the constitutional limits of federal legislative authority, E-SIGN applies only to "any transaction in or affecting interstate or foreign commerce". Courts have interpreted this legislative scope broadly, however, so that most, if not all, significant internet contracts will fall within the scope of E-SIGN. Under this authority, E-SIGN pre-empts any state law that is contrary to E-SIGN.

In order to promote voluntary compliance with the rules and basic principles of E-SIGN, and to promote the growth of e-commerce, E-SIGN exempts from preemption any state law that either a) adopts the 1999 version of UETA recommended by its drafters, or b) adopts an alternative set of rules that are consistent with E-SIGN, so long as they do not require, or give advantage to, any specific technology for creating, storing, generating, receiving, communicating or authenticating electronic records or electronic signatures.211 This arrangement is intended to allow experimentation and flexibility in the methods of electronic contract formation, contrary to a less flexible and more prescribed approach used by some national laws on electronic writings and signatures.

As of 2012, forty-seven states, the District of Columbia, and the Virgin Islands have adopted versions of UETA that are consistent with the rules of E-SIGN. The three states that have not adopted UETA, New York, Illinois and Washington, have adopted their own laws recognizing electronic contracts and signatures.212 Like E-SIGN, UETA includes a rule recognizing contracts formed by "electronic agents" (automated software programs).213 In addition to general validity rules parallel to those of E-SIGN214, UETA establishes rules regarding the effects of changes to, or errors in, electronic records215, and rules regarding the time and place of the sending and receipt of electronic records.216

Although E-SIGN and UETA permit writing and signature legal requirements to be satisfied by electronic writings and signatures, neither law requires a contract party to use electronic writings and signatures over their objection.217

CHAPTER 3 - Examples – "Shrink-wrap", "Browse-wrap", "Click-wrap" and Other Electronic Contracts

Datapoint#3

...U.S. wireless market...[spending] in 2012 rose 10.0 percent, the largest increase since 2007...The dominant driver will be the transformation of the market from primarily a voice service to primarily a data service. Voice and text messaging are declining while spending on wireless data is surging. In 2012, wireless subscribers for the first time spent more on data than they did on voice....By 2016, data will comprise more than 72 percent of total wireless services spending.

--from TIA's 2013 Market Review and Forecast – Wireless Preview (Telecommunications Industry Association)

a) "Shrink-wrap" Contracts

When most computer software programs were sold in retail stores and by mail order (instead of being downloaded on-line), they were physically stored on so-called floppy disks (or compact disks), which were "shrink-wrapped" in plastic to prevent theft or tampering. The earliest electronic contract lawsuits involved issues of identification of an offer and acceptance, and the terms of a contract for the sale of shrink-wrapped goods.

Although software is typically licensed, rather than sold, Uniform Commercial Code Article 2 applies to "transactions in goods", rather than only to sales.218 The UCC defines goods broadly.219 Software embedded in a computer program (like music on a CD or a lecture recorded in a book) has been considered to meet this definition by most judges.220

Software disks wrapped in plastic frequently include written notices or warnings on their covers, stating that the package contains the seller's contract terms, and that the use of the product, after the buyer has an opportunity to review the terms, serves as an agreement to those terms. The terms usually gave the buyer a period of time within which to review the terms and return the product, if dissatisfied with it. If the product is not returned within that time period, the buyer will be considered to have automatically agreed to all of the seller's contract terms.

Judges generally recognize the seller's shrink-wrapped terms as an "offer", and the buyer's acts, of opening the package and keeping the product beyond the return period, as an "acceptance".221 Most judges reject the argument that this type of "buy now--agree later" contract is always unconscionable, under the rules described in Part A, Chapter 7, d), because of the one-sided nature of the contract formation process. Specific contract terms, however, are subject to the unconscionability defense. For example, mandatory arbitration clauses for consumer disputes have sometimes been successfully challenged as unconscionable.

A few judges initially viewed a purchase request by a computer buyer as an offer, and the shipment of the goods by the seller as an "acceptance with additional terms", subject to the "battle of the forms" rules of UCC §2-207.222 Eventually, however, this analysis did not prevail among the majority of judges.

A buyer of consumer goods typically responds to specifications and contract terms on the exterior of a package of shelved goods in a retail store by offering to buy them at a cash register. If such goods contain a visible notice or warning of mandatory contract terms included within the package, however, this indicates that the seller is actually making the contract offer.

A money-back return period, for goods with detailed terms placed inside its package, is often provided in exchange for the seller's ability to disclose complex terms after the buyer initiates a contingent purchase. The greater complexity (and novelty) of electronic software-based goods argues in favor of both the seller's right to disclose the terms of sale inside the goods package, and in favor of the buyer's right to use the goods before completing the contingent purchase. In comparison, most consumer goods are obtained through repetitive purchases of items with well-known qualities for which neither a money-back trial period nor a right to disclose terms after purchase would be necessary or useful.

b) "Browse-wrap" Contracts

Browse-wrap contracts typically involve the use of information provided on a web site (or a screen presented by a program on a CD), which is conditioned on the information provider's "Terms of Use" that apply to all who access the information. The Terms of Use are usually presented on the first page of the web site through a hyperlink. The terms typically state that, by using the web site, the user automatically agrees to the provider's contract terms. Unlike many information downloads or registrations by web site users, browse-wrap Terms of Use do not require an express assent, such as by clicking on an "I Agree" button.

For example, an online newspaper begins its Terms of Service by stating

> These Terms of Service govern your use of the _____ .com website (the "Site"). By using this website (the "Site"), you agree to be bound by these Terms of Service and to use the Site in accordance with these Terms of Service, our Privacy Notice, and any additional terms and conditions that are referenced herein or that otherwise may apply to specific sections of the Site, or to products and services that we make available to you through the Site (all of which are deemed part of these Terms of Service). Accessing the Site, in any manner, whether automated or otherwise constitutes use of the Site and your agreement to be bound by these Terms of Service.

Most judges, who have confronted the issue, have decided that a formal act of acceptance by a site user is not required in order to bind them to such browse-wrap terms of use.223 A "contract by conduct", also called an "implied- in-fact" contract, has long been recognized as formed when a party who is offered a benefit, subject to the offeror's requirements, accepts the benefit, after having a reasonable opportunity to reject it, and with reason to know that the benefit was offered with the expectation that the offeree would comply with the offeror's requirements.224

Browse-wrap contract disputes have been resolved based on these common law contracts principles. Four requirements, which are frequently identified by judges as necessary for implied assent by a user to proposed browse-wrap terms, are 1) adequate notice to the user of the existence of the proposed contract terms (determined by visual presentation of content, or by actual knowledge by the user of contract terms despite inadequate notice), 2) a meaningful opportunity for the user to review the terms, which is usually before the time of acceptance of a contract offer (actual reading of the terms not being required, but being foregone at the user's risk), 3) adequate notice that a specified action by the user will manifest assent to the terms (including take-it-or-leave-it terms that a user cannot negotiate), and 4) the taking of the specified action by the user (although, if done by mistake, a user might be able to correct the mistake, such as through a confirmation screen or procedure).225

c) "Click-wrap" Contracts

The "wrap" analogy, which began with the comparison of "browse-wrap" web site terms of use to "shrink-wrap" contract terms on software disks and CD packages, has been extended to the most common method of agreement to contract terms for use of web sites or online software downloads. The act of clicking on an "I Agree" or "Agree" or "Accept" button at the end of a software license agreement is often required in order for users to access the functions of a web site, or to download an online software program. This procedure is called a "click-wrap" (or "click-through") agreement.

The legality of electronic contracting is taken for granted

by many internet users. A recent click-wrap contract for an online consumer software distributor, however, emphasizes the equivalence of electronic contracts with their physical counterparts, by stating

ELECTRONIC CONTRACTING

Your use of the Services includes the ability to enter into agreements and/or to make transactions electronically. YOU ACKNOWLEDGE THAT YOUR ELECTRONIC SUBMISSIONS CONSTITUTE YOUR AGREEMENT AND INTENT TO BE BOUND BY AND TO PAY FOR SUCH AGREEMENTS AND TRANSACTIONS. YOUR AGREEMENT AND INTENT TO BE BOUND BY ELECTRONIC SUBMISSIONS APPLIES TO ALL RECORDS RELATING TO ALL TRANSACTIONS YOU ENTER INTO ON THIS SITE, INCLUDING NOTICES OF CANCELLATION, POLICIES, CONTRACTS, AND APPLICATIONS. In order to access and retain your electronic records, you may be required to have certain hardware and software, which are your sole responsibility.

_____is not responsible for typographic errors.

As the growing judicial acceptance of browse-wrap contracts shows, the affirmative act of clicking on an "I Agree" button is not always required to bind a user of online information to an information provider's Terms of Use. In situations where online software is licensed for a fee, rather than offered for free, however, providers have regularly used click-wrap contracts. The advantage of click-wrap contracts over browse-wrap contracts is their more definite and demonstrable evidence of contract assent, which often eliminates arguments that a web site or software user either had no opportunity to learn of contract terms, or did not affirmatively accept them.

A service provider must still prove that a user either knew, or had reason to know of the contract terms that it agreed to by clicking on an "Agree" button. As an example, using facts from a case in Chapter 8, d) hereafter, a seller of a diamond ring wants to ship it by a delivery service to a buyer, and wants to require the carrier to collect the payment in cash before transferring the ring to the buyer. In response to the shipper-seller's inquiry whether the carrier will collect cash from the buyer before delivering the ring, the carrier employee tells the shipper that it will do so. The carrier's procedures, however, also require every shipper, before receiving a shipping label, to click on an "I Agree" button at the end of the Terms of Service on a monitor that processes shipping information. The terms include a statement that the carrier "will not accept currency in any amount for payment of C.O.D. shipments". The shipper clicks on the "I Agree" button. The carrier takes the diamond ring to the buyer, accepts a cashier's check in payment from him, and delivers the diamond ring to the buyer. The cashier's check is a forgery.

If the defrauded seller-shipper sues the carrier for breach of its promise to deliver the ring only after receiving cash payment from the buyer, a judge could decide that the seller-shipper should win, if he proves that he did not have any reason to know of the "no currency for C.O.D. shipments" rule in the Terms of Service that he accepted by clicking on the "I Agree" button.226

Most judges have determined that only "reasonable" or "adequate" notice of contract terms is required to be given to a party who clicks on an "I Agree" button, in order for their action to be an acceptance of the terms presented.227 In the previous diamond ring shipment example, a judge might give the seller-shipper a chance to prove that the notice given to him of the "no currency for C.O.D. shipments" contract term was not reasonable, because the reassuring statement of the carrier employee made it unreasonable to expect that a contrary statement would appear in the contract terms.

d) E-mail and Other Electronic Contracts

The Statute of Frauds for certain types of contracts described in Part A, Chapter 4, d), requires a "writing signed by the party" to be bound by the contract. No particular description of the "writing" or the "signature" is usually stated. Judges have often construed the writing and signature requirements liberally in order to avoid releasing a party from an otherwise binding contract, simply because of the informality of the writing or signature method used. Contracts written on brown paper bags, or contracts whose written terms must be gathered from separate pieces of paper, have been determined to be sufficient. Similarly, signatures written in crayon, or signatures consisting only of initials have been determined to be sufficient.

Neither the federal E-SIGN statute, nor the state statutes based on UETA, requires an electronic contract to take any particular electronic form. The "electronic signature" or "electronic record", used to authenticate an electronic contract as belonging to a particular person, is also not required to take any particular form. Specific methodologies for electronic signatures were intentionally avoided by these U.S. laws, as a rejection of the elaborate methodology of authenticated and encrypted "keys" kept by a central authority in some other nations and regions. Flexibility for future technological advances was preferred in the U.S. over uniformity of authentication methodology.

In response to the flexibility of methods allowed to satisfy the requirements of a writing or signature under E-SIGN and UETA, various types of electronic contracts and signatures have developed. The preceding sections described, as "browse-wrap", contracts accessed through a Terms of Service or a Terms of Use hyperlink, often located at the bottom of a web page. Contracts with terms presented on one or a series of pages, to which a buyer or user of software must affirmatively "click" agreement, were described as "click-wrap" contracts.

The methods for signing electronic contracts have been

as varied as the contract formats. Sometimes users or buyers have been required to type their names into a specific signature box at the end of an online contract. Sometimes a user or buyer's name has been placed on a signature line by the other party in response to telephone questions and answers. The number of possible methods of electronic signatures is limited only by imagination, with one important exception. As with printed signatures, the names or initials (or other symbols) used as a signature must have been made with the approval of the signer, and they must have been intended by the signer to indicate their approval of the related contract terms.

If two parties intend to establish a contract through an exchange of e-mail messages, these messages together can constitute a writing that satisfies the Statute of Frauds, and they can form a contract, if they include enough essential terms to enable a judge to enforce the exchanged promises. Similarly, if two parties intend that their names typed at the end of their e-mail messages should constitute their signatures to their e-mail contract, this will be sufficient under E- SIGN or UETA.228

e) Electronic and Quasi-physical Signatures

The possible forms that electronic signatures might take are as variable as their related contracts. "Type-your- name-in-the-box" e-signatures, and typed names at the end of e-mails are among the simplest forms. The ability of electronic tracing technologies to mimic ink-and-paper signatures has produced the electronic signature pads that are familiar to all of us at store checkout counters (for proof of credit card authorization), and as presented by package carriers (for proof of delivery). These types of e-signatures can provide a higher level of uniqueness (and therefore reliability, or at least familiarity) for authenticating approvals at crucial stages of sales or service contracts, compared to typed names. Like any authentication method, however, they can be subverted.

CHAPTER 4 - Formalities for an Electronic Contract?

In Part A, Chapter 4, d) and e), the requirements for, the formalities of, and the parties to a printed contract, were described. There are no differences between U.S. printed contracts and electronic contracts regarding the requirements for their formation, or their possible parties or beneficiaries. Statutes have been enacted, however, to reconcile the non-tangible nature of electronic contracts with the traditional Statute of Frauds requirements for printed writings and signatures, and to fulfill the purposes of those requirements.

a) Electronic Writings

The first purpose of the original Statute of Frauds in England (and its successors in U.S. state law) was to protect certain types of contracts from perjured testimony about their formation. Contracts that were considered most in need of such protection were identified either by a) their subject matter--such as contracts for the sale of land, for expensive goods, for other personal property, for the sale of securities, or for security interests in a debtor's property not held by the security interest holder, or b) the likely difficulty of proving the formation of the contract because of (i) the relationships of the purported contract parties--such as the executors of a will and the deceased will-making party, or a surety alleged to be liable for the debt of another person, or a contract party engaged to be married to the other contract party, or (ii) the possible passage of time, and reliable memories, between the alleged making of a contract and its proof at a trial or other forum--such as contracts that cannot be performed completely within one year of their formation.

The fraud protection of a printed writing and signature could sometimes be defeated through the creation of fraudulent documents and forged signatures. Generally, however, the protective formalities of a writing and signature served to relieve the process of proof of contract formation from the threats of biased or faulty memories, or lies.

Given the protective purposes of the writing requirement, the necessity to balance its benefits and detriments against the benefits of electronic contracts quickly followed the emergence of electronic commerce. The State of Utah attempted the first regulation of electronic contracts in the U.S. in 1994. It was soon followed by other U.S. states using various approaches. The United Nations (with encouragement of U.S. participants) recognized the advantage of a model law approach to required formalities for electronic contracts. In 1996, it promulgated its Model Law on Electronic Commerce (MLEC).229

The National Conference of Commissioners on Uniform State Laws (NCCUSL) followed the lead of the MLEC, and the Canadian Uniform Electronic Commerce Act, in 1999 with the Uniform Electronic Transactions Act (UETA). In 2000, the U.S. Congress enacted the Electronic Signatures in Global and National Commerce Act (E-SIGN) federal law approving electronically written and signed contracts as the legal equivalents of printed contracts, and pre-empting other U.S. state laws to the extent provided in E-SIGN.

MLEC Articles 5, 6 and 7, E-SIGN §101(a), and UETA §7 eliminate many (although not all) common law and statutory requirements for a printed writing or signature for enforcement of a contract. In their place, they permit an electronic contract or signature as the legal equivalent. UETA replaces the protections of printed writings and signatures with rules focused on the purposes of printed formalities, without assuming their inherent or unique reliability.

For example, under UETA §8, any legal writing requirement for a transaction is satisfied if the transaction information is provided, sent, or delivered in an electronic record capable of retention by the recipient at the time of receipt.230 For example, some click-wrap agreements are made capable of retention through a "Send By E-mail" hyperlink presented just above the "Agree" and "Don't Agree" buttons. E-SIGN adds an explicit requirement of accuracy to UETA's requirement of retainability, by specifying that "…the legal effect, validity, or enforceability of an electronic record of such contract or other record [as a writing] may be denied if such electronic record is not in a form that is capable of being retained and accurately reproduced for later reference by all parties or persons who are entitled to retain the contract or other record."231

To protect against possible fraud, an electronic record is treated by UETA as not capable of retention by the recipient, if the sender, or its information processing system, inhibits the ability of the recipient to print or to store the electronic record.232 If a sender inhibits the ability of a recipient to print or to store an electronic record, UETA provides that the electronic record is not enforceable against the recipient.233

b) Electronic Signatures

The second purpose of the original Statute of Frauds, and its U.S. legislative descendants, was to protect the types of contracts described above from inaccurate or perjured testimony regarding their authentication, through the requirement of a printed or handwritten signature.

The UETA rules for approval of electronic substitutes for printed signatures allow proof that a signature was made by a specific person in any manner, supported by evidence of the effectiveness of any security procedure chosen to assure that proof.234 The electronic signature's effect is determined from its context and the circumstances of its creation, including the parties' agreement, if any, and by applicable law.235 E-SIGN does not discuss how e-signatures might be created, but defines an electronic signature as "an electronic sound, symbol, or process, attached to or logically associated with a contract or other record and executed or adopted by a person with the intent to sign the record".236 UETA and E-SIGN each provide for notarizations, acknowledgements, verifications, and statements under oath to be made electronically, if an electronic signature is "attached to or logically associated with the signature or record" that it is intended to authenticate.237

By referring to security procedures that might be used to authenticate electronic signatures, and to the importance of the context and surrounding circumstances of their creation, the UETA rules recognize the varying and evolving reliability of different security techniques. U.S. law has left the details of techniques used to assure the security of electronic signatures to the contract parties. The European Union uses a more prescriptive approach to the security of electronic signatures, as reflected in the E.U. Electronic Signatures Directive adopted in 1999.238 The Model Law on Electronic Signatures (MLES) approved by the United Nations in 2002 follows the prescriptive approach of the E.U. Electronic Signatures Directive.239 Some U.S. members of the U.N. MLES drafting group preferred the more flexible U.S. approach to security techniques over the final MLES prescriptive approach.

Electronic signatures are sometimes used to authorize financial and other online transactions of great significance. A greater degree of technical effort used to assure the reliability of the methods used to approve such transactions is appropriate, and has become common. For example, unique and private user names and passwords are required for log-ins to many web sites that contain personal user information. Specific log-in questions and answers are often added as an extra layer of security. Cryptographic "public key" and "private key" technologies are sometimes used to limit access from exterior locations to business computer networks. The increased resources necessary to maintain a record of compliance with these security procedures are often justified by the greater risks posed by unauthorized users of financial, business or other personal data maintained behind security "firewalls".

The 2012 Michigan Court of Appeals decision in *Zulkiewski v. American General Life Insurance Company*240 analyzed the legal effects of security procedures used to prove an electronic signature. A husband applied, by a printed form, for a life insurance policy. He named his first wife as the primary beneficiary, with his parents as contingent beneficiaries. The insured later divorced his first wife. The primary beneficiary was changed by printed form to the insured's mother, and the contingent beneficiary to his father. The insured then re-married. Subsequently, an online account with the insurance company was opened in the insured's name, using his policy number, social security number, mother's maiden name and e-mail address. The company sent a notice to the insured that the account had been opened, and warned him to contact the company if he had not intended to open the online account.

On the same day the online account was opened, it was used to change the policy beneficiary designations to make the insured's new wife his primary beneficiary, and to make his mother the contingent beneficiary. The company sent an e-mail and a letter to the insured confirming the beneficiary changes.

After the insured's death, his wife and his mother submitted competing insurance claims. In the lawsuit involving the competing claims, the trial court determined, by summary judgment without trial, that there was no evidence offered that anyone other than the insured had changed the beneficiary designations. The trial court ordered the policy proceeds to be paid to the insured's wife.

On appeal, the insured's mother argued that, although UETA removes any challenge to the validity of a signature because it is in electronic form, UETA allows an electronic signature to be invalidated, unless there is sufficient proof of the security of the system used to process the electronic signature, and of the accuracy of the security system's attribution of the signature to the alleged signer. In other words, the insured's mother argued that the insurance company's security process should be presumed to have allowed the insured's signature to be forged.

The Michigan version of UETA provides

(1) An electronic record or electronic signature is attributable to a person if it is the act of the person. The

act of the person may be shown in any manner, including a showing of the efficacy of any security procedure applied to determine the person to which the electronic record or electronic signature was attributable.

(2) The effect of an electronic record or electronic signature attributed to a person under subsection (1) is determined from the context and surrounding circumstances at the time of its creation, execution, or adoption, including any agreements of the parties, and otherwise as provided by law.241

The appeals court rejected the argument that these rules require proof of the "efficacy of any security procedure" involving an electronic signature. It determined that this was only one of several methods by which to attribute an electronic signature to a particular person. In this case, the company sufficiently attributed the electronic signature to the insured through evidence of presentation of the insured's personal information, and through the e-mail and regular mail notices to the insured of the establishment of the online account and the beneficiary changes. The insured's wife also submitted an affidavit (sworn statement) that she was not involved in the beneficiary changes, that the insured was knowledgeable about computer use, and that he had also designated her as the beneficiary of other insurance policies.

c) Electronic "Originals"

The significance of an "original" writing, versus a "duplicate" writing, is, to some extent, related to the effects of the development of the technology of photocopying in the mid-twentieth century. Concerns about the authenticity of copies of contracts and other documents, however, had preceded photocopying by at least as many years as had witnessed human ingenuity in the intentional or unintentional misrepresentation of previously established agreements.

One of the most important legal reasons to identify a trustworthy "original" document relates to the so-called "Best Evidence Rule", derived from common law, and now frequently expressed in U.S. procedural statutes. For example, the Best Evidence Rule applies when a party wants to admit into evidence at trial the contents of a document, as in the following U.S. federal court rules of evidence.

ARTICLE X. CONTENTS OF WRITINGS, RECORDINGS, AND PHOTOGRAPHS

Rule 1001. Definitions

For purposes of this article the following definitions are applicable:

(1) Writings and recordings. "Writings" and "recordings" consist of letters, words, or numbers, or their equivalent, set down by handwriting, typewriting, printing, photostating, photographing, magnetic impulse, mechanical or electronic recording, or other form of data compilation.

(2) Photographs. "Photographs" include still photographs, X-ray films, video tapes, and motion pictures.

(3) Original. An "original" of a writing or recording is the writing or recording itself or any counterpart intended to have the same effect by a person executing or issuing it. An "original" of a photograph includes the negative or any print therefrom. If data are stored in a computer or similar device, any printout or other output readable by sight, shown to reflect the data accurately, is an "original".

(4) Duplicate. A "duplicate" is a counterpart produced by the same impression as the original, or from the same matrix, or by means of photography, including enlargements and miniatures, or by mechanical or

electronic re-recording, or by chemical reproduction, or by other equivalent techniques which accurately reproduces the original.

Rule 1002. Requirement of Original

To prove the content of a writing, recording, or photograph, the original writing, recording, or photograph is required, except as otherwise provided in these rules or by Act of Congress.

Rule 1003. Admissibility of Duplicates

A duplicate is admissible to the same extent as an original unless (1) a genuine question is raised as to the authenticity of the original or (2) in the circumstances it would be unfair to admit the duplicate in lieu of the original.

Rule 1004. Admissibility of Other Evidence of Contents

The original is not required, and other evidence of the contents of a writing, recording, or photograph is admissible if--

(1) Originals lost or destroyed. All originals are lost or have been destroyed, unless the proponent lost or destroyed them in bad faith; or

(2) Original not obtainable. No original can be obtained by any available judicial process or procedure; or

(3) Original in possession of opponent. At a time when an original was under the control of the party against whom offered, that party was put on notice, by the pleadings or otherwise, that the contents would be a subject of proof at the hearing, and that party does not produce the original at the hearing; or

(4) Collateral matters. The writing, recording, or photograph is not closely related to a controlling issue.

Rule 1005. Public Records

The contents of an official record, or of a document authorized to be recorded or filed and actually recorded or filed, including data compilations in any form, if otherwise admissible, may be proved by copy, certified as correct in accordance with rule 902 or testified to be correct by a witness who has compared it with the original. If a copy which complies with the foregoing cannot be obtained by the exercise of reasonable diligence, then other evidence of the contents may be given.242

Regarding the "original" of an electronic document, E-SIGN provides as follows.

RETENTION OF CONTRACTS AND RECORDS.—

(1) ACCURACY AND ACCESSIBILITY. –If a statute, regulation, or other rule of law requires that a contract or record relating to a transaction in or affecting interstate or foreign commerce be retained, that requirement is met by retaining an electronic record of the information in the contract or other record that—

(A) accurately reflects the information set forth in the contract or other record; and

(B) remains accessible to all persons who are entitled to access by statute, regulation, or rule of law, for the period required by such statute, regulation, or rule of law, in a form that is capable of being accurately reproduced for later reference, whether by transmission, printing, or otherwise.

(2) EXCEPTION.—A requirement to retain a contract or other record in accordance with paragraph (1) does not apply to any information whose sole purpose is to enable the contract or other record to be sent, communicated, or received.

(3) ORIGINALS.—If a statute, regulation, or other rule of law requires a contract or other record relating to a transaction in or affecting interstate or foreign commerce to be provided, available, or retained in its original form, or provides consequences if the contract or other record is not provided, available, or retained in its original form, that statute, regulation, or rule of law is satisfied by an electronic record that complies with paragraph (1).243

Similarly, a state UETA statute typically provides that

(a) If a law requires that a record be retained, the requirement is satisfied by retaining an electronic record of the information in the record which:

1. Accurately reflects the information set forth in the record after the record was first generated in final form as an electronic record or otherwise.

2. Remains accessible for later reference.

…(d)   If a provision of law requires a record to be presented or retained in its original form, or provides consequences if the record is not presented or retained in its original form, that law is satisfied by an electronic record retained in accordance with subsection (a).244

In order to avoid uncertainties in proof of the contents of a document through testimony or other secondary proof, a litigant of a contract issue might prefer that its electronic contract, offered as an original, be accepted as such by a trial judge. An electronic document would satisfy the descriptions of an electronic original in either E-SIGN or UETA, if it accurately reflects the information set forth in the contract and it remains accessible for later reference.

The E-SIGN and UETA criteria of originality alone, however, might not suffice to admit the contract into evidence at trial. Evidence that a printout or other readable output of a contract, or other document, reflects the data accurately might depend not only upon the reproduced informational content of the printout, but also upon the transmission and receipt "meta-data" context of the delivery of the contract, and the reliability of the authentication of the contract as the final agreement of the parties.

Context and reliability of printed contracts are usually proved simply from the "four corners" of the paper contract itself. The context and reliability of an electronic contract might, however, require evidence of data beyond the contract contents, related to transmission time, source and method, and evidence of separate data verifying the actual final approval of the contract contents by the contract parties.245 E-SIGN and UETA each disclaim any requirement that such delivery meta-data be retained in order to comply with record retention laws.246

CHAPTER 5 - Was a Contract Created, and When? (Time and Place of Sending and Receipt)

In Part A, Chapter 4, a), and b), the requirements of offer and acceptance in the formation of a contract were analyzed. Because very few offers are unlimited in their time for acceptance, it is sometimes important to determine exactly when and where an alleged acceptance was made. A mail postmark could prove the time of sending of a contract acceptance. A signed receipt could prove the time of receipt of an acceptance sent by mail or a delivery service. The non-tangible nature of an electronic offer or acceptance, however, requires statutory rules to determine the time and place of sending and receipt of electronic offers and acceptances.

Offers may be ambiguous as to the time, place and manner by which they must be accepted. If no specific requirements for an acceptance are stated in the offer, most U.S. state common law allows an acceptance in any reasonable time, place and manner, so long as the terms in the acceptance match those in the offer.247 U.S. common law developed the so-called "mailbox rule" to deal with offers that are revoked after an acceptance has been sent, but before it has been received. Under this rule, unless the offer provides otherwise, an acceptance, made as invited by the offer, is effective as soon as sent by the offeree, whether or not it ever reaches the offeror.248 This rule does not apply to offers of option contracts, and only applies to acceptances. Revocations of offers must actually be received in order to be effective.

UETA-based statutes allow parties to an electronic contract to make their own rules for when an acceptance is effective, and for when it is sent or received. If the parties do not provide otherwise, the U.S. common law "mailbox rule" will apply. (A different "mailbox rule" applies to international sale of goods contracts, as described in Part C, Section I, Chapter 3, f).) The UETA "default rules" for the time of sending and receipt of an electronic acceptance are:

(a) Unless otherwise agreed between the sender and the

recipient, an electronic record is sent when the record:

1. Is addressed properly or otherwise directed properly to an information processing system that the recipient has designated or uses for the purpose of receiving electronic records or information of the type sent and from which the recipient is able to retrieve the electronic record.

2. Is in a form capable of being processed by that system.

3. Enters an information processing system outside the control of the sender or of a person that sent the electronic record on behalf of the sender or enters a region of the information processing system designated or used by the recipient which is under the control of the recipient.

(b) Unless otherwise agreed between a sender and the recipient, an electronic record is received when the record enters an information processing system that the recipient has designated or uses for the purpose of receiving electronic records or information of the type sent and from which the recipient is able to retrieve the electronic record; and is in a form capable of being processed by that system.249

The place where a contract communication is made is usually less important than the time of its making. It can become important in some circumstances. For example, in determining whether or not a court has personal jurisdiction over the sender of an electronic (or other) communication, the test required by the U.S. Supreme Court to satisfy constitutional due process requirements is whether there are intentional contacts by a contract party with a geographic location, plus a balancing of state interests and party interests, which make it fair to require the communicator to answer to a court in that court location for disputes related to the communication.250

Printed communications sent through mail or courier

delivery are relatively simple to trace geographically. Electronic communications, however, have not had a long history. UETA "default rules" have once again filled the common law gap, by stating

(d) Unless otherwise expressly provided in the electronic record or agreed between the sender and the recipient, an electronic record is deemed to be sent from the sender's place of business and to be received at the recipient's place of business. For purposes of this paragraph, the following rules apply:

1. If the sender or recipient has more than one place of business, the place of business of that person is the place having the closest relationship to the underlying transaction.

2. If the sender or the recipient does not have a place of business, the place of business is the sender's or recipient's residence, as the case may be.251

Further rules are provided by UETA-based statutes regarding: 1) the time of receipt of an electronic record when the locations of a recipient's information processing system and its place of business are different (with no change to rule of receipt), 2) the rule of receipt not requiring an individual person to be aware of receipt by an information processing system, 3) the time of receipt rule not by itself establishing that the content sent corresponds to the content received, and 4) actual knowledge contrary to the results under the rules of sending and receipt, which requires the legal effect of the sending or receipt to be determined by other applicable law (including the common law mailbox rule).252

CHAPTER 6 - What Are the Terms of an Electronic Contract? (Mistake and Error)

In Part A, Chapter 7, e), the defenses against an alleged breach of contract related to mistake were reviewed. If a mutual mistake was made by both parties regarding a basic assumption on which the contract was made, and that mistake has a material adverse effect on a contract duty, the adversely affected party can sometimes avoid liability for not performing that contract duty.253

State common law usually makes it much more difficult, however, to avoid a contract duty because of a unilateral mistake by only one party. Some kind of unfair behavior by the non-mistaken party is usually required to allow the mistaken party to avoid contract liability for a unilateral mistake.254

UETA-based statutes provide rules regarding errors made in the transmission of contract-related electronic communications. These rules are somewhat similar to those of the state common law defense of mistake. For example, where contract parties have agreed to use a security procedure to detect changes or errors, but one party has not followed this security procedure, UETA-based statutes provide that only the party conforming to the procedure may avoid the effect of the changed or erroneous electronic record.255

UETA-based statutes provide a similar rule for the situation of an individual (real person) contracting with an automated electronic "agent" (software program), by stating

(b) In an automated transaction involving an individual, the individual may avoid the effect of an electronic record that resulted from an error made by the individual in dealing with the electronic agent of another person if the electronic agent did not provide an opportunity for the prevention or correction of the error and, at the time the individual learns of the error, the individual:

1. Promptly notifies the other person of the error and that the individual did not intend to be bound by the electronic record received by the other person.

2. Takes reasonable steps, including steps that conform to the other person's reasonable instructions, to return to the other person or, if instructed by the other person, to destroy the consideration received, if any, as a result of the erroneous electronic record.

3. Has not used or received any benefit or value from the consideration, if any, received from the other person.256

If these requirements for rescinding an electronic contract are not satisfied, UETA provides that the erroneous electronic record will have the effect provided by other law, or by the parties' contract. The parties may not, however, agree to change the UETA rules on electronic agent errors, and on the applicability of other laws.257 The failure of the party acting through an electronic agent, to provide an opportunity for prevention or correction of a human input error, is the element of unfairness under UETA that prevents that party from holding the human party liable for their unilateral contract mistake.

CHAPTER 7 - Who Can Act for the Parties to An Electronic Contract? (Automated Transactions and Electronic Agents)

In Part A, Chapter 4, e) i), the methods by which new parties may be substituted for the original parties to a contract were reviewed. Chapter 4, e) ii) analyzed how a third person could become a beneficiary of a contract to which she is not a party.

The rules, according to which a person, or a business entity, can be authorized to act for another person or entity, are the subject of the law of agency. Persons and businesses can authorize others to act for them through formal and informal procedures. Those authorizations can include the authorization of an agent to enter contracts on behalf of their principal.

Electronic contracts are frequently formed through electronic agents, which perform actions for their human or business principals through computer software programs. The substitution of electronic agents for humans can save time and money, especially for repetitive, routine contracts. Online agreements for the licensing of downloaded software programs are one example of an electronic contract formed by an electronic agent offering software to a user, with the human user accepting the offered terms by reading (or not reading) the software license agreement and clicking on an "I Agree" button. Like many agreements for non-electronic goods, the contract terms for many software products are offered on a "take-it-or-leave-it" basis.

"Adhesion" contracts offer only the choice of acceptance and product use, or non-acceptance and product avoidance. They are usually accepted by offerees as a trade-off between efficient, low-cost mass production and marketing of software goods, and less efficient, higher cost production and marketing of software goods with customized and negotiated contract terms. If a user requires the customization of contract terms in order to purchase a software product, they can expect to be charged more for the product as a cost of the extra effort required to create those customized terms, and for any increased risk of contract liability created by such terms.

Non-electronic contracts are sometimes formed through a combination of computer hardware and software operations. With the growth of self-service checkout registers in retail stores, gas stations, and other locations, they are becoming more common.

The advent of electronic contracting agents requires either an expansion of the law of agency, or new statutory adjustments. The same uniform statutes that legitimized electronic contracts generally have also been used to legitimize the formation of electronic contracts through electronic agents.

E-SIGN provides that

> A contract or other record relating to a transaction in or affecting interstate or foreign commerce may not be denied legal effect, validity, or enforceability solely because its formation, creation, or delivery involved the action of one or more electronic agents so long as the action of any such electronic agent is legally attributable to the person to be bound.258

By requiring an electronic agent's actions to be "legally attributable to the person to be bound", this rule defers to the law of agency the determination of whether an electronic agent's actions were authorized.

UETA-based statutes provide that

> In an automated transaction, the following rules apply:

> (a) A contract may be formed by the interaction of electronic agents of the parties, even if no individual was aware of or reviewed the electronic agents' action or the resulting terms and agreements.

(b) A contract may be formed by the interaction of an electronic agent and an individual, acting on the individual's own behalf or for another person, including by an interaction in which the individual performs actions that the individual is free to refuse to perform and which the individual knows or has reason to know will cause the electronic agent to complete the transaction or performance.

(c) The terms of the contract are determined by the substantive law applicable to the contract.259

These UETA-based statutes explicitly authorize contracts between two or more electronic agents that are implicitly authorized by E-SIGN. These types of contracts are more likely to occur between two or more business parties than between one business party and one consumer party. By eliminating the "legally attributable" requirement of E-SIGN, UETA was also intended to clarify that no proof of individual human intention to form a contract would be required. UETA's rules also describe a "take-it-or-leave-it" contract offer by a company to a human offeree, which would probably be accepted either by clicking on an "I Agree" button, or rejected by clicking on a "Decline" or "I Don't Agree" button. UETA's final rule emphasizes that general contract law determines what the terms are of an electronic contract that is formed by one or more electronic agents.

CHAPTER 8 - How Are Electronic Contracts Broken/Breached?

a) Early Shrink-wrap, Browse-wrap and Click-wrap Cases

Some aspects of electronic contracts are unique, such as the evidence of an electronic original, the time and place of sending and receipt of electronic offers and acceptances, and the procedures for correction of erroneous keystrokes. Most electronic contract issues, however, involve the same rules that apply to printed contracts.

The basic rules of U.S. contract law, presented in Part A, establish how electronic contracts are formed and breached, their defenses against claims of breach, and how they are enforced. The type of electronic contract that is at issue--"click-wrap", "browse-wrap", e-mail, or a combination thereof—will affect how the rules of contract formation are applied to them.

i) Shrink-wrap Cases

Brower v. Gateway 2000, Inc.260 involved a class action lawsuit by consumers who had purchased home computers by mail or telephone. When the plaintiffs-consumers sued the seller for breach of contract for failure to provide promised warranty service, the seller moved to dismiss the lawsuit. It argued that the "Standard Terms and Conditions Agreement" printed on the "shrink-wrap" packaging of the computers required that any dispute "be settled exclusively and finally by arbitration", using the services of the International Chamber of Commerce office in Chicago, Illinois. The agreement stated that, if a buyer kept the computer more than thirty days from the date of its delivery, the buyer accepted all the terms of this agreement.

A New York state trial judge dismissed the class action lawsuit, because the arbitration clause of the agreement provided that arbitration was the exclusive remedy for any dispute. On appeal, the buyers argued that the agreement had not been accepted by them under the "battle of the forms" rules of UCC §2-207, and that the arbitration clause was unconscionable because of the greater inconvenience and cost to the buyers of arbitration, compared to litigation in court.

The appeals court decided that the consumers had accepted the seller's contract offer by keeping their computers for more than thirty days, and that UCC §2-207 did not affect this result. Consumer buyers in retail stores might routinely make offers to sellers of goods who have advertised the terms of the offers they will accept. Gateway 2000, Inc., however, was like some other sellers of complex goods or services, such as airlines and insurers. It offered its computer for sale, with buyer payment and goods delivery preceding the buyer's receipt of the contract terms, including the method of acceptance, rather than occurring simultaneously. As the saying goes, the "seller is the master of the offer", and it dictates the offer's terms and its method of acceptance.

The appeals court determined that procedural unconscionability did not exist, because the buyers had a meaningful choice of whether or not to reject the seller's terms, by returning the computers to the seller, and then buying from a competitor. Unlike some states, however, New York allows substantive unconscionability alone to invalidate a contract, if its terms are unreasonable. The court decided that mandatory arbitration before the International Chamber of Commerce required excessive costs (including mailing copies of all documents to ICC headquarters in Paris, France). These costs unreasonably discouraged buyers from using the arbitration remedy, and left them with no practical remedy for a contract breach. The appeals court returned the case to the trial judge, instructing him to appoint a U.S.-based arbitrator, as a compromise between no arbitration and a costly arbitration hosted by a foreign organization that did not usually deal with consumer arbitration parties.

*Stenzel v. Dell, Inc.*261, a Maine appellate decision, involved another class action lawsuit that was defeated by an arbitration clause. This clause was included in Dell Computer's shrink-wrap Terms and Conditions agreement. The court discussed the facts of the two lead plaintiffs' purchases. One consumer plaintiff ordered a computer by telephone. The other ordered a computer through Dell's web site. Both objected to the seller's charging of sales taxes and to its shipping charges. Dell maintained that their complaints must be resolved through arbitration, as required by their shrink-wrap sales contract terms.

Although the consumers initiated the purchases, the court viewed the relevant contract offer as having been made by Dell in its Terms and Conditions agreement. As in the *Brower* case, the court decided that the contract offer was made by the seller, because Dell included in its delivered product package contract terms that it would not negotiate. Where goods are sold by a distant seller, rather than through stores (or if the goods are an expensive and/or complex product that requires set-up and installation), the offer terms often state that by retaining the product beyond a specific time period, the consumer buyer accepts the seller's offered contract terms.

The *Stenzel* court decided that each of the Dell computer buyers was given adequate notice of the mandatory arbitration term of the contract, because they were given three opportunities to review the terms: first, on Dell's web site; second, on their order acknowledgement forms; and third, in the shrink-wrap agreement.

Especially important to the court was the statement in capital letters at the beginning of the shrink-wrap agreement stating that it contained

...VERY IMPORTANT INFORMATION ABOUT YOUR RIGHTS AND OBLIGATIONS, AS WELL AS LIMITATIONS AND EXCLUSIONS THAT MAY APPLY TO YOU. THIS DOCUMENT CONTAINS A DISPUTE RESOLUTION CLAUSE.

Whether or not the consumers actually read the agreement was irrelevant, according to the court. As many other judicial opinions have stated, a contract party is not excused from complying with contract terms that they have accepted expressly (by words or signatures or conduct) or implicitly (by action or inaction), even if they failed to read the terms they accepted. Were the law otherwise, contract obligations could easily be later avoided by an initial refusal to read the contract. The court also rejected unconscionability arguments, in part because arbitration was not shown to be prohibitively expensive for the consumers.

In *DeFontes v. Dell, Inc.*262, a consumer class action was brought against the computer seller for deceptive collection of taxes on service contracts. Dell moved to dismiss the case and to compel arbitration, based on a mandatory arbitration clause in the Terms and Conditions agreement of sale, which was similar to the agreement in the *Stenzel* case. These terms were accessible through a hyperlink on the product website, were in the product shrink-wrap agreement, and were in the seller's acknowledgement of the buyers' orders. As described also in section ii) below, the browse-wrap contract was determined by the Rhode Island state trial judge to be insufficiently conspicuous to bind the consumer buyers. He also decided that the shrink-wrap agreement gave insufficient notice to the buyers of their rights to return the computers to the seller, and thereby to avoid its prescribed method of acceptance.

On appeal, the Rhode Island Supreme Court applied UCC §2-207 to this sale of goods. It determined that, for complex goods like a computer, the seller was the usual offeror and the consumer the usual offeree. Such a contract was formed only when the consumer accepts the seller's terms after having a reasonable opportunity to refuse them. The court determined, however, that Dell failed to sufficiently inform the buyers of their right to reject the goods by returning them. The terms stated that "[by] accepting delivery of the computer systems, related products, and/or services and support, and/or other products described on that invoice[,] You ('Customer') agrees to be bound by and accepts those terms and conditions." The agreement was determined to have failed to clearly inform the buyers of the time period beyond which they could not return their computers, and after which they would be deemed to have accepted the goods and related contract terms. For this reason, and unlike the *Stenzel* decision, the buyers were determined to not have accepted the seller's offered terms merely by keeping their computers. The mandatory arbitration agreement term was not enforced. Two different courts reached different results regarding the same basic agreement.

ii) Browse-wrap Cases of Sufficient Notice of Terms of Use

One of the first cases to enforce a browse-wrap agreement, by finding that the use of a web site contrary to browse-wrap Terms of Use was a contract breach, was *Register.com, Inc. v. Verio, Inc.*263, litigated initially in the federal trial court for the Southern District of New York [Manhattan]. In that case, Register.com issued domain names for web sites under its agreement with the Internet Corporation for Assigned Names and Numbers (ICANN). The ICANN agreement required Register.com to obtain from applicants certain identifying ("WHOIS") information, and to make that information available to the public without charge. Register.com also operated a web site development business that competed with Verio, Inc.'s web site services business. Verio created an automated software program to obtain daily updated WHOIS information from Register.com's web site, which Verio then used to solicit Register.com registrants through e-mail, telemarketing and direct mail.

Register.com's web site browse-wrap Terms of Use provided that

By submitting a WHOIS inquiry, you agree that you will use this data only for lawful purposes and that under no circumstances will you use this data to …support the transmission of mass unsolicited, commercial advertising or solicitation via email.

The browse-wrap terms also prohibited any user from accessing the WHOIS database using automated processes, such as software "robots" (or "bots"). Register.com received complaints from some of its registrants that Verio had sent them email solicitations for Verio's web site services that appeared to have been sanctioned by Register.com. These registrants had opted out of receiving commercial solicitations from Register.com. Register.com demanded that Verio stop its email solicitations in violation of the browse-wrap agreement.

Register.com's agreement with ICANN required it to permit the use of WHOIS data "for any lawful purpose except to...support the transmission of mass unsolicited solicitations via email (spam)." Register.com, after making its demand to Verio, also added, to its browse-wrap Terms of Use prohibition on the use of WHOIS data inquiries for email solicitations of customers, solicitations of customers "via direct mail...or by telephone." Verio ceased using Register.com's WHOIS information for mass solicitations by email, but continued to use it for mass solicitations by direct mail and telephone.

Register.com sued Verio, seeking a temporary restraining order and a preliminary injunction, to stop Verio from using Register.com's WHOIS information for direct mail and telephone marketing. The trial court granted these requests on grounds of both breach of the browse-wrap contract and trespass to personal property. On appeal, Verio argued that it was a third party beneficiary of the ICANN agreement's requirement of public access to WHOIS information, which did not specifically mention mass solicitations by telephone or direct mail in its prohibition of use of the information for email "spam".

The federal appeals court rejected Verio's third party beneficiary argument, because the ICANN agreement stated specifically that it was not intended to give contract benefits to third parties, and because the agreement provided a specific internal ICANN procedure for third parties to use to resolve disputes about use of registrant information. Regarding the browse-wrap contract issue, the court recognized that the Terms of Use appeared on the user's computer screen only with the results of a WHOIS inquiry, rather than on the initial web page presented to the public. Verio argued that this type of browse-wrap notice to users was inadequate to create an implicit assent to Register.com's terms simply by using the information on the screen, because it was presented only after the inquiries were made, and after the WHOIS information was displayed. Verio also argued that it could only be bound to Register.com's Terms of Use by clicking its assent to them after they were presented.

The appeals court focused on the likelihood of actual notice to a user, like Verio, of Register.com's browse-wrap procedures and policies. By focusing on the characteristics of, and context for, the party presented with web site Terms of Use, the court placed electronic web site contracts within the mainstream of basic contract law. This law emphasizes whether the actual user, who is alleged to have agreed to contract terms, received reasonable notice of those terms. The court noted that Verio was a daily user of Register.com's web site information. Verio even admitted that it actually knew the content of Register.com's Terms of Use, although it acted contrary to them.

The court stated that Verio was like a passerby, who might be excused from paying the first time, if he sees a posted price of apples for sale only after eating one from a roadside stand. The passerby would not be excused, however, for later unpaid snacks like this. Verio could not succeed with its argument of inadequate notice of the Terms of Use for its retrievals of Register.com's registration information, after its first robotic snack.

The court also rejected Verio's argument that it could only be bound to Register.com's Terms of Use through a "click-wrap" type of acceptance. As with any printed or oral contract, Verio accepted Register.com's offer of the benefits of use of Register.com's web site once Verio was given notice of the Terms of Use, and then silently accepted those benefits by using the web site. This created an implied-in-fact contract, or a "contract by conduct", under standard offer and acceptance rules described in Part A, Chapter 4, b).264

The court rejected Verio's argument that an "I Agree" click was necessary to bind a web site user to the web site provider's Terms of Use, or that a 2002 case in the same appellate court, *Specht v. Netscape Communications Corp.*265 always required a click-wrap type of acceptance of web site Terms of Use.

Specht involved a user agreement to arbitrate disputes with Netscape regarding its browser software. The agreement to arbitrate was contained in the terms of the offer of use of the software, which were posted on Netscape's web site, but which were not necessarily seen by typical customers downloading the browser software. This is because it was unnecessary to scroll to the bottom of the page where the terms of use were posted in order to download the browser software, and customers were not instructed to do so. Because there was no evidence that the customers had actually seen (or reasonably should have seen) the terms of the offer, the appellate court held that they could not be bound by those terms. This did not mean, however, that an offeree's acceptance of web site Terms of Use must always and only be made through a click-wrap agreement.

Register.com involved an implicit acceptance, by a commercial and repeat user of a web site, of browse-wrap Terms of Use. Later cases have analyzed whether, and how, a one-time, consumer user of a web site might accept an offer of browse-wrap contract terms by using a web site.

In *DeFontes v. Dell, Inc.*266(discussed previously as a shrink-wrap case), consumers complained that they were not bound by browse-wrap Terms of Use requiring arbitration of disputes. Although the terms were also presented in the shrink-wrap of the purchased computer, the judge decided that the browse-wrap arbitration terms were not accepted by the consumers' retention and use of the computer, because they were "inconspicuously located at the bottom of the webpage". This was insufficient notice of the arbitration terms for a one-time, consumer contracting party.

In *Southwest Airlines Co. v. BoardFirst, L.L.C.*267, BoardFirst tried to circumvent the airline's famous policy against reserved seating, by soliciting passengers to give BoardFirst their ticket information in order for it to use it to check-in on the airline's web site (in exchange for payment by the passengers). The web site Terms of Use, however, prohibited any third party from using it "for the purpose of checking Customers in online or attempting to obtain for them a boarding pass in any certain boarding group." Southwest had also notified BoardFirst, through cease-and-desist letters, that its continuing scheme was a violation of the Terms of Use. A federal trial judge in Texas decided that, despite its protestations that it had not read the web site browse-wrap terms, as in the *Register.com* case, BoardFirst had actual knowledge of the terms from Southwest's letters. Even without the letters, BoardFirst might have had sufficient notice of the Terms of Use, because, as in *Register.com*, a sophisticated internet business would probably expect such prohibitions, especially since BoardFirst repeatedly used the airline's web site for its own business purposes. Because Southwest was unable to quantify the money damages caused by BoardFirst's breach of contract, the judge only awarded Southwest a permanent injunction against BoardFirst's use of its web site in violation of the Terms of Use.

In *Druyan v. Jagger*268, an online buyer of a Rolling Stones concert ticket sued the seller, Ticketmaster, for her travel and hotel expenses resulting from an alleged breach of contract when an Atlantic City concert was cancelled. The web site Terms of Use, however, provided that, in the event of a concert cancellation, Ticketmaster "will not be liable for travel or any other expenses...". The browse-wrap Terms of Use also stated that Ticketmaster was not liable for incidental or consequential damages for any contract breach. After dismissing the claims against the band's lead singer, Mick Jagger, against the concert promoter, and against the plaintiff's hotel, the New York federal trial judge determined that the terms were "sufficiently conspicuous" to bind the ticket buyer to a contract.

Immediately above a "Look for Tickets" button, the statement appeared that "[B]y clicking on the 'Look for Tickets' button or otherwise using this web site, you agree to the Terms of Use". The Terms of Use were represented by a hyperlink. The judge determined that, by clicking on the button, the ticket buyer had agreed to the Terms of Use, whether or not she actually read them. The buyer had been using the Ticketmaster web site for five years.

iii) Unusual Click-wrap Cases

In *eBay, Inc. v. Bidder's Edge, Inc.*269, the online auction site eBay permitted bids on auctioned items only by users who had clicked on an "I Agree" box, which indicated their acceptance of the terms of the eBay User Agreement. The terms prohibited accessing the eBay web site through any device with a purpose to monitor or to copy its web pages or content without permission. eBay used "robot exclusion headers", which sent warning messages to computers that might use automated software programs to copy the contents of eBay's site, and then transmit it to other locations. Bidder's Edge was an auction site aggregator. It had entered a license agreement with eBay in 1998 to automatically research and compare a limited category of goods on eBay's site with those on other auction sites.

After negotiations failed, between Bidder's Edge and eBay, to allow Bidder's Edge to expand its license to new goods categories, Bidder's Edge nevertheless used "bots" programs to automatically copy and compare these new goods from eBay's website. eBay requested a court injunction ordering Bidder's Edge to stop accessing its site in this manner without a license. In 2000, the California federal trial judge granted the request on the basis of a property law argument of trespass against eBay's personal property.

Because Bidder's Edge had received a license from eBay to copy and re-transmit parts of its web site, it does not appear that it was actually bound by the click-wrap Terms of Use that would have applied to a normal user. Arguments might also have been made, however, that this was either a case of a contract breach by Bidder's Edge in violation of the terms of eBay's original license agreement, or a violation of the browse-wrap "robot exclusion header" User Agreement. The case was settled by the parties before an appeal of the trial judge's decision was completed.

In *Doe v. SexSearch.com* 270, a customer joined an online adult dating service. He contacted a person online, who described herself as eighteen years old, and he arranged to meet her. After they had sex, he learned that she had lied about her age, and that she was only fourteen years old. After his arrest for sexual misconduct with a minor, and subsequent damaging publicity, the customer sued SexSearch alleging breach of contract, alleging the unconscionability of the service's click-wrap contract terms limiting its liability, and arguing for the service's vicarious liability for the minor's misrepresentations because of its negligence.

The court of appeals determined that there was no contract breach, because the web site click-wrap terms and conditions stated that the service was not responsible for the accuracy of information provided by its users. It also found that there was neither fraud, nor negligent infliction of emotional distress against the customer, nor negligent misrepresentation of information, nor deceptive consumer sales practices by the service. The court also found that the service's limitation of liability was not unconscionable. *People v. Direct Revenue, LLC*, in subsection f) below, reached a similar conclusion about the non-liability of an intermediary online service provider for misrepresentations by a commercial third party user.

b) Cases of Contract Terms Located in Multiple Documents

i) A Case of E-mail Changes to Conditions of Employment

Not every electronic contract case involves the use of a web site or the purchase of computer hardware or software. Many contracts, such as employment contracts, do not involve the sale of goods. Most workers in the United States do not work under individual or union employment contracts. Nevertheless, courts have determined that an employer's discretion to change its employees' conditions of employment is sometimes limited by statements made by the employer in its employee handbook. Many courts have determined that a contract relationship is created when an employer requires its employees to comply with certain conditions stated in a handbook. This could be considered to be an offer of employment contract terms, which is accepted expressly, or implicitly through the employee's work after his receipt of notice of the conditions of employment and the handbook terms.

In a 2005 federal appellate case, *Campbell v. General Dynamics Government Systems Corp.*271, a company notified its employees of changes to its employment handbook through a mass e-mail. The employees were not required to acknowledge receipt of the changes or to indicate their understanding of them. The e-mail included hyperlinks through which the employees could learn further information, including the required arbitration of discrimination claims. Employees were not required to click on the hyperlinks, however, and the company did not track whether or not they did so.

When the company later attempted to force its employees to use arbitration to resolve discrimination claims, and they resisted, federal trial and appellate courts decided that notice of handbook changes through e-mail must be "enough to put a reasonable employee on inquiry notice of an alteration to the contractual aspects of the employment relationship" in order to be an enforceable contract offer. The courts found that this particular e-mail message failed to give such reasonable notice, given the lack of previous use of company e-mails to make binding changes to employment rules.

ii) A Case of Shrink-wrap Additions to a Printed Negotiated Agreement

A Kansas state court case assumed, as the *Campbell* courts did, that the terms of a printed contract could later be changed by adding additional terms. The Supreme Court of Kansas decided, however, that the manner of presentation of the offer of contract terms in *Wachter Management Co. v. Dexter & Chaney, Inc.*272 was insufficient to give adequate notice of the existence of a clause in added terms that chose a King County (Seattle) state trial court as the only proper forum for litigation of contract disputes.

A construction company buying accounting and project-management software was notified in a cover letter for a written and signed printed "proposal" (without an "entire agreement" merger clause) that further licenses were included in the proposal. The original proposal itself did not refer to or incorporate by reference any licenses. The shrink-wrap license for the delivered software (with a merger clause) included a choice of forum in a King County, Washington court.

Federal appeals courts had previously concluded that similar computer shrink-wrap license agreements were contract offers that (as stated in the license) would be accepted by the buyer's action of keeping the product for more than a certain number of days. The majority of the seven judges on the Kansas Supreme Court concluded, however, that, under the applicable rules of UCC §2-204 (Formation in General) and UCC §2-209 (Modification; Rescission and Waiver), this shrink-wrap license was an attempt to amend an existing contract.

The court distinguished this case from *Brower v. Gateway 2000, Inc.*, and similar cases that allow acceptance of a contract offer by use of goods shipped with additional shrink-wrap contract terms. The character of the buyer as a business, which had already negotiated and concluded its contract proposal terms, was a decisively distinctive fact for the majority of this court. This conclusion, however, seems out of the mainstream of most courts' analyses of the effectiveness of shrink-wrap agreement contract terms.

On the point of whether or not the Uniform Commercial Code applies to a sale of software as goods, however, the decision is in agreement with many court decisions, at least where the sale of software is the predominant purpose of the contract, and the services accompanying the software are of an incidental nature.

The *Affinity Internet, Inc. v. Consolidated Credit Counseling Services, Inc.* case discussed in Chapter 9, h) hereafter, and the *Hugger-Mugger, LLC v. NetSuite, Inc.* case discussed in Chapter 10 hereafter, each involved a printed agreement that "incorporates by reference" into it other contract terms located on a web site. Incorporation by reference is a standard contract drafting practice by which contract terms located in a different document are made a part of the agreement that is actually signed, through a reference to the other document in the signed agreement. This is usually done for purposes of convenience, where the different document was already written for another contract. The other terms are only referred to, rather than repeated in their entirety, in order to save space.

There is nothing wrong with drafting a contract in this manner, so long as the other terms are easily accessible to both contract parties, and so long as their incorporation by reference is stated clearly to the party who has not written or used the terms previously. If these requirements are met, then the "duty to read" of the party that has not written these terms creates a contract, when this duty is combined with an action of that party that appears to a reasonable person to be an expression of acceptance of those incorporated terms.

iii) Invoices that Incorporate (by Reference) Web Site Terms

In *International Star Registry of Illinois v. Omnipoint Marketing, LLC*273, two businesses entered multiple contracts by signing printed invoices. Each invoice stated that, by signing the invoice, the party indicated that it "read and agree[d] to…the terms and conditions posted" at the address of Omnipoint Marketing's web site.

A contract dispute arose that involved a disagreement concerning where the dispute should be resolved. Omnipoint, an electronic mail advertiser, argued that the forum selection clause, included in its web site terms and conditions, should apply as a part of the contract agreement, resulting in a transfer of the case to a federal trial court in Florida. Star Registry argued that the incorporation by reference of the web site terms into the invoice contract was insufficient to put it on notice that the forum selection clause was part of the contract.

The Illinois federal trial court decided that Star Registry was bound by the web site terms for invoices that it signed, because the terms were adequately described in the invoice, and the invoice clearly expressed the parties' intention that the web site terms become a part of their contract. The common law and the statutory law of contracts are very flexible about how a contract is documented. Although many contracts are written very formally, with lots of "legalese", these practices are neither necessary (nor sometimes sufficient) to form a binding, legal contract. Legally enforceable contracts can be documented informally in one or more writings. They can even be created without a written document in many cases. (See Part A, Chapter 4.)

*Manasher v. NECC Telecom*274 arose from a contract for consumer long-distance telephone service. The consumers agreed to begin service in response to telemarketer solicitations. After using the service, they received an invoice bill that included fees that the consumers disputed. When they tried to bring their dispute to court, the company noted on the second page of the invoice a statement that "NECC's Agreement 'Disclosure and Liabilities' can be found online at www.necc.us or you could request a copy by calling us at (800) 766 2642." Within the "Disclosure and Liabilities" document was a clause that compelled all disputes to be resolved through arbitration.

The federal trial judge rejected the company's argument that a single mention of the "Disclosure and Liabilities" was sufficient to incorporate by reference the arbitration clause into the long-distance service contract, because there was no statement in the invoice providing clear evidence of the parties' intention that the other document, and its terms, would become part of a binding contract. In doing so, the judge distinguished this case from the facts of *Treiber & Straub, Inc. v. United Parcel Service, Inc.*, discussed in section d) hereafter, because in *Treiber & Straub, Inc.* the consumer twice affirmed by clicking on a computer screen box that he had agreed to UPS's terms and conditions. In this case, the consumers never affirmatively indicated their agreement to NECC Telecom's contract terms. The judge also distinguished these facts from those in the *Hugger-Mugger, LLC v. Netsuite, Inc.* case discussed in Chapter 9, section j) hereafter, because, unlike in this case, in Hugger-Mugger the incorporation by reference was clearly stated and affirmatively agreed to in a click-wrap agreement.

*Greer v. 1-800-Flowers.com*275 involved a customer who ordered flowers for his girlfriend by telephone. The company sent a "Thank You" note to his home, which was opened by his wife. His wife requested and received a proof of purchase for the flowers. She also received information about the girlfriend's identity and the contents of the card accompanying the flowers. The customer sued the company in Texas for breach of its Privacy Policy and for damages connected with his divorce. The company moved to dismiss the suit based on the forum selection clause in its web site Terms of Use, which stated that all legal claims must be made in New York.

Prior to his ordering the flowers, and in response to the customer's telephone question about its Privacy Policy, the company told Greer that the policy could be viewed on its web site. Greer ordered the flowers based on the Privacy Policy on the web site. In his lawsuit, however, he argued that his contract for his telephone order for flowers included the Privacy Policy, but did not include the Terms of Use for the company's web site. The Texas federal trial judge noted that the telephone representative had told Greer that the company's web site contained the Privacy Policy. If he had read the policy, he would have seen first, that on the first page and in all capital letters it stated that it was part of the Terms of Use, second, that a link to the Terms of Use was located on the left-hand side of the Privacy Policy, and third, that the Terms of Use stated that they would be agreed to by any party accessing the web site. The terms contained the clause choosing New York as the forum for contract disputes. Although Greer ordered his flowers by telephone, his complaint involved the web site Privacy Policy, and the related Terms of Use forum selection clause applied to "any claim relating to this Web Site" or its content. The customer could not avoid the transfer of the case to New York by arguing that he was not sufficiently notified that the forum selection clause was a part of his contract. His failure to read the Terms of Use did not change this result.

c) Mandatory Arbitration and Forum Selection Clauses, and Hybrid Click-wrap Contracts

Contract terms that require private arbitration of disputes between parties, rather than litigation in public courts, are a frequent point of contention regarding the effectiveness of shrink-wrap, click-wrap and browse-wrap contract terms. Consumers and employees usually perceive arbitration as more favorable to businesses and employers than is litigation in public courts.

Forum selection (or choice-of-forum) clauses are another point of contention. Arbitration clauses choose how a contract dispute will be resolved. Forum selection clauses choose where a contract dispute will be resolved.

A successful legal argument might be made against these contract choices, such as unconscionability in the substance of an arbitration clause, or the procedure through which it was created and agreed to. Unfairness of the chosen forum or its applicable law, or violation of public policy arguments might be made against a forum selection clause. Otherwise, the parties are allowed to choose their dispute resolution procedure and their dispute resolution forum pursuant to their freedom of contract. (See Part A, Chapter 7, d)'s discussion of the defense of unconscionability.)

In a Pennsylvania federal trial court case in 2007, a tort lawyer, and Google customer, opened his AdWords account by navigating to a page that contained the AdWords contract terms and conditions. The page had a notice at the top stating "Carefully read the following terms and conditions. If you agree with these terms, indicate your assent below." The customer could scroll to the bottom of a box on the same page containing the terms, and click to indicate his agreement with the terms before opening his account. He could also obtain a printer-friendly version for printing or for viewing in a full screen. The terms included a forum selection clause choosing San Jose County, California. The customer was required to, and did, click a box below the scroll box to indicate his agreement. When his contract dispute arose, however, he argued that the forum selection clause was not enforceable against him, because the entire agreement was not visible at one time in the scroll box.

In *Feldman v. Google, Inc.*276, a lawyer-advertiser-customer complained of being charged by Google for improper use by others of his AdWords hyperlink on Google's search results page. The federal trial judge decided that the customer had received reasonable and adequate notice of the forum selection clause, even though it was not immediately visible at the beginning of the scroll box. The warning to read the terms was visible at the top of the web page before the forum selection clause. The click-wrap "I Agree" box was located at the bottom of the scroll box after the forum selection clause. Therefore, the customer had received reasonable and adequate notice of the contract terms and had indicated his agreement to those terms. Actual reading and understanding of the terms by the customer, as usual, was not necessary to bind him to those contract terms. The judge emphasized that the contract was legible in 12- point font and was only seven paragraphs, and that the customer had ample time to read and review its terms.

Another case in which the manner of presentation of a click-wrap agreement with an arbitration clause, and the context in which it was made available to be read and understood, determined its enforceability was the New York federal trial court case of *Bar-Ayal v. Time-Warner Cable, Inc.*277 A cable customer purchased software products and services pursuant to a click-wrap agreement located on a CD-ROM. He later brought a class action suit for allegedly excessive service charges.

Installation of the software required the customer to click on an "I Accept" graphic eight times during the installation process, including a final click that indicated that the buyer "had the opportunity to read and understand each and every term set forth" in the agreement, including section 13 which required arbitration of disputes. The customer argued that he could bring a class action lawsuit, and was not bound by the mandatory arbitration requirement of the contract, because it was hard to find. It required scrolling through 30 separate screen presentations to reach it. The federal trial judge rejected this argument, noting that "[i]t is not significantly more arduous to scroll down to read an agreement on a computer screen than to turn the pages of a printed agreement...". If printed, the agreement would have totaled nine pages. The arbitration requirement, unlike most of the terms, was in all capitalized letters. The judge compared the customer's clicking on the "I Accept" button, without scrolling to read all the contract terms, to signing a printed agreement without reading all of its terms. The objectively manifested action of assent was sufficient to create a binding contract, regardless of subjective intent.

In *Fteja v. Facebook, Inc.*278, a New York Facebook user, whose account was allegedly terminated without explanation, sued in a New York state court alleging religious and ethnic discrimination. The California-based social network removed the case to a New York federal court under federal "diversity jurisdiction". (See Part A, Chapter 2, b).) Facebook then moved to transfer the case to the federal trial court in Santa Clara County, California, as a more convenient venue, and pursuant to the Terms of Use for its service. These terms stated

> You will resolve any claim, cause of action or dispute ("claim") you have with us arising out of or relating to this Statement or Facebook exclusively in a state or federal court located in Santa Clara County. The laws of the State of California will govern this Statement, as well as any claim that might arise between you and us, without regard to conflict of law provisions. You agree to submit to the personal jurisdiction of the courts located in Santa Clara County, California for the purpose of litigating all such claims.

The former user claimed that he had not read these terms when he signed up to use the social network. In response, Facebook noted that all users are required to click on a "Sign

Up" button that states just below it: "By clicking Sign Up, you are indicating that you have read and agree to the Terms of Service." The phrase "Terms of Service" was highlighted and underlined, indicating a hyperlink to the text of the terms.

The rules developed in prior state and federal cases regarding click-wrap and browse-wrap contracts were applied by the New York federal trial court. It first determined that the former user could be bound by contract terms that he indicated assent to, regardless of whether he actually read or understood them, so long as the terms had been reasonably communicated. Facebook offered proof that the service could not be accessed without clicking the "Sign Up" button.

Unlike many click-wrap contracts, the text of the terms was not presented to the user on the same page on which he clicked his assent to the terms. Nevertheless, the user's own claims that he had used the service extensively indicated that he was a knowledgeable internet user who understood that the text of the terms was available through the hyperlink.

The trial judge compared the hyperlinked terms (in this hybrid click-wrap contract) to a sign above bins of apples at a roadside fruit stand that states "By picking up this apple, you consent to the terms of sales by this fruit stand. For those terms, turn over this sign." The judge also compared the hyperlinked terms to terms of sale, including a fine print forum selection clause, printed on the reverse side of a cruise ship ticket. This type of presentation of terms has been enforced by the U.S. Supreme Court.279 The judge ruled that "clicking the hyperlinked phrase is the twenty-first century equivalent of turning over the cruise ticket." However, "whether or not the consumer bothers to look is irrelevant" so long as the requirement of the terms in return for the service, and their location are reasonably communicated.

Although an assent to a forum selection clause contained in click-wrap terms of use does not by itself require a transfer of venue to the chosen forum, the New York federal trial judge determined that all other relevant factors also favored the transfer of the lawsuit to California. All records and witnesses pertaining to the claim of improper discrimination were located in California. The alleged breach of contract occurred in California. There was no factual connection to the New York federal district alleged by the plaintiff. There were no facts alleged by the plaintiff showing that he would be unable to litigate the case in California. Because no other reasons were presented to prevent the user from complying with this choice-of-forum contract duty, the lawsuit was transferred to the federal court in California.

In *Sherman v. AT&T Inc.*280, a residential internet service customer sued AT&T for breach of contract and unjust enrichment, alleging that AT&T had overcharged customers by advertising promotional plans, but billing customers at standard rates. Besides his own claims, Sherman sought to represent a class of similarly situated AT&T customers. The defendants moved to compel non-class arbitration pursuant to their click-wrap terms of service agreement, and to stay the federal district court proceedings pending the outcome of the arbitration.

The Illinois federal trial judge determined that Sherman had clicked his agreement to AT&T's terms of service agreement, as he was required to do in order to obtain residential internet service for his home computer. The click-wrap box, which Sherman was required to check, only showed a hyperlink "AT&T Terms of Service", rather than showing the actual terms. (As in *Fteja*, this is sometimes called a "modified" or "hybrid" click-wrap agreement to indicate its mixture of click-wrap and browse-wrap procedures.) Nevertheless, the click-wrap assent stated that "I have read and agree to the AT&T Terms of Service...". Sherman was later notified by e-mail of a change of address for the mandatory individual arbitration provision in the Terms of Service Agreement. The e-mail also provided only a link to the actual agreement terms, and stated that by continuing to use the service, customers would agree to the terms.

Sherman's arguments against the enforceability of the

arbitration agreement term were that the telephone sales representative he spoke with, to order his internet service, never mentioned the arbitration requirement, that the failure to present or expressly incorporate the Terms of Service in the click-wrap button presentation made their enforcement unconscionable, and that the Terms of Service agreement lacked mutuality of party obligations. The federal trial judge determined that the internet service purchase was a "purchase now, terms later" contract that fairly balanced reasonable notice of terms against consumer cost and inconvenience, like other telephone and retail sales that depend on a customer's duty to read the contract to which she agrees.

Regarding the adequacy of the hybrid click-wrap notice of contract terms, the judge relied on the decision in *Hill v. Gateway 2000, Inc.*, and the decision described in the next section in *Treiber & Straub, Inc. v. United Parcel Service.* He determined that adequate notice was provided of the actual terms, which provided "in clear and reasonable language, in capital letters" the mandatory arbitration requirement that waived Sherman's right to bring a class action.

Sherman's argument of procedural unconscionability, because of the presentation of the contract terms through a hyperlink, was rejected for similar reasons that "the Terms are not difficult to find, read or understand". The judge finally addressed the argument that the contract lacked mutuality, because only claims against AT&T were required to be arbitrated, while claims by AT&T were not. Under Illinois contract law, the judge determined that this type of mutual obligation was not required if Sherman received consideration in return for his agreement to arbitrate. The agreement provided for AT&T to pay all arbitration filing, administration and arbitrator fees, unless the complaint was frivolous, with a maximum customer cost of $125 for even frivolous claims of less than $10,000. The motion to compel arbitration and to stay litigation was granted.

d) The Diamond Ring Shipment Cases

Sometimes several cases involve such similar, and interesting, facts that they deserve to be analyzed together. Three court decisions have involved expensive diamond rings sent through United Parcel Service (UPS), which were later lost or stolen. When the shippers-customers tried to make claims against UPS for the value of the lost rings, the legal results showed some interesting "rules of the road" for click-wrap contracts.

In the first case, *Treiber & Straub, Inc. v. United Parcel Service, Inc.*281, a jeweler retailer arranged with UPS to return a diamond ring to its wholesaler. The jeweler used the UPS web site, where he thought he purchased, for a $174.65 premium, $50,000 insurance coverage for a ring with an actual value of $105,000. The customer listed on the airbill the actual value of the ring as $50,000. When the ring was lost in transit, the jeweler sued UPS for $50,000.

He had clicked twice on the click-wrap assent box on the UPS web site to indicate his agreement with its Terms and Conditions of Service. The terms stated that "excess value insurance does not provide any insurance protection for packages or letters having an actual value of more than $50,000…". Therefore, for items of "unusual value", defined as more than $50,000, there was no insurance coverage at all.

The customer argued that the insurance exclusions were not sufficiently clear and conspicuous to draw his attention. As a matter of federal common law, in furtherance of uniformity of law on common carrier liability for interstate shipping, the federal appellate court determined that the jeweler had received clear and reasonable notice of the limits of insurance, because they were presented both in the web site Terms and Conditions, and they were referred to in the UPS Tariff schedule, which was mentioned in the Terms and Conditions, and which was available on the web site.

Although the jeweler was a first-time user of the web site, he was a sophisticated customer sending an expensive product. If he did not read (and understand) the insurance limitations that he agreed to, he should have. UPS, according to the court, could choose how to limit its liability for expensive packages according to terms it reasonably disclosed. It could also avoid any liability for lost packages that were more expensive than the value listed by its customers.

In the next case, *Feldman v. United Parcel Service, Inc.*282, the shipper-customer purchased a $57,000 diamond ring from a web site under an arrangement with the seller that allowed the buyer to return the ring if he was dissatisfied. The dissatisfied Mr. Feldman took the ring to a local UPS store to return it to the seller. As instructed by an employee, the customer used the in-store "I-Ship Online" computer to complete his shipping label.

After typing in the required information, he was required to click a "Print" button on the computer screen, where he was instructed to "Please review everything carefully and then click Print to print your shipping request." Below the print button were two hyperlinks labeled "Terms of Service" and "Privacy Policy". If a customer clicked on the Terms of Service button, a pop-up window appeared with a statement that all shipments were subject to the UPS Tariff that was available on either the UPS web site or, upon request, from a store employee.

There was no actual hyperlink on the computer screen to the UPS Tariff, where an insurance prohibition for items with a value of more than $50,000 was stated. Without reading the Tariff, the customer printed the label and told the store employee that he wanted to insure the ring for $57,000. He claimed that the employee told him that $50,000 was the maximum insurance amount (rather than the maximum value of an insurable shipment). The customer then (thought that he) bought $50,000 of insurance for a $235.50 premium, based on this representation by the employee.

In Feldman's suit against UPS, for breach of contract for its later refusal to pay the $50,000 insurance amount after the ring was lost in transit, the New York federal trial judge denied UPS's request for a summary judgment in its favor. The judge decided that there was an unresolved fact question whether the customer had adequate notice of the insurance limitation.

The judge noted that, unlike the 2003 Tariff in the *Treiber & Straub* case, UPS's 2005 Tariff in this case "does not, however, contain any explicit statements about limitation of liability for insurance actually purchased." UPS could have eliminated any doubt about adequate notice by requiring the customer to agree to the insurance terms during the process of arranging for shipment, and by making those terms available to him at the time of shipment. These standard click-wrap procedures were not followed.

The label-printing computer did not connect to the internet to allow a reading of the UPS Tariff. The button clicked by the customer was labeled "Print", rather than something like "I Accept" or "I Agree", which might have indicated to the customer that he was accepting binding contract terms. There was no evidence that the Terms of Service, containing the insurance limitation, were available by request in the store location. This presentation and context, and the more ambiguous language of the 2005 Tariff, led to a different result than in *Treiber & Straub*.

In the third case, *Marso v. United Parcel Service, Inc.*283, the shipper-customer sold a $12,000 diamond ring to a buyer in another state. After allegedly confirming with a UPS store employee that he could ship the ring to the buyer and receive cash payment before delivery, the customer took the ring to that UPS store, where he used a store computer to print the shipping label information.

In this case, the computer terminal required the customer to click on an "I Agree" button before it would print the shipping label. The package was shipped with C.O.D. service, which by UPS's definition meant only "Collect On Delivery", rather than its other meaning of "cash on delivery". When UPS delivered the ring, instead of requiring the buyer to exchange cash for the ring, UPS accepted a cashier's check. The check was a forgery.

The shipper-customer sued UPS for the $12,000 value of the ring, claiming breach of contract. UPS defended the lawsuit by noting that, upon the shipper's clicking a "Print" button on an in-store computer, a pop-up screen appeared that referred the shipper to the UPS web site to view the Tariff/Terms of Service. It also stated that the shipper could obtain the terms from the counter attendant upon request. The Tariff/Terms were not actually visible on the in-store computer that printed the shipping label.

Before completion of the printing of the shipping label, the shipper was required to click an "I Agree" button that stated he agreed to the UPS Tariff/Terms of Service. These terms provided that "UPS will not accept currency in any amount for payment of C.O.D. shipments", and that all checks tendered for payment of a shipment would be accepted by UPS at the shipper's risk, including the risk of forgery.

In reversing the state trial judge's summary judgment in favor of UPS, the North Carolina appeals court decided that there was insufficient evidence that the customer had reason to know that the cash payment limitation on C.O.D. deliveries existed. The customer denied that he actually used the in-store computer, alleging that a store employee entered all the required information and assured him that he would receive a cash payment, which would be converted into a check from UPS to the customer. He also denied that he was informed of the existence of the Terms of Service. Because there were genuine issues of material fact as to first, whether the customer actual knew, or should have known, of UPS's shipping contract terms, and second, whether he agreed to them, a summary judgment (which decides a case based solely on undisputed fact allegations) was inappropriate.

e) Is a Web Site Advertisement a Contract Offer?

Part A, Chapter 4, a), discussed the requirement of a contract offer, and noted that advertisements are usually not considered to be contract offers in U.S. law. The main exception to this rule is for advertisements that state "first come, first served", or that otherwise indicate a commitment to complete an agreement with any reader who complies with any conditions required by the advertisement.

*Trell v. American Association for the Advancement of Science*284 applied this general rule to a claim by a writer that his submission of a manuscript, in response to a web site advertisement soliciting "news tips", created a unilateral contract that obligated the advertiser to publish his manuscript. The federal trial judge determined that the ad was not an offer to accept and publish any submissions, but was rather an invitation to readers to make their own offers of submitted articles to the advertiser in order for it to decide whether or not to accept them. An advertisement must be "definite, explicit and leave nothing open to negotiation" in order to be an offer. This ad did not meet these requirements. It was also not an offer of a prize or reward, although the submitted paper purported to solve a mathematical problem for which a Texas banker had offered a prize.

The idea behind the "ads are not offers" rule is that most advertisements are too general and indefinite to constitute offers. The advertisers would be in jeopardy of being bound to contracts with an unlimited and indeterminate number of readers, if every advertisement were a binding contract offer. If an advertisement is deceptive, this is a separate issue that is usually dealt with through consumer protection statutes.

f) Web Site Warranty Satisfying Magnuson Moss Warranty Act "Written Warranty" Requirement

In *In re McDonald's French Fries Litigation*285, McDonald's consumers with certain medical conditions sued the franchiser under a federal consumer protection statute, the Magnuson-Moss Warranty Act (MMWA), for economic harm resulting from breach of an express warranty that their "french fries" and "hash browns" potato products contained no allergens, and were wheat-free and gluten-free. Unlike some state commercial statutes, the MMWA does not require that an express warranty by a seller be made directly to the ultimate consumer. The MMWA does, however, require that the express warranty be a "written warranty".

The alleged warranty was located on the McDonald's corporate web site, as well as in restaurant menus. The Illinois federal trial judge decided that the consumers could sue based on the web site representations concerning the french fries. This decision is consistent with the terms and policies of E-SIGN and UETA to make promises recorded in electronic form as legally effective as printed promises.

g) Click-wrap Contract Providing "Conspicuous" Disclaimers of UCC Implied Warranties

In *Recursion Software, Inc. v. Interactive Intelligence, Inc.*286, a click-wrap software license agreement contained an all capital letters disclaimer of the Uniform Commercial Code (UCC) implied warranties of merchantability and fitness for a particular purpose. (See Part A, Chapter 5, c).) In order to exclude (avoid giving to a buyer) either of these warranties, UCC §2-316(2) requires a seller to use language that is "conspicuous".

Interactive Intelligence downloaded and used certain software without payment, believing it was permitted to do so, before Recursion acquired ownership of the software. When Recursion later sued to stop its use of the software, Interactive counter-sued Recursion for breach of implied warranties of merchantability and fitness for a particular purpose, because of alleged defects in the software. In response to Recursion's argument that Interactive was bound by a click-wrap agreement, which conspicuously excluded these implied warranties, Interactive argued that these exclusions were not conspicuous, because they were located in a scroll box that required the reader to scroll down to read the entire agreement.

UCC §1-201(10) defines "conspicuous" as "so written, displayed or presented that a reasonable person against which it is to operate ought to have noticed it." Whether or not a term is "conspicuous" is to be decided by the court."287 The Texas federal trial judge determined that the language in the scroll box was conspicuous, because it was in all capital letters, it was stated in plain language, and the license agreement was relatively short. When fact-related determinations like this are reserved by statute for judicial (rather than jury) determination, the statutory purpose is usually to promote more consistent guidance for parties to follow regarding how future, similar fact determinations will be made.

In *PDC Laboratories, Inc. v. Hach Company*288, a browse-wrap terms and conditions agreement for a sale of plates for recreational water quality testing disclaimed all warranties of sale, except for a one year express warranty allowing only a refund of the purchase price as damages. The dissatisfied buyer argued that the disclaimer of warranties was not sufficiently conspicuous under UCC §2-316(2), and was also procedurally unconscionable.

The terms and conditions were hyperlinked on three pages of the web site purchase process in contrasting color and underlined text. The last page of the order process instructed the buyer to "Review terms, add any comments, and submit order", followed by another hyperlink to the terms and conditions. The Illinois federal trial judge ruled that the inclusion of the disclaimers in the browse-wrap contract was not procedurally unconscionable.

CHAPTER 9 - What Defenses Are Possible Against a Claim of Breach?

a) Federal Trade Commission "Dot Com Disclosures" Guidance for Internet Advertisers Regarding Consumer Protections

In March 2013, the Federal Trade Commission (FTC) issued *.com Disclosures: How to Make Effective Disclosures in Digital Advertising* (2013 .com Disclosures).289 This guidance revised the FTC May 2000 *Dot Com Disclosures: Information about Online Advertising* (2000 Dot Com Disclosures)290, which was published as "information businesses should consider as they develop online ads to ensure that they comply with the [general principles of advertising] law." The 2013 guidance addresses "new issues...concerning space-constrained screens and social media platforms".

The 2000 guidance provided that, to the extent that an online advertiser could show its compliance with it, the advertiser would be protected from complaints of unfair or deceptive online advertising. The 2013 guidance, however, states that it is not "intended to provide a safe harbor from potential liability" and that "[w]hether a particular ad is deceptive, unfair or otherwise violative of a Commission rule will depend on the specific facts at hand".291 FTC guides only provide examples or direction on how to avoid unfair or deceptive acts or practices.

The basic principles of advertising law are described by the FTC as:

- Advertising must be truthful and not misleading;

- Advertisers must have evidence to back up their claims (substantiation); and

- Advertisements cannot be unfair.

The FTC Act's prohibition on "unfair or deceptive acts or practices"292 applies to internet advertising, marketing and sales. According to 2013 .com Disclosures, "Disclosures that are required to prevent an advertisement from being deceptive, unfair, or otherwise violative of a Commission rule, must be presented 'clearly and conspicuously.'"293

Some FTC rules and guides spell out the information that must be disclosed in connection with certain specific advertising claims. In many cases, these disclosures prevent a claim from being misleading or deceptive. Other FTC rules and guides require disclosures to ensure that consumers receive material information about the terms of a transaction, or to further consumer protection goals. Both types of disclosures must be clear and conspicuous.

To make material information clear and conspicuous, the 2013 guidance advises online advertisers to:

Place the disclosure as close as possible to the triggering claim.

Take account of the various devices and platforms consumers may use to view advertising and any corresponding disclosure. If an ad is viewable on a particular device or platform, any necessary disclosures should be sufficient to prevent the ad from being misleading when viewed on that device or platform.

When a space-constrained ad requires a disclosure, incorporate the disclosure into the ad whenever possible. However, when it is not possible to make a disclosure in a space-constrained ad, it may, under some circumstances, be acceptable to make the disclosure clearly and conspicuously on the page to which the ad links.

When using a hyperlink to lead to a disclosure, make the link obvious; label the hyperlink appropriately to convey the importance, nature, and relevance of the information it leads to; use hyperlink styles consistently, so consumers know when a link is available; place the hyperlink as close as possible to the relevant information it qualifies and make it noticeable; take consumers directly to the disclosure on the click-through page; assess the effectiveness of the hyperlink by monitoring click-through rates and other information about consumer use and make changes accordingly.

Preferably, design advertisements so that "scrolling" is not necessary in order to find a disclosure. When scrolling is necessary, use text or visual cues to encourage consumers to scroll to view the disclosure.

Keep abreast of empirical research about where consumers do and do not look on a screen.

Recognize and respond to any technological limitations or unique characteristics of a communication method when making disclosures.

Display disclosures before consumers make a decision to buy — e.g., before they "add to shopping cart." Also recognize that disclosures may have to be repeated before purchase to ensure that they are adequately presented to consumers.

Repeat disclosures, as needed, on lengthy websites and in connection with repeated claims. Disclosures may also have to be repeated if consumers have multiple routes through a website.

If a product or service promoted online is intended to be (or can be) purchased from "brick and mortar" stores or from online retailers other than the advertiser itself, then any disclosure necessary to prevent deception or unfair injury should be presented in the ad itself — that is, before consumers head to a store or some other online retailer.

Necessary disclosures should not be relegated to "terms of use" and similar contractual agreements.

Prominently display disclosures so they are noticeable to consumers, and evaluate the size, color, and graphic treatment of the disclosure in relation to other parts of the webpage.

Review the entire ad to assess whether the disclosure is effective in light of other elements — text, graphics, hyperlinks, or sound — that might distract consumers' attention from the disclosure.

Use audio disclosures when making audio claims, and present them in a volume and cadence so that consumers can hear and understand them.

Display visual disclosures for a duration sufficient for consumers to notice, read, and understand them.

Use plain language and syntax so that consumers understand the disclosures.294

As general advice, the FTC states that

In reviewing their ads, advertisers should adopt the perspective of a reasonable consumer. They also should assume that consumers don't read an entire website or online screen, just as they don't read every word on a printed page. Disclosures should be placed as close as possible to the claim they qualify. Advertisers should keep in mind that having to scroll increases the risk that consumers will miss a disclosure.

In addition, it is important for advertisers to draw attention to the disclosure.295

Regarding visual and email marketing methods, the 2000 guidance advised that

Rules and guides that apply to written ads or printed materials also apply to visual text displayed on the Internet.

If a seller uses e-mail to comply with Commission rule or guide notice requirements, the seller should ensure that consumers understand that they will receive such information by e-mail and provide it in a form that consumers can retain.

Direct mail solicitations include e-mail solicitations. If an e-mail invites consumers to call the sender to purchase goods or services, that telephone call and a subsequent sale must comply with the Telemarketing Sales Rule requirements.296

The 2013 .com Disclosures includes examples of twenty-two "mock" online advertisements with possibly unclear, deceptive or misleading elements in connection with the FTC's "clear and conspicuous" guidance. Methods of clarifying and improving those elements are suggested. The guidance clarifies that previous rules that applied to "written" or "printed" advertising also apply to visual text displayed on the internet. The guidance also discusses circumstances in which businesses may use e-mail to comply with an FTC rule or requirement to provide required notices or documents to consumers.

To the extent that online advertisers and sellers conform their web sites to the 2013 .com Disclosures guidance, it is likely that their online contract formation procedures will effectively and legally create contracts with their desired and expected terms. The analysis in the following sub-chapters regarding the successes or failures of challenges to various types of web site contracts and advertisements should be read with this FTC guidance in mind.

b) Dispute Resolution Examples:

1. The Credit Report 10-Day Free Trial

2. The Need for a "Corrections & Amplifications" Note in Revised Web Site Ads

3. Electronic Bill Pay Might Put You into Customer Service Purgatory

4. International Sale of Goods Arbitration

5. Unexpected Changes to a Printed Home Repair Contract

[See Appendix D]

c) The 2010 Federal and California Laws Restricting Unfair Internet Sales Practices- "Data Passing", "Negative Options", and "Automatic Renewals"

On December 29, 2010, the Restore Online Shoppers' Confidence Act (ROSCA) or the "Act"297 was signed into law by President Obama. It describes itself as "An Act to protect consumers from certain aggressive sales practices on the internet."

The Act restricts the practice of "data passing", whereby an initial internet seller passes to a third-party internet seller (usually without the consumer's knowledge) the credit card or other payment information of the consumer/buyer. The third-party internet seller then uses that credit or payment information to charge, or attempt to charge, the buyer for goods or services that they may be misled into thinking were part of the transaction with the initial seller. This practice has often been combined with a "free trial period", under which consumers must exercise a "negative option" in order to avoid their free trial period being automatically converted to a regular membership or subscription, which must be affirmatively canceled by the consumer in order to avoid charges.

ROSCA §3(a) 298 prohibits such third-party sellers from charging or attempting to charge consumers for internet transactions, unless—

(1) before obtaining the consumer's billing information, the post-transaction third party seller has clearly and conspicuously disclosed to the consumer all material terms of the transaction, including—

(A) a description of the goods or services being offered;

(B) the fact that the post-transaction third party seller is not affiliated with the initial merchant, which may include disclosure of the name of the post-transaction third party in a manner that clearly differentiates the post-transaction third party seller from the initial merchant; and

(C) the cost of such goods or services; and

(2) the post-transaction third party seller has received the express informed consent for the charge from the consumer whose credit card, debit card, bank account, or other financial account will be charged by—

(A) obtaining from the consumer—

(i) the full account number of the account to be charged; and

(ii) the consumer's name and address and a means to contact the consumer; and

(B) requiring the consumer to perform an additional affirmative action, such as clicking on a confirmation button or checking a box that indicates the consumer's consent to be charged the amount disclosed.

ROSCA §3(b) 299 reinforces the prohibition on undisclosed receipt of "data passes" by third-party internet sellers with a prohibition on the making of such "data passes" by initial internet sellers, by providing that

It shall be unlawful for an initial merchant to disclose a credit card, debit card, bank account, or other financial account number, or to disclose other billing information that is used to charge a customer of the initial merchant, to any post-transaction third party seller for use in an Internet-based sale of any goods or services from that post-transaction third party seller.

ROSCA §4 300 reinforces the prohibitions on "data passing" by restricting the use of the "negative option" technique that requires consumers to affirmatively "opt out" of otherwise automatic enrollments and renewals in memberships or services after the end of trial periods, by providing that

> It shall be unlawful for any person to charge or attempt to charge any consumer for any goods or services sold in a transaction effected on the Internet through a negative option feature (as defined in the Federal Trade Commission's Telemarketing Sales Rule in part 310 of title 16, Code of Federal Regulations), unless the person—
>
> (1) provides text that clearly and conspicuously discloses all material terms of the transaction before obtaining the consumer's billing information;
>
> (2) obtains a consumer's express informed consent before charging the consumer's credit card, debit card, bank account, or other financial account for products or services through such transaction; and
>
> (3) provides simple mechanisms for a consumer to stop recurring charges from being placed on the consumer's credit card, debit card, bank account, or other financial account.

The phrase "negative option feature" is defined by the FTC's Telemarketing Sales Rule as

> Negative option feature means in an offer or agreement to sell or provide any goods or services, a provision under which the customer's silence or failure to take an affirmative action to reject goods or services or to cancel the agreement is interpreted by the seller as an acceptance of the offer.301

The 2007 FTC workshop on how to make "clear and conspicuous disclosures" on the internet produced a January 2009 report on negative option marketing, such as by clubs that send periodic notices offering goods to consumers, magazines that automatically renew subscriptions, free trial period sellers that automatically enroll and charge at the end of the period, and agreements by consumers for periodic shipment of goods or receipt of services. If these arrangements operate to charge payments automatically, unless the consumer objects, they are "negative option" marketing plans.302

The Federal Trade Commission is authorized to enforce ROSCA. Section 5 of the Federal Trade Commission Act makes violations of its terms also violations of the FTC's unfair or deceptive acts or practices rules.303 Section 6 of the Federal Trade Commission Act authorizes state attorneys general to bring civil lawsuits against violators of the Act for injunctive relief in federal courts, unless at the time the suit is brought "the same alleged violation is the subject of a pending action by the Federal Trade Commission or the United States under this Act."304

On December 1, 2010 a new law took effect in the State of California that implemented Senate Bill No. 340.305 This law requires any business making an "automatic renewal" or "continuous service" offer to a consumer in California to make "clear and conspicuous" disclosures of the offer terms before completing the transaction (and to disclose later any material changes to the terms of an accepted offer). It also requires such businesses to obtain the affirmative consent of the consumer before making any charges pursuant to such offers, and to provide a retainable acknowledgement of that consent with the offer terms and cancellation policy.

The following definitions address the scope of the law and the requirements for the consumer disclosures:

(a) "Automatic renewal" means a plan or arrangement in which a paid subscription or purchasing agreement is automatically renewed at the end of a definite term for a subsequent term.

(b) "Automatic renewal offer terms" means the following clear and conspicuous disclosures: (1) That the subscription or purchasing agreement will continue until the consumer cancels. (2) The description of the cancellation policy that applies to the offer. (3) The recurring charges that will be charged to the consumer's credit or debit card or payment account with a third party as part of the automatic renewal plan or arrangement, and that the amount of the charge may change, if that is the case, and the amount to which the charge will change, if known. (4) The length of the automatic renewal term or that the service is continuous, unless the length of the term is chosen by the consumer. (5) The minimum purchase obligation, if any.

(c) "Clear and conspicuous" or "clearly and conspicuously" means in larger type than the surrounding text, or in contrasting type, font, or color to the surrounding text of the same size, or set off from the surrounding text of the same size by symbols or other marks, in a manner that clearly calls attention to the language. In the case of an audio disclosure, "clear and conspicuous" and "clearly and conspicuously" means in a volume and cadence sufficient to be readily audible and understandable."

(d) "Consumer" means any individual who seeks or acquires, by purchase or lease, any goods, services, money, or credit for personal, family, or household purposes.

(e) "Continuous service" means a plan or arrangement in which a subscription or purchasing agreement continues until the consumer cancels the service."306

The law also requires that

If the offer includes a free trial, the business shall also disclose in the acknowledgment how to cancel and allow the consumer to cancel before the consumer pays for the goods or services.307

To facilitate cancellations,

A business making automatic renewal or continuous

service offers shall provide a toll-free telephone number, electronic mail address, a postal address only when the seller directly bills the consumer, or another cost-effective, timely, and easy-to-use mechanism for cancellation....308

The law provides civil penalties for violations of its requirements, although it provides that "If a business complies with the provisions of this article in good faith, it shall not be subject to civil remedies."309

As a type of "self-help" remedy for direct enforcement by consumers, the law provides that

In any case in which a business sends any goods, wares, merchandise, or products to a consumer, under a continuous service agreement or automatic renewal of a purchase, without first obtaining the consumer's affirmative consent as described in Section 17602, the goods, wares, merchandise, or products shall for all purposes be deemed an unconditional gift to the consumer, who may use or dispose of the same in any manner he or she sees fit without any obligation whatsoever on the consumer's part to the business, including, but not limited to, bearing the cost of, or responsibility for, shipping any goods, wares, merchandise, or products to the business.310

Certain types of regulated businesses, alarm company operators, and financial institutions are exempted from the law's requirements.311

The clear and conspicuous disclosures required by this California law could require the actual offer terms to be presented above any "I Agree" button or similar method of consent. Only a click-wrap type of consent would be likely to satisfy the requirement of an "affirmative consent". E-mail or regular mailings of acknowledgements of consent, and of material changes, to offer terms might satisfy the requirements for retainability of these disclosures.

Section d) hereafter discusses the 2011 decision in *Van Tassell v. United Marketing Group, LLC*, in which a federal trial court used "ordinary principles of [Illinois] contract law" to deny a pre-trial motion to compel arbitration of class action claims based on common law contract, unjust enrichment, fraud and the federal Electronic Communications Privacy Act312. These claims involved "data passing" of buyer credit card information by online retailers to third-party consumer membership group marketers, with "negative option" and "automatic renewal" practices. The purchases occurred prior to either the federal ROSCA or California Senate Bill No. 340's enactment into law.

Section i) hereafter discusses the 2012 decision in *Schnabel v. Trilegiant Corporation, Affinion, Inc.*, in which a federal appeals court also used basic contract law rules to determine that consumer purchasers of services from online retailers had not agreed to "data passing" of their credit card information by these retailers to a third-party internet seller of discounted consumer goods and services. The third-party seller's purported contract also used "negative option" and "automatic renewal" techniques. Because the contract also was entered into before either the ROSCA or Senate Bill No.340 was enacted into law, these statutes did not apply to the transactions in the *Schnabel* case.

d) Cases of Insufficient Notice of Browse-wrap and Click-wrap Terms of Use/Service

In *Ticketmaster Corp. v. Tickets.com*, a series of three federal trial judge decisions addressed, as a defense to an alleged contract breach, the argument that Ticketmaster's browse-wrap Terms of Use were not violated by its rival, Tickets.com, because they were insufficiently conspicuous. The companies competed in the retail sale of tickets for entertainment events. Besides selling tickets on its own web site, Tickets.com provided information on how and where tickets could be bought on other web sites. It included on its pages event information copied from Ticketmaster's web site, with direct hyperlinks to Ticketmaster's web pages selling the related event tickets, which was contrary to Ticketmaster's web site Terms of Use.

Ticketmaster's home page contained a variety of instructions and hyperlinks, including a link at the bottom of the page that took a user to its Terms of Use. A user was not required to visit the page or to view the terms, however, in order to buy tickets for an event. Neither was a user required to click on any type of "I Agree" button referencing the terms in order to buy a ticket.

Ticketmaster sought a preliminary injunction against Tickets.com, arguing that its web site Terms of Use specifically prohibited copying and hyperlinking its web pages for commercial purposes. In the first stage of this litigation, the California federal trial judge determined that Ticketmaster's complaints did not amount to a breach of contract, because there was no allegation that Tickets.com was actually aware of Ticketmaster's Terms of Use, or that the terms were open and obvious, or hard-to-miss, like shrink-wrap terms or click-wrap terms.313

In Ticketmaster's second attempt to prevent Tickets.com from "deep-linking" to its event pages, contrary to its Terms of Use, the trial judge denied a request for a preliminary injunction against Tickets.com, because of lack of proof that Tickets.com knew of and agreed to Ticketmaster's Terms of Use.314

In the third and final decision denying a summary judgment request by Tickets.com, for the failure of Ticketmaster to show that Tickets.com had agreed to its Terms of Use315, the trial judge recognized that, although a click-wrap type of assent to terms might be preferable (because it is more provable than a browse-wrap assent), it was not always necessary. As in the shrink-wrap cases, an offeror could determine the method of acceptance by the offeree. If the offeree performed the clearly specified action of acceptance (such as by using the web page), it would be bound to the offeror's terms. By this time, further evidence had also emerged that Tickets.com had been warned by a letter from Ticketmaster that it was violating the Terms of Use, and that Tickets.com had explicitly rejected this warning.

The judge compared the presentation of the browse-wrap Terms of Use to the terms on the reverse side of a cruise ship ticket, to limitations of liability on a bill of lading, to air waybill or airline tickets, and to terms on the back of a parking lot receipt. Although it did not affect this case, by the time of the third ruling, Ticketmaster had wisely moved its notice of, and hyperlink to, its Terms of Use to the top of its home page, had increased the font size of the notice, and had added a statement that, by using the web site, users thereby agreed to the Terms of Use. The judge distinguished the facts of this case (plainly known use limits and a commercial user) from those in the following case.

*Specht v. Netscape Communications Corp.*316 involved a consumer complaint that a downloaded browser software "plug-in" had allegedly invaded user privacy by clandestinely transmitting private consumer information to the software provider, in violation of the federal Electronic Communications Privacy Act317 and the federal Computer Fraud and Abuse Act.318 When the consumers filed a class action lawsuit, Netscape moved to compel arbitration, pursuant to a mandatory arbitration provision in the plug-in download license agreement.

A federal appeals court (in an opinion written by future Supreme Court Justice Sotomayor) affirmed the trial judge's determination that the notice in the next paragraph, given by Netscape on a screen below the download button, and potentially visible only after the plug-in downloading process was completed, was inadequate to bind a consumer user to the arbitration requirement. The download process did not clearly require an "I Agree" click assent to the license agreement before downloading.

In addition, the eventual direction given by the following sentence was viewed by the trial judge as only suggesting an acceptance of the license agreement, without requiring it, by stating

> Please review and agree to the terms of the Netscape SmartDownload software license agreement before downloading and using the software.

This invitation contrasted with the click-wrap agreement for the basic Netscape browser software that clearly required a user assent before downloading. The hyperlink to the plug-in license agreement below the download button required a user to navigate through hyperlinks to two other web pages, where the user was finally presented with a click-wrap type of button by which to agree to the license terms. The appeals court agreed with the trial judge that a user would not necessarily have had "reasonably conspicuous notice" of the plug-in software license terms, or agreed to them, either by clicking his agreement to the browser software, which did not mention the plug-in software, or by accepting Netscape's invitation to download its browser plug-in software. The consumers had no duty to read contract terms that were not reasonably brought to their attention.

In *Williams v. America Online, Inc.*319, a Massachusetts state trial judge denied the internet service provider's motion to dismiss a lawsuit claiming damages that were allegedly caused by installation of its software. The software agreement required any suit to be brought in Virginia. The consumer objected that he had not knowingly agreed to this term. He had clicked "I Agree" twice, without overriding it by twice clicking the "Read Now" button that would take him to a page with the agreement terms. The judge determined that AOL had given the consumer too strong an incentive to agree without reading the terms. Because the harm to the user's computer occurred during software installation, before clicking "I Agree", the judge also decided that the harm had occurred even before any consent to the software agreement was possible.

As indicated in the FTC *Dot Com Disclosures* guide, described in section a) above, if the terms of an agreement are accessible from a web page only through hyperlinks, the links should be noticeable and easy to access, and their content and importance should be made obvious. The New York State Attorney General's office in 2001 settled its complaint against CompUSA320 that the amount of CompUSA's penalties for early termination of their three-year internet service agreement exceeded the amount of their related hardware rebate. The office complained that the agreement terms disclosing these penalties were buried behind a series of hyperlinks that the consumer had to navigate through. The settlement required that important disclosures be made adjacent to offers, or through a single, conspicuous web site link.

In two other stages of the "Turnitin" litigation (about the plagiarism-checking web site described in section e) hereafter), *A.V. v. iParadigms, LLC*321, students who were required to submit their academic papers to the web site for plagiarism checking tried to avoid the mandatory archiving required by the web site's click-wrap agreement by placing a unilateral disclaimer of any right to archive at the beginning of their papers. The Virginia federal trial judge's treatment of the site's click-wrap agreement is discussed in the next section. In addition to its argument that the agreement was enforceable against the students, the web site also argued that the students were required by a "Usage Policy", which was separate from its click-wrap agreement, to indemnify it (pay the web site owner's expenses) for defending the students' lawsuit. A hyperlink to the Usage Policy appeared on each page of the website.

The federal trial judge refused to enforce the indemnification provision, because it had not been made a part of the click-wrap agreement that the students assented to, which stated that it was the entire agreement between the parties. The judge also emphasized that the students had not actually seen or read the Usage Policy. This decision was made easier by the fact that the students appeared to be infrequent users of the web site (although they knew enough about its archiving requirement to try to avoid it with a written disclaimer).

The decision might have also been influenced by the unusual presence of an indemnification agreement in a consumer contract. In the United States, each party generally pays its own litigation costs, regardless of the outcome of a legal dispute. In order to enforce a requirement that a losing consumer pay a winning corporation's litigation expenses incurred in a good faith dispute, a judge might require even greater prominence for this term in a browse-wrap contract than is required for other browse-wrap terms.

In *Douglas v. United States District Court for the Central District of California*322, an America Online/TalkAmerica telephone service customer complained that the service violated his browse-wrap service contract by changing its posted online terms without notice to him. The changes added service charges, added a class action waiver, added a mandatory arbitration clause, and added a choice of New York governing law. The federal appeals court agreed that the customer's continued use of the service was not an agreement to purported contract changes that he was not aware of. He had no duty to continuously check the service's web site for proposed changes to his contract. In addition, changes to a contract proposed by one party are only offers, which must be accepted by the other party in order to become effective.

In *Hines v. Overstock.com, Inc.*323, a consumer web site user brought a class action on behalf of buyers of goods, who were charged a $30 "restocking fee" for returned goods that had been advertised as new, but which were in fact refurbished. Hines was only notified that she would be bound to a mandatory arbitration of disputes requirement in the site's Terms and Conditions by a statement in the first line of the terms that "[e]ntering this site will constitute your acceptance of these Terms and Conditions." The Terms and Conditions were referenced by a hyperlink in small print at the bottom of the home page that was unnecessary to view in order to place an order for a product on the web site. In response to the seller's motion to dismiss or to stay the action in favor of arbitration, the New York federal trial judge ruled that this was inadequate notice to bind the customer to the browse-wrap arbitration clause in the hyperlinked terms. The federal court of appeals agreed.

In *Nguyen v. Barnes & Noble, Inc.*324, a consumer purchased two tablet computers online for $101.95 each. The next day, the seller allegedly e-mailed the buyer with a cancellation of his order. The buyer sued the seller for breach of contract. The seller moved to stay the action, alleging that its web site Terms of Use required mandatory arbitration of any disputes arising out of any purchases from the web site.

The consumer argued, and the seller admitted, that the Terms of Use, including the arbitration requirement, were referenced on its web site only in a hyperlink at the bottom of each web page through which a buyer must navigate to make a purchase. The consumer argued that he did not affirmatively assent to the Terms of Use, nor was he required to read them before making his purchase.

The California federal trial judge determined that, whether an online agreement is a browse-wrap or a click-wrap agreement, a party must have either actual or constructive notice of its terms in order to be bound by them. The judge cited the facts of *Specht v. Netscape Communications Corp.* as one example of online contract terms that were not presented in a way to give reasonable notice of them to a consumer. *Hines v. Overstock.com, Inc.* was referred to as a similar example of online contract terms that a consumer was not bound by, because he was not prompted to review them before purchasing, and because the hyperlink to the terms was not prominently displayed so as to provide reasonable notice of them. The burden of proof is on the party offering the contract terms to show that a valid arbitration agreement was created, either because the offeree had actual notice of the terms, or because a reasonable user of the web site would have had notice of the contract terms. The computer seller failed to meet its burden of proof.

In *Hoffman v. Supplements Togo Mgmt.*325, a customer (and lawyer) purchased the dietary supplement known as

"Erection MD" from an online retailer. He sued the retailer for fraud, under New Jersey common law and a New Jersey consumer protection statute, for making false claims about the efficacy of the product without supporting scientific evidence. The New Jersey trial court dismissed the lawsuit, in part, because of a State of Nevada choice-of-forum clause that was located in the last sentence of a paragraph on the retailer's web site disclaiming FDA evaluation, medical advice, or disease-treating purposes for the supplement. The trial judge determined that the clause was sufficiently noticeable, even though it was only accessible by a "Disclaimer" located at the bottom of a page, which a customer was not required to scroll to after clicking a button to make a purchase.

On appeal, the New Jersey appellate court compared the click-wrap agreement approved by a New Jersey appellate court in *Caspi v. Microsoft Network* with the federal appeals court's disapproval of the browse-wrap agreement in *Specht v. Netscape Communications Corp.*, which that court determined was "submerged" at the bottom of a web page, where customers had no reason to scroll down to it, and were unlikely to find it. In this case, the appeals court concluded, contrary to the trial judge's finding that the disclaimer was prominently displayed, that Supplements Togo failed to provide reasonable notice of its disclaimer and choice-of-forum clause. The case was returned to the trial court to determine if the plaintiff had actual knowledge of the disclaimer clause.

In *Snap-On Business Solutions, Inc. v. O'Neil & Associates, Inc.*326, the winner of a jury verdict filed a motion for the award of attorney's fees based on a browse-wrap End User License Agreement accessible by a hyperlink on each page of its web site database. The agreement provided that database users would pay or reimburse Snap-On for reasonable legal fees incurred to protect or enforce its rights under the agreement.

The Ohio federal trial judge denied this motion, noting that Ohio contract law permits attorney fee obligations to be allocated by contract only where this was the result of a "free and understanding negotiation". The judge determined that this was not such a result, because the agreement provided only for payment of Snap-On's attorney's fees and not the end user's fees, and because the browse-wrap agreement did not require users to manifest their acceptance of, or to view, the agreement in order to use Snap-On's database. This decision implies, although it does not explicitly state, that the web site did not provide reasonable notice of the agreement to users.

In *In re Zappos.com Inc., Customer Data Security Breach Litigation*327, the computer servers of the online retailer Zappos suffered a security breach by computer hackers who obtained the personal information of customers. The customers filed lawsuits in various federal district courts to recover damages under federal and state statutory and common law. The defendants filed a motion to compel arbitration pursuant to the "Disputes" section of the Terms of Use agreement accessible on the Zappos.com web site. The Nevada federal judge analyzed, under Nevada contract law, whether or not the customers had agreed to the arbitration requirement in this section of the browse-wrap agreement.

Because there was no evidence presented that the customers had actual knowledge of the browse-wrap agreement, the judge analyzed whether they received reasonable notice of it. The Terms of Use hyperlink was located on each page of the web site, but was visible only if the user scrolled down the page. The hyperlink was viewed by the judge as "the same size, font, and color as most other non-significant links", and the web site did not direct the user to the Terms of Use when creating an account, logging in to an existing account, or making a purchase. In determining that no reasonable user would have reason to click on the Terms of Use, the judge compared this agreement to the agreements in the *Hines v. Overstock.com, Specht v. Netscape Communications Corp.*, and *Van Tassell v. United Marketing Group* cases and others, in which the arbitration clauses of similar browse-wrap terms were denied binding contract status. As stated in the droll conclusion of the *Hines* judge, "Very little is required to form a contract nowadays – but this alone does not suffice."328

The Terms of Use also provided that "We reserve the right to change this Site and these terms and conditions at any time." The customers argued that this sentence made the entire agreement an illusory promise, because it literally allowed Zappos to change the contract rules unilaterally, even retroactively, and without any notice to the customers. Zappos, in effect, made no binding promises. Without a binding promise, it failed to provide consideration and mutuality of obligation, and no contract was formed. The terms would bind Zappos' customers to arbitration, while allowing Zappos to avoid arbitration at its option through an "escape hatch". The judge agreed that, even if the customers had reasonable notice of the Terms of Use, the agreement made only non-binding, illusory promises, and did not create a contract. The judge denied the defendants' motion to compel arbitration.

In *Van Tassell v. United Marketing Group*, LLC329, purchasers of goods from online retailers brought a class action in an Illinois federal trial court complaining that the retailers used "data passing" to transfer their debit or credit card information to consumer membership group sellers, who used "negative option" and "automatic renewal" techniques to make recurring charges on the purchasers' debit or credit card accounts without their knowledge or permission. The defendants filed a pre-trial motion to compel arbitration, pursuant to a clause in the Terms and Conditions of the web sites used to make purchases, and the web sites of the third-party membership programs.

The trial judge ruled, regarding all except one retailer defendant, that the pre-trial evidence did not resolve whether the consumers completed a click-wrap agreement accepting the Terms and Conditions, or whether the online retailers provided this information to the third-party membership group sellers without permission. These defendants could renew their motion after presenting further evidence.

Regarding the retailer Pikes Peak Direct Marketing, Inc., the judge determined that the browse-wrap Conditions of Use, to which one plaintiff was directed through a hyperlink on online catalog web pages, did not provide reasonable notice of its terms. The hyperlink was not presented on the retailer's home page or checkout page. The agreement was accessible only through a "Customer Service" hyperlink at the bottom of the home page, which then required scrolling to the bottom of the "Customer Service" page to discover it. Alternatively, the Conditions of Use could be found by clicking on a hyperlink to "Conditions of Use, Notices & Disclaimers" near the end of a list of links on the "Customer Service" page.

The judge determined that "the Conditions of Use at issue here are even less obvious than those in Specht"330. Even if the Customer Service page was accessible through numerous hyperlinks, Pikes Peak failed to "provide any explanation as to why a user…would logically click on any of those links to find the Conditions of Use, especially when they are not mentioned anywhere else on the site."331 The buyer's "failure to scour the website for the Conditions of Use she had no notice existed" was not assent to its terms. The judge determined that there was no valid agreement to arbitrate, and denied Pikes Peak's motion to compel arbitration.

In *Jerez v. JD Closeouts, LLC*332, a New York retailer purchased 5,000 pairs of white tube socks from a Florida discount wholesaler. When the retailer's effort to return the socks as defective was rejected, it sued in New York state court. The wholesaler moved to dismiss pursuant to a choice-of-forum provision in its web site Terms of Sale notice that chose Broward County, Florida as the mandatory forum for any lawsuits related to its sales.

The New York trial judge reviewed internet sales cases described elsewhere in this book regarding the requirement of reasonable communication of terms to the offeree of a contract, including *Specht v. Netscape Communications Corp.*, *Hoffman v. Supplements Togo Management, LLC*, and *Fteja v. Facebook, Inc.* The contract terms in this case were not referenced in a click-wrap scroll box or related hyperlink. They were not incorporated by reference in another communication. The Terms of Sale that included the forum selection clause were presented only by a hyperlink on the "About Us" page of the seller's web site. The judge determined that, by this manner of presentation, "the terms were 'buried' and 'submerged' on a web page that could only be found by clicking on an inconspicuous link on the company's 'About Us' page".

The judge determined that "[e]specially in cases where the terms of an e-commerce transaction are negotiated…a seller must make an affirmative effort to 'reasonably communicate' the essential terms of sale to the buyer". The significance of the negotiation was that it showed that no additional effort would have been required for the seller to inform the buyer of its web site terms of sale, if it had not already made the terms conspicuous on the web site. The motion to dismiss because of an improper forum was denied.

e) Cases of Sufficient Notice of Click-wrap Terms of Use/Service

This section describes cases in which judges determined that reasonable notice of click-wrap terms of use/service was provided to the offeree of a contract. Reasonably presented click-wrap contracts are a more reliable method of online contract formation than browse-wrap contracts. Once reasonably presented, click-wrap contracts by their nature require an active manifestation of assent to terms (whether or not read and understood) by the offeree, which can be documented for later use. Their reliability has been confirmed by the judicial decisions in this section.

Browse-wrap contracts, by contrast, usually require an indirect and more passive assent by the offeree. The resolution of disputes over such passive consents puts greater emphasis on the reasonableness of the notice of the browse-wrap terms to compensate for the passive nature of the assent. Litigation decisions, in which reasonable notice of browse-wrap terms of use was determined to have been given, are distributed throughout the following sections.

A third trend of hybrid or modified click-wrap contracts should also be noted, in which a click-wrap button requires consent to terms of use accessible through a hyperlink. These contracts are also described throughout Chapters 8 and 9, particularly the *Fteja v. Facebook, Inc.* and *Sherman v. AT&T* cases in Chapter 8, section c), and the *Vernon v. Qwest Communications International, Inc.* and *Swift v. Zynga Game Network, Inc.* cases in Chapter 9, section k).

A Rhode Island trial judge decided in *Groff v. America Online Inc.*333 that an internet service provider's choice-of-forum and choice-of-law provisions in its service terms were validly agreed to, where the customer was presented with two options: either click "I Agree" on a button next to a "Read Now" sign directing him to the service terms, without actually reading the terms, or scroll through and read the terms in a box next to the "I Agree" button, and then click on another "I Agree" button at the end of the scroll box. The customer clicked on the first "I Agree" button without reading the terms. The judge decided that the agreement was validly assented to, under the general rule that a party can make a binding agreement, even if they choose to not read or do not understand what they are agreeing to. (The customer had been a Rhode Island lawyer for thirty years.) There was adequate disclosure of the agreement terms.

In *Caspi v. Microsoft Network*334, a New Jersey appellate court approved a similar acceptance procedure for a choice-of-forum clause in an internet service agreement. Subscribers protested "negative option billing", which moved them into more expensive service plans automatically, unless they opted out. The terms of the internet service agreement were placed in a scroll box next to "I Agree" and "I Don't Agree" buttons. The opportunity to read the membership agreement terms before assenting to them made their disclosure adequate according to the court, whether or not the member actually read them.

The rule applied by the court to a choice-of-forum clause is that the party objecting to it has the burden of showing that it was either obtained by fraud or duress, or that it violates a strong public policy of the state where the court hearing the objection is located, or that the clause would create serious inconveniences for conduct of a trial. The plaintiffs failed to prove any of these grounds for denying the selected forum in the State of Washington. The federal and state laws restricting "negative option billing" practices, referred to in section c) previously, were not in effect at the time of this case.

An Ontario, Canada judge in *Rudder v. Microsoft Corp.*335 decided that the State of Washington choice-of-forum clause in a similar click-wrap license agreement was binding on Canadian class action plaintiffs alleging improper credit card charges. The judge ruled that the Microsoft Network members were given a clear opportunity to read the license terms. The fact that the terms appeared on multiple screens was compared to a multi-page written agreement. The enrollment procedure required two "I Agree" clicks, and even warned members that they would be bound to all of the agreement terms, whether or not they actually read them. A lead plaintiff admitted that he had scanned the agreement, but he was only looking for cost information.

The dismissal of the lawsuit was justified as being consistent with the general deference by Canadian courts to choice-of-forum and mandatory arbitration clauses. This deference promotes international commercial certainty, legal comity, and freedom of contract. The fact that two of the plaintiffs were law graduates with "a professed familiarity with Internet services" made their complaints "particularly indefensible". Regarding the choice-of-forum clause itself, the members failed to show "strong cause" for it to not be enforced. It was noted that the same clause had been enforced in the *Caspi* litigation.

A New York federal trial judge decided similarly in *Novak v. Overture Services, Inc.*336, in which internet search results within a discussion group were alleged to have been improperly biased for financial reasons. The judge decided that the fact that the choice-of-forum clause of the discussion group click-wrap agreement could not be seen by a user without scrolling 300 lines down the screen, ten lines at a time, to view it did not deny the consumer the opportunity to read it before agreeing to it. Neither did the character of the agreement as a "form contract" make it unenforceable. The judge emphasized that the entire agreement was only seven-and-a-half pages long, and was presented in an easy-to-read font.

An Illinois federal judge decided similarly regarding a class action complaint that alleged improper accessing and use of user information and communications. *In re Real Networks, Inc., Privacy Litigation*337 involved a mandatory arbitration clause in an online license agreement. The agreement's required click-wrap assent was decided to not be unconscionable, through denial of a reasonable opportunity to understand the arbitration clause, although the clause appeared in a final paragraph entitled only "Miscellaneous", with choice-of-law and choice-of-forum clauses.

The decision occurred before enactment of the Electronic Signatures in Global and National Commerce Act (E- SIGN). The judge's determination that the click-wrap agreement was a "written agreement" under the Federal Arbitration Act338, because it could be printed and stored at the consumer's initiative, might not satisfy the consumer protection requirements in E-SIGN, which put the burden on businesses to provide consumers with simple methods to print or store electronic agreements.339

In *People v. Direct Revenue, LLC*340, the New York State Attorney General alleged deceptive practices pursuant to a click-wrap software license agreement that permitted "pop-up" advertising triggered by the consumer's internet browsing. The advertising broker, Direct Revenue, offered free games and free screensavers to induce consumers to view the ads. The New York trial judge rejected the deception allegation, because consumers were given adequate notice through a "Security Warning" and a "Yes" or "No" button to click to indicate their agreement to an "End User Licensing Agreement", to which they were directed by a hyperlink. The agreement provided that such advertisements would be permitted by stating that "[t]he software will collect information about websites you access and will use that information to display advertising on your computer." It was not necessary to force the user to read the agreement. Providing a clear hyperlink to its terms was sufficient to make the terms binding through the consumers' assent. The clear terms of the agreement regarding advertising prevented it from being deceptive.

In *A.V. v. iParadigms, LLC*341, students were required by their school to submit academic papers to the web site "Turnitin", which compared their papers with others to detect plagiarism. The students clicked on the web site's required "I Agree" button to indicate their assent to its user agreement, which permitted the archiving of submitted papers for later use. The agreement stated that "Turnitin and its services…are offered to you, the user…, conditioned on your acceptance without modification of the terms, conditions and notices contained herein."

The students had intended to avoid the archiving permission by placing a written disclaimer on their papers denying their consent to archiving. When the papers were later archived, the students sued for copyright infringement. The Virginia federal trial judge determined that, by clicking their assent to the user agreement, the students had agreed to the web site contract authorizing archiving. The students' disclaimer ploy had been anticipated and prevented by the "without modification" provision in the agreement. Even if it had not been, it is questionable whether the disclaimer would have been effective, if the students had known about the archiving policies of the web site and had known that no human would actually read their disclaimers.

A.V. v. iParadigms, LLC also considered a claim of the defense of minority (or "infancy") (discussed in Part A, Chapter 7, a) i)), which was raised by the student paper writers, who were below the minimum age at which they could generally agree to, and be legally bound to, contracts. Although the students were below the age of majority when they clicked their assent to the web site agreement, the judge applied a standard unjust enrichment exception to the "infancy" defense, which is that a minor is bound to the terms of the contract they agree to, if they keep the benefits of the contract once they have a chance to return, or reject, them. The students kept the benefit of meeting their course credit by using the web site. They were, therefore, bound to the terms of the web site click-wrap agreement.

In *Via Viente Taiwan, L.P. v. United Parcel Service, Inc.*342, a click-wrap license agreement of the delivery service required a customer's clicked acceptance of a service contract with a choice of forum of either federal or state court in Atlanta, Georgia for any litigation arising from service disputes. The customer tried to sue UPS in Texas, arguing that the agreement was unenforceable, because the service software, with the click-wrap agreement, had been installed at its place of business by a UPS employee. The Texas federal trial judge ruled, however, that the agreement was enforceable, because any computer user should not have been surprised by the required click-wrap agreement in the software, and a sophisticated business user especially should have expected a requirement of agreement to some license terms for the service. It would have been unfair to allow the customer to gain the benefits of the service without agreeing to the license terms. There was no evidence presented that the choice-of-forum clause was unenforceable for other reasons.

In *Scherillo v. Dun & Bradstreet, Inc.*343, a dissatisfied purchaser of an online company report objected to the choice-of-forum clause in the click-wrap contract he had agreed to. After he had purchased and acted on the report, the company he invested in was revealed to be a "Ponzi" scheme.

The user argued that the "I Agree" box he was required to check was located below a scroll box containing the contract terms. Because he could not read all the contract terms without scrolling through the entire box, he argued that the forum selection term was not reasonably communicated to him. The New York federal trial judge rejected this argument, comparing the scroll box contract to a multi-page printed contract. A person who refuses to read the contract text in a scroll box is like a person who refuses to read the pages preceding the signature page of a printed contract, the judge ruled. Each had the chance to learn what they were agreeing to, and each was bound by its signature. The judge rejected, as unlikely, the user's argument that he inadvertently checked the "I Agree" box by hitting the space bar on his keyboard, and then inadvertently confirmed this assent by hitting the return key, which took him to a page where he entered his credit card information. The judge was not persuaded that the choice-of-forum clause should not be enforced for any other reasons.

In 2009, the American Law Institute (ALI), a private organization, proposed in its *Principles of the Law of Software Contracts* a "safe harbor" rule of automatic validity for certain types of standard form (take-it-or-leave-it) click-wrap contracts for software transfers. These standard form click-wrap contracts would not be subject to further analysis of the adequacy of disclosure of their terms. Like the ALI's Restatement (Second) of Contracts, these principles have only a "persuasive" authority that is related to the quality of their analysis, and the expertise of their proponents. They can be, but are not required to be, considered by judges in deciding cases.

f) A Case of On-line "Puffing"?

In *Scott v. Bell Atlantic Corp.*344, a telephone company's web site advertised its DSL (digital subscriber line) internet service with enthusiastic descriptions in customer "testimonials". Its DSL click-wrap service agreement, however, included disclaimers of error-free or uninterrupted service or "access that meets your needs". A further, all-capital letters provision disclaimed all warranties, express or implied, including any warranty of merchantability or fitness for a particular purpose.

A New York state appeals court rejected a customer lawsuit for breach of contract, breach of warranty, and fraud through false and deceptive advertising, because of the servicer's "conspicuous, unequivocal" disclaimers. "A reasonably prudent consumer could not have relied on" the advertising, because of these disclaimers. The company's advertising of its maximum connection speed was not a guarantee of a typical connection speed. As Chapter 5, c) in Part A on warranties discusses, advertising claims that cannot be objectively proved or disproved (e.g. "best") are usually treated as just "hot air" or "puffing" or boasting, which cannot be relied upon by buyers responding to the advertising. In a sale of goods, UCC §2-316(1) prevents a disclaimer from being effective, if it contradicts an express warranty. The *Scott* case, however, involved a sale of services, and a disclaimer of all warranties, not just express warranties.

g) Sufficient Notice of Terms Through Agreement by Another Computer User or an Employee

In *Motise v. America Online, Inc.*345, the stepson of an AOL subscriber signed onto and used his stepfather's AOL account. Although the stepson had not agreed to AOL's terms of use, his stepfather had already agreed to them in a click-wrap member service agreement. When the stepson sued AOL in New York for disclosing his "screen name" on a "listserv", thereby causing an invasion of privacy and other harm, the New York federal trial judge decided that the terms the stepfather had agreed to also bound the stepson. These terms included a choice of forum of the state of Virginia for lawsuits. The judge characterized the stepson as a "sub-licensee of privileges that the defendant conditionally granted" to the stepfather. If an account user could obtain greater rights than those of the actual AOL member whose account was used, then the AOL terms of service could be easily circumvented. The forum selection clause itself was not unenforceable, because of any fraud, duress or great inconvenience to the plaintiff.

In *Mortgage Plus v. Doc Magic Inc.*346, a mortgage lender agreed to a click-wrap license agreement on a CD-ROM during installation of business software. The agreement included a choice of forum for disputes in Los Angeles, California. Later, the lender sued the software company in Kansas, alleging that the software program failed to produce documents complying with federal Truth-In-Lending Act disclosure requirements.

The lender argued that the employee who assented to the click-wrap agreement was not specifically authorized to do so, and therefore his employer was not bound by this agreement. The Kansas federal trial judge decided that, even if this were true, the lender-principal ratified this unauthorized assent by its employee-agent, after learning of it, by attempting to benefit from the contract, rather than by promptly repudiating it. These attempts to benefit were shown by the three occasions over a period of six years when other employees also clicked their assent to the agreement and processed hundreds of documents through the licensed software. The judge then decided that a balance of factors favored enforcement of the forum selection provision. The case was transferred to federal court in Los Angeles.

h) Sufficient Notice of Terms Through Agreement with An Intermediate Service Provider

In *People v. Direct Revenue, LLC*347(also discussed in section e) previously), software users, through a click-wrap agreement, authorized third-party advertisers to present to them "pop-up" ads based on web pages they visited. The New York state trial judge determined that the provider of the initial software, and the intermediary between the customers and the advertisers, Direct Revenue, was not liable for any deceptive practices by the ad distributors, because they were independent contractors, whom Direct Revenue did not control. Neither was there evidence that Direct Revenue ratified any misconduct by the advertisers after learning of it. Direct Revenue also provided users with a method to uninstall the software, which was used by many of them. *Doe v. SexSearch.com* 348, in Chapter 8, a) iii), reached a similar conclusion about the non-liability to a deceived customer of an intermediary online service provider for misrepresentations by another user of the service.

i) Cases of E-Mails Creating and Not Creating a Contract and Satisfying the Statute of Frauds

In Part B, Chapter 2, the electronic signature rules of UETA were described, which provide:

> "Electronic signature" means an electronic sound, symbol, or process attached to or logically associated with a record and executed or adopted by a person with the intent to sign the record.349 ...

> (a) An electronic record or electronic signature is attributable to a person if the record or signature was the act of the person. The act of the person may be shown in any manner, including a showing of the efficacy of any security procedure applied to determine the person to which the electronic record or electronic signature was attributable.

> (b) The effect of an electronic record or electronic signature attributed to a person under paragraph (a) is determined from the context and surrounding circumstances at the time of its creation, execution, or adoption, including the parties' agreement, if any, and otherwise as provided by law.350

The "effect" referred to in UETA §9(b) is the legal effect of the electronic record or signature. The "parties' agreement" is their agreement as to the purpose of the electronic record or signature.

The decision in *Brantley v. Wilson*351 illustrates how these UETA rules have been applied by a trial judge. Prospective real estate buyers exchanged eight different e-mails with land owners. When the owners decided not to sell, the would-be buyers sued for specific performance to have the property transferred to them. The owners argued that the exchanged e-mails were not writings and signatures satisfying the Statute of Frauds.

The e-mails collectively included descriptions of the price, financing requirements, closing costs and a detailed land description. A collection of e-mails, like a collection of printed letters, can collectively constitute a signed writing sufficiently describing the subject of a contract to satisfy the Statute of Frauds. The owners argued, however, that these descriptions were only negotiating points, and that any actual sale was intended to be made through a printed agreement, as referred to in one of the e-mails.

The Arkansas federal judge decided that the applicable state version of UETA allowed an electronic contract for the sale of land, but only when the parties intended to contract electronically.352 The facts were not clear enough for the owners to win their motion for summary judgment to end the litigation, without an actual trial of evidence of the parties' intention to contract electronically, and of evidence that the land seller intended her typed name on her e-mails to be her signature.

In the Massachusetts federal trial judge decision in *CSX Transportation, Inc. v. Recovery Express, Inc.*353, a purported buyer of old railcars presented himself as being from "interstate demolition and recovery express", and sent an offer to buy railcars through an e-mail message using the e-mail address albert@recoveryexpress.com. When his check for a purchase "bounced", CSX tried to recover the purchase price from Recovery Express. Albert, and the money he received from his re-sale of the railcars, had disappeared. Albert worked not for Recovery Express, but instead for Interstate Demolition, which only shared office space and e-mail service with Recovery Express. It later ceased operations, because of another fraud by Albert.

The trial judge determined that CSX could not rely either

on the buyer's e-mail address, or on his e-mail and telephone representations, as his "apparent authority" under agency law to do business for Recovery Express. Apparent authority (under agency law) must be created by the action of a principal, such as Recovery Express, that causes another to reasonably believe that a person is its agent. Interstate Demolition only had an office-sharing arrangement with Recovery Express, and the latter had allowed Albert to use an e-mail address with its domain name. The judge decided that CSX acted unreasonably in relying solely on this e-mail address as the basis for Albert's authority to enter a contract for Recovery Express. If this were not the law, then any subordinate employee with access to company letterhead, business cards, or a company car could bind that company to an unauthorized offer. CSX was careless, and it should have confirmed Albert's authority before transferring its property to him. A summary judgment was issued in favor of Recovery Express in CSX's suit for breach of contract and unjust enrichment.

In *Kerr v. Dillard Store Services, Inc.*354, a department store employer provided on its intranet an agreement that its employees must resolve any employment-related disputes through mandatory arbitration. After the plaintiff was fired and brought a discrimination lawsuit against Dillard's, the company claimed that the employee had agreed to mandatory arbitration by adding her initials to the online agreement. The former employee argued, however, that for five months she had refused to accept the arbitration requirement, and that another employee had placed her initials on the form without her consent while helping her to access the intranet to check her work schedule.

The Kansas federal trial judge determined that the Kansas UETA statute permitted the creation of an electronic written arbitration agreement that was enforceable pursuant to the Federal Arbitration Act. The proponent of an arbitration agreement must show that the other party knowingly and intentionally agreed to it. Given the employee's denial of her approval of the agreement, and absent persuasive evidence that someone else could not have placed the employee's initials on the online form, the judge ruled that there was insufficient proof that the employee had agreed to mandatory arbitration.

*Alliance Laundry Systems, LLC v Thyssenkrupp Materials, NA*355 concerned a purported sale of stainless steel. The parties had done business with each other several times. They had previously exchanged printed purchase orders that were sent by the buyer, and signed and returned by the seller, under a supply agreement. After the supply agreement was terminated, the seller offered some left-over steel to the buyer though several e-mail solicitations. The buyer responded with a price counter-offer by e-mail that was accepted by the seller.

The buyer then confirmed in an e-mail that its offer would be sent by "hard copy" to the seller. Meanwhile, the seller's credit department e-mailed the buyer a notice that, until overdue payments for previous shipments were received, it could not make any further shipments to the buyer. Communications between the parties continued intermittently. The seller eventually sold the steel originally offered to the buyer to other customers, and the buyer objected to this sale.

Because it concerned a sale of goods, the Wisconsin Uniform Commercial Code (UCC) rules applied to the buyer's suit for breach of contract, including the rule of UCC §2-104(1) that "[A] contract for sale of goods may be made in any manner sufficient to show agreement, including conduct by both parties which recognizes the existence of such a contract."356 The Wisconsin UETA also provides that "This [Act] applies only to transactions between parties each of which has agreed to conduct transactions by electronic means."357 The section provides further that "[w]hether the parties agree to conduct a transaction by electronic means is determined from the context and surrounding circumstances, including the parties conduct."358

The Wisconsin federal trial judge combined the UCC §2-104(1) rule, that the intention of the parties to form a contract can be shown from their conduct that indicates they have a contract, with the UETA §5(b) rule that the parties' agreement to conduct a transaction by electronic means is determined from their conduct. The judge found that these practices resulted in a set of "rules of the road" (a "course of performance" under UCC §2-208) that showed that the buyer's e-mail purchase order alone was not intended by both parties to create a binding contract. A printed "hard copy" of its purchase order was required to be sent by the buyer and returned by the seller.

The buyer's failure to object, when the seller's credit department withheld a shipment, because of overdue payments for previous shipments, was relevant to this issue. The buyer had previously objected promptly when shipments pursuant to printed purchase orders were late. Its failure to object in this case indicated that it might not have considered an e-mail purchase order alone to be sufficient to create a contract. The judge denied the buyer's motion for summary judgment, leaving the fact questions regarding contract formation for the decision of the jury.

In *Querard v. Countrywide Home Loans, Inc.*359, a customer exchanged e-mails with a mortgage lender about refinancing a mortgage. In a later lawsuit for breach of contract for failure to complete the refinancing, the court initially determined that, under California's Statute of Frauds, an oral/non-written commitment to lend (non-purchase) money secured by a deed of trust/mortgage was enforceable. The court decided that no single e-mail contained all the essential terms necessary to form a contract. When read together, however, the California state appeals court determined that the e-mails contained sufficient expressly stated essential terms (such as parties, loan amount, repayment schedule), and sufficient essential terms that could be "implied from industry custom and the terms of the parties' existing loan agreements" (such as late payment penalty, and rules for default and enforcement of the loan), to form a binding contract. The case shows that even a services contract, which is not subject to the Uniform Commercial Code (UCC), can be interpreted using implied terms taken from the "custom and usage", "course of dealing" and "course of performance" sources of contract interpretation described in Part A, Chapter 5, b).

In *diCaramate v Ginsglobal Index Funds*360, the parties created a printed Memorandum of Understanding about a joint venture to market investment products, which was not sufficient to establish a contract, but under which they did business. The memorandum choice-of-forum clause chose the law of the State of Delaware to apply to their agreement. Later e-mails modified the memorandum. The arrangement was later terminated.

In a breach of contract and unjust enrichment lawsuit, the California federal trial judge ruled that, even without a formal contract, the memorandum and the e-mails together contained sufficient essential terms to create a binding contract. The Statute of Frauds applied because the agreement had a five-year term. Delaware law made the e-mails sufficient writings, and made the typed names on the e-mails sufficient signatures.

In *MEMC Electronic Materials, Inc. v. BP Solar International, Inc.*361, a series of e-mails, as well as printed purchase orders and invoices, was exchanged between a seller and a buyer to cover a three-year period for the future supply of silicon powder for use in the manufacturing of solar panels. Printed agreements had been used for a previous three-year period for similar agreements. The silicon powder was a by-product of the seller's other operations.

When the buyer claimed that the seller had breached this future supply agreement by failing to supply powder for the third year of the agreement, the seller argued that the alleged three-year future supply contract did not satisfy the Statute of Frauds. Several e-mails from the buyer indicated an agreement, with one e-mail specifying a minimum quantity of the goods for each of the three years, and others indicating future prices and other terms that would be negotiated later between the parties. The buyer alleged that the parties' course of dealing and course of performance supplied all other essential contract terms. The seller's reply e-mail confirmed the buyer's stated e-mail terms without objection, although the seller later argued that its reply was only a continuation of negotiations.

The Maryland appeals court ruled that the e-mails satisfied both the signed writing requirements of the Statute of Frauds, and the "merchant's failure to object" to a confirmatory reply exception, under UCC §2-201(2), to the Statute of Frauds requirement of a writing signed by the party to be charged with liability. The only term necessary to be stated in the writings was the quantity of goods, which was stated. It affirmed a jury fact-finding of the existence of an output contract, and the jury verdict for almost $9,000,000 for "cover damages" created by the necessity to purchase the goods at a higher price from another source.

In *Orteck International Inc. v. TransPacific Tire & Wheel, Inc.*362, a tire distributor sued a tire manufacturer for breach of exclusive distributorship and warehouse purchase agreements, for promissory estoppel regarding statements leading the distributor to buy and improve a tire warehouse, and for unjust enrichment through direct manufacturer sales to the distributor's retail customers. A Maryland federal trial judge analyzed two e-mail messages to determine whether the messages, related to the proposed exclusive distribution agreement, satisfied the Statute of Frauds.

The judge ruled that the e-mails, by themselves, did not satisfy the Statute of Frauds regarding an exclusive distribution contract. Neither the "merchant's failure to object" exception, nor the "part performance" exception under UCC §2-201(3)(c), applied. The only e-mail message sent by the tire distributor plaintiff was only copied to, and not directed to, the tire manufacturer defendant. Neither the distributor's e-mail, nor the manufacturer's only signed e-mail, its reply, established a quantity term. Furthermore, the defendant manufacturer objected to the distributor's purported confirmation within 10 days of its receipt (the UCC §2-201(2) time period), thereby preventing the exception from applying in any event. The part performance exception was irrelevant to the distributor's complaint of a breach of contract to supply tires in the future, and its complaint of a breach of its exclusive right to distribute tires. The parties' course of dealing alone was inadequate to establish the existence of an exclusive distribution contract that satisfied the Statute of Frauds.

The distributor's evidence of an oral agreement with the manufacturer to share the costs of a tire warehouse was determined by the judge to be insufficient to establish a contract. There was no evidence that the manufacturer was unjustly enriched by using any customer information received from the distributor to solicit sales from those customers. The distributor's claims of promissory estoppel failed regarding the purported exclusive distribution and warehouse agreements, and the agreement to not sell to the distributor's retail customers, because: 1) it failed to prove clear and definite promises by the manufacturer on these subjects, and 2) the distributor failed to prove that it reasonably relied on any statements by the manufacturer on these subjects.

In *Schnabel v. Trilegiant Corporation, Affinion, Inc.*363, a federal court of appeals affirmed a trial judge's denial of a motion to require arbitration of a class action claim of "unlawful, unfair and deceptive practices" under federal and state consumer protection statutes, involving "data passing", "negative options", and "automatic renewals". These internet marketing practices have been described in section c) previously, and typically involve browse-wrap contract formation techniques. In *Schnabel*, the effect of these practices was addressed by the court in the context of contract formation by e-mail. The federal ROSCA, and California Senate Bill No. 340, restrictions on these practices did not apply to the *Schnabel* transactions, which occurred before the effective dates of these statutes.

Schnabel family members made separate purchases from the online travel web site Priceline.com and from the sports memorabilia web site Beckett.com. On the order confirmation screen pages for their purchases, they were presented with "enrollment offers" of membership in a discount club for consumer goods and services. The discount club was not affiliated with the online retailers from whom the purchases were made. The enrollment offer required the consumers to enter their personal information in order to enroll and receive the club benefits. It did not, however, require them to re-enter their credit card information, because this information was automatically transferred to the discount club through a "data pass" from the retailers.

The Schnabels claimed that they thought their enrollment was in a service provided by the same retailers from whom they had made their purchases. A hyperlink was provided to the third-party discount club, where a consumer could "Learn More" or "See Details". The enrollment page described a member's right to cancel membership before the end of a free enrollment period, but any further membership information was described in small print as being provided in a separate e-mail. Enrollees were required to click a "Yes" button with a statement that, by clicking the button, the purchaser acknowledged that he or she had read the Terms and Conditions of a membership agreement accessible from a hyperlink below the button.

After they clicked on the "Yes" buttons, both Schnabel enrollees received from Trilegiant e-mails, which contained Terms and Conditions, including a clause requiring either small claims court or binding arbitration resolution of any consumer disputes, and waiving any right to bring a class action lawsuit. The Schnabels sued to recover a series of monthly charges against their credit card accounts that they claimed were unauthorized. To defeat Trilegiant's motion to compel arbitration, the Schnabels argued that they had never agreed to the e-mailed Terms and Conditions, which required small claims or arbitration adjudication of their disputes.

The federal Connecticut trial judge agreed with the Schnabels' argument, concluding that the only contract they agreed to was the contract established through the online screens with their direct online retailers. These screens set forth the one-time goods and services purchased by the Schnabels and their costs and payment procedures. The trial judge determined that the arbitration provision (and a choice-of-law provision) in the e-mailed Terms and Conditions was sent after the conclusion of these purchases. It had not been sufficiently brought to the notice of the Schnabels in order for their clicking "Yes" on the screen inviting them to enroll in the discount club to also constitute an agreement to the arbitration clause.

On appeal, the federal circuit court applied to these facts the two basic requirements of acceptance of a contract offer. The first requirement is existence of an act of acceptance of an offer, objectively viewed. The second requirement is existence of reasonable notice to the offeree of the terms of the offer.

The court analyzed the purported e-mail contract as similar to a "contract now, terms later" shrink-wrap contract, where terms received after purchase are treated as agreed to, unless the purchase is returned within a certain time period. Alternatively, it analyzed it as a proposal for amendments to an existing purchase contract that would be treated as accepted, unless rejected within a certain time period by canceling the discount club membership. Under either analysis, the court determined that the post-purchase e-mails did not provide reasonable notice of the enclosed contract terms, of the relationship of those terms to the original goods or services purchased, or that failure to act regarding the third-party discount club offer would be treated as agreement to its contract terms.

The e-mail was unclear in its subject line, which only referred to "Important information about your membership privileges". The first twelve paragraphs of the e-mail referred to membership information, rather than to contract terms. The actual arbitration provision was stated in the twentieth paragraph. Finally, the failure of the offeror to require acknowledgement of receipt of the arbitration provision "undermines Trilegiant's assertion that the plaintiffs received sufficient notice to bind them to the additional terms through their inaction."364

The court stated that the test of reasonable notice of offered contract terms depends on various factors including, but not limited to, the conspicuousness of the term, the course of dealing between the parties, and industry practices. The same court's earlier decision in *Register.com v. Verio, Inc.* was cited as an example of an offeree receiving reasonable notice of browse-wrap terms, because of its business sophistication and its previous experience with the offeror's web site. Unlike shrink-wrap contracts, these e-mailed terms were separated in both time and (cyber-) space from the discount club enrollments they were related to, thereby providing less notice of their relevance to the offerees. According to the court, "Trilegiant effectively obscured the details of the terms and conditions and the passive manner in which they could be accepted….the [online enrollment screens] made it appear –falsely—that being a member imposed virtually no burdens on the consumer besides payment."365 The court did not rule on the offeror's argument that its hyperlink to the Terms and Conditions established a browse-wrap contract, because the argument was waived by not being raised at trial. It noted, however, that the court's earlier decision in *Specht v. Netscape Communications Corp.* ruled that a browse-wrap contract term presented only after a series of contract screens did not provide enough reasonable notice of its terms to be enforceable.366

In *Kwan v. Clearwire Corporation*367, two customers of Clearwire, an internet service provider, brought a class action claiming violation of statutory consumer protections in the procedures used for their introductory free trial periods of service. Clearwire, and its debt collectors, filed a motion to compel arbitration of the disputes, pursuant to the Terms of Service, to which it alleged the plaintiffs had agreed.

Clearwire stated that it sent order confirmation e-mails to both customers that included hyperlinks to the Terms of Service. The State of Washington federal judge determined, however, that these e-mails only included hyperlinks to Clearwire's internet home page. The home page only included another hyperlink at the bottom labeled "Legal", which led to a second page listing various links, including to a third linked page with the Terms of Service. The e-mail was stated by the plaintiffs to have referred to Terms of Service, without further reference to an arbitration requirement, only on its third page. The parties disagreed about whether one plaintiff, Ms. Brown, had actually clicked on an "I Agree" button showing her agreement to the Terms of Service, or whether a technician servicing a faulty modem at her house had clicked on the button.

The second Clearwire customer, Ms. Reasonover, received printed materials with her mobile internet service modem. Clearwire stated that these materials indicated that, by activating the service, the customer would be bound by the Terms of Service accessible at its web site home page. The federal judge determined that this instruction was stated only in smaller print at the bottom of a page welcoming the customer to the service, and that the included hyperlink (as in Ms. Brown's case) required clicks to three web pages to access the actual Terms of Service. Clearwire argued that Ms. Reasonover clicked on an "I Accept" button, but provided no evidence of this action. The customer stated that she did not click her acceptance of any contract terms, because she abandoned the service before actual use when she was unable to get an acceptable signal strength for her modem.

The federal judge applied the same contract formation requirements of reasonable notice of terms, and objective evidence of assent to those terms by the offeree, which were applied in the *Specht* and *Register.com* cases. Comparing Ms. Brown's notice of terms to the notice in *Specht*, he determined that "the breadcrumbs left by Clearwire to lead Ms. Brown to its [Terms of Service] did not constitute sufficient or reasonably conspicuous notice…".368 Because the parties disagreed on whether the customer, or the modem technician, clicked on the button agreeing to contract terms, the motion to compel arbitration was denied and a hearing to determine the facts of this alleged assent was ordered.

The notice of Terms of Service provided in the printed materials sent to Ms. Reasonover with her mobile service modem were determined to be inadequate for the same reasons as the notice in the e-mail to Ms. Brown. The judge rejected Clearwire's motion to compel arbitration, based only on Ms. Reasonover's access to a web page with Terms of Service, and an "I Accept Terms" button, to prove adequate notice to her of the terms or to prove her agreement to the terms. There was no actual evidence that the customer clicked on the acceptance button. Finally, Clearwire's debt collectors' ability to use Clearwire's arbitration clause to avoid litigation was determined to depend on whether the debt collectors were agents of Clearwire, or only independent contractors. This was a fact question requiring the presentation of evidence at a hearing.

j) Cases of Insufficient and Sufficient Incorporation by Reference of Web Site Terms into Written Agreements

In the 2006 case of *Affinity Internet, Inc. v. Consolidated Credit Counseling Services, Inc.*369, a printed agreement for computer and web hosting services provided that it was "subject to…terms, conditions, user and acceptable use policies" located on a specified web site. The web site terms included a mandatory arbitration provision, which was not described in the printed agreement. When the servicer defendant, in a lawsuit for breach of contract and unjust enrichment, tried to enforce the arbitration provision, the plaintiff argued that it had not received sufficient notice of it.

The Florida state appeals court determined that the web site arbitration requirement had not been sufficiently "incorporated by reference" into the printed agreement by simply stating that it was "subject to" the web site terms. There must be a clearer expression in the primary document of the parties' intention to be bound by the terms of the referenced document. The web site terms needed to either be attached to the printed agreement or provided to the other party, or the printed agreement needed to "sufficiently describe the document", or "so much of it as is referred to" in the printed agreement. This court's treatment of terms incorporated from an online source, as being less available to a party than terms incorporated from a printed source, might have been influenced by the defendant's offering, as proof of the web site terms, a web site with a different address than the address referred to in the printed agreement.

In the 2005 case of *Hugger-Mugger, L.L.C. v. NetSuite, Inc.*370, a Utah federal trial judge was presented with a printed software licensing agreement that provided that it was "subject to the terms of this agreement and the Terms of Service posted at www.NetSuite.com, or successor web site…This Agreement and Incorporated Terms of Service represent the entire agreement of the parties." A mandatory California choice-of-forum provision in these web site terms was objected to, when the customer, Hugger-Mugger, sued the internet service provider, NetSuite, in Utah for breach of warranty.

This incorporation by reference was judged against three requirements: 1) the reference to the outside document must be clear and unequivocal, 2) the reference must be brought to the attention of the other party and he must consent to the incorporation, and 3) the incorporated terms must be known or easily available to the parties. Finding all three requirements satisfied, the trial judge enforced the mandatory arbitration provision. In addition, the judge determined that an employee of Hugger-Mugger accepted NetSuite's click-wrap agreement with the mandatory choice-of-forum provision, using "ostensible" or apparent authority that Hugger-Mugger led NetSuite to believe the employee had been given to enter contracts. The judge determined that Hugger-Mugger did not meet its burden to show that the choice-of- forum provision was unenforceable, because it was unreasonable or unjust.

In *Spartech CMD, LLC v. International Automotive Components Group North America, Inc.*371, two businesses entered a series of contracts for the sale of goods. A dispute arose regarding pricing. The goods buyer, International, issued five purchase orders to the goods seller, Spartech. Four of the purchase orders included a term incorporating by reference "Purchase Order Terms and Conditions which are available through links provided on [buyer's] Web Site at [web address]…The Terms apply to all purchases by [buyer] and its affiliates under any purchase order." The Terms and Conditions included a paragraph requiring arbitration in Michigan of any dispute related to the purchase order. The fifth purchase was entered directly into the seller's computer system without a purchase order.

In response to all five purchases, the seller sent the buyer an Acknowledgement Form with Terms and Conditions of Sale. The seller's terms included a choice-of-forum clause providing that "[i]f Seller brings an action to enforce the terms of this agreement in any Pennsylvania or federal court, Buyer agrees to waive objections to personal jurisdiction and venue." The paragraph also chose Pennsylvania law as its choice of law. After the pricing dispute arose, the seller sued in Michigan federal court for an injunction to prevent arbitration of the dispute.

Before the Michigan federal judge, the seller, Spartech, argued that the conflict between its choice of forum in its Acknowledgement Form terms and the buyer's choice of arbitration for disputes in its four purchase orders created a "battle of the forms". Both parties agreed to resolve the legal issues under the Michigan version of UCC §2-207. For the fifth purchase made without a buyer's purchase order, or related terms, the seller argued that its choice of forum was the only relevant term.

The federal judge determined that the four purchase orders sent by the buyer sufficiently incorporated the web site contract terms by explicit reference. Any failure by the seller to read those terms did not prevent their application to the contract, because the buyer's "intent to incorporate the Terms is clear on its face". Without a purchase order, however, the fifth contract was only governed by the seller's

Acknowledgement Form terms, since there was no course of dealing or usage of trade that indicated disputes should be resolved by arbitration.

The seller argued that the buyer's arbitration requirement should be eliminated from their purchase order contracts under the "knockout rule" of UCC §2-207(2)(b), because it was a different and conflicting term that was a material alteration of the parties' contract. The Michigan federal judge read the parties' terms, however, as complementary, rather than conflicting. Their contract dispute could be resolved initially by arbitration. The arbitration award could then be taken to state or federal court for enforcement in a suit by the seller. The language of the seller's terms did not require all disputes to be resolved exclusively in court, nor did it refer to lawsuits initiated by the buyer. The judge denied the request for an injunction against arbitration of the four purchase order contracts. She permitted the litigation of the non-purchase order contract to continue, however, during the arbitration of the other contracts.

k) Defenses of Substantive and Procedural Unconscionability

The *AT&T Mobility LLC v. Concepcion* U.S. Supreme Court 2011 decision, discussed in Part A, Chapter 7, d), reversed a group of California state contract law decisions. These decisions had denied enforcement of class action waivers and mandatory arbitration clauses in consumer contracts as unconscionable, because the mandatory arbitration did not provide for group or class proceedings alleging deliberate fraud. Mandatory arbitration and other contract terms, however, might still be denied enforcement as unconscionable for other reasons under state contract law. What other reasons are, or are not, sufficiently similar to those found to be preempted by federal law under *AT&T Mobility LLC v. Concepcion* is currently unclear.

A federal trial judge applied State of Washington contract law in *Riensche v. Cingular Wireless*, LLC 372, a class action decided under diversity (of parties' state citizenship) jurisdiction. The action was brought claiming breach of contract and an improper tax surcharge. The federal judge first determined that Riensche could be bound by the click-wrap telephone service agreement terms, whether or not he read them before clicking "I Agree". To resolve the customer's claim that procedural unconscionability prevented the enforcement of class action waiver and mandatory arbitration terms in the agreement, three factors were analyzed: 1) the manner of entering the contract, 2) existence of a reasonable opportunity to understand the contract terms, and 3) whether "a maze of fine print" hid important contract terms.

The requirement that the consumer enter personal information on the web site, before he was presented with contract terms, was determined to not be an improper manner of contracting. The consumer had the option to cancel the transaction when the terms were presented. Neither did the "timing out" of the transaction after fifteen minutes of inactivity deny him a reasonable opportunity to understand the terms, given that the consumer could have read the terms separately without a time limit and returned later to enter personal information. A consumer could also terminate his service without a penalty after receiving his mailed welcome kit.

A sentence near the beginning of the agreement stated a requirement of "the use of arbitration to resolve disputes" and limited "the remedies available to you in the event of a dispute." The actual arbitration clause capitalized the word "ARBITRATION", stated that it "affects your rights", and provided a link to the American Arbitration Association for information on arbitration rules. This was determined to provide a reasonable opportunity for the arbitration terms to be understood. The agreement presentation in four pages of unbroken text was found to not hide important terms, because the agreement was legibly presented and could be read online, printed from the online agreement, or read in the printed agreement included in the welcome kit. Small print and the absence of section breaks did not make the agreement procedurally unconscionable under Washington law, especially given the all capital letters heading of the arbitration clause. Finally, Riensche was determined to have had a "heightened awareness" of the possibility of an arbitration clause, because of his past litigation against the same company.

Riensche prevailed, however, on his argument of substantive unconscionability, which, by itself, is sufficient to invalidate a contract under Washington law. The class action waiver was first determined to be substantively unconscionable, because it was "unilateral and excessively favors Cingular". This reason for invalidating the waiver would no longer be valid under *AT&T Mobility LLC v. Concepcion*. Finally, the judge ruled regarding the arbitration clause's limitation of injunctive relief remedies "only in favor of the individual party seeking relief and only to the extent necessary to provide relief warranted by that party's individual claim". This provision was determined to be substantively unconscionable, because it was "one-sided and overly harsh to consumers", and denies a remedy available under state consumer protection law. Whether this reason for invalidating the class action waiver is different enough from the reasons invalidated by *AT&T Mobility LLC v. Concepcion* so that it will provide this decision with future validity is questionable.

Some judges have issued conflicting decisions about the frequently stated requirement that a contract must present a party with an "absence of meaningful choice" in order to be procedurally unconscionable. For example, in a Pennsylvania federal trial court diversity jurisdiction case, California law was applied to resolve an argument arising out of participation in the "Second Life" virtual reality online game.

In *Bragg v. Linden Research*373, a customer of the online game claimed that its owner had improperly deprived him of virtual/intellectual property rights that he had obtained in its virtual world when it canceled his membership. Bragg had clicked "I Agree" to a click-wrap Terms of Service contract that included a requirement of mandatory arbitration of member/customer disputes. The Pennsylvania federal judge decided that the arbitration requirement was substantively unconscionable under California law, because it authorized Linden Research to suspend or terminate an account at any time for any reason or no reason, to retain any customer payments based on suspicions of fraud, and to amend the agreement at any time with a posting on its web site. This made the agreement one-sided when a dispute with a customer arose. In addition, the arbitration expenses of $17,500 for a $75,000 dispute, plus shared costs and fees, were determined to be higher in total than the expenses that would have been incurred in state or federal court. Finally, the mandatory California choice of forum was determined to be unreasonable and unconscionable, given the nationwide customer base of the online game.

The judge determined that, under California law, the contract was also procedurally unconscionable: first, because it was presented to Bragg on a "take-it-or-leave-it" basis, and "[a]lthough it is not the only virtual world on the Internet, Second Life was the first and only virtual world to specifically grant its participants property rights in virtual land"; second, because "Linden buried the TOS's arbitration provision in a lengthy paragraph under the benign heading 'GENERAL PROVISIONS'", and third, because "Linden also failed to make available the costs and rules of arbitration in the ICC by either setting them forth in the TOS or by providing a hyper-link to another page or website where they are available."

It is always difficult for a federal court in a diversity of citizenship case to try to predict how a state court would apply its law to the facts of a case (unless it specifically asks the state's highest court what it would do, which is a time-consuming procedure). Many, if not most, of the contracts that we encounter daily are "take-it-or-leave-it" contracts. Most judges have concluded that such contracts do present us with a meaningful choice, which is to either enter the contract, or to "walk away".

A later decision, by a federal district court in California, agreed with the *Bragg* judge's analysis of procedural unconscionability under California contract law. In *Brazil v. Dell Inc.*374, customers who bought computers from Dell's web site agreed to Dell's click-wrap Terms and Conditions of Sale, which were hyperlinked to its "I Agree" button. The customers were also reminded of the Terms and Conditions of Sale in an e-mail confirmation of the sale, and they received the agreement in their product shrink-wrap. The customers later sued Dell in a class action for breach of contract and unjust enrichment through alleged false advertising of price discounts.

Although the first paragraph of the terms, in all capital letters, directed the customer to read the document carefully and warned that it included a dispute resolution (mandatory arbitration) clause, the judge determined that the agreement, which included a class action waiver by the customer, used a "take-it-or-leave-it" manner of contracting, and denied the customer a meaningful choice. There was no unfair "surprise" of the buyers regarding the contract terms, which is an important, but not a required, element of procedural unconscionability under California law.

A greater degree of substantive unconscionability can overcome a lesser degree of procedural unconscionability under California law. The judge determined that there was sufficient substantive unconscionability to invalidate the agreement's prohibition of class actions because these facts involved an alleged scheme to deliberately cheat large numbers of consumers of small amounts of money. These reasons are similar to those given by the judge in the *Riensche v. Cingular Wireless, LLC* decision and, by themselves, would now appear to be insufficient to deny enforcement of a mandatory arbitration clause under the reasoning of *AT&T Mobility LLC v. Concepcion*.

Another federal trial judge opinion applied California law to invalidate a mandatory arbitration clause in a click-wrap terms and conditions agreement as unconscionable. In *Mazur v. eBay Inc.*375, the plaintiffs alleged a practice of fake bidding by auction house defendants, acquiesced in by eBay. The agreement was determined to be procedurally unconscionable, because it was both an "oppressive contract of adhesion", and was presented as "a single-spaced massive block of impenetrable text" with the arbitration clause "hidden in the prolix printed form" without any paragraph, section or heading breaks, thereby satisfying the "surprise" factor under California law. The bidders were not directed to any other web sites for easier-to-read versions of the agreement.

In applying the California "lack of mutuality" test of substantive unconscionability, the judge determined that the arbitration clause's selection of a two-person law firm that advertised itself as a "virtual corporate legal department" prevented these arbitrators from providing a "neutral and fair resolution of the dispute". The arbitration requirement's prohibition of the use of attorneys or witnesses, and its one-hour time limit to present arguments, was determined to have "lopsided adverse consequences" for a complaining bidder, although these rules also applied to the auction house. Therefore, the arbitration clause was determined to be unenforceable, because it was substantively unconscionable.

The judge further invalidated the arbitration requirement based on its practical effect of denying a class action type of remedy for a large group of customers with small monetary claims, who alleged a deliberate scheme to defraud them. This reason for invalidating a mandatory arbitration clause was overturned by the analysis of *AT&T Mobility LLC v. Concepcion*. The remaining reasons for the judge's decision, however, would probably be sufficient for a determination of unconscionability under California contract law.

In *Appliance Zone, LLC v. NexTag, Inc.*376, an Indiana online merchant alleging trademark infringement objected to the California choice-of-forum clause in a comparison shopping web site's click-wrap terms of service agreement that it had previously agreed to. The merchant first argued that its nineteen-year-old employee, who clicked its assent to the agreement, could not bind the merchant, because he was unauthorized to contract for it. This argument was rejected, because the employee of majority age had apparent authority to bind the merchant to the agreement. The merchant also argued that the clause was procedurally and substantively unconscionable, because it was inconspicuous, and was presented in a take-it-or-leave-it contract. The checkbox to accept the terms of service did not present the entire agreement, but only presented a hyperlink reading "Terms of Service".

The Indiana federal trial judge ruled that the agreement was "highly visible and easily accessible" and was presented in a manner more visible than Appliance Zone's own web site browse-wrap "Terms & Conditions". Its status as a multi-million dollar online merchant made Appliance Zone's unsubstantiated argument, that it was subjected to a disparity in bargaining power, unsuccessful. Finally, its argument that the choice-of-forum clause was substantively unconscionable was unsupported by facts, especially given that Appliance Zone's own browse-wrap terms of use were similar in substance. The choice-of-forum clause was determined to be enforceable.

In the post-*Concepcion* decision of *Vernon v. Qwest Communications International, Inc.*377, a class action lawsuit was brought in federal court by internet service customers for violation of consumer protection statutes by allegedly improper application of $200 early termination fees for their services. The Qwest defendants filed a motion to compel arbitration of the disputes pursuant to the mandatory arbitration clause in the customers' Subscriber Agreements. The customers argued that the arbitration clause was unconscionable under applicable state law, because it precluded class- wide arbitration of common complaints, and was therefore unenforceable.

The federal trial magistrate judge first noted that the Supreme Court in *Concepcion* determined that parties by contract "may agree to limit the issues subject to arbitration, to arbitrate according to specific rules, and to limit *with whom* a party will arbitrate its disputes."378 Qwest presented evidence that existing customers were informed by printed letter, with incorporation by reference to the Qwest web site "legal" page, of the Subscriber Agreement terms. New customers subscribing by telephone were informed by voice prompts of the existence of the agreement, and the availability of its terms at the web site page. Both of these types of customers were told that they would be deemed to have agreed to the terms if they did not cancel their service within thirty days. Customers subscribing through the internet were required to click on a button indicating their agreement to Terms and Conditions, including arbitration, which appeared in a scroll box on the same web page. They were reminded on the same checkout page to review the terms and conditions later, including arbitration, and to cancel their service within thirty days if they did not agree with them. All customers had to install the service software through a computer disk that instructed them to read the Subscriber Agreement, including the arbitration clause, and to click on a button to accept the agreement, without which the software would not be installed. A copy of the agreement could be printed from the same page. Every customer also received a Welcome Letter that informed them of the applicable Subscriber Agreement at the web site, which included an arbitration provision, and asked them to cancel their service within thirty days if they did not agree to it.

Applying the contract formation requirements of reasonable notice of contract terms, and an objective manifestation of agreement to them, the judge determined that the existing Qwest customers, who received printed letters informing them of the Subscriber Agreement, had reasonable notice of its terms, including the arbitration clause, even if the terms were not presented in the letters. The judge compared this to the decision in *Fteja v. Facebook, Inc.* described previously in Chapter 8, section c), approving the hybrid contract of a "click-wrap" agreement with "browse-wrap" terms available through a hyperlink. The hyperlinked terms "were not hidden or difficult to find."379 The customers' continued use of the service beyond the cancellation deadline was determined to be a manifestation of assent to the agreement. The judge rejected the argument that no agreement was formed because Qwest had the power to alter its terms in the future, making its promises illusory. Qwest was required to inform the customers of any changes, which they could avoid by then canceling their service. No such changes were actually made in this case.

The judge determined that the preclusion of a class-wide arbitration, despite the small monetary amounts at stake, did not by itself establish substantive unconscionability under Colorado contract law. Following the precedent of *Concepcion*, the argument that denial of a class-wide remedy was itself contrary to public policy was rejected. Neither was the contract viewed as procedurally unconscionable, because the offer of a contract on a "take-it-or-leave-it" basis does not alone create procedural unconscionability. The multiple communications to the customers gave them a reasonable opportunity to become familiar with the agreement and its terms. The defendants' motion to compel arbitration was granted.

In *Swift v. Zynga Game Network, Inc.*380, a hybrid contract required a game player using Facebook to assent to Terms of Service/Use by clicking on an "Allow" button, beneath which was a statement in smaller grey font that, by clicking, the user agreed to use of her Facebook information, and to hyperlinked Facebook Terms of Service, and to hyperlinked Terms of Service of the YoVille online game. The YoVille Terms of Service provided that Zynga could later unilaterally change its mandatory arbitration provision, and that use of the game, after notice of the change, would constitute acceptance of the changed terms.

In an attempted class action suit for unjust enrichment related to allegedly fraudulent offers of video game applications, the California federal judge distinguished this presentation of terms from those in *Specht* and *Hines*, which the plaintiff argued were similar cases of unreasonable notice of online terms. Unlike those cases, the judge determined that Zynga's terms were accessible by a hyperlink just below a click-wrap button, which, the user was informed, provided assent to those terms.

Zynga defended this litigation until the U.S. Supreme Court ruled in *AT&T Mobility LLC v. Concepcion* that federal arbitration law preempted the California common law making class action waivers in mandatory arbitration clauses always unconscionable. After *Concepcion*, Zynga moved to compel arbitration. The judge denied the plaintiffs' argument of unconscionability of the mandatory arbitration clause, because of the failure to present any specific facts supporting it. A general argument of unconscionability, because of the mandatory arbitration requirement alone, was unavailable after *Concepcion*.

l) Defenses of Adequate Notice of Permitted Unilateral Modifications

In section d) previously, the *Douglas* case decided that a browse-wrap contract gave insufficient notice to a consumer of a telephone service's power to unilaterally change its terms of use. *Margae v. Clear Link Technologies, LLC*381 addressed a similar issue regarding a click-wrap partner agreement between two internet marketing companies covering marketing services provided by Margae for Clear Link and its affiliates. The online agreement allowed Clear Link and its affiliates to "modify the agreement at any time by notifying the Sales Partner or by posting a new agreement" on its web site. The agreement was in fact modified unilaterally to require mandatory arbitration of disputes and was posted on the defendant's web site. Objections of failure of assent to this change, lack of consideration to support the new agreement, and unconscionability were raised in Margae's suit for breach of contract and unjust enrichment related to its marketing services.

Regarding failure to assent to the agreement changes, the Utah federal trial judge determined that Margae had assented to the original click-wrap agreement, which permitted notice of unilaterally changed terms by their posting to Clear Link's web site. Margae had business reasons to regularly visit the web site and should have monitored it for agreement changes. The continued payments that Margae was paid for its post-amendments marketing services were sufficient consideration to support the agreement, as amended. Finally, the amended agreement was not procedurally unconscionable, because Margae was a sophisticated business with bargaining power. Neither was it substantively unconscionable, because Margae was a sophisticated corporation that could have ended its business relationship in response to unacceptable agreement changes. The judge rejected Margae's argument that it was unfair to deny it the possibility of equitable court remedies under the new mandatory arbitration requirement, while leaving open that option for Clear Link, stating that "even if the arbitration clause were unfair, courts have the power to construe agreements to avoid inequities". The *Margae* decision shows that, unless special circumstances of misrepresentation or unfair practices are proved, as discussed in Part A, Chapter 7, c), business parties, unlike consumers, are usually expected to protect themselves from damage to their interests by negotiating favorable contracts.

*Harris v. Blockbuster Inc.*382 involved a lawsuit for violation of the Video Privacy Protection Act.383 Blockbuster entered an arrangement with Facebook whereby, when a Blockbuster customer rented a movie through Blockbuster Online, the customer's rental choice was communicated to her friends through the Facebook "Beacon" program. A click-wrap contract required Blockbuster Online customers to agree to its Terms and Conditions, which gave it the right to unilaterally change its service agreement with a consumer "at any time, and in its sole discretion…with or without notice", such changes to "be effective immediately upon posting." The terms of service agreement required consumers to periodically review the agreement terms. Their continued use of the service was deemed to constitute acceptance of any modified terms.

Blockbuster's arrangement for unilateral changes had a

fatal flaw. The consumer argued that the click-wrap agreement was illusory and not binding, because it did not expressly limit future contract changes only to disputes arising after the date of the contract change. The Texas federal trial judge agreed that, by not limiting its power to change the contract to post-change disputes only, Blockbuster had effectively not made any binding promises in its original contract. By failing to make a binding promise, Blockbuster had failed to provide legal consideration, and the contract, including its arbitration requirement, was not enforceable.

In *Harold H. Huggins Realty, Inc. v. FNC, Inc.*384, an online real estate appraisal service agreement had originally required mandatory arbitration of disputes, but it later was unilaterally modified twice. The original agreement required the real estate appraiser-user's clicked assent to any agreement changes after they were posted on the sign-in page. The first modification changed responsibility for arbitration fees, but allowed existing customers to continue using the service without clicking their agreement to these changes.

The second modification replaced the original service agreement entirely with a new version of the service agreement that eliminated the mandatory arbitration requirement. FNC only gave a banner notice of this change for several weeks on its home page, which, together with its presentation as the only user agreement on its website, implied that the new agreement applied to all users. When an appraiser customer brought a class action breach of contract lawsuit against the service for misuse of business information about the appraisers, the service argued that its attempted elimination of the arbitration requirement was ineffective, first because it did not require a clicked assent to the change, as required by the original agreement, and second, because it did not provide effective notice of the change.

The Maryland federal trial judge ruled that the original agreement did not actually require a clicked acceptance of all changes to the contract, but made changes "effective 30 days after the changes are posted". Although the agreement's language was ambiguous, because that ambiguity could benefit its drafter, the benefit of the doubt was given to the customer, using the standard contract interpretation rule that contract language "ambiguities are construed against the drafter" – here, the online service provider.

In addition, the judge determined that the appraiser plaintiffs waived (voluntarily and knowingly surrendered) their right to insist on a clicked assent to the agreement changes, as any contract party may do. The judge also applied the legal doctrine of "quasi-estoppel" against FNC's position that the arbitration requirement had not been eliminated by its agreement changes, by finding that 1) this argument was inconsistent with its prior statements in the web site banner and the hyperlink to the user agreement, and 2) permitting FNC to prevail in such a reversal of position, only for purposes of this litigation, would be "unconscionable". This type of unconscionability need not satisfy the procedural and substantive tests described in the previous section. The quasi-estoppel doctrine used by the judge also does not require proof of appraiser reliance on FNC's statements regarding agreement changes that the more common doctrine of "equitable estoppel" requires. Finally, the judge determined that FNC waived its rights to compel arbitration by its changes to the user agreement and its notices thereof to its users.

m) A Third-Party Beneficiary of Craigslist Terms of Use?

In *Jackson v. American Plaza Corp.*385, the click-wrap Terms of Use of the online classified advertising web site, Craigslist.org, prohibited multiple postings of the same real estate rental offer. The plaintiffs and defendants were competing rental advertisers on Craigslist, but there was no direct contract between them. The plaintiffs sued to enjoin the defendants from violating the Terms of Use through their admitted repetitive postings of the same ads within 48 hours. The plaintiffs claimed standing to sue as third-party beneficiaries of the Terms of Use contract between Craigslist and the defendants.

In denying the requested injunction, the New York federal trial judge applied the standard third-party beneficiary rules described in Part A, Chapter 4, e), ii). The judge determined that the plaintiffs failed to prove that they were intended beneficiaries of the contract. Especially important for this determination was the actual language of the Terms of Use, which stated that if users were dissatisfied with the service, their "only recourse was to immediately discontinue use." The contract also provided an internal grievance procedure to resolve complaints about use of the web site, stating that users should "report any violations of the TOU…by flagging the posting(s) for review…or by emailing . . . abuse craigslist.org". By implication, this procedure was viewed as eliminating litigation as a method to address violations of the Terms of Use. Finally, the purpose of the prohibition on repetitive posting was to benefit only the web service itself, which was indicated by the agreement's statement that "you agree not to . . . repeatedly post the same or similar Content or otherwise impose an unreasonable or disproportionately large load on our infrastructure."

n) Is Web Site Design and Building a Service or a Sale of Goods?

In *Conwell v. Gray Loon Outdoor Marketing Group, Inc.*386, a limited partnership hired a web site designer to build a web site and to host it. The designer was paid for the initial site building, but when it later altered the site at the client's request, it was not paid for the alterations. The designer eventually took down the web site as a form of "self- help". The designer also sued for non-payment, and the client countersued for conversion (the tort of unauthorized taking) of the web site. The web site was composed of computer software. Various courts have determined that software is "goods" under the Uniform Commercial Code (UCC). Where a contract covers a mixture of goods and services, however, a judge will look to see what the predominant purpose of the contract is, in order to classify it as either a goods contract subject to UCC law, or a services contract subject to common law.

The Indiana Supreme Court ruled that the "predominant thrust" of the contract was the providing of services. Therefore, the Indiana common law of contracts applied, under which a contract was determined to have been formed. Regarding the alleged tort of conversion, the judge ruled that, under copyright law, the partnership never actually owned the web site. It had only obtained a non-exclusive license to use the site. Therefore, it could not claim that it had been improperly deprived of its property.

o) E-mail Modification, and Text Message Circumvention, of No Oral Modification Contract Clauses

In *Copeland Corp. v. Choice Fabricators Inc.*387, a fixed price, three-year contract for the supply of stamped steel parts contained a "no oral modification" clause, as permitted by UCC §2-209(3). UCC §2-209(4), however, permits an attempted oral modification to operate as a waiver of the no oral modification clause.

After the price for the steel parts was increased by the seller, in response to drastic increases in its own costs, the buyer sent the seller several e-mails indicating that it had agreed to accept the higher price. When the surcharges began to be billed, the buyer sent seven letters indicating that it would pay the surcharges under protest. The buyer later sued the seller for breach of contract, resulting in a verdict for the seller at trial. The federal appeals court determined that the e-mails sent by the buyer, together with the original printed agreement, were a "writing" signed by the party to be charged that satisfied the Statute of Frauds requirement of UCC §2-201.

In *CX Digital Media, Inc. v. Smoking Everywhere, Inc.*388, a web site retailer of electronic cigarettes entered an agreement with a broker of internet advertising promotion to direct traffic to the retailer's web site. The original agreement required the retailer to pay a $45 fee (later increased to $51) to the broker for each sale of an electronic cigarette kit to a customer directed to the web site through the broker's network. The number of sales for which a fee would be paid was limited to 200 per day, and all internet customer traffic was to be directed to one specific web site page.

At the start of the third year of the contract, a vice-president of the broker and an account executive of the retailer engaged in an exchange of text messages. These text messages indicated that all customer traffic would be directed by the broker to two new web site pages. The messages also indicated that there would be no limit on the number of sales per day for which the broker would be paid for referrals. The Florida federal trial judge, applying Delaware law, first determined that the text message exchange indicated the parties' intent to switch customer referrals from the original web site page to two new pages. The judge then analyzed the following pertinent parts of the text message exchange to determine its effect on the original written contract, which contained a "no oral modification" clause.

> [Broker] "We can do 2000 orders/day by Friday if I have your blessing…And I want the AOR [agent of record] when we make your offer #1 on network."

> [Retailer] "NO LIMIT."

> [Broker] "awesome!"

When the retailer failed to pay the referral fees to the broker for customer sales directed through its network (both before and after this text message exchange), the broker sued the retailer for breach of contract. Broker-directed sales to the new web site pages had increased from an average of 39 per day, in the month before the text message exchange, to 1,244 per day in the following month. The judge determined that the broker's first message was an offer to raise the sales limit from 200 to 2,000 per day, which was rejected by the retailer's counter-offer of an unlimited number of sales per day for which it would pay a referral fee to the broker. The retailer's unlimited number counter-offer was then accepted by the broker's message "awesome!", and by the broker's actions to increase the number of referrals.

The original agreement stated that it "may be changed only by a subsequent writing signed by both parties". The trial judge determined that the text messages were unsigned, written modifications of the original agreement. Nevertheless, under Delaware common law, the messages operated as a waiver of, or promissory estoppel against, the retailer's argument that the absence of signatures prevented enforcement of the written modifications. Where parties' subsequent agreement to modify an earlier agreement fails to satisfy a signed writing requirement, a court may refuse enforcement of the signed writing requirement against a party that has materially relied on the subsequent agreement, if enforcement of the writing requirement would be unjust.389 After disposing of arguments by the retailer of lack of consideration, lack of authority to make the modifications, frustration of purpose, violation of the implied covenant of good faith and fair dealing, and mutual mistake, the judge entered an order requiring the retailer to pay to the broker $1,260,805.00 in referral fees, plus interest and attorney's fees and costs, as required by the original contract.

p) An Inadvertent Series of E-mail Messages Can Give Grounds for a Demand for Adequate Assurances

As described in Part A, Chapter 6, c), when a contract party is presented with reasonable grounds to believe that the other party will breach its contract duties, it may demand "adequate assurances" that the proper performance of those duties will be completed. Until it receives them, the party making the demand may suspend its own contract performance for which it has not already been compensated. For a sale of goods under the UCC, if the party making the demand does not receive within a reasonable time, not exceeding thirty days, such adequate assurances, it may treat the failure to provide them as an anticipatory repudiation of the contract by the other party, and it may sue for a total contract breach.

In *Validsa Inc. v. PDVSA Services Inc.*390, a Florida foods trader entered a contract with a representative of the Venezuelan government for nearly $150 million of food commodities, pursuant to which it received ten purchase orders. In order to fulfill its contract duties, the trader entered into several contracts with food suppliers. The buyer's agent accidentally sent a string of internal e-mails to the trader. This string of e-mails indicated that the final and the largest of the ten contracts should be cancelled and further payments suspended. $44 million in advance payments already made by the buyer were not mentioned. The trader demanded by letter an explanation of the situation and an immediate response from the buyer.

After an unsuccessful meeting between the parties on how to proceed, the trader sent another letter to the buyer requesting adequate assurances of performance within five days, to which the buyer responded with an objection to "a legal pre-claim communication" because of an e-mail that was misdirected. The trader responded with a third letter requesting the buyer to "normalize the late payments on the contracts", to which the buyer responded by sending an e-mail to the trader attaching a new draft agreement. The new agreement substituted the buyer's representative as the party responsible for payments to the seller on the pending food shipments. The trader responded to this communication with a suit for breach of contract to recover over $150 million in unpaid balances due for shipped foodstuffs, lost profits, consequential and incidental damages, costs and attorneys' fees. The buyer counterclaimed for breach of contract and unjust enrichment from the trader's failure to deliver foodstuffs.

The federal trial judge entered summary judgments for the trader for the buyer's failure to pay for delivered goods, and for the buyer's anticipatory repudiation regarding future scheduled deliveries. The trial judge denied the buyer's motions for summary judgment against the trader, and awarded the trader more than $40 million in damages, which were offset by the $44 million in advance payments made by the buyer.

Because the making of an anticipatory repudiation is usually a matter of fact determination, the federal appeals court could not overturn the trial judge's determination on this issue, unless it was unreasonable. The federal appeals court agreed with the trial judge that, even though the e-mails had been sent unintentionally: 1) they created reasonable grounds for insecurity that the buyer would perform its contract duties; and 2) the trader's letters to the buyer were written demands for adequate assurances. The appeals court determined, however, that fact questions remained as to whether the buyer provided adequate assurances, precluding summary judgment on this issue. The fact that the trader held over $44 million in advance payments from the buyer, which the buyer had not requested to be returned, was particularly important in this determination. Also important was the fact that the trader sued the buyer for anticipatory repudiation within thirty days of the buyer's last proposal to the trader, while UCC §2-609(4) gives a party "a reasonable time not exceeding thirty days [to provide] such assurance of due performance as is adequate under the circumstances of the particular case".391

q) An E-mail Message Can Be Used to Demand Adequate Assurances

In *Rocheux International of New Jersey, Inc. v. U.S. Merchants Financial Group, Inc.*392, a distributor sold plastic raw materials to buyers, who were providers of plastic product-packaging services. The buyers notified the sellers by e-mail that a large amount of their materials was defective. The sellers replied initially with an e-mail to the buyers notifying them that, if they did not pay their overdue balance, the sellers would take from the warehouse the remaining plastics that were delivered and not paid for, sell them, and sue for any remaining amount due. The buyers failed to make more than $3 million in payments for shipments of the plastics. The plastics were eventually sold by the sellers to a third party, and a suit was brought for the remaining amount due under UCC §2-706.

The buyers claimed that many of the materials delivered were defective, and were rejected by them, or their acceptance was revoked, for this reason. Therefore, the sellers' re-selling of the delivered and warehoused plastics without the buyer's consent was a breach of contract. Many of the defects were alleged to be discoverable only after processing of the materials into packaging. The buyers alleged that they had alerted the sellers to these types of problems on various occasions between 2000 and 2007, to which the sellers responded only a few times with their own inspections of the materials. Defective materials had previously been sold by the buyers for scrap, and the buyers alleged they had been told by the sellers that they would receive payment credits for defective materials.

The sellers alleged that there were only a very few occasions in the six year relationship when only minor defects were complained of and had necessitated payment credits. They also argued that the buyers had acknowledged their duty to pay for all delivered materials, they had not complained of any defects in the warehoused deliveries, and that they had initially blamed their non-payments on accounting software problems. The sellers' initial e-mail response to the buyers' e-mail notice of defects requested an opportunity to inspect for defects, and offered a full refund for defective materials. These communications were followed by various exchanges of letters between the parties. Most of the non-warehoused materials had already been sold for scrap by the buyers when the sellers' response was received.

The buyers argued against the sellers' motion for summary judgment for breach of contract by arguing that the sellers improperly repudiated the contract without making a required demand for adequate assurances from the buyers, and despite receiving such assurances from the buyers. The New Jersey federal trial judge ruled that the sellers had made a proper demand for adequate assurances under UCC §2-609 in their e-mail and subsequent letters. The judge ruled that as a matter of law, based on undisputed facts, the sellers had reasonable grounds for insecurity. The judge reserved for a fact determination by a jury, however, the issue of whether the buyers actually provided adequate assurances to the sellers in their responses to the sellers' reasonable and proper demands.

CHAPTER 10 - How Are Electronic Contracts Enforced, or How is Compensation Made for a Contract Breach?

Datapoint #4

The declining number of jury trials in both state and federal courts and in civil and criminal cases can undermine public confidence in the judicial system and decrease the skills of lawyers and judges when they actually do have a trial....according to The Florida Bar's Special Committee to Study the Decline of Jury Trials....It found that over past decades while the real number of cases filed has increased, those that are resolved by jury trials has declined both as a percentage and in real numbers. Those statistics apply to both state and federal cases in both civil and criminal dockets.

Among the committee's findings:

Between 1962 and 2002, the annual number of federal civil dispositions rose from 258,876 to 501,320, but the number resolved by jury trials declined from 5,802 to 4,569. The number tried declined from 11.8 percent to 1.8 percent.

During the same time, federal criminal filings went from 33,110 to 76,827, while the number resolved at trials declined from 5,097 (15 percent) to 3,573 (4.7 percent).

For Florida's circuit courts, the fiscal year 1986-87 saw 155,407 civil dispositions with 2,413 (1.6 percent) going to jury trials. By the 2009-10 fiscal year, there were 401,463 civil dispositions, but only 879 (0.2 percent) were resolved by jury trials.

Over the same period for circuit criminal cases, there were 130,575 criminal dispositions and 4,091 jury trials (3.1 percent) in 1986-87 and 200,710 dispositions and 4,112 jury trials (2.1 percent) in 2009-10.

An ABA study reviewed the trial statistics for 21 states and the District of Columbia between 1976 and 2002. The study included both bench [judge-only] and jury civil trials, with bench trials being the overwhelming majority. It found that in 1976, 528,567 out of 1,464,258 dispositions were by trial (36.1 percent) and by 2002 that number had dropped to 487,200 trials out of 3,087,857 dispositions (15.8 percent). For criminal trials over the same period, the disposition by trials dropped from 8.5 percent to 3.3 percent. The report cited several reasons for the decline in jury trials. On the civil side, it noted there is an increasing use of mediation, arbitration, and other alternative dispute resolution methods. "Another factor is the expense involved, not just in conducting a trial, but in preparing a case for trial," the report said. "These costs include the expenses involved in discovery, the costs of expert witnesses, the ability of the client or the attorney to fund the case, and the attorney's fee. Another factor is the amount of time it takes to bring a case to trial and any delays that occur along the way."

-from *Panel fears the declining number of jury trials may undermine public confidence*, by Gary Blankenship, The Florida Bar News, January 15, 2012

a) U.S. Contract Law Enforcement by Injunctive Remedies

In the click-wrap case, *eBay, Inc. v. Bidder's Edge, Inc.* discussed in Chapter 8, a) iii), the web auction site requested, and was granted by the trial judge, an injunction preventing Bidder's Edge from using its automated software "bots" to copy the contents of eBay's web site and to transmit it to other locations for its own commercial purposes. The injunction was granted on the basis of a tort argument of trespass against personal property. It might have also been granted, however, on the basis of a breach of a click-wrap contract. Equitable remedies, including injunctions, are available for a breach of contract (as described in Part A, Chapter 8, g), where a plaintiff proves that the usual money damages remedy would not compensate her adequately.

Register.com v. Verio, Inc., discussed in Chapter 8, a) ii), also involved the use of software robots by a web site user contrary to its browse-wrap contract terms of use. As in the *Bidder's Edge* case, the web site owner requested the trial court to issue a temporary restraining order preventing the site user from deploying its "bots" to copy information from a web site and use it for its own commercial purposes. A temporary restraining order is like a short-term injunction prohibiting a party from engaging in specific actions. The trial court issued the temporary restraining order, and subsequently issued a permanent injunction prohibiting the same activity, because of the violation of the browse-wrap contract terms of use.

Temporary restraining orders, and preliminary and permanent injunctions are equitable remedies that order a party to not do something. In contrast, a court may also grant an equitable remedy that orders a party to do something with an order of specific performance. As with all equitable remedies, the plaintiff must first prove that the usual money damages remedy would be inadequate as a remedy for the contract breach. For example, in *Hugger-Mugger, LLC v. NetSuite, Inc.*, discussed in Chapter 9, j), a mandatory arbitration requirement located in a terms of service contract was enforced by a court order.

b) E.U. Contract Law, Enforcement and Remedies

The contract law of various European nations is primarily national law. Since the advent of the European Union, however, E.U. legislation has added several layers to national contract law.

E.U. Directives, proposed by the E.U. Commission, and adopted by the E.U. Parliament and Council, serve as guidance for implementing legislation of member States. Directives establish the goals that must be achieved by national legislation, and the deadlines for such legislation, but allow flexibility in the methods of achieving those goals. E.U. Regulations, also proposed by the E.U. Commission, and adopted by the E.U. Parliament and Council, are binding law that supersedes any contrary national legislation.

If a member State fails to enact legislation in compliance with a Directive, the E.U. Commission can refer this violation to the European Court of Justice. The Directive can be substituted for non-complying national legislation through "direct effect". Violations of E.U. Regulations by contrary national legislation can be similarly enforced.

Often the E.U. Commission proposes both a Directive and a Regulation on a particular subject. The Directive is likely to be adopted much sooner than the related Regulation, because of the binding effect of the provisions of the Regulation. This complicated process of multi-national legislation and enforcement, however, leaves both E.U. Directives and Regulations with less immediate and less predictable effects than U.S. federal legislation, or U.S. uniform state law, such as the Uniform Commercial Code.

The E.U. 1993 Directive on Unfair Contract Terms in Consumer Contracts393("Unfair Terms Directive") was enacted to "harmonize" substantive consumer contract law among European Union member nations. The Unfair Terms Directive applies to all standardized (non-negotiated) contracts offered by merchants to consumers.

Subsequent European Union directives have also prescribed acceptable methods of selling to E.U. consumers, including the 1997 E.U. Directive on the Protection of Consumers in Respect of Distance Contracts ("Distance Selling Directive")394 applicable to transactions between remote merchants and consumers, the 1999 E.U. Directive on Certain Aspects of the Sale of Consumer Goods and Associated Guarantees ("Sales Guarantees Directive")395, and the 2005 E.U. Directive on Unfair Business-to-Consumer Commercial Practices ("Unfair Commercial Practices Directive").396

In 2011 the European Union approved a new E.U. Directive on Consumer Rights ("Consumer Rights Directive")397, which will replace the Distance Selling Directive, and a directive related to sales at a consumer home or a business, as of June 13, 2014. The other consumer sales directives will remain in effect.

United States consumer contract law is primarily developed through common law judicial decision-making in individual court cases. The primary statutory contract law, the state versions of Article 2 of the Uniform Commercial Code, applies only to transactions in goods (primarily sales). In the nations of the European Union, and in many other civil law nations, a more statutory and regulatory approach to consumer contract law prevails. For example, the United Kingdom Office of Fair Trading ("OFT") issued its IT Consumer Contracts Made at a Distance398 guidance in 2005, applying the U.K. unfair contract terms law to internet contracts "to help distance sales businesses ensure their terms and conditions comply with the relevant regulations." OFT interpretations of individual contract terms have also been available as "case reports" since the mid-1990s.

European national regulatory agencies provide binding guidance on the validity of specific contract terms, and enforce that guidance through administrative actions. For example, national contract laws, in general, are more likely to invalidate the take-it-or-leave-it mandatory arbitration clauses, and the company headquarters state choice-of-forum clauses, which are frequently approved by U.S. courts for consumer contracts.399

The typical definition of "consumer" in U.S. cases and statutes is similar to that of the Electronic Signatures in Global and National Commerce Act (E-SIGN) definition.

Consumer. The term "consumer" means an individual who obtains, through a transaction, products or services which are used primarily for personal, family, or household purposes, and also means the legal representative of such an individual.400

In contrast, the definition of "consumer" in the E.U. Unfair Contract Terms Directive specifies

> "consumer" means any natural person who, in contracts covered by this Directive, is acting for purposes which are outside his trade, business or profession.401

The Distance Selling Directive, the Sales Guarantees Directive, the Unfair Commercial Practices Directive and the Consumer Rights Directive have similar consumer definitions. The E.U. directives definitions of "consumer" appear to include businesses and professionals acting outside their own area of expertise, even though they are otherwise contracting for commercial purposes. The European Court of Justice ("ECJ") has limited the application of these directives to certain businesses and professionals on a case-by-case basis. However, unless so excluded, businesses and professionals will qualify as consumers under this broad type of definition. The ECJ has also tried to limit the use of consumer protection laws by businesses to harass their commercial competitors by applying a requirement that alleged "deceptive" advertising be shown to have actually misled a significant number of consumers to whom it was addressed.402

CHAPTER 11 – European Union Consumer Contract Law

a) E.U. Unfair Contract Terms Directive

Besides the difference in scope of coverage arising from the wider definition of "consumer" under the E.U. consumer directives, compared to U.S. contract law, the substance of the directives' rules is more favorable to consumers in many situations. For example, Article 3.1 of the Unfair Terms Directive provides that "A contractual term that has not been individually negotiated shall be regarded as unfair if, contrary to the requirement of good faith, it causes a significant imbalance in the parties' rights and obligations arising under the contract, to the detriment of the consumer."403 Compared to the U.S. consumer defense of unconscionability, this "significant imbalance" protection appears to provide much greater protection to E.U. consumers.

The implementation of the Unfair Terms Directive in Germany, France and the United Kingdom illustrates how this difference might affect online contracts in practice. Since 1993, CLAB Europa, The European Database on Unfair Terms in Consumer Contracts, has collected abstracts/summaries of judicial and administrative proceedings, and settlements and arbitration awards.404 Some examples of these decisions are described below.

In German litigation, a contract clause of an eBay seller that limited to thirty days a buyer's right to return goods without a reason was determined to violate the Unfair Terms Directive Annex 1(q) prohibition of terms "excluding or hindering the consumer's right to take legal action or exercise any other legal remedy, particularly by requiring the consumer to take disputes exclusively to arbitration not covered by legal provisions, unduly restricting the evidence available to him or imposing on him a burden of proof which, according to the applicable law, should lie with another party to the contract".405

In 2003, the French Unfair Contract Terms Commission ("UCTC") recommended that French courts treat 28 types of contract terms as unfair under the French implementation of the Unfair Contract Terms Directive.406 A French consumer advocacy group sued America Online in 2003 claiming that 36 of AOL's online service contract terms were unfair, according to the UCTC's recommendations. In *AOL France v. Union Federale des Consommateurs-Que Choisir*407, a French trial court ruled in 2004 that 31 of the 36 contract terms complained of were unfair and unenforceable. Among these terms were:

- automatic termination without notice for a subscriber's failure to update their personal information

- limitation of a subscriber's remedy, for breach of the agreement by AOL, to termination of the service agreement

- a binding assumption of receipt of e-mail notices two days after delivery

- the right of AOL to share the subscriber's personal information with third parties without their prior consent

- AOL's right to modify the agreement, payment terms and the subscriber's user name without their consent

- AOL's right to terminate the agreement without cause

- AOL's right to suspend or terminate the agreement without prior notice for minor breaches by the subscriber

- The inability of a subscriber to terminate the agreement early for cause without paying for the entire remaining period of the agreement

- AOL's right to add 15 seconds to each invoiced connection and to charge in full for each full service minute used

- AOL's disclaimer of liability for service interruptions, errors, and other failures

Other contract terms found by the court to be illegal, and null and void, included:

- AOL's unilateral right to modify the agreement, even with prior notice and a subscriber's right to terminate upon notice

- Failure to object to payment term changes constitutes acceptance

- Failure to object to invoiced amounts within 90 days constitutes acceptance

- A license for AOL to use all content put online by a subscriber

- A right to terminate the agreement for risk of non-payment

- A limitation of liability of AOL to the last six months of service fees

- AOL's right to reasonable attorney's fees for a subscriber's breach408

Like the U.S. defense of unconscionability, if a contract term is "unfair" under national legislation implementing the Unfair Terms Directive, the term will not be enforced, and the entire contract may be avoided by the complaining party.409 Under U.K. law, a consumer can obtain an injunction against enforcement of such a term or contract in an action by a qualifying governmental body or non-governmental consumer organization.410

In a 2006 settlement with the U.K. Office of Fair Trading, Dell Corporation agreed to revise its consumer contract terms, which had previously limited its liability for negligence to the price of the product, excluded liability for consequential losses, excluded liability for oral representations not confirmed in writing, and required consumers to notify Dell immediately of any errors in its confirmation of the consumer's purchase order.411

The trend of national cases implementing the Unfair Terms Directive has been to provide greater protection to E.U. consumers presented with non-negotiable contracts than is provided to U.S. consumers through litigation. The E.U. prohibitions of choice-of-forum clauses favoring sellers, and mandatory arbitration clauses, are particularly noteworthy.412

Another procedural protection afforded by the Unfair Terms Directive that, in theory at least, exceeds comparable U.S. consumer contract protections is in Article 5 of the Unfair Terms Directive, which provides

> In the case of contracts where all or certain terms offered to the consumer are in writing, these terms must always be drafted in plain, intelligible language. Where there is doubt about the meaning of a term, the interpretation most favourable to the consumer shall prevail....413

"Plain language" and "Plain English" laws have grown in popularity in the U.S. within the past several decades. Their intended consumer benefits are sometimes undermined, however, by the combination of lengthy consumer disclosures, the "duty-to-read" rule of U.S. contract law, and "take-it-or-leave-it" standard form contracts. As discussed in Chapter 9, k), the unconscionability defense to breaches of onerous contract terms is becoming a more porous shelter for U.S. consumers.

Rather than requiring consumer contract terms to be evaluated for their legality on a case-by-case basis, the Unfair Terms Directive Article 3 supplies an "Annex [of]... an indicative and non-exhaustive list of the terms which may be regarded as unfair." Among those contract terms listed are

1. Terms which have the object or effect of:

...(b) inappropriately excluding or limiting the legal rights of the consumer vis-à-vis the seller or supplier or another party in the event of total or partial non-performance or inadequate performance by the seller or supplier of any of the contractual obligations, including the option of offsetting a debt owed to the seller or supplier against any claim which the consumer may have against him;...

(h) automatically extending a contract of fixed duration where the consumer does not indicate otherwise, when the deadline fixed for the consumer to express this desire not to extend the contract is unreasonably early;

(i) irrevocably binding the consumer to terms with which he had no real opportunity of becoming acquainted before the conclusion of the contract;...

(q) excluding or hindering the consumer's right to take legal action or exercise any other legal remedy, particularly by requiring the consumer to take disputes exclusively to arbitration not covered by legal provisions, unduly restricting the evidence available to him or imposing on him a burden of proof which, according to the applicable law, should be with another party to the contract.

The first part of 1(q) of the Annex is contrary to the evolving direction of U.S. Supreme Court decisions limiting the overturning of mandatory arbitration clauses in consumer contracts represented by *AT&T Mobility LLC v. Concepcion.*

b) Other E.U. Consumer Protection Directives

The 1997 E.U. Distance Selling Directive, which is effective until June 13, 2014 (unless replaced sooner by national legislation implementing the 2011 Consumer Rights Directive), applies to contracts for goods or services by, among other methods, "Videotex (microcomputer and television screen) with keyboard or touch screen" and "Electronic mail".414 Besides harmonizing national law to establish a 7 day right of withdrawal by the consumer (with specified exceptions and with a related right to reimbursement), and a 30 day time period within which a consumer purchase must be completed by the supplier, the Directive requires the supplier to provide specified information related to the transaction.415

The 1999 E.U. Sales Guarantees Directive harmonizes national laws to mandate, for consumer goods sales, three warranties similar to the warranties for sales of goods in the U.S. Uniform Commercial Code described in Part A, Chapter 5, c). These are first, an express warranty that consumer goods "comply with the description given by the seller and possess the qualities of the goods which the seller has held out to the consumer as a sample or model"416, second, the implied warranty of merchantability that goods are "fit for the purposes for which goods of the same type are normally used"417, and third, the implied warranty that goods are "fit for any particular purpose for which the consumer requires them and which he made known to the seller at the time of conclusion of the contract and which the seller has accepted".418 The Directive provides procedures for implementation of consumer rights under these mandated warranties.419 It also provides rules for standardization of express guarantees provided by sellers in a manner similar to the U.S. Magnuson-Moss Warranty Act (MMWA).420

The 2000 E.U. Directive on Electronic Commerce421 harmonizes E.U. member nation laws to require online service providers and senders of online commercial communications to disclose specified information about themselves and their goods or services, including the rights of recipients to opt-out from receiving future unsolicited communications (spam).422 The Directive requires the national laws of member States to permit contracting by electronic means, with specified exceptions.423 It establishes requirements for provider disclosure of "the different technical steps to follow to conclude the contract", including acknowledgement of consumer orders by online service providers, and identification and correction of input errors by consumers.424 The Directive provides rules for protection of online service providers from legal liability for the content of online communications.425 In an interesting embrace of alternative dispute resolution, Article 17 of the Directive encourages the use of national laws promoting "out-of-court dispute settlement" between online service providers and their customers. Article 18, on court actions, encourages national legislation implementing the directive to provide for "interim measures" (such as injunctions) to protect against "alleged infringement" of legal interests.

The 2005 E.U. Directive on Unfair Business-to-Consumer Commercial Practices426, which must be implemented by member nations by June 12, 2013, harmonizes national laws to prohibit three types of unfair business-to-consumer commercial practices: 1) any commercial practice "contrary to the requirements of professional diligence" and that "materially distort or is likely to materially distort the economic behaviour with regard to the product of the average consumer whom it reaches"; 2) misleading commercial practices; and 3) aggressive commercial practices.427

"Professional diligence" is defined as "the standard of special skill and care which a trader [business] may reasonably be expected to exercise towards consumers, commensurate with honest market practice and/or the general principle of good faith in the trader's field of activity."428 This standard appears to be similar to the UCC §1-203 requirement that "Every contract or duty within this Code imposes an obligation of good faith in its performance and enforcement."429

Distorting unfair commercial practices are defined similarly to the U.S. common law contract defense of undue influence, discussed in Part A, Chapter 7, b), by use of the standard of the "perspective of the average member of that group" who is "particularly vulnerable to the practice or the underlying product because of their mental or physical infirmity, age or credulity in a way which the trader could reasonably be expected to foresee".430

The prohibition of "aggressive" commercial practices includes specific prohibitions of "harassment, coercion, including the use of physical force, or undue influence that significantly impairs or is likely to significantly impair the average consumer's freedom of choice or conduct".431 "Undue influence" is defined as "exploiting a position of power in relation to the consumer so as to apply pressure, even without using or threatening to use physical force, in a way which significantly limits the consumer's ability to make an informed decision".432 Besides the obvious parallel to the U.S. contract common law of undue influence, these provisions also include a "coercion" prohibition that is similar to the U.S. common law contract defense of duress, discussed in Part A, Chapter 7, b).433

Annex I of the Directive lists thirty-one commercial practices that are in all circumstances considered unfair, because they are either misleading or aggressive. One example of an unfair misleading practice is "[e]stablishing, operating or promoting a pyramid promotional scheme".434 Another is "[u]sing editorial content in the media to promote a product where a trader has paid for the promotion without making that clear in the content".435 Another example of an unfair misleading practice is "[m]aking persistent and unwanted solicitations by telephone, fax, e-mail or other remote media except in circumstances and to the extent justified under national law to enforce a contractual obligation".436 Another unfair misleading practice is "[i]ncluding in an advertisement a direct exhortation to children to buy advertised products or persuade their parents or other adults to buy advertised products for them."437

c) 2011 E.U. Directive on Consumer Rights

As of June 13, 2014, the 1997 E.U. Distance Selling

Directive, and the 1985 E.U. Doorstep Selling Directive, will be repealed and replaced by the 2011 E.U. Directive on Consumer Rights.438 It is focused primarily on "distance selling" business-to-consumer contracts made without face-to-face contact. The Directive also establishes certain standards for contract information disclosure for "doorstep" or "off-premises" selling business-to-consumer contracts (made face-to-face but away from the business premises), and for certain other business-to-consumer contracts, unless they "involve day-to-day transactions which are performed immediately at the time of their conclusion."439 As with other E.U. Directives, the Consumer Rights Directive is intended to be implemented through national laws.

The information required to be provided to a consumer "in a clear and comprehensible manner" for a contract other than a distance or off-premises contract, prior to binding the consumer to such a contract, includes: a) the main characteristics of the goods or services, b) the identity of the trader [business], c) the total price of the goods or services, d) the arrangements for payment, delivery, performance of services, and complaint procedures, e) guarantees [warranties] required by law, f) the duration of the contract and conditions for its termination, g) the functionality [methods of operation] of any "digital content" [data produced and supplied in digital form], including digital rights management software that limits consumer copying of digital content, and h) any interoperability of digital content with hardware or software that the trader is aware of, or can reasonably be expected to be aware of.440

Similar categories of information must be provided by businesses to consumers in distance and off-premises contracts. A greater emphasis is placed on disclosure of business contact information for these contracts. In addition, information about the consumer's right of withdrawal from the contract must be disclosed. Disclosure is required of voluntary business codes of conduct, as defined in the 2005 Unfair Commercial Practices Directive. Other information must be provided regarding minimum duration of a consumer's obligations, and deposit or other financial guarantee requirements of the consumer. Businesses must also disclose "where applicable, the possibility of having recourse to an out-of-court complaint and redress mechanism, to which the trader is subject, and the methods for having access to it."441 Information on right of withdrawal procedures may be disclosed by following Model Instructions set forth in Annex I(A).

Regarding the manner of required information disclosures, the Directive provides

If a distance contract to be concluded by electronic means places the consumer under an obligation to pay, the trader shall make the consumer aware in a clear and prominent manner, and directly before the consumer places his order, of the information [required regarding characteristics of goods or services, price, contract duration, and minimum duration of consumer obligations]....

The trader shall ensure that the consumer, when placing his order, explicitly acknowledges that the order implies an obligation to pay. If placing an order entails activating a button or a similar function, the button or similar function shall be labelled in an easily legible manner only with the words "order with an obligation to pay" or a corresponding unambiguous formulation indicating that placing the order entails an obligation to pay the trader. If the trader has not complied with this subparagraph, the consumer shall not be bound by the contract or order.442

The "explicit acknowledgement" requirement quoted above appears to permit only click-wrap online consumer contracts for the purchase of goods or services.

The Directive requires business disclosure of delivery and method of payment restrictions at the beginning of the ordering process. It permits abbreviated disclosures of certain information where the method of communication "allows limited space or time to display the information". Confirmations of distance contracts must be provided to a consumer within a reasonable time after the conclusion of the contract and before delivery of the goods or performance of the service begins.443

The Directive standardizes national periods for the right of withdrawal from a consumer purchase as "14 days to withdraw from a distance or off-premises contract without giving any reason, and without incurring any costs" other than those provided for in the Directive.444 The withdrawal period begins at the conclusion of the contract for a service or digital content contract, or from the day of last delivery of physical goods (or first delivery of regularly delivered goods).445

Businesses have "not later than 14 days from the day on which he is informed of the consumer's decision to withdraw from the contract" to reimburse all payments received from the consumer, including, if applicable, the costs of delivery. The reimbursement must be made using the same means of payment as the consumer used for the initial transaction, unless the consumer expressly agrees otherwise, and without any extra fees for such reimbursement by standard delivery. The reimbursement may be withheld until the business has received back the goods, or evidence that they have been sent back, whichever is earliest.446

Consumers must return goods not later than 14 days from the notice to the business of withdrawal.447 Exceptions to the right of withdrawal apply for various goods or services, including "sealed audio or sealed video recordings or sealed computer software which were unsealed after delivery" and "contracts concluded at a public auction".448

The Directive also includes rules for charges by a business of fees for the use of a means of payment (such as credit cards or lines)449, the passing of the risk of loss or damage to goods from the business to the consumer450, and rules regarding charges by businesses for any "extra payment in addition to the remuneration agreed upon for the trader's main contractual obligation", including a prohibition of "default options" requiring a consumer to "opt out" of extra payments that were not expressly agreed to by the consumer.451

The Directive prohibits the "inertia selling" of unsolicited goods or services, thereby denying the transformation of consumer silence into consent.452

PART C. INTERNATIONAL CONTRACTS

Section I of Part C discusses the substantive law of international commercial (business-to-business) contracts-- the law that applies to formation, duties, interpretation, breach, defenses and remedies. Section II discusses the law of formation of international commercial contracts through electronic communications. Section II also discusses current proposals for, and laws requiring, online dispute resolution of international consumer (business-to-consumer) contracts.

SECTION I. COMMERCIAL CONTRACTS

Summary of Part C, Section I

International contract law is in the process of development. International contracts between businesses have existed for millennia. The law that applies to those contracts, however, has until recently been national or local law, or private organization rules, with specific changes to those default rules negotiated by the parties. These laws or rules have either been chosen by the parties, or chosen for them by a court with jurisdiction over their contract dispute through a conflict-of-laws analysis. (This is also sometimes called private international law analysis.)

In 1980, the United Nations approved a commercial law treaty, the Convention on Contracts for the International Sale of Goods (CISG). The CISG is designed to provide a country-neutral law that automatically applies to international sale of goods contracts between commercial parties with contract-related places of business in nations that have ratified the CISG, unless the contract parties opt out of its application to their contract. As of March 4, 2013 (with ratification by Brazil), 79 nations, including the U.S., have ratified the CISG.

Few legal decisions in the U.S. have so far reported the use of the CISG in contracts involving U.S. businesses. Some of those reported cases have applied the CISG based on principles of the Uniform Commercial Code (UCC) that are more familiar to U.S. judges. As more major trading nations ratify the CISG, however, its use by U.S. businesses in international contracts, and its application by U.S. courts according to its own principles, will increase.

The Principles of International Commercial Contracts (PICC) was first published in 1994 by the International Institute for the Unification of Private Law (French acronym UNIDROIT). It is designed to serve as a Restatement of the Law for international commercial contracts.

As the use and understanding of the CISG, and the PICC, increase in the U.S. and other nations, their rules and principles will provide a framework for the application of future country-neutral international commercial electronic contract law, such as the Convention on the Use of Electronic Communications in International Contracts (the Electronic Contracts Convention). The Electronic Contracts Convention was approved by the United Nations in 2005, and became effective on March 1, 2013.

Increased use and understanding of the CISG, the PICC and the Electronic Contracts Convention will facilitate the eventual enactment of widespread regional and international online alternative dispute resolution arrangements for consumer contracts. Such arrangements could provide benefits for consumers, businesses and international commerce by expediting, streamlining and reducing the costs of fair resolution of consumer complaints for sales of goods across international borders.

CHAPTER 1 – Choice-of-Forum and Choice-of-Law Clauses

Parties might actively negotiate a contract, or a contract might be a "take-it-or-leave-it", or "adhesion" (you are stuck with it) contract in which a stronger party (like a business) dictates its terms to a weaker party (like a consumer). Any limitations on dictated terms would be created by contract law and consumer protection law. In either negotiated or take-it-or-leave-it contracts, two of the most important terms are the choice-of-forum clause and the choice-of-law clause.

The choice of forum determines where any dispute related to the contract will be resolved. In a take-it-or-leave-it contract, the forum will usually be either a state or federal court in the geographic headquarters of the stronger business party, or the office of an arbitration organization. In a negotiated contract, the forum might be located at the geographic location of one of the parties, or at a neutral location, where neither party has any continuous physical presence.

The nature of the forum might be a government court or a private arbitration organization. Businesses in different nations negotiating contracts involving large sums of money often choose a geographically neutral location and a forum with experience in business disputes, such as a state or federal trial court in Manhattan, New York (near Wall Street), or a state or federal trial court in the State of Delaware, or a court in the City of London, or in Switzerland, or the International Chamber of Commerce arbitration organization in Paris.

When the choice of forum specifies that a contract dispute will be resolved by arbitration, the chosen arbitration organization will usually accept the parties' choice as a simple matter of accepting new business, if its rules are followed and its fees are paid. A government court will often accept the choice of private parties to resolve their dispute in its courtroom (and at its taxpayers' expense), however, only if there is a substantial connection of the contract, or of one of the contract parties, to that forum.

The substantial connection requirement ensures that it will serve the interests of the local taxpayers to resolve the dispute, and ensures that the court will have the power of "personal jurisdiction" to resolve the dispute by effectively compelling the losing party to obey its orders and judgments.453 Otherwise, a court has the power to dismiss a case with no, or little, connection to its location on grounds of forum non conveniens (an inconvenient forum).454

A negotiated choice of law will usually be a body of law that a mutually chosen forum has experience in applying to disputes. This is the normal case for both practical and legal reasons. If a forum were directed to apply unknown or unfamiliar law, it would create practical difficulties for the judge and the parties to learn or to prove that law, with additional related costs. Common law or statutes might also limit certain contracts' choice of the law of a forum that has no relationship to the subject of the contract for these reasons of expense and inconvenience to the forum court.455

UCC §1-105(1) gives limited support to the requirement of a choice of law that is familiar to the chosen forum, by providing:

(1) Except as provided in this section, when a transaction bears a reasonable relation to this state and also to another state or nation, the parties may agree that the law either of this state or of such other state or nation will govern their rights and duties. Failing such agreement, this code applies to transactions bearing an appropriate relation to this state.456

This rule requires that a transaction have (at least) a "reasonable relation to this [forum] state and also to another state or nation" in order for the parties' choice of the law of that other state or nation to override the applicability by default of the forum state UCC. Paragraph (2) of UCC §1-105 is usually a statement of specific forum state laws applicable to commercial transactions that cannot be opted out of through a party choice of law, such as funds transfers laws, rights of sellers' creditors in goods sold, bank deposits and collections, letters of credit, investment securities, security interests, and leases.457

A different rule on parties' choice of law has been recommended in the 2004 revision to UCC §1-105, which eliminates for businesses any requirement of a choice of law with "a relation to the State designated" as the choice of forum. As of 2011, and ten years after its proposal, however, this revision has only been adopted by the U.S. Virgin Islands.458

The Convention on Choice of Court Agreements (COCA)459 was promulgated in 2005 by the Hague Conference on Private International Law, an intergovernmental organization with 71 nation-state members and one regional organization member (the European Union). It was signed by the United States in 2009, but the U.S. has not yet ratified COCA. Only Mexico has ratified COCA to date.460

The COCA Convention is designed to be the civil commercial litigation parallel to the New York Convention on the Recognition and Enforcement of Foreign Arbitral Awards.461 It would apply primarily for contracts between parties residing in different ratifying nations. A court in a ratifying nation would be required accept jurisdiction if it is selected under a choice-of-court contract clause, unless there is no connection to that forum. A court not chosen would be required to refuse jurisdiction. Courts in ratifying nations would be required to recognize and to enforce the judicial decision of a court in another ratifying nation that was the chosen dispute forum.

The U.S. Department of State originally proposed the ratification of COCA through a process of "cooperative federalism", requiring either the adoption by states of a uniform state law, or the default application of COCA through federal implementing legislation. This process would be similar to the use of the Electronic Signatures in Global and National Commerce Act (E-SIGN) to promote adoption of uniform state versions of the Uniform Electronic Transactions Act (UETA). It has never before been used for treaties.

A difference in opinion between state and federal authorities on the law applicable by federal judges in diversity jurisdiction cases, however, has stalled this process of ratification and implementation. The most recent State Department proposal is for implementation by a federal statute only.

U.S. businesses with international business transactions favor COCA for several reasons. First, COCA would avoid jurisdiction battles between courts by allocating jurisdiction to the court chosen in a valid contract. Second, U.S. courts are currently more likely than the courts of some other nations to enforce choice-of-court clauses and to enforce foreign judgments.462 Third, the increasing expense of arbitration, relative to litigation, makes court judgment enforcement attractive to businesses with limited budgets. As was the case with the New York Convention, ratification by other nations might be required before U.S. ratification is politically possible.

Many international contracts between businesses choose the law of the State of New York as their choice of law, and choose New York state or federal courts as their choice of forum. Many choose English law (especially admiralty law) as their choice of law, and the courts of the City of London as their choice of forum. Swiss law is also a popular choice. As international trade grows, however, and where permitted by the law of the forum, an increasing number of parties choose a neutral international commercial contract law. This law is described in the next chapter.

CHAPTER 2 - The Convention on Contracts for the International Sale of Goods

Many of the activities of the United Nations do not involve commerce. The United Nations Commission on International Trade Law (UNCITRAL), however, has a large impact on commerce through its analysis, creation and promotion of international commercial treaties, model laws and best practices. Model laws are templates and prototypes for national laws, such as the United Nations Model Law on Electronic Commerce (MLEC)463, which was a precursor to the United States' Uniform Electronic Transactions Act (UETA).

The most important commercial treaty created by the United Nations, and promoted for ratification by U.N. members, is the New York Convention on the Recognition and Enforcement of Foreign Arbitral Awards464 (the "New York Convention"). This treaty has been adopted/ratified by more than 150 nations, including the United States in 1970. It is important, because commercial parties to international business contracts often prefer to resolve their disputes through the "private courts" of arbitration organizations rather than through government courts. (See the discussion of the obstacles to enforcement of foreign court judgments in the previous chapter.)

Arbitration is often considered to provide faster, cheaper, and more technically informed resolutions of complicated business disputes than court judgments or verdicts. The reasons for an arbitration decision (or "award") are not required to be disclosed to the public by the arbitration organization, if the parties desire to keep them confidential. Such non-disclosure prevents the reasons for an award from becoming a precedent that could bind other parties in a future arbitration dispute with similar facts. (The reasons stated for an appellate court decision establish a precedent for future trial and appellate court decisions in common law countries under the judicial doctrine of *stare decisis*.)

Arbitrators, who can be individually selected from a panel by the parties, are also believed to harbor less bias in favor of a contract party of the same nationality than do judges of government courts. The New York Convention requires the courts of ratifying nations to recognize and enforce the legitimate "awards" of arbitration organizations regarding disputes resolved by them pursuant to a contract choice-of-forum clause.

What law is applied by an arbitration organization to an international commercial contract dispute? What law is applied by a public court to such a dispute, if the parties choose to have their dispute resolved by a government court? It is usually impractical to apply one body of law to resolve some parts of a dispute, and another law to resolve other parts of a dispute. Therefore, a single body of law is usually chosen. If the law chosen is that of the nation or state of only one of the parties, the other party is likely to believe itself disadvantaged. If the law chosen is that of a forum with which neither party is familiar, both might believe themselves to be disadvantaged.

In part to avoid such a disadvantage for either or both parties to an international commercial contract, the Convention on Contracts for the International Sale of Goods (CISG)465 was developed and promoted by UNCITRAL. The CISG has been adopted/ratified by 79 nations, including the United States in 1986. The CISG, like Article 2 of the U.S. Uniform Commercial Code (UCC), applies only to contracts for the sale of goods, and not to services. It also excludes from its scope the sale of various goods regulated by special laws. Unlike the UCC, the CISG does not apply to consumer contracts, with very limited exceptions for inadvertent sales to consumers.466

Under CISG Article 1(a), the CISG automatically "applies to contracts of sale of goods between parties whose place of business are in different States [nations]" if each of those nations has adopted/ratified the CISG treaty. In some ratifying nations, under Article 1(b), a court may also apply the CISG to an international sales contract through "conflict-of-laws" rules (also called "private international law" in international law terminology). The United States has, like some other nations, however, pursuant to CISG Article 95, ratified a version of the CISG that does not include Article 1(b).

Ratifying nations have the power to make various "declarations" under Articles 92, 93, 94, 95, 96 and 97 that limit the effectiveness of various CISG rules in the version of the Convention adopted by those nations. This flexibility of treaty versions has encouraged widespread CISG ratification, with the trade-off of a proliferation of CISG versions that can inhibit the use of the Convention by contract parties, because of the extra analysis and due diligence required by them (or their lawyers) to determine which national version of the CISG is preferable. The highest reported number of judicial opinions applying the CISG to international sales of goods has been from Germany.

Even if the "place of business" (as defined in Article 10) of each party to a contract were located in a nation that has ratified the CISG, under CISG Article 6 "[t]he parties may exclude the application of this Convention or...derogate from or vary the effect of any of its provisions." The parties may not, however, change the effect of CISG Article 12, which permits a ratifying nation to require that a contract be "in writing" under its national CISG version.

One effect of Article 6 is to permit parties, whose contract would otherwise be governed by the CISG, because of CISG Article 1(a), to avoid the CISG as their contract governing law by choosing a different applicable law.467 Any U.S. party seeking to exclude the application of the CISG, by substituting the law of a U.S. state, must be careful to choose not only, for example, "the law of the State of New York", but also to specifically exclude the CISG as applicable law with a phrase such as "and the CISG shall not apply to this contract." This additional phrase is necessary because U.S. courts have determined that the CISG is a part of the law of every U.S. state through the operation of the "supremacy clause" of Article VI of the U.S. Constitution. This article makes U.S. treaties the "supreme Law of the Land...[the] Laws of any State to the Contrary notwithstanding." Therefore, to choose a particular state law for a contract is not by itself enough to exclude the applicability of the CISG, because the CISG is also the law of every U.S. state. The exclusion of the CISG must be specifically stated in a choice-of-law contract term.468

Where a buyer and a seller with principal places of business in different CISG-ratifying nations create a contract through the exchange of pre-printed forms, this so-called "battle of the forms" could create a further problem. If the seller and buyer forms differ in their choice of the law applicable to the contract, the final decision of which law applies (and whether or not a contract was formed at all) would be left to the forum in which the dispute arises. If each party's place of business is in a nation that ratified the CISG, the "battle of the forms" rules of CISG Article 19 (discussed below) would apply.

The CISG was adopted in six official languages-Arabic, Chinese, English, French, Russian and Spanish, each of which is a text that is "equally authentic".469 Nevertheless, the lack of exact equivalence among these and other languages can make the translation of certain CISG legal terms and concepts difficult.

CHAPTER 3 - The CISG Compared to the UCC470

(a) Sphere of Application, Applicable Law, Statutes of Limitations and Required Notices of Breach

The CISG has been adopted both by common law nations, in which judicial precedent supplements statutes, and by civil law nations, in which judicial opinions have a much more limited role as sources of law. Most native English-speaking nations use some form of a common law system.

UCC §1-103 provides

Unless displaced by the particular provisions of this code, the principles of law and equity, including the law merchant and the law relative to capacity to contract, principal and agent, estoppel, fraud, misrepresentation, duress, coercion, mistake, bankruptcy, or other validating or invalidating cause shall supplement its provisions.471

The principles of law and equity referred to include common law judicial precedent. The law merchant referred to includes customary law, such as usages of trade.

Similarly, CISG Article 4 provides

This Convention governs only the formation of the contract of sale and the rights and obligations of the seller and the buyer arising from such a contract. In particular, except as otherwise expressly provided in this Convention, it is not concerned with:

(a) the validity of the contract or of any of its provisions or of any usage;

(b) the effect which the contract may have on the property in the goods sold.472

Thus, under (a), defenses to an alleged breach of an international commercial contract are governed by national law, customary international commercial law, or general international commercial law principles, often referred to as *lex mercatoria*. Many of these defenses are described in the Principles of International Commercial Contracts analyzed in Chapter 4.

The CISG does not expressly exclude specific defenses, such as UCC §1-203's "obligation of good faith in the performance or enforcement" of sale of goods contracts, from application to CISG-governed contracts. The wide variation of contract defenses among different national legal systems made it impossible to reach a consensus on this issue. Instead, the CISG expresses a compromise position on the relevance of some defenses in CISG-governed contracts in Article 4, as quoted above, and in CISG Article 7, which provides

> (1) In the interpretation of this Convention, regard is to be had to its international character and to the need to promote uniformity in its application and the observance of good faith in international trade.

> (2) Questions concerning matters governed by this Convention which are not expressly settled in it are to be settled in conformity with the general principles on which it is based, or in the absence of such principles, in conformity with the law applicable by virtue of the rules of private international law.

Although it is perhaps an unsatisfying compromise, the first subparagraph's meaning is fairly clear. What is the meaning of paragraph (2)? The "general principles on which [the CISG] is based" are those expressed in its legislative history, and in the civil law and common law antecedents of its rules. The "rules of private international law" are the international conflict-of-laws rules, according to which the laws of one jurisdiction, or one legal source, are chosen by the forum to apply to a dispute. These rules generally determine the appropriate law based on the degree of physical and transactional connection of the geographic source of the law to the dispute. As described above, however, with limited exceptions, CISG Article 6 also allows the contract parties to choose their own rules to apply to different aspects of their commercial international sale of goods contract.

"Statutes of limitations" establish time periods within which a lawsuit for a breach of contract must be commenced. In the U.S., they are established in individual state statutes. UCC §2-725 proposes a uniform statute of limitations period of four years from the time of a contract breach, but the actual limitations period varies among state UCC versions.473 A separate Convention on the Limitation Period in the International Sale of Goods (CLPISG) (ratified by the U.S. and more than twenty other nations) provides for a general four year claim period from the time that a breach of contract occurs.474 Like the CISG, the CLPISG applies only to non-regulated commercial contracts475, excludes personal injury claims476, applies only to the immediate parties to the contract477, and, with some restrictions, allows contract parties to derogate from or vary their contract rules from the CLPISG rules.478 For example, the parties may not extend the limitation period to more than ten years.479

Although some U.S. state laws treat statutes of limitations as procedural rights, which are waived unless timely argued by the party having the right, other state laws treat these statutes as jurisdictional and substantive matters that absolutely bar legal remedies, whether or not a statute of limitations is timely argued by a party. The CLPISG Article 24 appears to follow the procedural approach by providing that "[e]xpiration of the limitation period shall be taken into consideration in any legal proceedings only if invoked by a party to such proceedings."

CISG Article 39(1) imposes requirements that a buyer claiming lack of conformity of goods must give notice of such to the seller within "a reasonable time after he has discovered it or ought to have discovered it" and "at the latest within a period of two years from the date on which the goods were actually handed over to the buyer, unless this time limit is inconsistent with a contractual period of guarantee."480 CISG Article 44, however, permits the buyer to "reduce the price in accordance with article 50 or claim damages, except for loss of profit, if he has a reasonable excuse for his failure to give the required notice." UCC §2-607(3)(a) similarly requires that after acceptance of goods "[t]he buyer must within a reasonable time after he or she discovers or should have discovered any breach notify the seller of breach or be barred from any remedy".481

b) No Statute of Frauds

Unlike UCC §2-201, there is no Statute of Frauds in the CISG. (See Part A, Chapter 4, d)). Under CISG Article 11, a sale of goods contract "may be proved by any means, including witnesses."482 Under CISG Article 12, however, any nation adopting the CISG may make a declaration excepting itself from the elimination of a writing requirement for a contract. If a national version of the CISG with a writing requirement applies to a contract, for example because the "place of business" of a party to the contract is located within such a nation, under Article 12 "the parties may not derogate from or vary the effect of [such a declaration]".

Using their power under Article 6 to derogate from or vary the effect of any of [the CISG's] provisions "subject to Article 12", the contract parties may generally impose their own requirements for a written contract. Under CISG Article 29(2), a written contract may require "any modification or termination" of the contract to also be in writing, subject to the waiver of this requirement by conduct that is relied upon by the other party. UCC §2-209(2),(4) and (5) provide similar "no oral modification" and waiver rules.

c) No Parol Evidence Rule

If the parties make a written contract, a Parol Evidence Rule, such as in UCC §2-202, might become important. (See Part A, Chapter 5, a)). UCC §1-205(4) also provides that, in case of conflict, "…express terms control both [prevail over inconsistent] course of dealing and usage of trade and course of dealing controls usage of trade."

The CISG does not have a Parol Evidence Rule. CISG Article 8(3) provides

> In determining the intent of a party or the understanding a reasonable person would have had, due consideration is to be given to all relevant circumstances of the case including the negotiations [course of dealing], any practices which the parties have established between themselves [course of performance], usages [of trade] and any subsequent conduct of the parties [course of performance]. (Language in brackets added.)

Contrary to the UCC Parol Evidence Rule, under the CISG evidence from negotiations prior to formation of a contract can be used to contradict final written contract terms.483 Would a negotiated "merger clause", which states that the written contract is the entire contract, prevent the use of such pre-contract evidence? A merger clause that expressly states its intention to use the parties' power under CISG Article 6 to "derogate" from the rule of CISG Article 8(3) would probably be more effective than a standard U.S. merger clause, which might be considered to be only one more "circumstance of the case".484

d) Open Price Term

UCC §2-204(3) requires the terms of a contract to be sufficiently definite to "provide a reasonably certain basis for giving an appropriate remedy."485 UCC §2-305(1) provides rules to determine "a reasonable price" for a contract for which neither a price, nor a method to determine it, is expressed in the contract, or where the expressed method to determine the price is not complied with.486

In contrast, CISG Article 14(1) provides that, regarding its subject, a proposed contract "is sufficiently definite if it indicates the goods and expressly or implicitly fixes or makes provision for determining the quantity and the price." No discretion is provided for a judge or arbitrator to determine "a reasonable price". CISG Article 55, however, provides

> Where a contract has been validly concluded but does not expressly or implicitly fix or make provision for determining the price, the parties are considered, in the absence of any indication to the contrary, to have impliedly made reference to the price generally charged at the time of the conclusion of the contract for such goods sold under comparable circumstances in the trade concerned.

e) Irrevocable Offer

The common law of contracts may determine if an offer has been made irrevocable, either expressly or impliedly. Consideration or detrimental reliance to support irrevocability is usually required, because offers are usually revocable until they are accepted. UCC §2-205 provides for the automatic limited irrevocability of a "firm offer" by a merchant, as discussed in Part A, Chapter 4, b) i).487

CISG Article 16(2) provides rules similar to those of the common law, by providing

> ...an offer cannot be revoked:

> (a) If it indicates, whether by stating a fixed time for acceptance or otherwise, that it is irrevocable; or

> (b) If it was reasonable for the offeree to rely on the offer as being irrevocable and the offeree has acted in reliance on the offer.

Unlike the UCC, the CISG applies only to non-consumer, commercial contracts. Therefore, most parties to a CISG-governed contract will be similar to a UCC "merchant". CISG Article 16, however, has neither a "signed writing" requirement like UCC §2-205, nor an irrevocability time period limitation, like UCC §2-205's three month limitation. The CISG also appears to allow irrevocable offers to be created by more general contract language than does the UCC. UCC §2-205 requires for irrevocability an offer "which by its terms gives assurance that it will be held open". Like other CISG rules, Article 16(2) is an attempted compromise, in this case between the contract rules of civil law nations favoring the irrevocability of offers and the rules of common law nations favoring revocability.488

f) Different Mailbox Rule

The "mailbox rule" of the U.S. common law of contracts makes the acceptance of an offer effective upon its dispatch through a method that is invited by the offer. If the offeror revokes his offer after an acceptance has been thus dispatched by the offeree, or if the acceptance is lost by the delivery agent, the contract has been formed and the risk of a breach of contract is placed on the offeror. (See Part B, Chapter 5.)

CISG Article 18(2) provides that "An acceptance of an offer becomes effective at the moment the indication of assent *reaches* the offeror." (emphasis added) By itself, this would prevent an acceptance from becoming effective upon dispatch. CISG Article 16(1), however, also provides that "Until a contract is concluded an offer may be revoked if the revocation reaches the offeree before he has *dispatched* an acceptance." (emphasis added) In other words, an otherwise revocable offer cannot be revoked if the acceptance is sent by the offeree before she receives the revocation. The effect is the same as the U.S. "mailbox rule", except that, because CISG Article 18(2) requires receipt of an acceptance to form a contract, if the acceptance is lost in the delivery system, the revoking offeror will not be liable for a breach, because no contract was concluded/formed.

Except for this risk of dispatched, but lost, acceptances, for which U.S. common law makes revocation of offers more difficult, CISG Article 16(1) and 18(2)'s "mailbox rules", combined with CISG Article 16(2)'s irrevocability requirements (discussed in the preceding section), make it easier for offers to become (and remain) irrevocable than does U.S. common law or the UCC. Like U.S. common law, under CISG Article 18(1) "[s]ilence or inactivity does not in itself amount to an acceptance", and under CISG Article 18(2) an acceptance is not effective if it fails to reach the offeror "within a reasonable time, due account being taken of the circumstances of the transaction".

g) "Battle of the Forms"

The "battle of the forms" rule of UCC §2-207(1) provides generally that an acceptance remains an acceptance "even though it states terms additional to or different from those offered or agreed upon, unless acceptance is expressly made conditional on assent to the additional or different terms."489 Under UCC §2-207(2), the additional, or different, terms in the acceptance will become part of the contract, if they are expressly accepted by the offeror, or, so long as both parties are "merchants" (as defined by the UCC), automatically so long as the offer does not expressly limit acceptance to the terms of the offer, and the additional terms do not materially alter the contract, and the offeror does not object to the additional terms.490 Finally, UCC §2-207(3) provides that

> Conduct by both parties which recognizes the existence of a contract is sufficient to establish a contract for sale although the writings of the parties do not otherwise establish a contract. In such case the terms of the particular contract consist of those terms on which the writings of the parties agree, together with any supplementary terms incorporated under any other provisions of this Code.491

Both UCC §2-207(3), and CISG Articles 18(3) and 19(2), provide rules by which a contract may be formed, despite variations in terms between an offer and an acceptance, if goods have been delivered, accepted, and paid for without objection to the additional or different contract terms. CISG

Article 19(1) generally provides that "A reply to an offer which purports to be an acceptance but contains additions, limitations or other modifications is a rejection of the offer and constitutes a counter-offer." An exception to this general rule in CISG Article 19(2), however, allows the additional or different terms to become part of the contract if they "do not materially alter the terms of the offer…unless the offeror, without undue delay, objects…".

CISG Article 18(3) permits an acceptance by a practice established between the parties (course of dealing or performance) or a trade usage "such as one relating to the dispatch of the goods or payment of the price". In case of such an acceptance by action, CISG Article 19(2) would also establish the terms of the contract as the terms of the offer and of any non-material additional or different terms in the acceptance.492 As with U.S. law, under CISG Article 18(1), "[s]ilence or inactivity does not in itself amount to acceptance." CISG Article 19(3)'s examples of material alterations to offer terms narrows substantially the possibilities for additional or different terms in an acceptance to become CISG contract terms through an exchange of forms, compared to the UCC.

h) No Buyer Duty to Inspect Upon Seller Demand and Permitted Disclaimers

UCC §2-316(3)(b) denies a buyer the protection of any implied warranty by stating

> When the buyer before entering into the contract has examined the goods or the sample or model as fully as he or she desired or has refused to examine the goods, there is no implied warranty with regard to defects which an examination ought in the circumstances to have revealed to him.493

The Official Comment to this section clarifies that it applies only when the seller has demanded that the buyer inspect the goods in order to put her on notice that she is assuming the risk of defects that the examination ought to reveal. In contrast, CISG Article 35(3) prevents the seller from becoming liable for breach of implied warranties "…if at the time of the conclusion of the contract the buyer knew or could not have been unaware of such lack of conformity." No buyer duty to examine goods upon the seller's demand is stated under the CISG, nor is it stated that a failure to inspect precludes implied warranties. The parties could, and probably should, address such a duty in their contract terms.

UCC §2-316(1) and UCC §2-316(2) specify certain limitations on the disclaimer of UCC express warranties, warranties of merchantability and warranties of fitness for a particular purpose. UCC §2-719(2) and UCC §2-719(3) restrict the effectiveness of contract terms limiting the remedies for a breach, and limiting consequential damages, respectively. The CISG has no similar automatic restrictions on contract limitations of remedies and damages. Any such restrictions must be specifically provided for by contract terms, but the CISG does not provide any guidance on how sales warranties may be effectively modified or disclaimed, as does UCC §2-316.

i) No Damages for Personal Injury or Death

Regarding damages for breach of contract, CISG Article 5 provides that "This Convention does not apply to the liability of the seller for death or personal injury caused by the goods to any person." In contrast, UCC §2-714(3) and UCC §2-715(2)(b) permit, as a buyer's consequential damages for breach after acceptance of goods, "[i]njury to person or property proximately resulting from any breach of warranty."494 The potential disparity among national systems of compensation for personal injury is one reason for the CISG Article 5 damages exclusions.

j) Adequate Assurances of Performance

UCC §2-609 codifies the common law contract rules on the right of a party to demand adequate assurances that the other party's contract duties will be performed. Section 2-609(1) permits a party to demand such assurances "[w]hen reasonable grounds for insecurity arise". "[U]ntil he or she receives such assurance [the demanding party] may if commercially reasonable suspend any performance for which he or she has not already received the agreed return."495

UCC §2-609(2) provides that "Between merchants the reasonableness of grounds for insecurity and the adequacy of any assurance offered shall be determined according to commercial standards."496 UCC §2-609(4) provides that "After receipt of a justified demand failure to provide within a reasonable time not exceeding 30 days such assurance of due performance as is adequate under the circumstances of the particular case is a repudiation of the contract."497 By "repudiation", the UCC means an unjustified breach.

In contrast, CISG Article 71 provides

(1) A party may suspend the performance of his obligations if, after the conclusion of the contract, it becomes apparent that the other party will not perform a substantial part of his obligations as a result of:

(a) A serious deficiency in his ability to perform or in his creditworthiness; or

(b) His conduct in preparing to perform or in performing the contract....

(3) A party suspending performance, whether before or after dispatch of the goods, must immediately give notice of the suspension to the other party and must continue with performance if the other party provides adequate assurance of his performance.

CISG Article 72 provides

(1) If prior to the date for performance of the contract it is clear that one of the parties will commit a fundamental breach of contract, the other party may declare the contract avoided.

(2) If time allows, the party intending to declare the contract avoided must give reasonable notice to the other party in order to permit him to provide adequate assurance of his performance.

(3) The requirements of the preceding paragraph do not apply if the other party has declared that he will not perform his obligations.

Unlike UCC §2-609(1), CISG Article 71 does not require a demand for adequate assurances based on "reasonable grounds for insecurity". On the other hand, the CISG rules of Article 71(1) ("apparent...will not perform" and "serious deficiency") and 72(1) ("it is clear...will commit a fundamental breach") might be construed to require a more objective test of contract insecurity than the UCC rules.

A "fundamental breach", similar to a U.S. common law "total breach", is required for contract "avoidance" under CISG Article 81. CISG Article 25 provides

A breach of contract ...is fundamental if it results in such detriment to the other party as substantially to deprive him of what he is entitled to expect under the contract, unless the party in breach did not foresee, and a reasonable person of the same kind in the same circumstances would not have foreseen, such a result.

A CISG Article 72 "fundamental breach", for failure to provide adequate assurances of a contract performance, applying the standards of CISG Article 25, probably requires greater evidence of insecurity than does a UCC failure to provide adequate assurances amounting to contract repudiation. UCC repudiation can be triggered by merely reasonable grounds for insecurity. This higher burden serves the legislative purpose of the CISG to promote performance of CISG contracts, because a breach would have more numerous and severe practical consequences for goods shipped across, rather than merely within, national boundaries.

k) Specific Performance

If a buyer breaches a sale of goods contract, the seller has an "Action for the Price" under UCC §2-709. When the seller breaches, however, the buyer's right to specific performance to compel the seller to provide the goods, under UCC §2-716, is more limited, in accordance with common law requirements of uniqueness of the goods or inadequacy of money damages.

CISG Article 28 allows a remedy of specific performance to either the seller or buyer, if it is otherwise available under the law of the forum, by providing

> If, in accordance with the provisions of this Convention, one party is entitled to require performance of any obligation by the other party, a court is not bound to enter a judgement for specific performance unless the court would do so under its own law in respect of similar contracts of sale not governed by this Convention.

CISG Article 46(1) also provides a default right of the buyer to compel performance by the seller, by stating

> The buyer may require performance by the seller of his obligations unless the buyer has resorted to a remedy which is inconsistent with this requirement.

In general, the courts of civil law nations are more likely to provide specific performance orders as remedies for contract breaches than are the courts of common law nations. Specific performance availability also serves the CISG purpose to promote the performance of, and to avoid breaches of, international sale of goods contracts.

l) No Perfect Tender Rule and Right to Cure Late Delivery

Under the U.S. common law of contracts, a party's failure to completely perform its duties will create a total breach of contract only if the party has also failed to make a "substantial performance". (See Part A, Chapter 6, b).) Under UCC §2-601, however, for single delivery contracts, unless the parties agree otherwise,

> if the goods or the tender of delivery fail in any respect to conform to the contract, the buyer may
>
> (1) reject the whole; or
>
> (2) accept the whole; or
>
> (3) accept any commercial unit or units and reject the rest.498

In contrast, CISG Article 49 provides generally that

> (1) The buyer may declare the contract avoided:
>
> (a) If the failure by the seller to perform any of his obligations under the contract or this Convention amounts to a fundamental breach of contract...

CISG Article 51(2) also provides (regarding partial deliveries or partially conforming deliveries) that

> (2) The buyer may declare the contract avoided in its entirety only if the failure to make delivery completely or in conformity with the contract amounts to a fundamental breach of the contract.

Similarly, CISG Article 64 provides generally that

> (1) The seller may declare the contract avoided:
>
> (a) If the failure by the buyer to perform any of his obligations under the contract or this Convention

amounts to a fundamental breach of contract...

For the purposes of Articles 49, 51 and 64, Article 25, as previously quoted in section j), provides the applicable definition of fundamental breach.

The CISG rules effectively, like the common law of contracts, apply a substantial performance/material breach rule to determine whether a total contract breach has occurred. These rules promote contract performance in order to avoid the complex problems of contract remedies in a cross-border context. For example, a seller's transportation expenses for goods rejected by a buyer for a minor defect could be much greater for an international sale than for a domestic sale of goods.

One specific type of imperfect tender of goods by a seller is a late delivery. UCC §2-508(1) only permits a seller to "cure" a non-conforming delivery of goods rejected by the buyer if "the time for performance has not yet expired".499

UCC §2-508(2) provides that

Where the buyer rejects a nonconforming tender which the seller had reasonable grounds to believe would be acceptable with or without money allowance the seller may if he or she seasonably notifies the buyer have a further reasonable time to substitute a conforming tender.

In contrast, CISG Article 48(1) provides

Subject to article 49, the seller may, even after the date for delivery, remedy at his own expense any failure to perform his obligations, if he can do so without unreasonable delay and without causing the buyer unreasonable inconvenience or uncertainty of reimbursement by the seller of expenses advanced by the buyer.

CISG Article 48, and the requirements for a fundamental breach in Articles 49 and 51 for the remedy of contract avoidance, prevent a CISG buyer from cutting off a CISG seller's opportunities to remedy the non-conformity of their tender or delivery of goods, regardless of the state of the seller's beliefs regarding the acceptability of the goods or their tender. These differences in the seller's rights could make a substantial difference in the buyer's remedies under the CISG compared to the UCC. Preservation of a seller's options is easier, and promotion of contract performance is greater under the CISG.

m) Consequential Damages Foreseeability

As described in Part A, Chapter 8, d), the U.S. common law of contracts requires that consequential damages be reasonably foreseeable by the breaching party in order for them to be recovered by the non-breaching party. Similarly, UCC §2-715(2)(a) requires that, in order for a buyer of goods to recover consequential damages, they must be of the kind that "the seller at the time of contracting had reason to know and which could not reasonably be prevented by cover or otherwise...".500 A seller's consequential damages are not addressed in the UCC, leaving them subject to common law rules by operation of UCC §1-103.501

In contrast, CISG Article 74 provides regarding consequential damages that

> Such damages may not exceed the loss which the party in breach foresaw or ought to have foreseen at the time of the conclusion of the contract, in the light of the facts and matters of which he then knew or ought to have known, as a *possible* consequence of the breach of contract. (Emphasis added.)

If this wording creates a rule of "possible foreseeability", in contrast to the "reasonable foreseeability" UCC and U.S. common law rules, the effects of this difference could be substantial.

n) "Force Majeure" Defense

As described in Part A, Chapter 7, f), if a party believes that it might be prevented from performing a contract duty because of events beyond its control (such as a war, labor strike, or natural disaster), it will try to negotiate a *"force majeure"* clause into its contract to avoid liability for non-performance because of such an event. U.S. common law-governed contracts, and UCC-governed sale of goods contracts, require such a clause to be negotiated, because no general default rule provides for it.

U.S. contracts common law does recognize the defense of impossibility, because of the death or incapacity of a person, or the destruction or non-existence of a thing necessary for performance, if the capability of the person or the necessary thing was assumed by both parties. Impossibility by a supervening governmental regulation or order is also recognized as a common law defense. The defenses of impracticability (much greater cost to perform than assumed by both parties) and frustration of purpose (much lesser benefit from contract performance than assumed by both parties) are also recognized by common law, although these defenses have been reluctantly applied by courts.

UCC §2-613 governs a seller's duties and a buyer's rights when goods identified to be sold are destroyed or damaged "without fault of either party before the risk of loss passes to the buyer."502 UCC §2-614 governs a seller's duties and a buyer's rights when "without fault of either party" the agreed delivery of goods fails, or becomes unavailable or commercially impracticable. UCC §2-615 provides a "commercial impracticability" defense to a non-performing seller for delay in delivery or non-delivery "by the occurrence of a contingency the nonoccurrence of which was a basic assumption on which the contract was made or by compliance in good faith with any applicable foreign or domestic governmental regulation or order whether or not it later proves to be invalid.503

In contrast, CISG Article 79 provides

> (1) A party is not liable for a failure to perform any of his obligations if he proves that the failure was due to an impediment beyond his control and that he could not reasonably be expected to have taken the impediment into account at the time of the conclusion of the contract or to have avoided or overcome it or its consequences.

> (2) If the party's failure is due to the failure by a third person whom he has engaged to perform the whole or a part of the contract, that party is exempt from liability only if:

> (a) He is exempt under the preceding paragraph; and

> (b) The person whom he has so engaged would be so exempt if the provisions of that paragraph were applied to him.

> (3) The exemption provided by this article has effect for the period during which the impediment exists.

> (4) The party who fails to perform must give notice to the other party of the impediment and its effect on his ability to perform. If the notice is not received by the other party within a reasonable time after the party who fails to perform knew or ought to have known of the impediment, he is liable for damages resulting from such non-receipt....

Although it cannot recover damages, a buyer can avoid a contract for "fundamental breach", or attempt to reduce the price for the goods under Article 50, if the seller was unable to perform under the circumstances of Article 79.

What is the difference between the CISG and the UCC rules on impossibility or impracticability? The Official Comments to UCC §2-615 indicate three possible differences. First, Comment 4 states that increased cost alone does not excuse performance, unless the rise in cost is due to some unforeseen contingency, which alters the essential nature of the performance. It states further that a severe shortage of raw materials or of supplies due to a contingency such as war, embargo, local crop failure, unforeseen shutdown of major sources of supply or the like is within the contemplation of this section. It states that where a particular source of supply is exclusive under the agreement and fails through casualty, §2-615 applies. It states that the same holds true where a particular source of supply is shown by the circumstances to have been contemplated or assumed by the parties at the time of contracting. However, there is no excuse for the seller, unless it has employed all due measures to assure itself that its source will not fail.

Whether or not the CISG defense to liability will be applied more liberally than the UCC defense, as its language appears to permit, will be determined by future cases. Official Comment 8 to UCC §2-615 emphasizes that business risks that should be addressed in contract negotiations are not intended to be covered by this defense. The UNIDROIT Principles of International Commercial Contracts (discussed in the next chapter), which are often used to supplement the text of the CISG, also indicate that CISG Article 79's defense should apply to events fundamentally altering a party's performance that could not reasonably have been contemplated when the contract was made.

o) Shipment Terms

UCC §2-319, §2-320, §2-503 and §2-504 provide rules for allocation of the responsibilities of the contract parties through the use of the shipment terms "F.O.B.", "F.A.S.", "C.I.F." and "C. & F.". The CISG has no similar rules regarding shipment terms. CISG Article 31 makes a seller responsible for transportation of sold goods only up to the point of handing them over to the first transportation carrier, unless otherwise agreed by the parties.

The general practice of international goods buyers and sellers is to incorporate by reference into their contracts so-called INCOTERMS promulgated by the International Chamber of Commerce. These terms (including "C. & F.", "C.F.R.", "C.I.F.", "F.O.B.", "F.A.S.", and others) function to allocate transportation-related risks and responsibilities between the parties. The contract terms that allocate such responsibilities (such as "destination contracts" and "shipment contracts") are triggered by different INCOTERMS abbreviations. INCOTERMS rules might also apply to a CISG contract as a "trade usage" or customary law under CISG Article 9(2).

CHAPTER 4 - The Principles of International Commercial Contracts

The Principles of International Commercial Contracts (PICC) has sometimes been referred to as the "International Restatement of Contract Law".504 Like the Restatement (Second) of Contracts (the "Restatement 2d") published by the American Law Institute (ALI), the PICC is "soft law". The PICC is not a statute. The Uniform Commercial Code becomes a statute after it is enacted by a U.S. state legislature. The PICC is not a treaty. The Convention on Contracts for the International Sale of Goods becomes a treaty after it is ratified by a national legislature.

Neither the PICC nor the Restatement 2d has the binding force of common law judicial precedent, or a statute, or a treaty. For this reason, they are each referred to as "soft law". They are often cited, however, as authoritative descriptions of existing law. Judges often cite the Restatement 2d as a source of "persuasive authority". Commercial arbitrators similarly refer to the PICC.

The PICC might also be treated as international customary law, including law that applies to CISG-governed contracts. Under CISG Article 7(2)'s "general principles" rules of interpretation, and CISG Article 9(2)'s incorporation of international trade usage, PICC rules might be referred to in order to explain or to supplement CISG rules. The PICC rules might be specifically chosen as applicable law by international commercial contract parties, or they might apply indirectly as general principles of international commercial law or as *lex mercatoria*, if these principles or customary law is selected as applicable law under a choice-of-law clause.

Whether applied as persuasive authority by judges or arbitrators, or selected by the parties as their choice of law, the PICC can serve an important role in "filling the gaps" of commercial treaty law. For example, under CISG Article 4(a), the CISG "is not concerned with...[t]he validity of the contract or of any of its provisions or of any usage". In other words, the CISG does not address the entire subject of contract defenses. Chapter 3 of the PICC, however, includes twenty articles addressing issues of contract validity, including defenses of impossibility, mistake, fraud, and duress. As an authoritative description of existing international commercial law, as general principles of international commercial law, as customary law, as trade usage, or as party-chosen law, the PICC, like U.S. common law, must yield to any superseding statutes or treaties.

a) PICC Purposes, Uses and General Requirements

The International Institute for the Unification of Private Law (French acronym UNIDROIT) was originally created by the League of Nations in 1926. It is currently an intergovernmental organization operating pursuant to a multilateral agreement among its 61 nation-state members.505 In 1994, it published the first version of its Principles of International Commercial Contracts (PICC). The third version of the PICC was published in 2010.506 The PICC has five official language versions in English, French, German, Italian and Spanish. The third edition of the PICC adds a number of new rules, including rules similar to the common law rules expressed in the American Law Institute Restatement (Third) of Restitution related to unjust enrichment, and rules related to restitution as a remedy for contracts that are "unwound" because of various defenses.

Like the CISG, and unlike the UCC, the PICC applies only to commercial, not consumer, contracts. Unlike both the UCC and the CISG, the PICC is not limited to contracts for the sale of goods, but also applies to services contracts. The PICC and the Restatement 2d each function like a treatise on contract law written by legal experts. Because each was written by a diverse collection of experts (professors, lawyers and judges), however, the PICC and the Restatement 2d have greater persuasive authority than a treatise written by only one, or only a few, legal experts.

The PICC and the Restatement 2d attempt primarily to

describe the rules of international and U.S. contract law respectively, as they currently exist. Because of variation among U.S. states' contract law rules, and because of variation among nations in rules of international contract law, each set of rules must sometimes choose a majority legal rule, or a preferable legal rule. Because U.S. states operate mostly within a shared common law system and national culture, a majority U.S. legal rule is easier to identify and to promote than is a majority international legal rule. Where no consensus rules exist, this wider variation in international contract law rules has led the PICC to choose to promote legal rules considered by it to be preferable rules (based on practical, theoretical and philosophical reasons) more often than majority rules.507

The Preamble to the PICC states as its purposes that

[1]These Principles set forth general rules for international commercial contracts.

[2]They shall be applied when the parties have agreed that their contract shall be governed by them.

[3]They may be applied when the parties have agreed that their contract be governed by general principles of law, the lex mercatoria [Latin for the law of merchants] or the like.

[4]They may be applied when the parties have not chosen any law to govern their contract.

[5]They may be used to interpret or supplement international uniform law instruments.

[6]They may be used to interpret or supplement domestic law.

[7]They may serve as a model for national and international legislators. [Numbers added]508

The second and third preamble sentences highlight the

use of the PICC as the choice of law by contract parties to govern their specific contract. As PICC Article 1.1, Freedom of Contract, emphasizes, "The parties are free to enter into a contract and to determine its content."

The second preamble sentence contemplates a specific choice of the PICC as governing law by the parties. Arbitration forums have been more receptive than government courts to a choice of the PICC as governing law. Most courts have thus far preferred that the parties choose the domestic law of a particular nation-state, with the PICC being used only to supplement that law. Official Comment 2 to the 2004 Revised UCC §1-302 would permit parties to choose the PICC as a governing law, except as specifically prohibited by other UCC rules. In practice, however, there are no reported U.S. cases of parties choosing the PICC as applicable law for their commercial contracts. This might stem from concerns that U.S. judges will not recognize the PICC as law that is enforceable like statutes or common law precedents, and from the unfamiliarity of U.S. judges with PICC rules.509

Although the drafters of the proposed revised §1-301 of the UCC attempted to permit a choice of international commercial law for international transactions, without regard to party contacts with the dispute forum, this proposal has met with very limited success. Unless and until compelled to accept the PICC as governing law by non-U.S. parties, there may be little incentive for U.S. parties to abandon familiar U.S. law for PICC soft law that is not even binding by default to certain international contracts, as is the CISG.510

The third preamble sentence contemplates an implied choice of the PICC as governing law, because it is considered to be a persuasive and authoritative expression of the general principles of international commercial contract law. Some contract law rules that enforce national public policy, particularly defenses to an alleged breach of contract such as unconscionability, are mandatory. According to PICC Article 1.4, these rules cannot be opted out of by the parties. Most contract law rules are voluntary default rules, however, which the parties may choose to apply, or not, to their contract pursuant to PICC Article 1.1 and PICC Article 1.5.

As the fourth preamble sentence indicates, if the parties fail to choose applicable law, the most relevant international contract rules will be applied to a dispute by a judge or arbitrator according to so-called private international law/conflict-of-laws rules. There are no reported decisions of U.S. judges finding the PICC to be applicable contract law, either through a specific party choice of law, or as general principles of law, or because of party failure to choose any governing law that leads to a conflict-of-laws judicial decision.

One U.S. federal trial court case affirmed an arbitration award that was challenged, in part, for allegedly improperly using the PICC as a source of law.511 The International Chamber of Commerce arbitration award was affirmed, and was enforced pursuant to the New York Convention on the Recognition and Enforcement of Foreign Arbitral Awards (the "New York Convention"). Another federal trial court denied a request to refuse to compel arbitration pursuant to a contract agreement based on the "unfairness" general principle of the PICC discussed in subsection f) below.512

If the parties choose an "international uniform law instrument" (such as the CISG) as the primary source of law governing their contract (or if it is found through conflict-of-laws analysis to apply to a contract between parties from nations whose ratified versions of the CISG permit this), the fifth preamble sentence permits the use of the PICC to interpret or to supplement the uniform law instrument's rules. The following section b) discusses the possible use of the PICC as a CISG "gap-filler".

The sixth preamble sentence contemplates the use of the PICC by judges, lawyers and others to interpret or supplement existing national contract law.

The seventh preamble sentence contemplates the use of the PICC by nation-state and international legislators as a model for proposed national and international contract law, respectively. It appears to have been used for this purpose by a variety of national and regional law drafting bodies, including its use by the Organization for the Harmonization of Business Law in Africa for its proposed Uniform Law on Contracts.513

Chapter 1 of the PICC sets forth general principles that are mostly similar to those of U.S. common law and statutory contract law. PICC Article 1.1 recognizes party freedom of contract.514 PICC Article 1.7 recognizes a requirement of good faith and fair dealing.515 PICC Article 1.8 provides that "A party cannot act inconsistently with an understanding that it has caused the other party to have and upon which that other party reasonably has acted in reliance to its detriment."516 This is a rule that is similar to the U.S. common law concept of equitable estoppel.

PICC Article 1.9(1) provides that contract parties are "bound by any usage to which they have agreed and by any practices which they have established between themselves."517 The agreed "usage" referred to is similar to the mutual subjective meaning, which U.S. parties are allowed to create for their contract terms, in the Restatement (Second) of Contracts §201(1). The established "practices" referred to are similar to the "course of dealing" to create a contract and the "course of performance" of an existing contract referred to in Restatement 2d §202(4) and (5) and §203(b). Article 1.9 recognizes these aids to contract interpretation, as well as international commercial trade usage, in parallel with Restatement 2d §202(4) and §203(b). Article 2.1, regarding the absence of a writing requirement, is discussed in Chapter 5.

b) The PICC as a Filler of CISG Gaps for International Contracts

The CISG only applies to contracts for the sale of goods. The PICC has been applied, mostly in arbitration cases, to a variety of international sales contracts, including contracts for services, such as construction, transportation and distribution, for licenses, for shareholder and partnership agreements, for corporate merger and acquisition agreements, and for natural resource and car parts supply contracts.518

CISG Article 7(1) provides that "In the interpretation of this Convention, regard is to be had to its international character and to the need to promote uniformity in its application…". CISG Article 7(2) states that "Questions concerning matters governed by this Convention which are not expressly settled in it are to be settled in conformity with the general principles on which it is based or, in the absence of such principles, in conformity with the law applicable by virtue of the rules of private international law."

Even though the CISG preceded the PICC, many view the PICC as expressing general principles of international contract law on which the CISG is based. It has been used, for example, by an arbitrator to fill the gap in the CISG Article 78 rule as to what rate of interest applies to defaulted payments.519

Another arbitration decision applied the PICC as CISG Article 9(2) "usage of which the parties knew or ought to have known and which in international trade is widely known to, and regularly observed by, parties to contracts of the type involved in the particular trade concerned."520 This is a parallel to the UCC §1-205(2) "usage of trade" (or "trade usage") that, according to UCC §1-205(5), "shall be used in interpreting the agreement", and which, according to UCC §2-202's Parol Evidence Rule, may explain or supplement a final written expression of a contract. UCC §1-205(4) places express contract terms above pre-contract course of dealing, and places course of dealing above usage of trade in the hierarchy of interpretation tools in case of contradictions among them.

Because, as CISG Article 4 states, the CISG applies only to "the formation of the contract of sale and the rights and obligations of the seller and the buyer arising from such a contract", the CISG does not address assignment of rights and delegation of contract duties. PICC Chapter 9 provides extensive rules on these subjects.

While the CISG does not address the rights of possible third-party contract beneficiaries, PICC Chapter 5 does address these rights. Finally, the CISG does not address the right of "set-off", which is a type of self-help remedy by which a party reduces its own contract performance duty to account for a breach by the other party. PICC Chapter 8 provides rules on this subject.

CHAPTER 5 - The PICC Compared to the Restatement 2d of Contracts and UCC

a) No Statute of Frauds and No Parol Evidence Rule

PICC Article 1.2 states

Nothing in these Principles requires a contract, statement or any other act to be made in or evidenced by a particular form. It may be proved by any means, including witnesses.521

PICC Article 1.4, however, provides

Nothing in these rules shall restrict the application of mandatory rules, whether of national, international or supranational origin, which are applicable in accordance with the relevant rules of private international law.522

Therefore, although the PICC itself does not require a written contract, it will not supersede any such mandatory requirement of applicable national law, such as a U.S. state Statute of Frauds. PICC Article 1.11 provides a definition of "writing" for that contingency as "any mode of communication that preserves a record of the information contained therein and is capable of being reproduced in tangible form."

PICC Article 1.2's admission of "any means" to prove a contract and its terms is expanded upon by PICC Article 4.3(a)'s rule that, in determining the intention of the parties from their statements and other conduct, "regard shall be had to all the circumstances, including (a) preliminary negotiations between the parties…". Given this exclusion of a PICC Parol Evidence Rule, a contract must itself exclude any pre-contract negotiations from contradicting its terms, such as by use of a "merger clause" (discussed in Part A, Chapter 5, a)). PICC Article 2.1.17 addresses the effectiveness of a merger clause by stating

A contract in writing which contains a clause indicating

that the writing completely embodies the terms on which the parties have agreed cannot be contradicted or supplemented by evidence of prior statements or agreements. However, such statements or agreements may be used to interpret the writing.523

The use of pre-contract statements or agreements to interpret written contract terms is similar to the rules of Restatement 2d §202(1), §214(c), §215, and UCC §2-202.

b) Good Faith Obligation in Negotiations

Restatement (Second) of Contracts §205 provides that every contract imposes upon each party a duty of good faith and fair dealing in its performance and enforcement.524

UCC §1-203 provides

Every contract or duty within this code imposes an obligation of good faith in its performance and enforcement.525

UCC §1-102 provides

The obligations of good faith, diligence, reasonableness and care prescribed by this code may not be disclaimed by agreement, but the parties may by agreement determine the standards by which the performance of such obligations is to be measured if such standards are not manifestly unreasonable...526

UCC §1-201(20) (2004 revision) adds a definition that

"Good faith," except as otherwise provided in this code, means honesty in fact and the observance of reasonable commercial standards of fair dealing.527

The UCC §1-201(20) 2004 revised good faith definition had been preceded by a separate sale of goods "good faith" definition for "merchants" in existing UCC §2-103 that

"Good faith" in the case of a merchant means honesty in fact and the observance of reasonable commercial standards of fair dealing in the trade.528

It is not yet clear what additional good faith duties will bind non-merchants in U.S. states adopting the revised 2004 version of UCC §1-201(20), because it is not clear what reasonable commercial standards they should be responsible for knowing.

Because the common law and the statutory requirements for good faith apply literally only to the performance and enforcement of contracts, the general rule applied by U.S. courts has been "anything goes" in pre-contract negotiations, short of fraud and other intentional torts. Many exceptions to this general rule, however, have been created by individual judicial decisions. How much of this general rule remains after these exceptions is questionable.

PICC Article 1.7 provides

(1) Each party must act in accordance with good faith and fair dealing in international trade.

(2) The parties may not exclude or limit this duty.529

PICC Article 2.1.15 provides

(1) A party is free to negotiate and is not liable for failure to reach an agreement.

(2) However, a party who negotiates or breaks off negotiations in bad faith is liable for the losses caused to the other party.

(3) It is bad faith, in particular, for a party to enter into or continue negotiations when intending not to reach an agreement with the other party.530

PICC Article 2.1.16 adds:

Where information is given as confidential by one party in the course of negotiations, the other party is under a duty not to disclose that information or to use it improperly for its own purposes, whether or not a contract is subsequently concluded. Where appropriate, the remedy for breach of that duty may include compensation based on the benefit received by the other party.531

The PICC does not otherwise define good faith or provide examples of bad faith. Liability for bad faith in negotiations is a familiar concept in civil law legal systems, but is unfamiliar to most common law legal systems. This is, in part, because tort law in some civil law nations does not provide a tort remedy for fraud in contract negotiations, while common law legal systems do provide such a tort remedy. Therefore, contract law bears the burden of imposing liability for pre-contractual wrongdoing in such civil law nations.532

Liability for bad faith negotiations in the U.S. can also be based on grounds other than the tort of misrepresentation. Companies that owe a special duty to serve the public without discrimination, such as public utilities and common carriers, must accept offers to contract on their standard terms. Refusals to negotiate in order to illegally restrain trade violate both tort law and antitrust statutes. Refusals to negotiate in order to improperly discriminate may violate tort and statutory law. Employers and unions have a duty to negotiate collective bargaining agreements in good faith under labor laws.

In non-regulated contracts, some courts have enforced pre-contractual liability for misappropriation of ideas disclosed during contract negotiations. This liability may be based on theories of unjust enrichment, a special duty of confidentiality, or trade secrets. Where one contract party, such as an architect or builder, has provided services upon request of the other prospective contract party, such as a real estate developer, a court has occasionally provided restitution where the services have been requested and used in bad faith, and the contract is later awarded to a different party.533

Promissory estoppel has been used as a basis for pre-contractual liability where specific promises of benefits have been made to prospective contract parties, such as prospective franchisees, if they make certain expenditures in order to qualify for a contract relationship.534 Although it is not clear that greater pre-contractual liability is created by PICC rules, compared to U.S. common law and UCC rules, the potentially significant differences between them should be considered by parties negotiating international contracts.535

c) Enforcement of Contract Conditions

The 2010 PICC adds a new section on contract conditions precedent and conditions subsequent. Under U.S. common law, conditions are created by the parties' agreement, or by an interpretation of their agreement by a court.536

PICC Article 5.3.1, however, provides

A contract or contractual obligation may be made conditional upon the occurrence of a future uncertain event, so that the contract or the contractual obligation only takes effect if the event occurs (suspensive condition) or comes to an end if the event occurs (resolutive condition).537

Comment 1 to this article clarifies that

Conditions governed by the Principles include both those that determine whether a contract exists and those that determine obligations within a contract. Accordingly, application of the Principles may in some circumstances impose duties even in the absence of a contract.

These possible pre-contractual duties are consistent with the civil law duty to negotiate in good faith, but are not generally part of the common law of contracts. Common law restitution/unjust enrichment law or promissory estoppel law, however, might apply in these circumstances.538

d) Different PICC Mailbox Rule

PICC Article 2.1.6 provides for the same type of rule regarding when an acceptance of an offer becomes effective as does the CISG Article 18(2) rule discussed in Part C, Section I, chapter 3, f). Under the PICC, the acceptance becomes effective "when the indication of assent reaches the offeror."539 PICC Article 2.1.9(2) also provides

> If a communication containing a late acceptance shows that it has been sent in such circumstances that if its transmission had been normal it would have reached the offeror in due time, the late acceptance is effective as an acceptance unless, without undue delay, the offeror informs the offeree that it considers the offer as having lapsed.540

The PICC "mailbox rule" is thus much narrower than the common law U.S. rule. It applies only to late acceptances that have been sent by "normal" transmissions, and which have not been rejected, without undue delay, by the offeror. The U.S. rule applies to acceptances sent by a method invited by the offeror. The U.S. rule does not allow the offer to be revoked after a timely acceptance is dispatched.

Regarding revocation of offers, PICC Article 2.1.4 provides

> (1) Until a contract is concluded an offer may be revoked if the revocation reaches the offeree before it has dispatched an acceptance.
>
> (2) However, an offer cannot be revoked
>
> (a) if it indicates, whether by stating a fixed time for acceptance or otherwise, that it is irrevocable; or
>
> (b) if it was reasonable for the offeree to rely on the offer

as being irrevocable and the offeree has acted in reliance on the offer.541

This is the same rule as in CISG Article 16. PICC Article 2.1.4 is similar to the U.S. common law "option contract" rules.542 PICC Article 2.1.4(2)(a) lacks the consideration requirement of the common law rule in Restatement 2d §87(1)(a) (although only a minority of U.S. courts may actually require recital of a "purported consideration"). Article 2.1.4(2)(b) is, however, similar to Restatement 2d§87(2)'s rule of an "option contract" created by reasonable and detrimental reliance.

e) Battle of the Forms Rules

PICC Article 2.1.22 states

Where both parties use standard terms and reach agreement except on those terms, a contract is concluded on the basis of the agreed terms and of any standard terms which are common in substance unless one party clearly indicates in advance, or later and without undue delay informs the other party, that it does not intend to be bound by such a contract.543

This rule has elements that are similar to the so-called "battle of the forms" rules of UCC §2-207 and CISG Article 19, both of which apply only to contracts for the sale of goods. The general rule for U.S. common law contracts is the "mirror image" rule requiring offers and acceptances to match their terms exactly in order to form a contract.

f) No Consideration (or Detrimental Reliance) Requirement

PICC Article 3.2 states

A contract is concluded, modified or terminated by the mere agreement of the parties, without any further requirement.544

Thus, there is no requirement under the PICC for consideration, or for detrimental reliance, in order to justify the legal enforcement of a promise. For almost all sales of goods, and for other commercial contracts between businesses, the common law consideration requirement is usually and obviously satisfied, and its purposes are fulfilled. UCC §2-205 eliminates the requirement of consideration for a "firm offer"/irrevocable offer, and UCC §2-209(1) eliminates the consideration requirement for agreements modifying an existing contract. These rules are motivated by presumptions of the seriousness of commercial promises, and the appropriateness of their legal enforcement without further evidence of party intent. Therefore, there is no practical difference between U.S. law and the PICC elimination of a consideration, or detrimental reliance, requirement, at least for any non-consumer, commercial contracts.

g) Authority of Agents Rules

PICC Chapter 2, Section 2 contains various rules on the authority of agents. The Restatement 2d does not address this subject, which is covered in the Restatement of the Law (Third) of Agency as a separate area of U.S. common law.

h) Force Majeure and Hardship Defenses

PICC Article 7.1.7 provides a default "*force majeure*" defense against liability for non-performance of a contract duty that is very similar to the CISG Article 79 defense discussed in Part C, Section I, Chapter 3, n).545 The PICC rule does not address directly failure of performance caused by third party agents of the party responsible for performance. The PICC rule goes beyond the narrower common law contract defenses of impossibility, impracticability and frustration of purpose.

The PICC articles on the subject of "hardship" in performance add a mixture of rules that are both familiar and unfamiliar to common law lawyers, stating

Article 6.2.1 Contract to Be Observed

Where the performance of a contract becomes more onerous for one of the parties, that party is nevertheless bound to perform its obligations subject to the following provisions on hardship.

Article 6.2.2 Definition of Hardship

There is hardship where the occurrence of events fundamentally alters the equilibrium of the contract either because the cost of a party's performance has increased or because the value of the performance a party receives has diminished, and

(a) the events occur or become known to the disadvantaged party after the conclusion of the contract;

(b) the events could not reasonably have been taken into account by the disadvantaged party at the time of the conclusion of the contract;

(c) the events are beyond the control of the disadvantaged party; and

(d) the risk of the events was not assumed by the disadvantaged party.

Article 6.2.3 Effects of Hardship

(1) In case of hardship the disadvantaged party is entitled to request renegotiations. The request shall be made without undue delay and shall indicate the grounds on which it is based.

(2) The request for renegotiation does not in itself entitle the disadvantaged party to withhold performance.

(3) Upon failure to reach agreement within a reasonable time either party may resort to the court.

(4) If the court finds hardship it may, if reasonable,

(a) terminate the contract at a date and on terms to be fixed, or

(b) adapt the contract with a view to restoring its equilibrium.

Articles 6.2.1 and 6.2.2 are similar to the rules of the common law defenses of impossibility, impracticability and frustration of purpose. Article 6.2.3's procedural rights of a disadvantaged party, and possible remedies by a court for hardship, including re-writing of the contract "with a view to restoring its equilibrium", are not familiar to common law lawyers.

i) Specific Performance

In U.S. common law, the "default rule" of remedies requires a party to accept money damages for a breach of contract. A judge can compel a performance of a contract duty by the breaching party only if money damages would not be adequate to protect the interests of the injured party.546 Other common law limitations on specific performance availability apply where uncertain contract terms make enforcement difficult, where specific performance would be unfair, where public policy prevents it, and where a contract imposes a duty of personal service that would be difficult (and unconstitutional under the 13th Amendment) for a court to enforce.

Under the UCC, the seller has the right to recover the price of goods sold to a non-paying buyer547, and a buyer has a right to recover certain goods from a defaulting seller where they are already paid for, in whole or part548, and where the goods are unique "or in other proper circumstances".549

In contrast, PICC Article 7.2.2 states a general rule permitting specific performance as a contract breach remedy, with specified exceptions limiting this default rule, as follows

Where a party who owes an obligation other than one to

pay money does not perform, the other party may require performance, unless

(a) performance is impossible in law or in fact;

(b) performance or, where relevant, enforcement is unreasonably burdensome or expensive;

(c) the party entitled to performance may reasonably obtain performance from another source;

(d) performance is of an exclusively personal character; or

(e) the party entitled to performance does not require performance within a reasonable time after it has, or ought to have, become aware of the non-performance.550

As a penalty for non-compliance with a specific performance order, PICC Article 7.2.4 provides

(1) Where the court orders a party to perform, it may also direct that this party pay a penalty if it does not comply with the order.

(2) The penalty shall be paid to the aggrieved party unless mandatory provisions of the law of the forum provide otherwise. Payment of the penalty to the aggrieved party does not exclude any claim for damages.551

j) Right to Cure Non-Performance After Contract Termination

U.S. common law and the U.C.C. does not give a party that has committed a total breach of contract a right to "cure" (retroactively fulfill) its contract performance duty. To calculate their recoverable damages, however, U.S. common law and the U.C.C. require injured parties to reduce, or "mitigate", their damages. Accepting an offer by a breaching party, after a total breach, to perform might in some circumstances be required in order to mitigate damages.

PICC Article 7.3.1(1) provides that "A party may terminate the contract where the failure of the other party to perform an obligation under the contract amounts to a fundamental non-performance."552 PICC Article 7.3.1(2) sets forth various factors to determine whether or not a fundamental non-performance has occurred. The PICC concept of a "fundamental non-performance" is similar to the U.S. common law concept of a "material and total breach", which is determined by similar factors related to the circumstances of the breach and the actions of the parties553. Both a fundamental non-performance and a total breach allow the injured party to end its own performance duties and to sue the breaching party for damages.

PICC Article 7.3.2(1) states that "The right of a party to terminate the contract is exercised by notice to the other party."554 PICC Article 7.1.4 provides, in addition

(1) The non-performing party may, at its own expense, cure any nonperformance, provided that (a) without undue delay, it gives notice indicating the proposed manner and timing of the cure; (b) cure is appropriate in the circumstances; (c) the aggrieved party has no legitimate interest in refusing cure; and (d) cure is effected promptly.

(2) The right to cure is not precluded by notice of termination.

(3) Upon effective notice of cure, rights of the aggrieved party that are inconsistent with the non-performing party's performance are suspended until the time for cure has expired.

(4) The aggrieved party may withhold performance pending cure.

(5) Notwithstanding cure, the aggrieved party retains the right to claim damages for delay as well as for any harm caused or not prevented by the cure.555

The PICC right of a defaulting party to cure its default is consistent with the PICC (and CISG) emphasis on preserving the possibility of performance of an international contract, in recognition of the greater difficulties of enforcement of international remedies for breach of contract.

k) Effective Assignment of Non-Monetary Contract Rights Despite Changes or Prohibition

Restatement 2d §317(2) states a rule generally allowing assignment of rights to a contract performance, so long as there is no material change in the duty of the obligor, or material increase in the burden or risk imposed on him, or material impairment of his chance of obtaining return performance, or material reduction of the contract's value to him.556   Assignment of performance rights can also be prohibited by statute or by common law judicial decision on grounds of public policy.557 Contract prohibitions on assignment have been restricted through interpretation and remedies rules.558

PICC Article 1.4 recognizes applicable national and other statutory prohibitions on contract assignment.559   PICC Article 9.1.9(2) does not prohibit contract assignments on the basis of increased burden on the obligor.560

PICC Article 9.1.9(2) provides

The assignment of a right to other [than payment of a monetary sum] performance is ineffective if it is contrary to an agreement between the assignor and the obligor limiting or prohibiting the assignment. Nevertheless, the assignment is effective if the assignee, at the time of the assignment, neither knew nor ought to have known of the agreement. The assignor may then be liable to the obligor for breach of contract.

l) Multiple Obligors and Obligees

Chapter 11 of the 2010 PICC adds extensive rules regarding the contract duties and rights, as obligors and obligees, of multiple contract parties including rules on joint and several liability.561 The Restatement does not include rules on multiple contract parties, which is left to the law of individual U.S. states to resolve.

m) Affirmative Defense Statute of Limitations

PICC Chapter 10 provides rules for limitations periods that prevent a claimant from suing for breach of contract after a certain period of time. PICC Article 10.2 sets a general limitation period of three years from when the injured party knew or should have known of the facts giving rise to her claim, with a maximum period of ten years from "the day after the day the right can be exercised."562 PICC Article 10.3 allows the parties to vary these periods by agreement within certain limits.563

PICC Article 10.9 provides

(1) The expiration of the limitation period does not extinguish the right.

(2) For the expiration of the limitation period to have effect, the obligor must assert it as a defence.

(3) A right may still be relied on as a defence even though the expiration of the limitation period for that right has been asserted.564

Limitations periods for domestic contracts are set by U.S. state statutes. They vary in their time periods and in how they are calculated. U.S. statutes also vary in their effects on contract rights. In some states, a statute of limitations is "jurisdictional", meaning that, after the period expires, the right to sue expires, and an appeals court can overturn any judgment obtained under a time-barred lawsuit. In other states, a statute of limitations is only an "affirmative defense", meaning that, unless it is timely argued as a defense to a lawsuit, the ability to use the limitations period as a defense is forever waived. It cannot be later argued as a bar to the lawsuit or to a judgment recovered under the lawsuit.

The intention and effect of the PICC statute of limitations, as PICC Article 10.9 makes clear, is that the PICC statute of limitations operates only as an affirmative defense. If a jurisdictional U.S. statute of limitations applies to a lawsuit through PICC Article 1.4, and if its period were shorter than the PICC period, it could automatically supersede the longer PICC period as a "mandatory rule" of applicable law.565 If an applicable limitations period is longer than the PICC period under a jurisdictional U.S. statute, the PICC period could nevertheless apply, if it is an internal contract rule chosen by the parties.566

If an affirmative defense U.S. state limitations period is shorter than the PICC period, it would supersede the longer PICC period only if timely raised as a defense to a lawsuit. A shorter PICC period than an affirmative defense U.S. limitations period would have to be proved to be an internal contract rule chosen by the parties and timely pleaded. Shorter periods of limitation chosen by the parties are not usually as much of a concern to courts as are party agreements to extend limitations periods, because they do not involve issues of evidence weakened by the passage of time.

SECTION II. INTERNATIONAL ELECTRONIC CONTRACTS LAW AND ONLINE DISPUTE RESOLUTION PROPOSALS

Datapoint #5

More smartphones are forecast to be shipped globally than feature phones in 2013, the first such occurrence in the mobile phone market on an annual basis. According to the International Data Corporation (IDC) Worldwide Quarterly Mobile Phone Tracker, vendors will ship 918.6 million smartphones this year, or 50.1% of the total mobile phone shipments worldwide... By the end of 2017, IDC forecasts 1.5 billion smartphones will be shipped worldwide, which equates to just over two-thirds of the total mobile phone forecast for the year....

-- from *Smartphones Expected to Outship Feature Phones for First Time in 2013, According to IDC*, March 4, 2013, Source: IDC

Summary of Part C, Section II

International electronic commercial contracts are currently subject either to: 1) the law chosen by the contract parties, or 2) customary law applied to the contract, as determined by a court or arbitrator in a contract dispute, or 3) the national or state law applied by a court through a conflict-of-laws analysis, or 4) the automatic application of the Convention on Contracts for the International Sale of Goods (CISG) to a contract between parties whose places of business related to the contract are located in nations that have ratified the CISG, if the parties have not opted out of its application to their contract.

If the CISG applies to an electronic contract, a non-binding CISG advisory committee opinion treats the formation of CISG-governed contracts through electronic communications to be equally effective as formation through printed contracts. If a party-chosen, or a court or arbitrator-applied, national or state or customary law governs the contract, the effectiveness of the electronic communications used to form the contract will depend on the rules of those national or state or customary laws.

There is currently a limited amount of binding, country-neutral international treaty law validating international electronic commercial contracts. International customary law depends on industry and trade-specific practices. National law rules regarding the validity of electronic contracts continue to vary, despite the approval by the United Nations in 1996 of the Model Law on Electronic Commerce.

These obstacles to the recognition of the validity of international electronic contracts prompted the United Nations to approve the Convention on the Use of Electronic Communications in International Contracts (the Electronic Contracts Convention) in 2005. The Electronic Contracts Convention became effective on March 1, 2013 for three ratifying nations. The Electronic Contracts Convention establishes binding default rules regarding the effectiveness of international electronic commercial contracts, and the electronic communications used for their formation. Like the CISG, these rules automatically apply to contracts between parties whose contract-related places of business are located in nations that have ratified the treaty, unless the parties opt out of the application of the rules to their contract.

Recognition of the validity of international electronic commercial contracts under the Electronic Contracts Convention is expected to result in clearer rules for their formation and effectiveness, leading to increased international trade, and more reliable and uniform dispute resolutions. Similar benefits are expected from current proposals for online dispute resolution of international electronic consumer contracts. These consumer contracts increase in number each year despite the absence of standard cross-industry arrangements for cheap, reliable and fair resolution of consumer disputes.

The online alternative dispute resolution mechanisms of

mediation and arbitration, which are available to businesses for commercial contracts, are, and will likely remain, too expensive for international purchases of consumer goods and services. Some types of reliable online dispute resolution for international online purchases of consumer goods and services may be required in order to provide consumers with the confidence to increase their purchases to the levels made possible by technological advances.

CHAPTER 1 - Electronic Contracts Under Non-ECC Law

The United Nations Convention on the Use of Electronic Communications in International Contracts (CUECIC, Electronic Contracts Convention, or ECC) has been signed by eighteen nations and ratified by three nations.567 It became effective for those ratifying nations on March 1, 2013.568 The non-ECC international law on electronic contracts will be analyzed before presenting an analysis of the ECC.

a) CISG Rules and Electronic Communications

i) "Writings", "Signatures", and "Originals" in Contract Formation

International electronic commercial contracts continue to proliferate. International treaty and customary commercial law, meanwhile, is being stretched to cover such contracts (unless other law applies), until the ECC becomes more widely adopted.

The Convention on Contracts for the International Sale of Goods (CISG) was ratified by the U.S. and many other nations prior to the advent of the internet. The CISG does not contemplate or specifically address computer communications. Nevertheless, the rules of the CISG are flexible enough to accommodate some of the issues raised by electronic communications.

The only CISG rules that specifically mention contracts formed by writings are CISG Article 11 (no writing or form requirements), CISG Article 12 (Article 96 national treaty declarations requiring written contracts allowed), CISG Article 13 (stating that "[f]or purposes of this Convention 'writing' includes telegram and telex"), CISG Article 21(2) (effect of mis-transmission of late written acceptance), and CISG Article 29(2) (effect of written contract requiring modification or termination in writing).

CISG Article 7(2)'s rule of statutory construction allows CISG rules to be supplemented, by providing

> Questions concerning matters governed by this Convention which are not expressly settled in it are to be settled in conformity with the general principles on which it is based or, in the absence of such principles, in conformity with the law applicable by virtue of the rules of private international law.569

CISG Article 11 states

> A contract of sale need not be concluded in or evidenced by writing and is not subject to any other requirement as to form. It may be proved by any means, including witnesses.570

CISG Article 11's flexibility toward contract form requirements is a "general principle" of CISG Article 7, under which CISG Article 13's "writing" definition should be extended to include electronic communications, so long as they fulfill the same functions as printed writings. These functions are the reliable storing and later reproduction of the relevant communication.

Although no (non-national version) CISG rule requires a signature, or an original writing, electronic communications might also fulfill the functions of these requirements. These are the reliable authentication of the approval of a communication through a signature, and the reliable authentication of the unaltered terms of a communication through an original.

The Advisory Council of CISG experts issued its first (non-binding) opinion in 2003 on the subject of electronic communications. This opinion agreed that Article 11 permits the formation and proof of contracts through electronic communications571, and that Article 13's "writing" definition includes "any electronic communication retrievable in perceivable form".572 The opinion applied a test of functionality for equivalence with a printed communication, which is the ability for the communication to be saved and to be understood when retrieved. Therefore, a presumption applies for any CISG-governed contract that writings include electronic communications. The parties may depart from this presumption, and may deny electronic communications a status equivalent to printed communications, through their CISG Article 6 power to limit the applicability of most CISG rules to their contract. They may also strengthen or weaken the presumption through their prior conduct or trade usages.573

ii) Time of Sending and Receipt of Communications

The terms "send," "give," "made," "deliver," and "dispatch" are used by the CISG regarding the acts of a sender of a communication, while the terms "reach" and "received" are used regarding the recipient.

CISG Article 24 defines the term "reach" as

For the purposes of this Part of the Convention [Part II. Formation of the Contract], an offer, declaration of acceptance or any other indication of intention "reaches" the addressee when it is made orally to him or delivered by any other means to him personally, to his place of business or mailing address or, if he does not have a place of business or mailing address, to his habitual residence.

In contrast, for purposes of performance of contracts in Part III of the CISG, Sale of Goods, CISG Article 27 states

Unless otherwise expressly provided in this Part of the Convention, if any notice, request or other communication is given or made by a party in accordance with this Part and by means appropriate in the circumstances, a delay or error in the transmission of the communication or its failure to arrive does not deprive that party of the right to rely on the communication.

Rules in Part II, to which Article 24's definition of "reaches" applies, include Article 15(1) (offer effective when it reaches offeree), Article 15(2) (offer withdrawal reaching offeree before, or at same time as offer, is effective), Article 16(1) (revocable offer may be revoked, if revocation reaches offeree before dispatch of acceptance), Article 17 (all offers terminated when rejection reaches offeree), Article 18(2) (acceptance effective when it reaches offeror within time fixed by offeror, or reasonable time otherwise), Article 20(1) (time for acceptance set by offeror in instantaneous communication runs from moment offer reaches offeree), Article 21(2) (mis-transmitted written late acceptance that normally would have reached offeror on time is effective, unless offeror, without delay, objects), and Article 22 (acceptance withdrawal effective if it reaches offeror before or at same time it would have become effective).

Rules in Part III requiring receipt of communications include Article 47(2) (buyer receipt of notice from seller of nonperformance required before remedies for contract breach available), Article 48(4) (buyer receipt of seller request to buyer to accept late performance), Article 63(2) (seller receipt of notice from buyer of nonperformance required before remedies for contract breach available), and Article 79(4) (receipt of notice from either nonperforming party of *force majeure* excuse for nonperformance required to avoid damages).

Rules in Part III requiring only the "giving" of notice, whether or not actually received, pursuant to CISG Article 27, include Article 32(1) (seller duty to give buyer notice of consignment of goods to carrier), Article 67(2) (passing of risk of loss of goods to the buyer by giving of notice to buyer that goods have been identified to the contract), and Article 71(3) (notice must be given of suspension of performance in response to likely anticipatory breach).

Regarding CISG Article 24's definition of "reaches" for purposes of contract formation, CISG Advisory Council Opinion No. 1 states

The term "reaches" corresponds to the point in time when an electronic communication has entered the addressee's server, provided that the addressee expressly or impliedly has consented to receiving electronic communications of that type, in that format, and to that address.

The term "orally" includes electronically transmitted sound and other communications in real time provided that the addressee expressly or impliedly has consented to receive electronic communications of that type, in that format, and to that address.574

CISG Advisory Council Opinion No. 1 applies these definitions to the use of the term "reaches" in Articles 15, 16(1), 17, 18(2), 20(1), 21(2), 22 and to the use of the term "oral" in articles 18(2) (an oral offer must be accepted immediately unless the circumstances indicate otherwise) and 21(2) (offeror must orally or by sending notice inform offeree that offer has lapsed).

CISG Article 20(1) establishes a start time for a period for acceptance of offers sent by telegram or letter that does not depend on the time of receipt by the offeree, stating

A period of time for acceptance fixed by the offeror in a telegram or a letter e-mail communication begins to run from the moment the telegram is handed in for dispatch or from the date shown on the letter or, if no such date is shown, from the date shown on the envelope. A period of time for acceptance fixed by the offeror by telephone, telex or other means of instantaneous communication, begins to run from the moment that the offer reaches the offeree.

CISG Advisory Council Opinion No. 1, however, applies a receipt-based rule for "real-time" electronic communications, and a dispatch-based rule for e-mail communications, stating

A period of time for acceptance fixed by the offeror in electronic real time communication begins to run from the moment the offer enters the offeree's server.

A period of time for acceptance fixed by the offeror in e-mail communication begins to run from the time of dispatch of the e-mail communication.

"Means of instantaneous communications" includes electronic real time communication.

The term "reaches" is to be interpreted to correspond to the point in time when an electronic communication has entered the offeree's server.575

The "dispatch" treatment of e-mails is justified as based on the ability to determine when they were sent, and their nature as "functional equivalents of letters".576 The opinion does not address when the time for an acceptance period begins for an offer from a "passive web site".577"Chat room" communications are given as an example of instantaneous electronic communications in the opinion. Their similarity to oral communications is the basis for their receipt-based rule for the start of an acceptance period.578

Other applications of the Advisory Council Opinion interpretations of the terms "writing", "oral" and "notice" to include electronic communications are made regarding Article 21(1)'s rule on effectiveness of a late acceptance, with an offeror oral or dispatched notice to that effect to the offeree, and Article 21(2)'s rule on the effectiveness of late acceptances by a letter or other writing because of faulty transmission, absent offeror oral or dispatched notice to the offeree of a lapse in the offer.

The Advisory Council Opinion applies a complementary interpretation for the term "dispatch", as used in CISG Articles 16(1) (offer revocation reaching offeree before he dispatches an acceptance), 19(2) (offeror objection to additional or different terms in acceptance by dispatch of notice to offeree), 20(1) (time for acceptance of offer beginning at handing in of telegram for dispatch), 21(1) (offeror dispatch of notice to offeree that late acceptance is effective), 21(2) (offeror dispatch of notice of lapse of offer to offeree sending late acceptance). The opinion defines dispatch in the context of notice by electronic communications, stating

> The term "dispatch" corresponds to the point in time when the notice has left the offeree's server. A prerequisite is that the offeree has consented expressly or impliedly to receiving electronic messages of that type, in that format, and to that address.579

> Although the first sentence of the above paragraph refers to the "offeree's server", the discussion following it in the opinion makes it clear that it is intended to refer to a dispatch of notice from the offeror's server.580

The Advisory Council applies an interpretation of the term "specifications" of features of the goods for sale in Article 65, stating

> Specifications and communications may be electronic provided that the addressee expressly or impliedly consented to receiving such communications.581

Finally, the Advisory Council interpretation of the term "notice" states

> The term "notice" includes electronic communications provided that the addressee expressly or impliedly has consented to receiving electronic messages of that type, in that format, and to that address.582

This definition is applied to the use of the term "notice" in CISG Articles 19(2) (offeror notice of objection to additional or different terms in acceptance), 21(1) (offeror notice to offeree of effectiveness of late acceptance), 21(2) (offeror notice to offeree of lapse of offer making late acceptance ineffective), 26 (declaration of avoidance of contract effective only by notice to other party), 27 (delay of, error in, or failure to arrive of notice properly made does not deprive sender of right to rely upon it), 32(1) (required seller notice to buyer of consignment of goods to carrier), 39 (required buyer notice to seller of lack of conformity of goods), 43 (required buyer notice to seller of claim of right of third party in goods delivered), 47 (buyer receipt of notice from seller that he will not perform within additional period for performance fixed by buyer), 63 (seller receipt of notice from buyer that he will not perform within additional period for performance fixed by seller), 67 (risk of loss of goods passing to buyer requiring notice to buyer that goods have been identified to contract), 71 (immediate notice to other party by party suspending performance because of other party's serious deficiency in ability to perform or conduct making substantial nonperformance likely), 72 (reasonable notice required to allow adequate assurance of performance), 79 (notice to other party of prevention of performance by impediment beyond performing party's control), and 88 (notice of intention to sell goods that a party was bound to preserve after unreasonable delay by other party).

b) Customary International Law and Electronic Communications

i) Customary International Law Scope and Requirements; CISG and UCC Trade Usage

The International Court of Justice (ICJ) is located in The Hague, Netherlands. The ICJ was created by the United Nations to resolve disputes between member nations. The Statute of the ICJ states

The Court, whose function is to decide in accordance with international law such disputes as are submitted to it, shall apply:

...international custom, as evidence of a general practice accepted as law...583

This statute provides a useful definition of and a test for customary international law. First, it must be a general practice of international business, government, or other interactions (sometimes called "*jus cogens*"-a general practice). Second, the general practice must be treated by those who engage in it as not discretionary, but as a mandatory, legally required practice (sometimes called "*opinio juris*"). Just as the parties to a contract can create (many of) their own rules as the "law of the contract", business people can create their own rules for the conduct of their business or trade. This is the customary law of their business or trade.

If international customary electronic contract law exists for a legal issue, it supplies rules of law for international contracts that are not governed by the CISG. For CISG-governed contracts, such customary law could supply "general principles" on which the CISG is based, pursuant to the CISG Article 7(2) provision that

> Questions concerning matters governed by this Convention which are not expressly settled in it are to be settled in conformity with the general principles on which it is based or, in the absence of such principles, in conformity with the law applicable by virtue of the rules of private international law.

International customary electronic contract law could also supply supplemental CISG rules pursuant to the CISG Article 9(2) trade usage provision that

> The parties are considered, unless otherwise agreed, to have impliedly made applicable to their contract or its formation a usage of which the parties knew or ought to have known and which in international trade is widely known to, and regularly observed by, parties to contracts of the type involved in the particular trade concerned.

CISG Article 8(3) provides further

In determining the intent of a party or the understanding a reasonable person would have had [regarding contract-related statements or conduct of a party], due consideration is to be given to all relevant circumstances of the case including the negotiations, any practices which the parties have established between themselves, usages and any subsequent conduct of the parties.

Thus, customary law in the form of trade usages can be used: 1) to supply rules for non-CISG governed international contracts; 2) to "fill the gaps" in CISG rules under Article 7(2); 3) to supplement CISG rules under Article 9(2); and 4) to interpret the meaning of party statements and conduct under CISG Article 8(3).

CISG Article 18(3) provides, regarding methods of acceptance of offers

However, if by virtue of the offer or as a result of practices which the parties have established between themselves or of usage, the offeree may indicate assent by performing an act, such as one relating to the dispatch of the goods or payment of the price, without notice to the offeror, the acceptance is effective at the moment the act is performed, provided that the act is performed within the period of time laid down in [paragraph (2)].

The equivalence of customary law to U.S. contract law trade usage is evident from a brief review of relevant UCC rules. UCC §1-102 provides

(1) This code shall be liberally construed and applied to promote its underlying purposes and policies, which are:... (b) To permit the continued expansion of commercial practices through custom, usage, and agreement of the parties...584

UCC §1-205 provides in part

(3) A "usage of trade" is any practice or method of dealing having such regularity of observance in a place,

vocation or trade as to justify an expectation that it will be observed with respect to the transaction in question. The existence and scope of such a usage are to be proved as facts. If it is established that such a usage is embodied in a written trade code or similar record, the interpretation of the record is a question of law.

(4) A course of performance or a course of dealing between the parties or usage of trade in the vocation or trade in which they are engaged or of which they are or should be aware is relevant in ascertaining the meaning of the parties' agreement, may give particular meaning to specific terms of the agreement, and may supplement or qualify the terms of an agreement. A usage of trade applicable in the place in which part of the performance under the agreement is to occur may be so utilized as to that part of the performance…

(6) Evidence of a relevant usage of trade offered by one party is not admissible unless that party has given the other party notice that the court finds sufficient to prevent unfair surprise to the other party.585

The Official Comments to UCC §1-205 state that, by adopting the term usage of trade, the UCC rejects case law disapproving its use to interpret contract language and to supplement other applicable law.586 The UCC §1-205(3) trade usage requirement of "regularity of observance" does not require "ancient or immemorial", "universal" or similar observance, as was stated in some English common law cases, and thereby allows the creation of new trade usage, such as in trade codes, and usages followed only by a majority of trade participants.587 Trade usages have a presumption of reasonableness, and must be proved to not be reasonable.588

The UCC §1-205 rules and comments on custom and trade usage provide useful guidance for the purpose, scope of application, and proof requirements of international electronic contracts customary law. Any such rules of international customary law would not displace mandatory national laws, such as a Statute of Frauds/written contract requirement, which embody legislative policies applicable to all contracts.589 Customary law rules should only be "gap-fillers" that give meaning to contract terms that the parties have failed to define, expressly or implicitly, through their course of contract performance, or implicitly through their pre-contract negotiations course of dealing.

Proof of international electronic contracts customary law should follow the flexible standards of UCC §1-205 by requiring only a) regularity of observance, b) a presumption of reasonableness, and c) observance only in a dominant pattern of practice, which allows for minority variations in practices.590 These rules should facilitate the rapid development and adaptation of new customs and usages in a manner appropriate to the business realities of "internet time".

The requirement of the ICJ Statute that international custom be "evidence of a practice accepted as law" has sometimes been construed to require proof of a subjective belief by parties in the legally binding effect of the practice. Such proof is often difficult, if not impossible. Its purpose should be satisfied for international electronic contracts customary law by a UCC type of requirement of regularity of observance of the practice, showing the objective recognition by the majority of trade participants of the binding character of the practice.

ii) Sources and Examples of International Electronic Contracts Customary Law

One example of an electronic business-to-consumer contract procedure, which has become international customary law through regular practice by a clear majority of businesses, might be the practice of displaying to a prospective customer all of the steps necessary to conclude an electronic contract before it can become effective. This practice is required by the 2000 European Union Directive on Electronic Commerce.591 It is supported by the 2000 Federal

Trade Commission (FTC) Dot Com Disclosures: Information about Online Advertising guidance that businesses should make clear and conspicuous disclosures "to ensure that consumers receive material information about the terms of a transaction".592 One survey of international internet vendors showed adherence to this practice by at least seventy-five percent of respondents.593

Another source of customary international electronic contract law is the Model Law on Electronic Commerce (MLEC), written and promoted by the United Nations Commission on International Trade Law.594 The MLEC serves as a prototype for national legislation establishing the equivalency of electronic and printed contracts, including the 1999 U.S. Electronic Signatures in Global and National Commerce Act (E-SIGN)595 and the state Uniform Electronic Transactions Act (UETA).596

Like the Restatement (Second) of Contracts for U.S. law, and the Principles of International Commercial Contracts for international commercial law, the MLEC was intended to serve "as a tool for interpreting existing international conventions and other international instruments that create legal obstacles to the use of electronic commerce... to recognize the use of electronic commerce and obviate the need to negotiate a protocol to the international instrument involved."597 The supplementation of statutes in order to facilitate commercial transactions is a traditional function of customary law and trade usage.598

Examples of such supplementation of statutes by customary international internet law might be seen in the parallel provisions of the MLEC and the Convention on the Use of Electronic Communications in International Contracts (CUECIC) on various subjects, such as electronic writings, signatures and originals, and time and place of dispatch and receipt of electronic communications, as discussed hereafter.

CHAPTER 2 - The United Nations Convention on the Use of Electronic Communications in International Contracts (CUECIC, the Electronic Contracts Convention, or the ECC)

a) Electronic Contracts Convention History, Status, Purpose, Scope and Applicability

i) History and Status

In 1998, the United States delegation recommended to the United Nations Commission on International Trade Law (UNCITRAL) that it develop an international convention on electronic contracts based on the principles of the Model Law on Electronic Commerce (MLEC).599 These MLEC principles (later followed by the U.S. E-SIGN and UETA legislation) include technological neutrality, national source neutrality, and party freedom in the choice of applicable contract law and rules.600 The MLEC allows various versions of national electronic commerce law, and a variety of such laws proliferated. A major motivation for the U.S. and other nations to establish the Electronic Contracts Convention was to harmonize international rules on electronic commerce, and to foster uniformity in the domestic enactments of the MLEC.601

The Convention on the Use of Electronic Communications in International Contracts (CUECIC, Electronic Contracts Convention, or ECC) was adopted by UNCITRAL and the General Assembly of the United Nations in 2005.602 Eighteen nations have signed the ECC, indicating their intention to consider it for ratification. The three nations that have ratified it to date are Singapore, Honduras and the Dominican Republic.603 It became effective for those three nations on March 1, 2013.604

In 2006, the American Bar Association (ABA), a voluntary national lawyer organization, formally recommended that the United States ratify the ECC.605 In an April 2010 report of the Cyberspace Committee of the ABA

Section of Business Law (2010 Report), various methods for implementation of the ECC as U.S. law were analyzed.606 The issue of treaty implementation gained increased importance following the 2008 U.S. Supreme Court decision in *Medellin v. Texas*.607

The *Medellin* decision determined the effects of the ratification by the U.S. of the Vienna Convention on Consular Relations (VCCR)608 on a Texas state court criminal trial that led to the imposition of the death penalty against a Mexican citizen. The Supreme Court rejected the argument that the failure of Texas law enforcement officers to notify the Mexican defendant of his VCCR right to contact the Mexican consulate after his arrest prevented the enforcement of the death penalty. In reaching this conclusion, the Supreme Court reasoned that only "self-executing" treaties, and treaties directly implemented by federal legislation, imposed duties on states pursuant to the U.S. Constitution "supremacy clause". This clause provides that "all Treaties made...under the Authority of the United States, shall be the supreme Law of the Land; and the Judges of every State shall be bound thereby...".609 The Supreme Court decided that the VCCR was neither self-executing nor directly implemented by federal legislation. It was not made a "self- executing" treaty merely by the President's statement to that effect.

In order to avoid post-*Medellin* issues regarding the effects of a ratified Electronic Contracts Convention on U.S. state contract law, the 2010 Report recommended that the ECC be ratified with directly implementing federal legislation. The report rejected a "cooperative federalism" approach, similar to the "E-SIGN plus UETA" method of federal law implementation.

The direct federal implementation approach was considered more effective and appropriate for a treaty, such as the ECC, whose application was limited to international contracts. The direct federal implementation method was viewed as better suited to promote a policy of limited federal encroachment on state powers, increased certainty in the effectiveness of contracts, continued confidence by foreign nations in U.S. treaty negotiations, and efficiency and transparency in the application of commercial treaty law in the U.S., particularly regarding the use of electronic communications in transactions subject to the Convention on Contracts for the International Sale of Goods (CISG).610

Direct implementation of the ECC through a federal statute will also eliminate practical problems in researching and finding the ECC and judicial decisions referring to it, after its enactment, because it will be located in a specific United States Code section. In contrast, the implementation of the CISG through Senate ratification only, without implementing legislation, relegated the text of the CISG to an appendix to the U.S. Code, where it is difficult for researchers to find, and where it does not have annotations, in annotated versions of the Code, of decisions and articles referring to it.611

Several further elements of the ratification process are being considered for recommendation by the American Bar Association. These elements reflect some of the goals of the Uniform Law Commission (ULC), a non-profit organization of state government-appointed experts in harmonization of U.S. state law. One ULC goal is to avoid unnecessary pre-emption of state law by international treaties.612

The ABA is currently considering a recommendation for the U.S. to include two declarations in its ratification of the ECC in order to clarify its effects on existing U.S. state law.613 The first declaration would state that the ECC applies only to electronic communications covered by Article 2 (Sale of Goods) and Article 2A (Leases) of the Uniform Commercial Code, and not to any other transactions covered by the Code. It would also state that the ECC does not apply either to electronic communications excluded from the scope of the Uniform Electronic Transactions Act (UETA), as recommended by the Uniform Law Commission, or to those excluded from the scope of the Electronic Signatures in

Global and National Commerce Act (E-SIGN).

The second declaration would limit the application of the ECC to the treaties currently in force and described in Article 20(1) of the ECC614. It would prohibit the ECC from applying to any future U.S. treaties, unless specifically provided for in a future U.S. declaration pursuant to Article 20(3).

Separate "understandings" are also being considered for inclusion in the instrument of ratification of the ECC. These understandings would become part of the legislative history of the convention, with significant influence on future judicial interpretations and applications of its terms.

The first relates to Article 3's allowance for contract parties to exclude the automatic ECC coverage of their contract, which would otherwise apply, if their principal places of business are in nations that have ratified the ECC.615

The same type of "opt out" provision in the Convention on Contracts for the International Sale of Goods (CISG) has been narrowly interpreted by U.S. judges as requiring very specific contract language in order to be effective.616

The proposed understanding would state that parties to a contract, to which the ECC would otherwise apply, may exclude its application, or change its terms, "expressly by the words used or by implication". This would allow judicial interpretation of party intent to opt out based on business practices, incompatible contract terms, course of dealing and other evidence of party intent, as well as contract language. This legislative history might prevent the technicalities of constitutional law from creating a "trap for the unwary" contract party. Future judicial decisions would implement the details of this rule of "exclusion by implication". One detail is whether, and to what extent, a presumption of ECC applicability is created by a contract between parties with places of business in ratifying nations, and, if so, whether, and to what extent, it must be overcome by proof of contrary party intention.

The second understanding would clarify that contract parties can by agreement neither change the scope of application of the ECC, nor change its procedural treaty rules. An example of the latter is the date when the ECC comes into force.

The third understanding would clarify that the rules for the time and place of dispatch of electronic communications under Articles 10.1 and 10.3 treat communications as dispatched only if "effectively directed or addressed to an addressee/recipient".

The fourth understanding would state that Article 10.2's presumption, that a communication is capable of being received when it reaches the addressee's electronic address, is rebuttable. The presumption could be rebutted by evidence, such as technical failure or service interruption, to show that the communication was delayed or not actually received.

ii) Purpose, Scope and Applicability

Like the Model Law on Electronic Commerce (MLEC), and national laws based on it, the purpose of the ECC is to "remove obstacles to the use of electronic communications in international contracts" formation and performance.617 Although the substantive ECC rules are similar to the MLEC rules, the ECC procedural rules are, in many ways, similar to the CISG.618

The Electronic Contracts Convention, like the CISG, applies to contracts between parties whose "places of business" are in different "States".619 Place of business is defined in the ECC as

> any place where a party maintains a non-transitory establishment to pursue an economic activity other than the temporary provision of goods or services out of a

specific location.620

The CISG requires both contract parties' places of business to be in ratifying nations in order for it to apply to their contract, absent a party choice or a forum application of the CISG as applicable law621. The ECC would also apply to a contract between parties whose places of business are in different ratifying nations. The ECC would only require the law of one contract party's place of business to be that of an ECC-ratifying nation, if the law of that nation applies to the contract through conflict-of-laws/private international law rules. Each party's place of business must, however, be located in a different nation.622

ECC rules are limited in application to the same types of international commercial contracts that are covered by CISG rules.623 Non-commercial contracts for "personal, family or household purposes", contracts of government-regulated entities, and negotiable instruments and documents of title are excluded from coverage.624 There is no exception, as there is in the CISG, for the ECC to apply to a personal, family or household contract whose purpose as such was not apparent to a commercial party. Commercial contracts on subjects other than the sale of goods are covered by the ECC, however, including contracts for services, licenses, auctions, barter and others.

Like the CISG625, the Electronic Contracts Convention allows contract parties to "opt-out" of ECC coverage, or to change individual ECC rules.626 Like the CISG627, ECC rules favor interpretation of their meaning with regard "to its international character and to the need to promote uniformity in its application and the observance of good faith in international trade."628 Like the CISG629, questions governed by the ECC "but not expressly settled in it are to be settled in conformity with the general principles on which it is based or, in the absence of such principles, in conformity with the law applicable by virtue of the rules of private international law."630

CUECIC Article 20.1 provides that the ECC applies to the use of electronic communications in connection with the formation or performance of a contract that is subject to six specified international conventions, to which an ECC-ratifying nation is, or may become, a party:

Convention on the Recognition and Enforcement of Foreign Arbitral Awards (New York, 10 June 1958);

Convention on the Limitation Period in the International Sale of Goods (New York, 14 June 1974) and Protocol thereto (Vienna, 11 April 1980);

United Nations Convention on Contracts for the International Sale of Goods (Vienna, 11 April 1980);

United Nations Convention on the Liability of Operators of Transport Terminals in International Trade (Vienna, 19 April 1991);

United Nations Convention on Independent Guarantees and Stand-by Letters of Credit (New York, 11 December 1995);

United Nations Convention on the Assignment of Receivables in International Trade (New York, 12 December 2001).631

CUECIC Article 20.2 allows the automatic future application of the ECC to the use of electronic communications in the formation or performance of contracts governed by future international conventions, treaties or agreements of a ratifying nation. Ratifying nations may also choose, under Article 20.3, specific treaties whose related electronic communications for contract formation or performance will be governed by ECC rules. Under Article 20.4, they may choose specific treaties whose related electronic communications for contract formation or performance will not be governed by ECC rules.

b) Electronic Contracts Convention Rules

i) Definitions

CUECIC Article 4 provides definitions for important terms used in the ECC, including

(a) "Communication" means any statement, declaration, demand, notice or request, including an offer and the acceptance of an offer, that the parties are required to make or choose to make in connection with the formation or performance of a contract;

(b) "Electronic communication" means any communication that the parties make by means of data messages;

(c) "Data message" means information generated, sent, received or stored by electronic, magnetic, optical or similar means, including, but not limited to, electronic data interchange, electronic mail, telegram, telex or telecopy[.]632

ii) Validity of Electronic Communications, Contracts, "Writings", "Signatures" and "Originals"

CUECIC Article 8.1 recognizes the validity and enforceability of communications and contracts in the form of electronic communications.633 CUECIC Article 8.2 clarifies that there is no requirement to use or accept electronic communications, but a party's agreement to do so may be inferred from its conduct. CUECIC Article 9.1 states that "[n]othing in this Convention requires a communication or a contract to be made or evidenced in any particular form."634

CUECIC Article 9.2 provides regarding electronic writings

Where the law requires that a communication or a contract should be in writing, or provides consequences for the absence of a writing, that requirement is met by an electronic communication if the information contained therein is accessible so as to be useable for subsequent reference.

CUECIC Article 9.3 provides regarding electronic signatures

Where the law requires that a communication or a contract should be signed by a party, or provides consequences for the absence of a signature, that requirement is met in relation to an electronic communication if:

(a) A method is used to identify the party and to indicate that party's intention in respect of the information contained in the electronic communication; and

(b) The method used is either:

(i) As reliable as appropriate for the purpose for which the electronic communication was generated or communicated, in the light of all the circumstances, including any relevant agreement; or

(ii) Proven in fact to have fulfilled the functions described in subparagraph (a) above, by itself or together with further evidence.

CUECIC Article 8.4 and CUECIC Article 8.5 provide, regarding electronic originals

4. Where the law requires that a communication or a contract should be made available or retained in its original form, or provides consequences for the absence of an original, that requirement is met in relation to an electronic communication if:

(a) There exists a reliable assurance as to the integrity of the information it contains from the time when it was first generated in its final form, as an electronic communication or otherwise; and

(b) Where it is required that the information it contains be made available, that information is capable of being displayed to the person to whom it is to be made available.

5. For the purposes of paragraph 4(a):

(a) The criteria for assessing integrity shall be whether the information has remained complete and unaltered, apart from the addition of any endorsement and any change that arises in the normal course of communication, storage and display; and

(b) The standard for reliability required shall be assessed in the light of the purpose for which the information was generated and in the light of all relevant circumstances.

iii) Time and Place of Dispatch and Receipt of Electronic Communications

CUECIC Article 10 provides rules for the dispatch and receipt of electronic communications, including

1. The time of dispatch of an electronic communication is the time when it leaves an information system under the control of the originator or of the party who sent it on behalf of the originator or, if the electronic communication has not left an information system under the control of the originator or of the party who sent it on behalf of the originator, the time when the electronic communication is received.

2. The time of receipt of an electronic communication is the time when it becomes capable of being retrieved by the addressee at an electronic address designated by the addressee. The time of receipt of an electronic communication at another electronic address of the addressee is the time when it becomes capable of being retrieved by the addressee at that address and the

addressee becomes aware that the electronic communication has been sent to that address. An electronic communication is presumed to be capable of being retrieved by the addressee when it reaches the addressee's electronic address.

3. An electronic communication is deemed to be dispatched at the place where the originator has its place of business and is deemed to be received at the place where the addressee has its place of business, as determined in accordance with article 6.635

4. Paragraph 2 of this article applies notwithstanding that the place where the information system supporting an electronic address is located may be different from the place where the electronic communication is deemed to be received under paragraph 3 of this article.636

iv) Invitations for Offers, Electronic Agents and Communication Errors

CUECIC Article 11 provides an electronic communication rule counterpart to the general contract rule regarding advertisements to the public, or "invitations for offers", by stating

A proposal to conclude a contract made through one or more electronic communications which is not addressed to one or more specific parties, but is generally accessible to parties making use of information systems, including proposals that make use of interactive applications for the placement of orders through such information systems, is to be considered as an invitation to make offers, unless it clearly indicates the intention of the party making the proposal to be bound in case of acceptance.637

CUECIC Article 12 provides a rule regarding contract formation by "electronic agents" by stating

A contract formed by the interaction of an automated

message system and a natural person, or by the interaction of automated message systems, shall not be denied validity or enforceability on the sole ground that no natural person reviewed or intervened in each of the individual actions carried out by the automated message systems or the resulting contract.638

CUECIC Article 14 provides a rule regarding the effects of electronic communication errors, by stating

1. Where a natural person makes an input error in an electronic communication exchanged with the automated message system of another party and the automated message system does not provide the person with an opportunity to correct the error, that person, or the party on whose behalf that person was acting, has the right to withdraw the portion of the electronic communication in which the input error was made if:

(a) The person, or the party on whose behalf that person was acting, notifies the other party of the error as soon as possible after having learned of the error and indicates that he or she made an error in the electronic communication; and

(b) The person, or the party on whose behalf that person was acting, has not used or received any material benefit or value from the goods or services, if any, received from the other party.

2. Nothing in this article affects the application of any rule of law that may govern the consequences of any error other than as provided for in paragraph 1.639

CHAPTER 3 - Major Differences Between Current Rules and ECC Rules

a) Comparison with CISG Rules

The Electronic Contracts Convention Article 9.2 "writing" test of "accessible so as to be usable for subsequent reference" improves upon the CISG Advisory Council test of "retrievable in perceivable form"640 by implying a requirement of continued accessibility. The ECC provides an electronic "signature" test641, but the CISG Advisory Council provides none.

ECC rules for the dispatch and receipt of electronic communications are broader and more flexible through references to "information systems"642, compared to the CISG Advisory Council opinion on the time when offers and acceptances reach a party, which refers to computer "servers", and to addresses designated for electronic communications.643 The ECC's legislative history also makes it clear that "it does not deal with the rights and obligations of intermediaries" such as the owners of computer servers.644

The ECC, like E-SIGN and UETA, provides for contracts through electronic agents or other automated processes645, while the CISG does not.646

The ECC provides a test for "original" electronic communications.647 The ECC rules on "original" communications provide rules for the authentication of electronic communications, while allowing the supplementation of those rules with custom, trade usage and party practices.648 The CISG Advisory Council has no definition of, or rules about, an "original" writing or communication. Any contract requirement of, or preference for, an "original" in a CISG- governed contract would require an analysis of applicable non-CISG law, such as national law, custom or trade usage.

The ECC establishes rules for determining a party's place of business.649 The narrower CISG rule only addresses situations in which a party has multiple places of business, or has no place of business.650

The ECC establishes rules for errors in the transmission of communications, which specifically address the situation of "human error" in information input when dealing with electronic agents of another party, and the developing internet custom that offers at least one opportunity to correct that error.651 In contrast, the CISG rule on communication errors only provides a rule that a properly sent communication, under Part III of the CISG, may be relied upon by the sender, despite a delay or error in transmission (without specifying the source of the delay or error).652 The ECC error rules are similar to the error rules of the Uniform Electronic Transactions Act (UETA) regarding input errors by individuals dealing with electronic agents.653 Both the ECC and UETA provide more useful rules than the CISG for addressing how the burden of a human error-induced loss should be shifted between parties.

Unless and until the ECC applies to their contracts, international commercial electronic contract parties, and courts or arbitrators, must interpret CISG rules to determine whether they permit contract formation and enforcement through electronic communications. They must analyze the text and legislative history of the CISG, CISG advisory opinions, and the domestic/municipal law of the nations where the parties have their places of business. The ECC binds each ratifying nation to recognize electronic contracts and signatures in the formation and enforcement of international commercial contracts. This is a simpler, more effective and more efficient method to facilitate e-commerce than current law.

b) Comparison with Customary International Law Rules

Customary international law rules for electronic communications in commercial contract formation and performance have two primary sources: 1) trade usage; and 2) the U.N. Model Law on Electronic Commerce (MLEC).

Trade usage is the most recent and adaptable source of customary law, but it is also the most difficult to identify. Customary law must be "widely known" and "regularly observed" according to CISG Article 9(2), or "generally accepted" as a "practice of Law" according to the International Court of Justice statute.654

Evidence of customary international law of electronic contracting is likely to require empirical data of trade customs, such as interviews, surveys and statistical data and analysis. Such information is available. Trade associations and government regulators might be sources of information on trade practices, and their acceptance and prevalence.

The reliance on trade custom and usage as a source of law has the potential disadvantage of delegating to the private marketplace policy choices that might affect the general public, and that should be influenced by their elected representatives.

The U.N. Model Law on Electronic Commerce (MLEC) was written, in part, to serve as

> a tool for interpreting existing international conventions and other international instruments that create legal obstacles to the use of electronic commerce, for example by prescribing that certain documents or contractual clauses be made in written form."655

By providing rules for the functional equivalence of electronic and printed contract communications, the MLEC serves as a type of trade usage or customary international law in aid of legislative interpretation.

For example, the function-based MLEC rules on "originals"656 have been closely followed by the ECC657(and to a lesser extent by UETA658). These rules may serve as a source of customary international law where the ECC does not apply to an international commercial contract. The MLEC recognition of the legal effectiveness of electronic communications establishes an important international norm. It is unlikely, however, to prevail over applicable national legal requirements for printed "writings", "signatures" and "originals".

Where national law requirements for printed documents do not apply, the MLEC rules on time of dispatch and receipt of "data messages"659 employ the terminology of "enters into an information system", which is similar to the later terminology of the ECC rules. Although not as detailed as the ECC rules, the MLEC rules may serve as a customary law basis for interpretation of non-ECC rules for electronic communication.

The MLEC rules on the place of dispatch and receipt of communications depend on an undefined "place of business".660 The rules defining a contract party's "place of business" in ECC Article 6 make its place of dispatch rules more useful.

The MLEC rule on data message errors only addresses the recipient's presumptive right to rely on the message content as received.661 Its lack of a rule on a sender's right to correct errors in data input might require contract parties to resort to evidence of trade usage where the ECC is not the governing law.

c) Comparison with E-SIGN and UETA Rules

The U.S. statutes on electronic contract communications that are comparable to the Electronic Contracts Convention are: 1) the Electronic Signatures in Global and National Commerce Act662(E-SIGN), which applies to transactions in or affecting interstate or foreign commerce663 (unless replaced, with respect to U.S. state law only, either by state legislation incorporating the version of the Uniform Electronic Transactions Act recommended by the National

Conference of Commissioners on Uniform State Laws in 1999 or by sufficiently similar legislation664); and 2) the Uniform Electronic Transactions Act665(UETA). Because E-SIGN, UETA and the ECC each derive many of their rules from the U.N. Model Law on Electronic Commerce, they are very similar. Major differences between ECC rules and either E-SIGN or UETA rules are described below.

The ECC broadly excludes from its application "[c]ontracts concluded for personal, family or household purposes"666, with further exclusions for various types of regulated contracts667 and financial contracts.668 E-SIGN exempts from its application various wills and estates law, family law and commercial contracts (other than sales and leases), but it applies generally to consumer contracts.669 UETA also excludes wills and estates-related contracts, and other contracts specified by state law, but it also applies generally to consumer contracts.670

The ECC671 and UETA672 allow their applicable rules to be changed by agreement of the contract parties. The ECC allows the parties to exclude the convention from applying to their contract at all.673 UETA applies only if the contract parties have agreed to conduct transactions by electronic means.674 Although E-SIGN may be replaced by UETA with respect to U.S. state law on electronic contracts675, E-SIGN's rules, particularly regarding consumer disclosure and consumer protection, will remain mandatory law for all transactions in or affecting interstate or foreign commerce.676

E-SIGN677 and UETA678 include various rules regarding presentation of electronic versions of notices and disclosures, and receipt of electronic records, particularly those required for consumer protection. The ECC does not apply to consumer contracts, and disclaims any effect on requirements for information disclosure under other laws.679

CUECIC Article 9.2 provides functional tests for proof of the existence of an electronic writing, by requiring that "the information contained therein is accessible so as to be useable for subsequent reference."680 E-SIGN and UETA do not include similar tests.

CUECIC Article 9.3 provides functional tests for proof of an electronic signature by a contract party. E-SIGN and UETA do not include similar tests, although UETA allows proof that an electronic signature was the act of a specific person "by a showing of the efficacy of any security procedure applied to determine the person".681

CUECIC Article 9.4 provides functional tests for proof of an electronic original. E-SIGN and UETA provide functional tests for retention of records 682, and original documents683, pursuant to other laws. E-SIGN and UETA also provide rules for the electronic retention of bank checks.684

The ECC685 and UETA686 provide rules for the time and place of sending and receipt of electronic communications for contract transactions. E-SIGN does not include these types of rules.

CUECIC Article 11 provides a rule on invitations for offers.687 Neither E-SIGN nor UETA provides a similar rule.

The ECC688 and UETA689 provide similar rules for the correction of input errors in communications between individuals and automated systems. E-SIGN does not include this type of rule.

CHAPTER 4 – A Short History of Alternative Dispute Resolution (ADR)

a) A Short History of Arbitration

Alternative Dispute Resolution (ADR) is the term applied to a variety of procedures used to resolve legal disputes outside of formal litigation in government courts. These procedures have increased in number and importance in national and international law since the mid-twentieth century. Before then, arbitration was used primarily to resolve disputes between nations and, in the United States, to resolve labor disputes.

Arbitration is a set of procedures agreed to by parties to resolve their legal dispute according to the decision of a private, independent arbitrator, or panel of arbitrators. The arbitrators examine the facts of the dispute according to informal procedures and rules. For example, there are no formal rules of evidence, like the hearsay rule, or formal discovery procedures, like depositions.

Arbitration is usually agreed to, either before or after a legal dispute arises, for four reasons: 1) arbitration is believed to be a faster way to resolve the dispute than court litigation; 2) arbitration is believed to be a less expensive way to resolve the dispute than court litigation; 3) arbitration is believed to be a better way to resolve the dispute than court litigation, because (unlike litigation where the parties cannot choose their judges) the parties can choose arbitrators who have technical and/or legal experience with the subject matter of the dispute; and 4) the facts of the dispute and the details of the arbitrators' decision may be kept confidential, unlike the public record of court litigation.

Merchants' guilds and other trade organizations arbitrated disputes among their members for many centuries. The first major arbitration of a legal dispute between nations was the case between the United Kingdom and the United States of America of the *Alabama* warship. After the U.S. civil war, an ad hoc arbitration panel was created by the U.K. and the U.S. to resolve a U.S. claim that the U.K. had violated its duties as a neutral state under international law in the U.S. civil war. The U.K. was alleged to have allowed the Confederate States to build a warship, the *Alabama*, in an English port, which later fought against the U.S. The arbitration panel decided in favor of the U.S. and ordered a monetary award against the U.K. The award was voluntarily paid by the U.K. The arbitrators had no power to enforce the award. The success of the Alabama arbitration led to other arbitrations of disputes between nations in the 19th century. The value of arbitration as an alternative to war eventually led to the creation of the Permanent Court of Arbitration in The Hague, Netherlands, as a permanent forum for such international disputes.

Non-state arbitrations entered U.S. law primarily as an adjunct to union-management labor agreements, which recognized the rights of labor unions to collectively negotiate labor contracts for their members. When contract negotiations failed, or when grievances governed by contracts arose, arbitration was sometimes required by the agreements, and was enforced through federal labor laws.690

Beginning in the 1970s, the use of arbitration outside of union contract negotiations increased. In that decade, many federal and state consumer protection laws were enacted, such as the Truth-In-Lending Act, the Fair Credit Reporting Act, and the Equal Credit Opportunity Act. In litigation, a new "class action" procedure began to be used successfully by lawyers to seek monetary damages for groups of consumers. These consumers had suffered similar injuries through the similar negligence of, or the contract breaches of, a seller of goods or services. In both class actions and individual lawsuits, tort punitive damages sometimes greatly increased the size of money judgments.

Because of these large judgments, defendants selling goods or services to consumers in mass markets in the 1980s began to try to restrict access to class actions by requiring consumers to agree to arbitration of future legal disputes in take-it-or-leave-it, non-negotiable contracts. (The contract cases discussing these arbitration clauses in the context of electronic contracts are discussed in Part B.) Few arbitration procedures conducted under these contracts allow for arbitration of group claims in a manner similar to class action litigation. Even if class arbitration of claims is allowed, defendants will often prefer arbitration rather than litigation of group claims, because there are no juries in arbitration, arbitrators are more likely to understand the technical facts in a case, consumer lawyers are less likely to win large fee awards, and the details of arbitration decisions and awards are confidential and will not be disclosed to the public.

In many cases, however, arbitration can be as beneficial for consumers as it is for businesses. Accelerated resolution of disputes, because arbitration cases are not placed behind criminal and other civil cases on court dockets, and lower costs from more informal fact-finding procedures may encourage consumers to prefer arbitration to litigation. This is especially true if arbitration costs and fees are agreed to be paid by business defendants.

b) Mediation and Small Claims Courts

Sometimes the resolution of a legal dispute can be made easier through the actions of a neutral third party to bring the disputing parties together to discuss the reasons for their problems and possible solutions. A mediator will not have authority to resolve the dispute, and will usually not make any recommendation on possible resolutions. The mediator's role is to open and maintain the "lines of communication" between the parties so that they understand each other's perspectives and positions, and have an informal forum in which to discuss settlement of their dispute.

Many civil (non-criminal) cases filed in U.S. state and federal courts are resolved before trial through voluntary settlements. Many courts require civil case litigants to participate in mediation meetings prior to trial, because such meetings will often lead to offers for settlements, which, if accepted, save significant government (and taxpayer) expense by avoiding expensive trials.

Many legal disputes, especially those involving consumers, involve a small amount of money relative to the cost of litigation. Small claims court is a popular alternative, in the United States, to class action group litigation for small dollar legal disputes, which do not involve facts common to many consumers. Small claims courts are actual state government courts whose jurisdiction covers only civil claims for money damages below a specified threshold. In 2012, $5,000 is a typical "ceiling" for the jurisdiction of a small claims court.691 If a consumer and a provider of goods or services are both within the personal jurisdiction of a small claims court, its procedures may provide many of the advantages of arbitration. These are: 1) informal procedures for the presentation of facts and legal arguments that do not require legal education or training; 2) faster scheduling and resolution of hearings than regular litigation; and 3) lower expense for the consumer than regular litigation, because the consumer can (and usually does) represent herself in small claims court, thereby avoiding attorneys' fees and costs.

CHAPTER 5 - Organization of American States (OAS) Proposals for Consumer Dispute Resolution

Online consumer purchases across national borders of goods and services have increased with the growth of the internet. Individual consumers do not have the same bargaining power as businesses, however, to negotiate their desired methods of dispute resolution. For consumers to gain confidence in their ability to resolve their disputes with international online retailers, a means for resolution of their disputes will probably need to come either from the retailers themselves (through, for example limited money-back guarantees), or through procedures established through multi-lateral governmental forums. Litigation for relatively small consumer transactions is often cost-prohibitive, even in domestic forums. Foreign or international litigation of consumer disputes would add even higher costs for travel, transportation and language translation. Therefore, most proposals for resolution of international online consumer contract disputes focus on dispute resolution conducted online through the internet.

The New York Convention on the Recognition and Enforcement of Foreign Arbitral Awards (New York Convention)692 covers arbitral awards involving consumers. It allows ratifying nations, however, to exclude by declaration from their version of the convention non-commercial arbitral awards.693 The existing New York Convention procedures for recognition of foreign arbitral awards could, therefore, be applied to international electronic contracts between consumers and businesses, especially if any nations that have made declarations excluding non-commercial awards amend them to allow the convention to apply to consumer disputes. This is the basis for one of several online dispute resolution mechanisms for such contracts being considered by the Organization of American States.

a) OAS Proposals for Consumer Online Dispute Resolution (ODR)

The Organization of American States (OAS) was created in 1948 as a regional organization of member nations.694 The OAS has promoted its goals of regional democracy, human rights, security and development through "hard law" treaties/conventions, through "soft law" model laws, and through networks of government representatives providing technical assistance for the implementation of treaties and agreements.

In 2008, Brazil, Argentina and Paraguay made a revised proposal for an OAS Convention on Consumer Protection and Choice of Law (the Buenos Aires Proposal), which is designed to establish choice-of-law rules that favor consumers in international contracts between them and business providers of goods and services.695 The U.S. delegation to the OAS expressed doubts regarding the utility of a binding international convention for consumer protection, given the expense of litigation and the uncertainties of application and enforcement of complex conflict-of- laws and jurisdiction rules.696

As an alternative to the Buenos Aires Proposal, the U.S. delegation proposed four complementary approaches to the resolution of disputes related to international sales of goods and services by businesses to consumers through the internet697: 1) promotion of, and adoption by members of, legislation based on a Model Law/Cooperative Framework for Electronic Resolution of Cross-Border E-Commerce Consumer Disputes (Model Law on ODR)698; 2) promotion of, and adoption by members of, legislation based on a Model Law for Alternate Dispute Resolution of Consumer Payment Card Claims (Model Law on Payment Card ADR)699; 3) promotion of, and adoption by members (who do not already have such procedures) of, legislation based on a Model Law on Small Claims700; and 4) promotion of, and adoption by members of, legislation based on a Model Law on Government Redress for Consumers Including Across

Borders (Model Law on Government Redress).701

In presenting these proposals to the OAS, the U.S. delegation noted the European Union Parliament's preference for procedures progressing through the following sequence based on the extent of effort required by individual consumers.702 The proposed procedures address only consumer complaints against businesses.703 They begin with complaints to consumer organizations and public authorities, advance to collective alternative/online dispute resolution, advance to individual alternative/online dispute resolution, advance to small claims court litigation, and culminate with class action/collective litigation or individual litigation. The following description of the U.S. proposals proceeds in the same order and also recognizes the corresponding extent of legal innovation required to accomplish the proposals.

Many OAS member-nations have legislation or credit card systems that protect consumers from unauthorized charges due to loss or theft. Fewer members protect consumers against non-conformity or non-delivery of goods.704

Like the U.S. Fair Credit Billing Act (FCBA) and Electronic Fund Transfer Act discussed hereafter, the Model Law on Payment Card ADR would permit consumers to make claims to their credit card issuers of alleged errors, unauthorized or incorrect charges, or charges for goods or services not accepted or delivered as agreed (but excluding quality disputes).705

A time limit for consumer notice of a claim to a card issuer of 60 days from receipt of an erroneous statement would apply.706 A card issuer would be required to investigate and resolve the consumer claim within certain time limits, or would have to re-credit the consumer's account. Various other rules would apply regarding collection of credit charges and re-crediting of debit charges during an investigation, and consumer cooperation with the issuer's investigation. As in the FCBA, a consumer could defend an action by the card issuer to collect the disputed charge on the same grounds that it could use in good faith to defend a collection action by the seller of goods or services.707

The Model Law on ODR would establish state-sponsored arrangements for online resolution of small consumer disputes related to international transactions. Nations with existing online dispute resolution (ODR) systems would use the proposal as a cooperative framework, while nations without such systems would implement their version of the model law in national legislation. The proposed system could be operated on a trial basis to determine whether it should be implemented permanently.708

A multi-state online system would be created to facilitate negotiations between businesses and consumers. Business participation in the ODR system would be voluntary. Businesses would possibly be motivated to participate by the assurance to their customers of a state-sponsored method of inexpensive online redress for their complaints. Businesses would pay all of the cost of the online arbitration.709

If a negotiated settlement were not reached, an online arbitrator would be appointed by a government entity in the location of the business to make a binding decision and award. The same limited appeals of ODR awards would be permitted as are provided by national law for other arbitration awards.710 All information or documents submitted by a party to an ODR provider/arbitrator would remain confidential, but ODR providers/arbitrators would be allowed to inform government consumer protection authorities about possible fraud by a business.711

The Model Law on Government Redress would establish national consumer protection authorities, empower them to obtain redress for consumers, and enable them to cooperate with their foreign counterparts, and to pursue enforcement across borders of judgments for consumer redress.712 The 2006 U.S. SAFEWEB Act is cited as an example of this type of international cooperation for consumer protection.713

Public authorities would be able to obtain monetary redress for economic harm to consumers from fraudulent or deceptive commercial practices through administrative, civil, criminal or collective actions. They would have the power to investigate and to preserve the confidentiality of business or personal information. Judgments obtained by authorities for consumers would be recognized for enforcement purposes by foreign courts as equivalent to judgments obtained by consumers.

Current OAS member laws on small claims judicial procedures vary significantly.714 European Union regulations established common small claims court rules and procedures in 2007.715 The proposed Model Law on Small Claims covers only business sales to consumers. It would provide redress for damages for breach of contract, damages to personal property, personal injury to the claimant or other economic harm.716 Claimants and businesses (their agents or owners) would be allowed to represent themselves, or be represented by other non-lawyers. Hearings would be based on written submissions, unless requested by a party and permitted by the court, or unless required by a court. Hearings through audio, video or other communications technology would also be allowed. Courts could provide remedies of damages, rescission, restitution, reformation and specific performance.717 Appeals of judgments would not require representation by a lawyer.718

The U.S. proposal encourages member states to adopt legislation permitting representational or collective legal actions for consumer with common claims.719 In the U.S., these are known as "class actions". Like small claims lawsuits, they are promoted as a practical way for the redress of legal grievances that are individually too small to justify the usual expense of hiring a private attorney. This proposal would allow consumers of one member state to participate in a collective action brought in the courts of a different member state.720

b) U.S. Fair Credit Billing Act and Electronic Fund Transfer Act Chargeback Rules

The proposed Model Law on Payment Card ADR adopts elements of two consumer finance protection laws enacted in the United States during the 1970s. The Fair Credit Billing Act721(FCBA) requires credit card issuers to provide, for credit card transactions, procedures by which consumers can dispute alleged billing errors. These errors include:

- charges not authorized by the consumer
- charges in the wrong amount
- charges for goods and services not accepted by the consumer
- charges for goods and services not delivered as agreed
- failure to properly reflect payments or credits to an account
- calculation errors
- charges for which that the consumer requests clarification or proof722

The FCBA gives consumers 60 days from receipt of their credit card billing statement to send a written dispute of the alleged error to their card issuer. The card issuer must respond to the dispute, investigate the alleged error, and either correct the error by crediting the consumer's account, or explain why no error occurred.723

If a credit card issuer fails to comply with the FCBA billing error procedures, it loses the right to collect the disputed amount and any related finance charges, but only up to $50.724 Consumers may bring private individual lawsuits against card issuers to recover disputed amounts.725 The Federal Trade Commission is responsible for the administrative enforcement of the FCBA and a complaint may be filed with this agency by a consumer regarding card issuer violations of the FCBA.726

The Electronic Fund Transfer Act727(EFTA), and Regulation E of the Federal Reserve Board728 implementing the EFTA, provides procedures for consumers to resolve alleged errors in the electronic transfer of funds by financial institutions. These errors include unauthorized electronic transfers, incorrect transfers, and failure to document or clarify electronic transfers pursuant to a consumer request made to determine whether an error exists.729

Consumers must notify the financial institution within 60 days of receipt of the statement in which the alleged error is first reflected. The financial institution is required to investigate, determine whether an error occurred, and report its findings to the consumer within certain time limits. For example, if the financial institution does not complete its investigation of the alleged error within 10 business days of notice by the consumer, it may take another 45 days to complete its investigation, but it may be required to provisionally credit the consumer's account in the disputed amount.730 A financial institution that fails to follow these rules to re-credit an account, and fails to either make a good faith investigation or to have a reasonable basis for believing in the absence of an error, may be liable to a consumer in a private lawsuit for triple the amount of actual damages plus attorney's fees.731 Class actions are also permitted against financial institutions for violations of the EFTA and Regulation E.732 Various regulatory agencies, including the FTC are responsible for enforcing the EFTA and Regulation E.

CHAPTER 6 – European Union Proposals for Consumer Online Dispute Resolution

In 2011, the European Commission proposed a Regulation on Online Dispute Resolution for Consumer Disputes733(Consumer ODR Regulation) for the online sale of goods or services between a member state "trader" and a member state consumer. A related Proposal for a Directive on Alternative Dispute Resolution for Consumer Disputes734(Consumer ADR Directive) would require all member states to enact legislation to enable all disputes between a consumer and a trader to be submitted to alternative dispute resolution, including online dispute resolution.

On March 12, 2013, the European Parliament adopted at first reading the proposed Consumer ODR Regulation.735 Under the Regulation, a clearinghouse online ODR platform would receive all trader or consumer requests for alternative dispute resolution. It would then transfer the requests to a registered member state ADR platform that would be competent to resolve it under its own rules of procedure. Traders engaging in cross-border e-commerce within the European Union would be required to inform consumers about the ADR platform.

Consumers and traders would be obligated to use a specific ADR entity, however, only if they agree to do so.736 ADR decisions could be either binding or non-binding on the parties.737 The results of online dispute resolution, therefore, would not always preclude either consumers or traders from exercising their rights to seek redress through litigation. Therefore, the system could act like a non-binding mediation, which could limit its attractiveness to some traders and consumers.

CHAPTER 7 - United Nations Proposals for Consumer Online Dispute Resolution

As of July 2012, the proposals of the Working Group III of the United Nations Commission on International Trade Law (UNCITRAL) for online dispute resolution (ODR) for cross-border electronic commerce transactions contemplate their application only to low-value transactions for goods and services for both business-to-business and business-to-consumer transactions.738 All procedures would be voluntarily agreed to by contract. They would not override mandatory domestic law, and they would not prevent either party from resort to litigation. Three phases of ODR would be covered: 1) party negotiations; 2) arbitrator-facilitated settlement of the dispute; and 3) arbitration by a neutral/arbitrator leading to a binding decision. ODR arbitral decisions would be final, binding and not subject to appeals on the substance of the dispute.

The proposals recognize that enforcement procedures for voluntary dispute settlements vary greatly among different legal systems and may not be amenable to harmonization either through treaties or model laws. Voluntary compliance by businesses with arbitral awards against them is the primary expected mode of enforcement.739

If judicial enforcement of an arbitral award becomes necessary, the New York Convention on the Recognition and Enforcement of Foreign Arbitral Awards ("New York Convention") could serve as a vehicle for enforcement. It has been adopted by more nations than any other U.N. commercial treaty. It requires common national legislative standards for the recognition of arbitration agreements, and for court recognition and enforcement of foreign arbitral awards.

Article 20 of the United Nations Convention on the Use of Electronic Communications in International Contracts (CUECIC, the ECC, or the Electronic Contracts Convention) provides that its rules apply to communications in connection with the formation or performance of a contract to which the New York Convention applies, if a nation ratifying the ECC has also ratified the New York Convention.740 The ECC became effective on March 1, 2013.

The ECC does not apply to consumer contracts. Nevertheless, the principles of functional equivalence between printed and electronic communications, expressed in the ECC, the UNCITRAL Model Law on International Commercial Arbitration, and in various national laws based on the U.N. Model Law on Electronic Commerce, should be applied to foreign arbitration awards subject to the New York Convention, which does not specify any form requirements for an award. If binding online arbitration awards were enforceable under the New York Convention, they should include awards in business-to-consumer contract disputes in which the agreement to arbitrate is documented by a click-wrap agreement. Similarly, the procedural requirements of an original and signed version of the arbitration award to be enforced should be satisfied by their electronic equivalents under the principles of these international laws.741

The validity of pre-dispute consent by consumers to arbitration agreements, and the eligibility for arbitration of consumer disputes, would depend on national law.742 Voluntary compliance by businesses with arbitral awards could be encouraged through independent certifications of merchant compliance and related notices to consumers.743 The issue of the applicable substantive law that would apply to ODR disputes remains to be resolved.744

PART D - CONCLUSION

Most United States common law and statutory requirements for contract formation and enforcement remain essentially as they have been for many decades. These requirements change very slowly through the "conservative incrementalism" that is a practical requirement of any effective legal system.745 Offer and acceptance, objective evidence of agreement to contract terms, consideration or detrimental reliance justifying legal enforcement of promises, absence of defenses to contract enforcement, and limited remedies provided for contract breach are the main issues of the U.S. law of contracts.

The resolution of disputes regarding these issues involves every type of commercial and personal activity in which people, and the organizations through which they act, are involved. The proliferation of individual electronic communications through the internet in the late 20th century raised novel questions about the application of writing and signature requirements under long-existing Statute of Frauds state and federal statutes in the U.S., and under similar requirements in other nations. New national and sub-national statutes, such as the E-SIGN federal statute and the UETA state statutes in the U.S., have mostly resolved the basic questions of the legal equivalence of electronic communications with printed communications in the formation and enforcement of commercial and consumer contracts.

Legal issues that are less amenable to statutory rules are addressed in the U.S. through judicial decisions in "adversary proceedings" litigation concerning actual controversies between parties with specific interests. For example, the requirement of objective evidence of acceptance of contract offer terms, and the applicability of the unconscionability defense, have necessitated judicial application of old principles of the common law of contracts to new contexts of web site pages, hyperlinks, e-mail and text messages. In nations with civil law, rather than common law, legal systems, control of specific types of electronic contracts for the protection of businesses, and especially for the protection of consumers, is more likely to develop from administrative regulation rather than from litigation in courts.

The transnational structure of the internet eliminates geographic and temporal barriers to contracting. The first of the important remaining barriers to increased international trade in goods and services through the internet is the absence of country-neutral international electronic contract law (other than international customary law) for the sale of goods between businesses. The ratification of the Convention on the Use of Electronic Communications in International Contracts by the United States (its primary proponent) and by other major trading nations will provide an important starting point for the gradual development of this type of law.

The second remaining important barrier to increased international trade through the internet is the lack of confidence of consumers in the availability of fair and expedited dispute resolution procedures for contract-related complaints. Although multilateral treaties have been proposed to establish legal rules for international sale of goods and services to consumers, the variety of public policies expressed in national consumer protection laws and procedures make such treaties difficult to establish. Experimentation with various dispute resolution procedures has been proposed by the United States to the Organization of American States, and has been implemented to a certain extent by the European Union. These proposals might provide consumer purchasers of goods and services across national borders with increased confidence in the fairness of dispute resolution for their complaints sooner than would treaty solutions. These proposed procedures include international standards for small claims courts, government representation of consumers with common complaints against businesses, voluntary and certified business compliance with dispute resolution procedures that are fair to consumers, and neutral clearinghouses for inexpensive and expedited online resolution of consumer disputes.

Scientists and engineers are developing methods of electronic communications that stretch the imagination. It is the duty of lawyers, judges, legislators, diplomats, and business and consumer advocates to work to develop laws and procedures that support the benefits of these technologies, while also providing the protection and fairness to businesses and consumers of contract law as an essential element of economic development and human progress.

ADDITIONAL ONLINE RESOURCES

Additional information and resources on contract law are available at the web sites

www.every1sguide.com

www.charleshmartin.com

Appendix A – Annotated Example Contract

[Because contracts, like people, come in all shapes and sizes, I have included this sample contract for your possible enjoyment. This is an example of a contract that a "reality tv" or "game show" contestant might be required to sign in order to appear on a program. It might be combined with an application to appear on the program. It contains many of the typical terms of an entertainment services contract, and, unless you are already a performer with negotiating leverage, would not be negotiable. Sections of the contract that contain legal concepts and rules referred to in the chapters of this book have annotations in brackets referring to the places where these concepts and rules are discussed. Because this sample contains only some of many possible provisions included in such a contract, it should not be considered representative of any particular contract.]

I. TERMS AND CONDITIONS

1. I am 18 years of age or older.

[See Part A, Chapter 7, a) i) on defense of minority/age-based incapacity to contract.]

2. I will not compete against, or appear on the program with any person who is an acquaintance, friend or relative, unless the Producer has been notified of such relationship prior to my appearance on any such program, and a determination regarding my eligibility shall be made by the Producer.

3. I agree not to participate in any manner on any other game show or reality show until six (6) months after the initial broadcast of each and any of my appearances on the program. I have not taped an appearance on any other television game or reality show which has been (or may be) aired within one year of my appearance on this program. I recognize that a breach by me of any part of this paragraph would cause Producer irreparable injury and damage that cannot be reasonably or adequately compensated by damages

in an action at law and, therefore, I hereby expressly agree that Producer shall be entitled to injunctive and other equitable relief to prevent and/or cure any breach or threatened breach of this paragraph by me.

[See Part A, Chapter 7, d) on public policy and covenants not to compete.] [See Part A, Chapter 8, g) on injunctive relief enforcement of contract duties.]

4. I am not a candidate for any public office, and I agree not to accept any candidacy until after the initial broadcast of my appearance on the program.

5. I will not make any unauthorized mention or "plug" of any commercial product, service, venture or thing on the air, including the name of my employer. Neither I nor anyone acting for me is giving or receiving any monies or other valuable consideration to get me on the program or to mention anything on the program. I am aware that my giving or receiving any such monies or other valuable consideration is a Federal offense (payola) punishable by fine and/or imprisonment. I am further aware that it is a Federal offense punishable by fine and/or imprisonment for anyone to rig the outcome of the program with the intent to deceive the viewing public, or to offer or accept any special or secret assistance in connection with the program. I agree that I will not participate in any such acts, and that if anyone tries to induce me to do any such acts, I will immediately notify a representative of _____.

[See Part A, Chapter 6, a) i) on express conditions.]

6. I understand that Producer's selecting me as a contestant for the program, or for any special program thereof, is within Producer's sole discretion irrespective of any tests I may have taken, any score I may have achieved, any prize(s) I may have won or otherwise, and that Producer's inviting me to the studio or other location does not guarantee my appearance on the program. If I am selected to participate on the program, Producer nevertheless is under no obligation to

afford me the opportunity to appear, and if I appear on a recorded program, or any part thereof, Producer has no obligation to broadcast the program, or any part thereof. If I do appear on the program, Producer may terminate my participation at any time, at Producer's discretion. I agree that the Producer's decision on all discretionary matters, including but not limited to all decisions regarding the correctness or incorrectness of all contestant responses given in the course of the program, shall be final. If I notice any irregularity or impropriety in contestant selection, briefing, or the taping or play of the program, I shall inform a representative of ____. I agree that all travel in connection with my qualification for or participation on the program except as otherwise expressly agreed in writing between myself and Producer, is my sole responsibility, risk, cost, and expense, regardless of whether or not I am selected to be on the program.

[See Part A, Chapter 5, b) on implied contract terms, including good faith in performance.][See Part A, Chapter 6, a) i) on express conditions, a) ii) on implied constructive conditions, and b) on total, partial and material breach.]

7. I understand that any appearance that I may make on the program is strictly for the purpose of participating in the program as a contestant. Except as specifically provided herein or as otherwise authorized by Producer, I will not myself, or authorize others to, advertise or promote my appearance on the program or receive or generate any monetary advantage from my appearance on the program. Without limiting the foregoing in any way, I will not myself, or authorize others to, prepare or assist in the preparation of any written work, any audio work, and/or any visual work that depicts, concerns, or relates in any way to my appearance on the program. I agree not to disclose winners, outcome or any content of any episode of the program prior to telecast. I recognize that a breach by me of this paragraph would cause Producer irreparable injury and damage that cannot be reasonably or adequately compensated by damages in an action at law and, therefore, I hereby expressly agree that

Producer shall be entitled to injunctive and other equitable relief to prevent and/or cure any breach or threatened breach of this paragraph by me.

[See Part A, Chapter 8, g) on injunctive relief enforcement of contract duties.][See Part A, Chapter 6, c) on anticipatory repudiation.] [See Part A, Chapter 5, b) on implied contract terms, including good faith in performance.] [See Part A, Chapter 6, a) i) on express conditions, a) ii) on implied constructive conditions, and b) on total, partial and material breach.]

8. Prior to my appearance on the program, I was advised in detail of all the rules regarding the program and agree to abide by them. Further, I understand that Producer reserves the right to change, add to, delete from, modify, or amend the rules at Producer's sole discretion.

[See Part A, Chapter 5, b) on implied contract terms, including good faith in performance.]

9. I have observed, and will continue to abide by, any and all rules and decisions made by Producer concerning my qualifications, participation on the program, selection of opponents, interviews with me, and the selection and awarding of prizes, cash or gifts, if any. Further, I have observed and will abide by all of the other rules and regulations prescribed by the Producer, and will follow all of the Producer's directions regarding my qualifications for, and participation on, the program. I understand that my selection as a contestant on the program is based upon my acceptance of all of the terms and conditions contained in this form. Any breach of this agreement by me will entitle Producer to terminate my participation in the program.

[See Part A, Chapter 5, b) on implied contract terms, including good faith in performance and enforcement.][See Part A, Chapter 6, b) on total, partial and material breach.]

10. I hereby grant to Producer, its successors, licensees, and

assignees, the non-exclusive but irrevocable perpetual and worldwide right and license to photograph me and/or to use my likeness, voice, name, biographical material and any remarks I may make in connection with the production, distribution, exhibition, advertising and other exploitation of the program throughout the universe by any method and in all media now known or hereafter devised, including, without limitation, the right to use the program or any portion of the program in which I appear in any interactive, online or computer-assisted media for any purpose whatsoever, without further compensation to me. I agree that the telecast or other exploitation of the program in which I appear will not entitle me to receive any additional prizes, cash or gifts. I shall cooperate by making available and furnishing any information or material that is requested of me. The photographs, tapes, movies and recording of everything I say or do on the program will be owned by Producer to do with as Producer wishes at any time in the future, as often as Producer wishes; the program or any part thereof can be rearranged or added to other material without payment to me of any kind whatsoever.

[See Part A, Chapter 5, b) on implied contract terms, including good faith in performance.]

11. All information that has been, is hereby or at any time will be related by me to the Producer is true and accurate, including all information regarding my occupation. If at any time, I become aware of any information related about or attributed to me which is inaccurate or misleading, I will immediately inform the Producer. If any disclosures or representations made by me hereunder are false or if I breach any provisions hereof, Producer may withhold any prize which I would otherwise have won and Producer may make any explanation, announcement, on-air or otherwise, which Producer and _____ may choose. I hereby agree to indemnify Producer and all those Released Parties described below in Paragraph _____, and hold Producer and them harmless from all liability, claims, actions, damages, expenses,

and losses of any nature whatsoever caused by or arising out of any statement or action of mine made on or in connection with my participation on the program.

[See Part A, Chapter 5, b) on implied contract terms, including good faith in performance and enforcement.][See Part A, Chapter 6, a), i) on express conditions.][See Part B, Chapter 9, d) on notice of terms, including *A. V. v. iParadigms, LLC* "Turnitin" case with indemnification requirement.]

12. I certify that all of the statements herein contained are true. I understand that contestants must meet all eligibility requirements for all purposes, including the right to receive cash or prizes. I further understand that the Producer reserves the right to require me to forfeit my appearance on the program and/or all prizes and awards credited to me, if any, if the information or representations made by me in this form are false whether by intention, inadvertence, or mistake, or if I fail to abide by this agreement, whether or not the program on which I appear is broadcast.

[See Part A, Chapter 5, b) on implied contract terms, including good faith in performance and enforcement.]

13. After my first appearance, I agree that I may continue to appear on the program as long as I am the winning contestant. I may choose to forfeit my right to continued appearances as returning champion upon notification prior to the taping of the next scheduled program to the Producer, which shall be confirmed in writing. I understand that my continued appearance as returning champion is subject to my availability for the next regularly scheduled tape date and/or for the taping of the next scheduled program, and that if I am unable to appear on that date and/or that time, I forfeit my right to any continued appearances on the show.

[See Part A, Chapter 5, b) on implied contract terms, including good faith in performance.]

14. Any prizes will be delivered to my address indicated above, or to the closest feasible place for pickup by me. I shall pay all shipping costs for deliveries outside the continental United States. Producer shall not be responsible for any delays in delivery of a prize, or for the condition in which it is delivered.

15. Any travel and lodging won by me cannot be assigned, transferred, exchanged, sold or redeemed for cash or credit. Only I may take any trip I win. I must take any trip within one year of the program's original airdate. All trips originate in Los Angeles, California.

[See Part A, Chapter 4, e) i) on assignability of rights.]

16. My refusal to accept any prize, or my failure to advise Producer within twelve (12) months of the original air date of the program in which I appear of the failure to receive any prize, shall release Producer and all others connected with the program of all obligations in connection with such prize. If for any reason the prize I win cannot be supplied, I shall accept either a prize of comparable value or a cash amount equal to the actual out-of-pocket cost to Producer of the prize I won, at Producer's sole discretion. If I wish to forfeit for income tax or other purpose any prize, cash or gift received, I shall give written notification of such forfeiture within two (2) weeks of my participation on the program. I acknowledge that my forfeiture of any prize releases Producer of all obligations to me in connection with such prize, cash or gift.

[See Part A, Chapter 5, b) on implied contract terms, including good faith in performance.]

17. If I decide to sell any item given to me by reason of my participation on the program, I agree not to advertise, directly or indirectly, in any media, that such item was given to me, or received by me, on the program.

18. I agree to pay federal, state and city taxes including

income, use or sales taxes or any other governmental charges imposed on prizes, cash or gifts, if any, given to me, or received by me, by reason of my participation on the program, and I release and indemnify the Producer from any liability therefore. I authorize the Producer to deduct or withhold any such taxes or charges or require their payment prior to delivery of said prizes, cash or gifts. [See Part B, Chapter 9, d) on notice of terms, including *A.V. v. iParadigms, LLC* "Turnitin" case with indemnification requirement.]

19. The provisions of this agreement shall be binding upon me and my heirs, executors and administrators and the rights herein granted to you may be assigned by you to any person, firm or corporation.

[See Part A, Chapter 4, e) on contract parties.]

20. The name given below is my legal name. Any other name(s) or alias(es) used by me are noted above. The Social Security number furnished is my true Social Security number and not that of any other person.

21. I RELEASE THE PRODUCER OF ___ , AND ALL OF THE DIRECTORS, OFFICERS, EMPLOYEES, SUCCESSORS, ASSIGNEES, AGENTS AND LICENSEES AND EACH OF THEM (HEREIN THE "RELEASED PARTIES") FROM ANY AND ALL CLAIMS ARISING OUT OF MY INJURY OR DAMAGE TO ME AS A RESULT OF, OR BY REASON OF, MY PARTICIPATION ON _____, OR FROM ANY USE OF ANY PRIZE OR GIFT AWARDED TO ME ON ____. I AGREE THAT I WILL NOT BRING OR BE A PARTY TO ANY LAWSUIT OR CLAIM AGAINST THE RELEASED PARTIES, BASED UPON OR ARISING FROM MY PARTICIPATION ON THE PROGRAM OR AN EXPLOITATION THEREOF, OR FROM ANY GIFTS OR PRIZES GIVEN TO ME ON _____OR ANY LEGAL THEORY (INCLUDING, BUT NOT LIMITED TO, PERSONAL INJURY, RIGHTS OF PRIVACY AND PUBLICITY OR DEFAMATION) WHATSOEVER. IN THE EVENT A LAWSUIT OR CLAIM SHOULD BE BROUGHT TO ENFORCE THE TERMS OF THIS CONTESTANT APPLICATION, RELEASE AND CONSENT, THE PREVAILING PARTY SHALL BE AWARDED ALL ATTORNEY'S FEES AND COSTS INCURRED.

[See Part A, Chapter 5, b) on implied contract terms, including good faith in performance and enforcement.][See Part A, Chapter 8, d) on restrictions on incidental and consequential damages.][See Part B, Chapter 9, d) on notice of terms, including *A.V. v. iParadigms, LLC* "Turnitin" case with indemnification requirement.]

ANY CONTROVERSY OR CLAIM ARISING OUT OF OR RELATING TO THIS AGREEMENT, ITS ENFORCEMENT, ARBITRABILITY OR INTERPRETATION SHALL BE SUBMITTED TO FINAL AND BINDING ARBITRATION, TO BE HELD IN LOS ANGELES COUNTY, CALIFORNIA, BEFORE A SINGLE ARBITRATOR, IN ACCORDANCE WITH

CALIFORNIA CODE OF CIVIL PROCEDURE §§ 1280 ET SEQ. THE ARBITRATOR SHALL BE SELECTED BY MUTUAL AGREEMENT OF THE PARTIES OR, IF THE PARTIES CANNOT AGREE, THEN BY STRIKING FROM A LIST OF ARBITRATORS SUPPLIED BY THE AMERICAN ARBITRATION ASSOCIATION OR JAMS/ENDISPUTE. THE ARBITRATION SHALL BE A CONFIDENTIAL PROCEEDING, CLOSED TO THE GENERAL PUBLIC. THE ARBITRATOR SHALL ISSUE A WRITTEN OPINION STATING THE ESSENTIAL FINDINGS AND CONCLUSIONS UPON WHICH THE ARBITRATOR'S AWARD IS BASED. THE PARTIES WILL SHARE EQUALLY IN PAYMENT OF THE ARBITRATOR'S FEES AND ARBITRATION EXPENSES AND ANY OTHER COSTS UNIQUE TO THE ARBITRATION HEARING (RECOGNIZING THAT EACH SIDE BEARS ITS OWN DEPOSITION, WITNESS, EXPERT AND ATTORNEYS' FEES AND OTHER EXPENSES TO THE SAME EXTENT AS IF THE MATTER WERE BEING HEARD IN COURT.) NOTHING IN THIS PARAGRAPH SHALL AFFECT EITHER PARTY'S ABILITY TO SEEK FROM A COURT INJUNCTIVE OR EQUITABLE RELIEF AT ANY TIME TO THE EXTENT SAME IS NOT PRECLUDED BY ANOTHER PROVISION OF THIS AGREEMENT.

[See Part A, Chapter 7, d) on unconscionability and public policy.][See Part B, Chapter 9, k) on defenses of substantive and procedural unconscionability.]

I have read the ____Privacy Policy and agree to the terms thereof.

I hereby certify that I have the right to grant the permission and the rights hereby conveyed to you, that the consent of no other party is required to constitute a valid release and consent, that I fully understand the meaning and effect thereof, and I declare under penalty of perjury that the foregoing is true and correct and, intending to be legally bound, I have signed it on

_____

(DATE)

_____

(SIGNATURE)

_____

(PRINT NAME)

Appendix B – Annotated Example Electronic Contract

[This sample electronic contract contains many of the typical terms of a click-wrap contract that you might accept when purchasing digital goods or services on the internet. Sections of the contract that contain legal concepts and rules that are referred to in the chapters of this book have annotations in brackets referring to the places where these concepts and rules are discussed. Because this sample contains only some of many possible provisions included in an online contract, it should not be considered representative of any particular contract.]

TERMS OF SERVICE

THE LEGAL AGREEMENTS SET OUT BELOW GOVERN YOUR USE OF THE SERVICES OF THE COMPANY. TO AGREE TO THESE TERMS, CLICK "AGREE." IF YOU DO NOT AGREE TO THESE TERMS, DO NOT CLICK "AGREE," AND DO NOT USE THE SERVICES.

A. STORE TERMS OF SALE

PAYMENTS, TAXES, AND REFUND POLICY

The Store services ("Services") accept these forms of payment: credit cards issued by U.S. banks and Gift Certificates. If a credit card is used for a transaction, the Company may obtain preapproval for an amount up to the amount of the order. Billing occurs at the time of or shortly after your transaction. If a Gift Certificate is used for a transaction, the amount is deducted at the time of your transaction. When making purchases, a Gift Certificate is used first. Your credit card is then charged for any remaining balance.

You agree that you will pay for all products you purchase through the Services, and that the Company may charge your credit card for any products purchased and for any additional amounts (including any taxes and late fees, as applicable) that may be accrued by or in connection with your Account. YOU ARE RESPONSIBLE FOR THE TIMELY PAYMENT OF ALL FEES AND FOR PROVIDING THE COMPANY WITH VALID CREDIT CARD DETAILS FOR PAYMENT OF ALL FEES. All fees will be billed to the credit card you designate during the registration process. If you want to designate a different credit card or if there is a change in your credit card status, you must change your information online in the Account Information section; this may temporarily disrupt your access to the Services while the Company verifies your new payment information.

Your total price will include the price of the product plus any applicable sales tax; such sales tax is based on the bill-to address and the sales tax rate in effect at the time you download the product. We will charge tax only in states where digital goods are taxable.

All sales and rentals of products are final.

Prices for products offered via the Services may change at any time, and the Services do not provide price protection or refunds in the event of a price reduction or promotional offering.

If a product becomes unavailable following a transaction but prior to download, your sole remedy is a refund. If technical problems prevent or unreasonably delay delivery of your product, your exclusive and sole remedy is either replacement or refund of the price paid, as determined by the Company. [See Part A, Chapter 8, e), i) on UCC buyer's remedies.]

Neither Issuer nor the Company is responsible for lost or stolen Gift Certificates.

The Company reserves the right to close accounts and request alternative forms of payment if a Gift Certificate is fraudulently obtained or used on the Service.

THE COMPANY, ISSUER, AND THEIR LICENSEES,

AFFILIATES, AND LICENSORS MAKE NO WARRANTIES, EXPRESS OR IMPLIED, WITH RESPECT TO GIFT CERTIFICATES, OR THE STORE, INCLUDING, WITHOUT LIMITATION, ANY EXPRESS OR IMPLIED WARRANTY OF MERCHANTABILITY OR FITNESS FOR A PARTICULAR PURPOSE.

[See Part A, Chapter 5, c) on warranties and their disclaimers for sale of goods contracts pursuant to UCC §2-316, Exclusion or Modification of Warranties.] [See Part B, Chapter 8, g) on click-wrap contract conspicuous disclaimers of warranties.]

IN THE EVENT THAT A GIFT CERTIFICATE IS NONFUNCTIONAL, YOUR SOLE REMEDY, AND OUR SOLE LIABILITY, SHALL BE THE REPLACEMENT OF SUCH GIFT CERTIFICATE. [See Part A, Chapter 8, e), i) on UCC buyer's remedies.]

THESE LIMITATIONS MAY NOT APPLY TO YOU. CERTAIN STATE LAWS DO NOT ALLOW LIMITATIONS ON IMPLIED WARRANTIES OR THE EXCLUSION OR LIMITATION OF CERTAIN DAMAGES. IF THESE LAWS APPLY TO YOU, SOME OR ALL OF THE ABOVE DISCLAIMERS, EXCLUSIONS, OR LIMITATIONS MAY NOT APPLY TO YOU, AND YOU MAY ALSO HAVE ADDITIONAL RIGHTS.

[See Part A, Chapter 5, c) on warranties and their disclaimers for sale of goods contracts pursuant to UCC §2-316, Exclusion or Modification of Warranties.] [See Part B, Chapter 8, g) on click-wrap contract conspicuous disclaimers of warranties.]

GIFTS

Gifts purchased from the Services may be purchased only for, and redeemed only by, persons in the United States, its territories, and possessions. Gift recipients must have compatible hardware and parental control settings to utilize some gifts. [See Part A, Chapter 6, a) on conditions to performance.]

PRE-ORDERS

By pre-ordering products, you are authorizing the Services to automatically charge your account and download the product when it becomes available. You may cancel your pre-order prior to the time the item becomes available.

[See Part A, Chapter 6, a) on conditions to performance.] [See Part A, Chapter 4, b) on revocable offers.]

ELECTRONIC CONTRACTING

Your use of the Services includes the ability to enter into agreements and/or to make transactions electronically. YOU ACKNOWLEDGE THAT YOUR ELECTRONIC SUBMISSIONS CONSTITUTE YOUR AGREEMENT AND INTENT TO BE BOUND BY AND TO PAY FOR SUCH AGREEMENTS AND TRANSACTIONS. YOUR AGREEMENT AND INTENT TO BE BOUND BY ELECTRONIC SUBMISSIONS APPLIES TO ALL RECORDS RELATING TO ALL TRANSACTIONS YOU ENTER INTO ON THIS SITE, INCLUDING NOTICES OF CANCELLATION, POLICIES, CONTRACTS, AND APPLICATIONS. In order to access and retain your electronic records, you may be required to have certain hardware and software, which are your sole responsibility.

[See Part B, Chapter 4, b) on proof that an electronic signature was the act of a particular person, and the legal effect of the e-signature under UETA §9.]

The Company is not responsible for typographic errors.

[See Part B, Chapter 6, on mistake and error.]

B. STORE TERMS AND CONDITIONS

THIS LEGAL AGREEMENT BETWEEN YOU AND THE COMPANY GOVERNS YOUR USE OF THE STORE SERVICE (THE "SERVICE").

THE STORE SERVICE

The Company is the provider of the Service, which permits you to purchase or rent digital content ("Content") for end user use only under the terms and conditions set forth in this Agreement.

[See Part A, Chapter 4, e) on contract parties.]

REQUIREMENTS FOR USE OF THE SERVICE

This Service is available for individuals aged 13 years or older. If you are 13 or older but under the age of 18, you should review this Agreement with your parent or guardian to make sure that you and your parent or guardian understand it.

[See Part A, Chapter 7, a) i) on minority defense to contract breach.]

The Service is available to you only in the United States, its territories, and possessions. You agree not to use or attempt to use the Service from outside these locations. The Company may use technologies to verify your compliance.

Use of the Service requires compatible devices, Internet access, and certain software (fees may apply); may require periodic updates; and may be affected by the performance of these factors. High-speed Internet access is strongly recommended for regular use and is required for video. The latest version of required software is recommended to access the Service and may be required for certain transactions or features and to download products previously purchased from the Service. You agree that meeting these requirements, which may change from time to time, is your responsibility. The Service is not part of any other product or offering, and no purchase or obtaining of any other product shall be construed to represent or guarantee you access to the Service.

[See Part A, Chapter 6, a) on conditions to performance.]

YOUR ACCOUNT

As a registered user of the Service, you may establish an account ("Account"). Don't reveal your Account information to anyone else. You are solely responsible for maintaining the confidentiality and security of your Account and for all activities that occur on or through your Account, and you agree to immediately notify the Company of any security breach of your Account. The Company shall not be responsible for any losses arising out of the unauthorized use of your Account.

[See Part A, Chapter 8, d) on restrictions on incidental and consequential damages.]

You agree to provide accurate and complete information when you register with, and as you use, the Service ("Registration Data"), and you agree to update your Registration Data to keep it accurate and complete. You agree that the Company may store and use the Registration Data you provide for use in maintaining and billing fees to your Account.

CONTENT AVAILABILITY

The Company reserves the right to change content options (including eligibility for particular features) without notice.

USAGE RULES

(i) You shall be authorized to use Products only for personal, noncommercial use.

(ii) You shall be authorized to use Products on authorized devices at any time, except for Content Rentals (see below).

(iii) You shall be able to store Products from up to different Accounts at a time on compatible devices, provided that each device may sync Products with only a single authorized device at a time, and syncing a device with a different authorized device will cause Products stored on that device to be erased.

(iv) You shall be authorized to burn an audio playlist up to _____ times.

(v) You shall not be entitled to burn video Products or Products.

(vi) Content Rentals

Some Products, including but not limited to Content rentals, may be downloaded only once and cannot be replaced if lost for any reason. It is your responsibility not to lose, destroy, or damage Products once downloaded, and you may wish to back them up.

[See Part A, Chapter 8, d) on restrictions on incidental and consequential damages.]

The delivery of Products does not transfer to you any commercial or promotional use rights in the Products. Any burning or exporting capabilities are solely an accommodation to you and shall not constitute a grant, waiver, or other limitation of any rights of the copyright owners in any content embodied in any Product.

You acknowledge that, because some aspects of the Service, Products, and administration of the Usage Rules entail the ongoing involvement of the Company, if the Company changes any part of or discontinues the Service, which it may do at its election, you may not be able to use Products to the same extent as prior to such change or discontinuation, and that the Company shall have no liability to you in such case.

[See Part A, Chapter 5, b) on implied contract terms, including good faith in performance and enforcement.][See Part A, Chapter 8, b) on reliance damages and d) on restrictions on incidental and consequential damages.]

SUBMISSIONS TO THE SERVICE

The Service may offer interactive features that allow you to submit materials (including links to third-party content) on areas of the Service accessible and viewable by the public. You agree that any use by you of such features, including any materials submitted by you, shall be your sole responsibility, shall not infringe or violate the rights of any other party or violate any laws, contribute to or encourage infringing or otherwise unlawful conduct, or otherwise be obscene, objectionable, or in poor taste. You also agree that you have obtained all necessary rights and licenses. You agree to provide accurate and complete information in connection with your submission of any materials on the Service. You hereby grant the Company a worldwide, royalty-free, nonexclusive license to use such materials as part of the Service, and in relation to Products, without any compensation or obligation to you. The Company reserves the right to not post or publish any materials, and to remove or edit any material, at any time in its sole discretion without notice or liability.

[See Part A, Chapter 5, b) on implied contract terms, including good faith in performance.] [See Part A, Chapter 5, c) on warranties.]

The Company has the right, but not the obligation, to monitor any materials submitted by you or otherwise available on the Service, to investigate any reported or apparent violation of this Agreement, and to take any action that it in its sole discretion deems appropriate, including, without limitation, termination hereunder or under its Copyright Policy (http://www. _____).

[See Part A, Chapter 5, b) on implied contract terms, including good faith in performance.] [See Part B, Chapter 9, j) on incorporation by reference of terms posted on web sites.]

THIRD-PARTY MATERIALS

Certain content, Products, and services available via the Service may include materials from third parties. The Company may provide links to third-party websites as a convenience to you. You agree that the Company is not responsible for examining or evaluating the content or accuracy and it does not warrant and will not have any liability or responsibility for any third-party materials or websites, or for any other materials, products, or services of third parties. You agree that you will not use any third-party materials in a manner that would infringe or violate the rights of any other party and that the Company is not in any way responsible for any such use by you.

[See Part A, Chapter 5, c) on warranties.][See Part A, Chapter 8, e), i) on UCC buyer's remedies.][See Part B, Chapter 9, h) on third-party provided content.]

OBJECTIONABLE MATERIAL

You understand that by using the Service, you may encounter material that you may deem to be offensive, indecent, or objectionable, and that such content may or may not be identified as having explicit material. Nevertheless, you agree to use the Service at your sole risk and the Company shall have no liability to you for material that may be found to be offensive, indecent, or objectionable. Product types and descriptions are provided for convenience, and you agree that the Company does not guarantee their accuracy.

[See Part A, Chapter 8, b) on reliance damages, and d) on restrictions on incidental and consequential damages.][See Part B, Chapter 9, h) on third-party provided content.]

IMPORTANT SAFETY INFORMATION

To avoid muscle, joint, or eye strain during your use of the products offered through the Service, you should always take frequent breaks, and take a longer rest if you experience any soreness, fatigue, or discomfort. A very small percentage of people may experience seizures or blackouts when exposed to flashing lights or patterns, including but not limited to while playing video games or watching videos. Symptoms may include dizziness, nausea, involuntary movements, loss of awareness, altered vision, tingling, numbness, or other discomforts. Consult a doctor before using the products offered through the Service if you have ever suffered these or similar symptoms, and stop using such products immediately and see a doctor if they occur during your use of such products. Parents should monitor their children's use of the products offered through the Service for signs of symptoms.

[See Part A, Chapter 8, b) on reliance damages, and d) restrictions on incidental and consequential damages.]

INTELLECTUAL PROPERTY

You agree that the Service, including but not limited to Products, graphics, user interface, audio clips, video clips, editorial content, and the scripts and software used to implement the Service, contains proprietary information and material that is owned by the Company and/or its licensors, and is protected by applicable intellectual property and other laws, including but not limited to copyright. You agree that you will not use such proprietary information or materials in any way whatsoever except for use of the Service in compliance with this Agreement. No portion of the Service may be reproduced in any form or by any means, except as expressly permitted in these terms. You agree not to modify, rent, lease, loan, sell, distribute, or create derivative works based on the Service in any manner, and you shall not exploit the Service in any unauthorized way whatsoever, including, but not limited to, by trespass or burdening network capacity.

[See Part A, Chapter 6, a) i) on express conditions.]

Notwithstanding any other provision of this Agreement, the Company and its licensors reserve the right to change, suspend, remove, or disable access to any Products, content, or other materials comprising a part of the Service at any time without notice. In no event will the Company be liable for making these changes. The Company may also impose limits on the use of or access to certain features or portions of the Service, in any case and without notice or liability. [See Part A, Chapter 5, b) on implied contract terms, including good faith in performance.] [See Part A, Chapter 8, b) on reliance damages and d) on restrictions on incidental and consequential damages.]

All copyrights in and to the Service (including the compilation of content, postings, links to other Internet resources, and descriptions of those resources) and related software are owned by the Company and/or its licensors, who reserve all their rights in law and equity. THE USE OF THE SOFTWARE OR ANY PART OF THE SERVICE, EXCEPT FOR USE OF THE SERVICE AS PERMITTED IN THIS AGREEMENT, IS STRICTLY PROHIBITED AND INFRINGES ON THE INTELLECTUAL PROPERTY RIGHTS OF OTHERS AND MAY SUBJECT YOU TO CIVIL AND CRIMINAL PENALTIES, INCLUDING POSSIBLE MONETARY DAMAGES, FOR COPYRIGHT INFRINGEMENT.

The Company, and other Company trademarks, service marks, graphics, and logos used in connection with the Service are trademarks or registered trademarks of the Company in the U.S. and/or other countries. Other trademarks, service marks, graphics, and logos used in connection with the Service may be the trademarks of their respective owners. You are granted no right or license with respect to any of the aforesaid trademarks and any use of such trademarks.

As an Account holder of the Service in good standing, you may be provided with limited access to download certain album cover art for music stored in your application. Such access is provided as an accommodation only, and the Company does not warrant, and will not have any liability or responsibility for, such album cover art or your use thereof. You may access album cover art only for music for which you are the lawful owner of a legal copy. Album cover art is provided for personal, noncommercial use only. You agree that you will not use album cover art in any manner that would infringe or violate this Agreement or the rights of any other party, and that the Company is not in any way responsible for any such use by you.

[See Part A, Chapter 5, c) on warranties.]

TERMINATION

If you fail, or the Company suspects that you have failed, to comply with any of the provisions of this Agreement, the Company, at its sole discretion, without notice to you may: (i) terminate this Agreement and/or your Account, and you will remain liable for all amounts due under your Account up to and including the date of termination; and/or (ii) terminate the license to the software; and/or (iii) preclude access to the Service (or any part thereof).

[See Part A, Chapter 5, b) on good faith obligation in performance and enforcement.][See Part A, Chapter 6, b) on total, partial and material breach, and c) on anticipatory repudiation.]

The Company reserves the right to modify, suspend, or discontinue the Service (or any part or content thereof) at any time with or without notice to you, and the Company will not be liable to you or to any third party should it exercise such rights.

[See Part A, Chapter 5, b) on good faith obligation in performance and enforcement.][See Part A, Chapter 8, b) on reliance damages and d) on restrictions on reliance and consequential damages.]

DISCLAIMER OF WARRANTIES; LIABILITY LIMITATION

THE COMPANY DOES NOT GUARANTEE, REPRESENT, OR WARRANT THAT YOUR USE OF THE SERVICE WILL BE UNINTERRUPTED OR ERROR-FREE, AND YOU AGREE THAT FROM TIME TO TIME THE COMPANY MAY REMOVE THE SERVICE FOR INDEFINITE PERIODS OF TIME, OR CANCEL THE SERVICE AT ANY TIME, WITHOUT NOTICE TO YOU.

[See Part A, Chapter 5, c) on warranties.] [See Part A, Chapter 8, e) i) on UCC buyers' remedies.] [See Part B, Chapter 8, g) on click-wrap contract conspicuous disclaimers of warranties.]

YOU EXPRESSLY AGREE THAT YOUR USE OF, OR INABILITY TO USE, THE SERVICE IS AT YOUR SOLE RISK. THE SERVICE AND ALL PRODUCTS AND SERVICES DELIVERED TO YOU THROUGH THE SERVICE ARE (EXCEPT AS EXPRESSLY STATED BY THE COMPANY) PROVIDED "AS IS" AND "AS AVAILABLE" FOR YOUR USE, WITHOUT WARRANTIES OF ANY KIND, EITHER EXPRESS OR IMPLIED, INCLUDING ALL IMPLIED WARRANTIES OF MERCHANTABILITY, FITNESS FOR A PARTICULAR PURPOSE, TITLE, AND NONINFRINGEMENT. BECAUSE SOME JURISDICTIONS DO NOT ALLOW THE EXCLUSION OF IMPLIED WARRANTIES, THE ABOVE EXCLUSION OF IMPLIED WARRANTIES MAY NOT APPLY TO YOU.

[See Part A, Chapter 8, e) i) on UCC buyers' remedies.] [See Part B, Chapter 8, g) on click-wrap contract conspicuous disclaimers of warranties.]

IN NO CASE SHALL THE COMPANY, ITS DIRECTORS, OFFICERS, EMPLOYEES, AFFILIATES, AGENTS, CONTRACTORS, OR LICENSORS BE LIABLE FOR ANY DIRECT, INDIRECT, INCIDENTAL, PUNITIVE, SPECIAL, OR CONSEQUENTIAL DAMAGES ARISING FROM YOUR USE OF ANY OF THE SERVICE OR FOR ANY OTHER CLAIM RELATED IN ANY WAY TO YOUR USE OF THE SERVICE, INCLUDING, BUT NOT LIMITED TO, ANY ERRORS OR OMISSIONS IN ANY CONTENT, OR ANY LOSS OR DAMAGE OF ANY KIND INCURRED AS A RESULT OF THE USE OF ANY CONTENT (OR PRODUCT) POSTED, TRANSMITTED, OR OTHERWISE MADE AVAILABLE VIA THE SERVICE, EVEN IF ADVISED OF THEIR POSSIBILITY. BECAUSE SOME STATES OR JURISDICTIONS DO NOT ALLOW THE EXCLUSION OR THE LIMITATION OF LIABILITY FOR CONSEQUENTIAL OR INCIDENTAL DAMAGES, IN SUCH STATES OR JURISDICTIONS, THE COMPANY'S LIABILITY SHALL BE LIMITED TO THE EXTENT PERMITTED BY LAW.

[See Part A, Chapter 8, b) on reliance damages, d) on restrictions on incidental and consequential damages, and e) i) on UCC buyers' remedies.] [See Part B, Chapter 8, g) on click-wrap contract conspicuous disclaimers of warranties.]

THE COMPANY SHALL USE REASONABLE EFFORTS TO PROTECT INFORMATION SUBMITTED BY YOU IN CONNECTION WITH THE SERVICE, BUT YOU AGREE THAT YOUR SUBMISSION OF SUCH INFORMATION IS AT YOUR SOLE RISK, AND THE COMPANY HEREBY DISCLAIMS ANY AND ALL LIABILITY TO YOU FOR ANY LOSS OR LIABILITY RELATING TO SUCH INFORMATION IN ANY WAY.

[See Part A, Chapter 6, a) ii) on implied constructive conditions.] [See Part A, Chapter 8, b) on reliance damages, d) on restrictions on incidental and consequential damages, and e) i) on UCC buyers' remedies.]

THE COMPANY DOES NOT REPRESENT OR GUARANTEE THAT THE SERVICE WILL BE FREE FROM LOSS, CORRUPTION, ATTACK, VIRUSES, INTERFERENCE, HACKING, OR OTHER SECURITY INTRUSION, AND THE COMPANY DISCLAIMS ANY LIABILITY RELATING THERETO. SOME PRODUCTS CAN BE DOWNLOADED ONLY ONCE; AFTER BEING DOWNLOADED, THEY CANNOT BE REPLACED IF LOST FOR ANY REASON. YOU SHALL BE RESPONSIBLE FOR BACKING UP YOUR OWN SYSTEM, INCLUDING ANY PRODUCTS PURCHASED OR RENTED FROM THE STORE.

[See Part A, Chapter 8, b) on reliance damages, d) on restrictions on incidental and consequential damages, and e) i) on UCC buyers' remedies.] [See Part B, Chapter 8, g) on click-wrap contract conspicuous disclaimers of warranties.]

WAIVER AND INDEMNITY

BY USING THE SERVICE, YOU AGREE, TO THE EXTENT PERMITTED BY LAW, TO INDEMNIFY AND HOLD THE COMPANY, ITS DIRECTORS, OFFICERS, EMPLOYEES, AFFILIATES, AGENTS, CONTRACTORS, AND LICENSORS HARMLESS WITH RESPECT TO ANY CLAIMS ARISING OUT OF YOUR BREACH OF THIS AGREEMENT, YOUR USE OF THE SERVICE, OR ANY ACTION TAKEN BY THE COMPANY AS PART OF ITS INVESTIGATION OF A SUSPECTED VIOLATION OF THIS AGREEMENT OR AS A RESULT OF ITS FINDING OR DECISION THAT A VIOLATION OF THIS AGREEMENT HAS OCCURRED. THIS MEANS THAT YOU CANNOT SUE OR RECOVER ANY DAMAGES FROM THE COMPANY, ITS DIRECTORS, OFFICERS, EMPLOYEES, AFFILIATES, AGENTS, CONTRACTORS, AND LICENSORS AS A RESULT OF ITS DECISION TO REMOVE OR REFUSE TO

PROCESS ANY INFORMATION OR CONTENT, TO WARN YOU, TO SUSPEND OR TERMINATE YOUR ACCESS TO THE SERVICE, OR TO TAKE ANY OTHER ACTION DURING THE INVESTIGATION OF A SUSPECTED VIOLATION OR AS A RESULT OF THE COMPANY'S CONCLUSION THAT A VIOLATION OF THIS AGREEMENT HAS OCCURRED. THIS WAIVER AND INDEMNITY PROVISION APPLIES TO ALL VIOLATIONS DESCRIBED IN OR CONTEMPLATED BY THIS AGREEMENT.

[See Part A, Chapter 7, d) on unconscionability and public policy.] [See Part A, Chapter 8, b) on reliance damages, d) on restrictions on incidental and consequential damages, and e) i) on UCC buyers' remedies.] [See Part B, Chapter 9, d) on notice of terms, including *A.V. v. iParadigms, LLC* "Turnitin" case with indemnification requirement.]

CHANGES

The Company reserves the right at any time to modify this Agreement and to impose new or additional terms or conditions on your use of the Service. Such modifications and additional terms and conditions will be effective immediately and incorporated into this Agreement. Your continued use of the Service will be deemed acceptance thereof.

[See Part A, Chapter 7, g) on contract modifications.][See Part B, Chapter 9, l) on notice of permitted unilateral contract modifications.]

MISCELLANEOUS

This Agreement constitutes the entire agreement between you and the Company and governs your use of the Service, superseding any prior agreements between you and the Company. You also may be subject to additional terms and conditions that may apply when you use affiliate services, third-party content, or third-party software. If any part of this

Agreement is held invalid or unenforceable, that portion shall be construed in a manner consistent with applicable law to reflect, as nearly as possible, the original intentions of the parties, and the remaining portions shall remain in full force and effect. The Company's failure to enforce any right or provisions in this Agreement will not constitute a waiver of such or any other provision. The Company will not be responsible for failures to fulfill any obligations due to causes beyond its control.

[See Part A, Chapter 5, a) on interpretation of contract language, including "merger"/"entire agreement" clauses.] [See Part A, Chapter 6, b) on total, partial and material breach.] [See Part A, Chapter 7, f) on impossibility, impracticability and frustration defenses.][See Part C, Section I, Chapter 3, n) and Chapter 5, h) on "*force majeure*" defense.]

The Service is operated by the Company from its offices in the United States. You agree to comply with all local, state, federal, and national laws, statutes, ordinances, and regulations that apply to your use of the Service. All transactions on the Service are governed by State of ___ law, without giving effect to its conflict of law provisions. Your use of the Service may also be subject to other laws. You expressly agree that exclusive jurisdiction for any claim or dispute with or relating in any way to your use of the Service resides in the courts in the State of _____ . Risk of loss and title for all electronically delivered transactions pass to the purchaser in the State of _____ upon electronic transmission to the recipient. No Company employee or agent has the authority to vary this Agreement.

[See Part B, Chapter 7 on automated transactions and electronic agents][See Part C, Section I, Chapter 1 on choice-of-law and choice-of-forum clauses.]

The Company may notify you with respect to the Service by sending an email message to your Account email address or a letter via postal mail to your Account mailing address, or by a posting on the Service. Notices shall become effective immediately.

[See Part B, Chapter 9, e) on notice of click-wrap contract terms of use.]

The Company reserves the right to take steps it believes are reasonably necessary or appropriate to enforce and/or verify compliance with any part of this Agreement. You agree that the Company has the right, without liability to you, to disclose any Registration Data and/or Account information to law enforcement authorities, government officials, and/or a third party, as it believes is reasonably necessary or appropriate to enforce and/or verify compliance with any part of this Agreement (including but not limited to the Company's right to cooperate with any legal process relating to your use of the Service and/or Products, and/or a third-party claim that your use of the Service and/or Products is unlawful and/or infringes such third party's rights). [See Part A, Chapter 5, b) on good faith obligation in performance and enforcement.]

Last Updated:

Appendix C – Rules for Negotiating Contracts

18 RULES FOR CONTRACT DRAFTING AND NEGOTIATION

I developed these rules based, in part, on more than thirty years of law practice for private and government clients, and on academic analyses of negotiating theory and practice. These rules apply, of course, only when you are in a position to negotiate some of, or all of, the terms of a contract.

1. WAIT! Take whatever time is allowed to you before committing yourself to a contract. If you have already committed yourself, state consumer protection statutes allow consumers to rescind many contracts within three days of signing. Many mistakes have been made by consumers and businesses by rushing into a contract without taking time to check the reputation of the other party, the contract terms, or even the necessity for the transaction.

2. Don't ask the other side for anything without being prepared to explain why you need it and why it's fair for them to give it to you. (Don't say "My _____ told me to ask for this.")

3. Don't ask for any general rights or protections that you are not prepared to give to the other side (e.g. no liability for consequential damages).

4. Don't forget to try to disclaim liability for consequential damages if you have a duty of performance that involves more than just paying money.

5. Don't forget the "entire agreement"/merger/integration clause.

6. Don't forget the choice-of-law clause.

7. Don't forget the choice-of-forum clause.

8. Don't forget a *force majeure*/"Act of God" clause if you

have a duty of performance for more than just paying money.

9. Don't forget the "no oral modifications" (NOM) clause.

10. Don't forget the "no oral waivers" (NOW) clause.

11. Don't forget the severability clause (i.e. if any provision of the contract is found to be unenforceable, that provision is "severed" from the rest of the contract, and the rest of the contract and its enforceable provisions remain in effect).

12. Protect yourself against omissions (things that should be in the contract, but you didn't think about) as well as commissions (things that should be changed).

13. Avoid ambiguity, unless you are certain that ambiguity favors you. (Don't be cute, be clear.)

14. Create definitions for important contract terms/language, preferably in a single definitions section/paragraph.

15. Modify any satisfaction or notice or consent requirements (especially if they affect you) by a qualification of reasonableness.

16. Remember that, even if it's a one-time deal, your reputation for honesty and fairness is at stake.

17. Remember that, if future deals are contemplated with the other side, what you might gain by deception (and more) will be lost, because of lost trust and confidence in later business deals.

18. Consider whether or not contract rights should be assignable or contract duties should be delegable, or whether either or both should be prohibited.

Resources: Getting to Yes: Negotiating Agreement Without Giving In by Roger Fisher and William Ury, Bruce Patton (editor), and other books published in connection with the Harvard Negotiation Project.

Appendix D – Dispute Resolution Examples

1. The Credit Report 10-Day Free Trial

You've seen the ads—"Free Credit Score". You've heard the advice—"It's the most important number for your financial well-being", "Everyone should check their credit score at least once a year". Being always open to good advice, and not having checked his score since he applied for a bank loan many years before, John decided to check his credit score.

The home page of the credit score company looked promising. At its top half, John could see the words he was looking for on a big red banner – "Get my Credit Score FREE*". The information after the asterisk read in smaller type "*IMPORTANT INFORMATION: When you order your free Credit Score here, you will begin your 10-day trial membership in Credit Report. If you don't cancel your membership within the 10-day trial period, you will be billed $14.95 for each month that you continue your membership. A three month minimum subscription applies. You may cancel your trial membership anytime within the trial period without charge."

John clicked on the button to get his free credit score. On the page requiring registration information (and including a description of the "10-day Free Trial" terms in larger type), John created his member profile and submitted credit card information. He received his credit score. He also received an e-mail telling him that he was enrolled in a Credit Report "Free Trial". Next to these quoted words an asterisk referred to a small print footnote "3 month minimum required". At the bottom of the e-mail in a green colored box were the statements "About your FREE 10-Day Trial: If you do not cancel prior to the end of the 10-day trial, you will be billed at the monthly subscription rate of $14.95 when the 10-day trial expires. A three month minimum subscription applies."

A week later, John received another e-mail telling him that there was no activity to report regarding credit bureau updates from his creditors. This e-mail also stated that his free trial would expire in 3 days. It was the holiday season. John was busy. He made a mental note to remember to cancel the report subscription since it didn't seem very useful, but he knew he had some more time to actually cancel. He thought the service would warn him again before his free trial period ended.

John received another e-mail notice of his credit bureau report the following day. This e-mail made no mention of his free trial period, or that it would expire in two days. Two days later, John received an e-mail that he was now subscribed to Credit Report and that his credit card had been charged for the first month of the three month subscription.

John called the 800 number for customer service for the credit score company to ask that his subscription be cancelled after one month, because he had intended to cancel within the free trial period. The customer service agent refused to allow John to cancel any part of the three month minimum subscription period. John asked to speak to a supervisor. The supervisor refused to allow John to cancel any part of the three month minimum subscription. John asked for the supervisor's name.

John then looked at the web pages and e-mails he had clicked through to see how he had so easily missed the free trial cancellation deadline that he had intended to meet. John noticed near the bottom of the company home page a sign "BBB – Accredited Business". John knew that this meant that the company had been approved by the Better Business Bureau.

John accessed the Better Business Bureau website, supplied the necessary information about the company and the supervisor he had spoken to, and filed the following complaint (acknowledged by e-mail):

Location Involved: (Same as above) Consumer's Original Complaint:

Credit Report product terms are not clear and conspicuous per FTC Dot Com Disclosure business guide in telling customers of free 10-day trial that they will be charged three times over three months if they do not cancel within 10 days.

Any other online subscription I have had has allowed cancellation after the first month's charge. _____ says they are like an insurance company. They are not. If they were, they would maintain a higher standard of service to the public.

I will also submit this complaint to the Federal Trade Commission. Consumer's Desired Resolution:

Refund of $ ___ subscription charge for second and third months.

BBB Processing

/   /2011 web BBB Complaint Received by BBB

The day following John's filing of his complaint, the Better Business Bureau sent him an e-mail acknowledging the receipt of the complaint and stating that it had been reviewed by one of their Dispute Resolution Specialists and forwarded to the business for their response. One week later, John received an e-mail from the company stating that his credit card had been credited for the amount of the first month's subscription, and a second e-mail stating that he would not be charged for the two following months of the subscription period.

What are the lessons of this story?

1. Customer service reps for many companies are not as helpful as you might think they would be. Don't take it

personally. They are often encouraged to discourage complaints as a kind of "firewall" between customers and companies providing poor service. See http://www.emilyyellin.com/web/?p=96 for tips on dealing with customer service reps based on her book Your Call is (Not That) Important to Us, and "10 Things Customer-Service Reps Won't Tell You" by Jen Wieczner, Smart Money, January 18, 2012.

2. Don't stop with the first customer service rep you speak to if they have not resolved your complaint to your satisfaction. Ask to speak to their supervisor. The supervisor may not satisfy you either, but he or she usually has more authority to make compromises with customers. Supervisors also usually have more power to investigate the service problems alleged by customers.

3. Remember the names of the reps and supervisors you speak to. If none of them takes your complaint seriously, and you believe you have a legitimate reason to complain, consider using a third party to help you. In this case, the Better Business Bureau (BBB) is a well-known and long-existing private, voluntary organization that is dedicated to maintaining high standards of business behavior. Businesses that belong to the BBB get the "reputation marketing" benefit that membership confers on them. They feel more pressure to respond to the BBB than to an individual customer. Before you do business with a company, check to see if it is a member of the BBB or a comparable organization.

4. When you make a complaint, be specific about whom you spoke to, what you complained about, and how you think the business failed to meet appropriate business standards. Knowledge is power, and this book is intended to give you information about what those standards might be, depending on the context. In this case, John's complaint, through the BBB, probably received a better response than a general complaint of unfairness once it was framed in the context of the business's web site, and its emails' failure to disclose

contract terms in a clear and conspicuous manner, according to the Federal Trade Commission (FTC) 2013 .com Disclosures Guide and 2000 Dot Com Disclosures Guide. [See Part B, Chapter 9, a) on FTC consumer protection and internet advertisers.]

5. Although it probably won't get you a quick response from the government, if necessary file an appropriate complaint with an agency like the FTC. Mention that you have filed the complaint in your complaint letter. Businesses might take you more seriously if they know that you are aware of the laws that govern their activities.

2. The Need for a "Corrections & Amplifications" Note in a Changed Web Site Advertisement

Jane changed her health insurance plan. When she reviewed the online benefits summary of the plan, the "Deductible" line under the column for the plan she chose stated that a $2,000 deductible applied as a "combined medical & prescription deductible". Further down the summary was a separate line – "Rx Deductible". On this line, under her plan column was the statement "NA".

Jane assumed that "NA" meant there was no deductible for prescriptions for the plan she chose. She ordered a prescription. When she received it, she was billed $250 for a bottle of pills that had cost her only $25 under her previous plan. Jane complained to customer service about the size of her bill. She was told that the bill represented the fact that a $2,000 deductible applied to her prescription order. Until her deductible was satisfied, she would be required to pay the full cost of the prescription with no insurance company payment.

Jane complained to the insurance company customer service rep and to a supervisor that the benefits summary had indicated that there was no deductible that applied to her insurance plan. Unlike all other plans that had a specific dollar amount listed on their "Rx Deductible" line, her plan's line stated "NA". In response, the insurance company directed

Jane to a benefits summary version that had been altered from the version she saw when she chose her plan. The altered version had an asterisk next to the lines for "Deductible (medical)" and "Rx Deductible". This new asterisk referenced a footnote that stated "Deductibles, copays and coinsurance apply to the out-of-pocket maximum". When Jane spoke to the customer service supervisor, the supervisor told her that Jane could file an appeal for the denial of her benefits claim. Jane filed this appeal.

1. Specific benefits provision in benefits summary:

When I enrolled in the_____ Option 2 on _____ , the online benefits summary page did not have any note next to the first benefits line under "Deductible type" --"Deductible (medical)". The online benefits summary page also did not have a note next to the first benefits line under "Prescription Drugs"—Rx Deductible". After I enrolled in this plan, a note was added to both of these benefit lines. The reference added by the note stated "In-network (or formulary) deductibles, copays and coinsurance apply to the out-of-pocket maximum."

At the time I enrolled, and currently, the benefits summary, under the column for _____Option 2 benefits on the "Rx Deductible" line, states "NA" [meaning "Not Applicable"].

The only benefits summary description of the _____Option 2 Deductible, at the time I enrolled, stated "NA". There was no further noted explanation, as there is currently, that the deductible applied to the out-of-pocket maximum. This indicated to me that there was no deductible amount for the prescription drug benefit. The note that was later added was an obvious clarification of the previous misleading description of the prescription drug benefit deductible.

Attached is a computer print-out of the online benefits summary page from _____ , and a copy of the changed benefits summary page sent to me after I ordered my prescription under the mistaken impression caused by the online benefits summary page.

2. Reasons why the deductible should not be applied to my prescription bill:

Attached is a copy of the invoice from _____for _____my ___order of _____ . As indicated on the invoice, I was charged the full $250 cost of this prescription, with no insurance benefit paid.

The following laws and principles support the reimbursement by you to me of the $250 (minus the regular charge) cost of my prescription.

> Federal Trade Commission (FTC) Guidance prohibits web site unfair and deceptive advertising

> The Federal Trade Commission (FTC) enforces federal laws against "false and misleading" and "unfair and deceptive" advertising.

> The FTC Dot Com Disclosures guidance for internet advertisers of May 2000 explains how federal laws on advertising apply to internet web sites and require "clear and conspicuous" disclosures of contract terms in order to avoid deceptive advertising.

Among the duties of internet advertisers described in the guidance are "If qualifying information is necessary to prevent an ad from being misleading, advertisers must present the information clearly and conspicuously" (page 4), "Disclosures must be effectively communicated to consumers before they make a purchase or incur a financial obligation" (page 11), "It's the advertiser's responsibility to draw attention to the required disclosures" (page 12), and "To ensure that disclosures are effective, consumers must be able to understand them" (page 18). Also, "Advertisers should use clear language and syntax and avoid legalese or technical jargon" (page 14). [See Part B, Chapter 9, a) FTC "Dot Com Disclosures" guidance for internet advertisers.]

The benefits summary in its original online version was ambiguous and misleading. The addition of a clarifying note to the description of the _____ Option 2 Deductible was not drawn to my attention before I enrolled and ordered a prescription, it is only in small print at the bottom of the page, and does not refer to the dollar amount of the deductible ($2,000) in the same way that the other option deductibles are referred to. It fails to meet these FTC standards for online advertising.

For the reasons state above, I respectfully request that you reimburse me for the $250 charged to me for my prescription for _____ minus the normal charge, and without the deductible.

This appeal was denied by the insurer with the following stated reasons:

> The benefit brochure that was provided upon enrollment is the complete statement of benefits available to members.

> As indicated on page 61 of the brochure, "the calendar year deductible does not apply for the [other insurance plans]." In the online benefits summary, for the Option 2 plan, it states at the top, "A combined medical and prescription deductible." For the [other plans] it states "separate medical & prescription deductible." The "NA" indicated [on the line under Option Rx for prescription benefits] is appropriate because there is not a separate Rx deductible for the Option 2 plan."

What are the lessons of this story?

1. Insurance companies are subject to less competition than other types of companies. As a result, they are less responsive to customer service complaints. Reading and understanding their customer information can be like putting together a jigsaw puzzle. Don't assume that your view of how the pieces fit is the same as the company's view. If a company or

employer representative is available to explain to you how the plans work, use those resources before you commit to an insurance plan to make sure you understand its requirements.

2. Check to see what appeal procedures might exist for a denial of a claim by an insurance company. If the customer service representative (or supervisor) doesn't mention it, search the company web site.

3. If the company denies your appeal, it is still possible to seek redress in the small claims branch of your local courts. You can represent yourself without a lawyer, and the procedures are simple and faster than regular litigation. [See Part C, Section II, Chapter 4, b) on mediation and small claims courts]

4. If you encounter a business practice that seems unfair to you, don't give up just because you don't know specific legal rules that the practice might violate. Contract law is intended to serve the interests of justice. If a practice is unfair, it might be illegal too. Check the contract law rules in this book, and the sources it cites, to see if there is a rule that applies to your situation. Search the Federal Trade Commission web site to see if there are any relevant FTC rules or guides at www.ftc.gov.

3. Electronic Bill Pay Might Put You into Customer Service Purgatory

By now you know that just about any interaction with a business that doesn't care about good customer service can lead you into "customer service purgatory". There are some interactions, however, that involve federal consumer protections that might help you if you find yourself in this situation.

Mary had her mortgage loan paid for ten years through a monthly automatic payment from her bank checking account. For the first time, in April, she received a message on her answering machine that her payment was overdue, and that she should contact her mortgage servicer to resolve it.

Mary looked at her online checking account statement. It showed a debit from her checking account in the amount of the loan payment to the mortgage servicer on the same day of the month that her previous payments had been made. It showed that the electronic check had been cashed by the mortgage servicer.

Mary wrote down the identification number of the electronic payment and related information. She called customer service at the mortgage servicer, and spoke to a representative. The representative told her that if she had her checking account bank send a copy of the electronic check to the mortgage servicer, the matter would be resolved.

Mary contacted her checking account bank and requested that they send a copy of the electronic check to the mortgage servicer. The checking account bank sent the copy.

The customer service rep whom Mary originally spoke to said that she would be available to speak with Mary again on Friday at 9:00 a.m. When Mary called the rep at that time, she received a voice message that the rep was not available. Mary left a message for the rep to call her. The rep did not return Mary's call. Later that afternoon, Mary called customer service again and asked to speak to the rep's supervisor. The supervisor told Mary that the first rep was not in the office that day. Mary told the supervisor her problem. The supervisor told Mary to have her checking account bank send another copy of the electronic check payment to the mortgage servicer to resolve the problem.

Mary had her checking account bank send another copy of the electronic check payment to the mortgage servicer. On the following business day, Mary called the supervisor she previously spoke to, but received only a voice mail message. One week after speaking to the original customer service rep, and after speaking to other reps and supervisors, Mary was able to speak again to the original customer service rep. The rep told Mary that, although Mary's checking account bank's records showed that the mortgage servicer had cashed her loan payment check, the copy of the electronic check sent by the bank did not prove this because there was no stamped endorsement on the back of the electronic check, as there usually was, and as there had been on previous checks.

Mary spent the next three weeks speaking to various customer service reps at the mortgage servicer and the checking account bank trying, without success, to find out what happened to the funds for her mortgage loan payment that had been debited from her checking account, but had not been credited to her mortgage loan payment. As the date for her next monthly loan payment approached, Mary dreaded seeing another payment amount debited from her checking account without being credited to her mortgage loan payment.

Mary researched what consumer rights she might have in this situation. She found the Electronic Fund Transfer Act (EFTA)746 during her search. Mary noted the following provisions of the EFTA that could help her.

§902. Congressional Findings and Declaration of Purpose [15 U.S.C. §1693]

...(b) It is the purpose of this title to provide a basic framework establishing the rights, liabilities, and responsibilities of participants in electronic fund transfer systems. The primary objective of this title, however, is the provision of individual consumer rights....

§908. Error Resolution [15 U.S.C. §1693f]

(a) If a financial institution, within sixty days after having transmitted to a consumer documentation pursuant to section 906(a), (c), or (d) or notification pursuant to section 906(b), receives oral or written notice in which the consumer—

(1) sets forth or otherwise enables the financial institution

to identify the name and account number of the consumer;

> (2) indicates the consumer's belief that the documentation or, in the case of notification pursuant to section 906(b), the consumer's consent, contains an error and the amount of such error; and

> (3) sets forth the reasons for the consumer's belief (where applicable) that an error has occurred,

> the financial institution shall investigate the alleged error, determine whether an error has occurred, and report or mail the results of such investigation and determination to the consumer within ten business days. The financial institution may require written confirmation to be provided to it within ten business days of an oral notification of error if, when the oral notification is made, the consumer is advised of such requirement and the address to which such confirmation should be sent…

(b) If the financial institution determines that an error did occur, it shall promptly, but in no event more than one business day after such determination correct the error, subject to section 909 [consumer liability limits for unauthorized transfers], including the crediting of interest where applicable.

(c) If a financial institution receives notice of an error in the manner and within the time period specified in subsection (a) of this section, it may, in lieu of the requirements of subsections (a) and (b) of this section, within ten business days after receiving such notice provisionally recredit the consumer's account for the amount alleged to be in error, subject to section 909, including interest where applicable, pending the conclusion of its investigation and its determination of whether an error has occurred. Such investigation shall be concluded not later than forty-five days after receipt of notice of the error. During the pendency of the investigation, the consumer shall have full use of the funds provisionally recredited.

(d) If the financial institution determines after its investigation pursuant to subsection (a) or (c) of this section that an error did not occur…

(e) If in any action under section 915, the court finds that—

(1) the financial institution did not provisionally recredit a consumer's account within the ten-day period specified in subsection (c) of this section, and the financial institution (A) did not make a good faith investigation of the alleged error, or (B) did not have a reasonable basis for believing that the consumer's account was not in error; or

(2) the financial institution knowingly and willfully concluded that the consumer's account was not in error when such conclusion could not reasonably have been drawn from the evidence available to the financial institution at the time of its investigation,

then the consumer shall be entitled to treble [triple] damages determined under section 915(a)(1)….

§915 Civil Liability [15 U.S.C. §1693m]

(a) Except as otherwise provided by this section and section 910, any person who fails to comply with any provision of this title with respect to any consumer, except for an error resolved in accordance with section 908, is liable to such consumer in an amount equal to the sum of

(1) any actual damage sustained by such consumer as a result of such failure;

(2)(A) in the case of an individual action, an amount not less than $100 nor greater than $1,000; or

(B) in the case of a class action…

(3) in the case of any successful action to enforce the foregoing liability, the costs of the action, together with a reasonable attorney's fee as determined by the court…

(e) A person has no liability under this section for any failure to comply with any requirement under this title if, prior to the institution of an action under this section, the person notifies the consumer concerned of the failure, complies with the requirements of this title, and makes an appropriate adjustment to the consumer's account and pays actual damages or, where applicable, damages in accordance with section 910 [financial institution liability for damages proximately caused by failure to make an electronic fund transfer].

(f) On a finding by the court that an unsuccessful action under this section was brought in bad faith or for purposes of harassment, the court shall award to the defendant attorney's fees reasonable in relation to the work expended and costs.

(g) Without regard to the amount in controversy, any action under this section may be brought in any United States district court, or in any other court of competent jurisdiction, within one year from the date of occurrence of the violation.

When Mary discovered this EFTA information, it had been nine business days since she had first called her checking account bank to tell them about the error in the transfer of her loan payment to her mortgage servicer. She called her checking account bank one more time. Mary told the customer service rep that, "Unless the error in the transfer of my payment is corrected, or I am credited for the amount of this missing payment by the next business day, in accordance with the Electronic Fund Transfer Act, I will be forced to take legal action."

On the next business day, Mary took all of her relevant checking account and mortgage payment account records, her notes of her calls to the customer service reps at the bank and the loan servicer, and the copies of her missing electronic fund transfer record to the branch of her checking account bank where she had previously had her signature on financial documents guaranteed by a bank officer. When Mary arrived at the bank branch, she told the receptionist that she needed to speak to a bank officer.

Mary was ushered into the office of a bank vice president after a few minutes of waiting in the reception area. She explained her problem to the officer, and that she was aware of her right under the EFTA to a re-credit of her checking account in the amount of the missing payment, if the bank did not resolve her problem by the end of the business day. The officer looked at her records, and at the online version of her bank account. The officer then called a number at the mortgage servicer, telling them that she was an officer of the bank.

After about thirty minutes spent by the bank officer in finding the right person to speak to at the mortgage servicer, and after the mortgage servicer's investigation of the problem, Mary had good news. The bank officer told Mary that her electronic payment had been "incorrectly posted" on the day it was debited from her checking account (26 days earlier). The mistake had been found within the last week. The payment had been correctly credited to Mary's mortgage loan account, and it had been backdated to its original due date. Mary had not been told any of this by her mortgage servicer.

What are the lessons of this story?

1. If you have a problem with an error in an automatic payment from, or deposit to, a financial account, be aware of your rights and responsibilities, and the rights and responsibilities of the financial institutions involved under the Electronic Fund Transfer Act (EFTA).

2. When you attempt to resolve the error with a customer service representative of a bank by telephone, tell them that you are giving them a ten business day notice under the EFTA within which they must investigate the error and respond to you, or else re-credit your account in the amount of the erroneous transfer.

3. If the telephone customer service representatives do not respond appropriately to your requests for assistance, or if the ten business day period has expired without a correction or response, consider speaking to a local officer of the financial institution in person. Bank officers usually have information about whom to contact at other financial institutions that you will not receive from telephone customer service reps. A call from your bank's vice president asking for a resolution of your well-documented problem will usually receive a much more serious and faster response than a call from a consumer service rep will receive. Get to know your friendly local bank officers and remember to thank them when they help you. Your loyalty to your bank will usually be rewarded by their personal assistance when you need it.

4. International Sale of Goods Arbitration747

Mike Bender is the wine buyer for Avanti Stores in the country of Alimentia. Boris Thomson is the sales manager for the BT Vineyards in the country of Napania. After they met at a wine trade fair, and completed their sales negotiations, on 1 June 2011 Mike mailed to Boris an order for 10,000 cases of BT's "Red Sunset 2010" wine at a price of US$60 per case, for a total price of US$600,000.

The wine was to be delivered in three shipments. The first shipment of 5,000 cases was due on 1 August 2011. The second shipment of 2,500 cases was due on 1 September 2011. The third shipment of 2,500 cases was contingent on sales of Red Sunset having reached 5,000 cases by 15 September 2011. The cover letter with the order required an acceptance by 12 June 2011. Otherwise, Avanti would need to make other buying arrangements for its Autumn sales promotions.

The purchase order arrived when Boris Thomson was on a business trip. Boris's secretary e-mailed Mike Bender that Boris was out of the office until 10 June. Mike responded by e-mail that the secretary should have Boris sign and send the offered contract immediately upon his return. Boris signed the contract when he returned from his trip on 10 June 2011, and returned it by courier to Mike Bender, who received it before the 12 June deadline.

On 10 June 2011, after the contract was signed and sent by courier, Boris received an e-mail from Mike stating that he had withdrawn the purchase offer. The e-mail had been received by the computer server at BT on 9 June 2011, but due to a server malfunction was not delivered until 10 June 2011. The reason given in the e-mail for the withdrawal was that a newspaper account reported that BT Vineyards was suspected of adulterating more than 200,000 bottles of wine by deliberately mixing grapes from different vineyards to hide the poor quality of certain prized vintages.

Boris immediately responded to Mike's e-mail, telling him that a manager had mistakenly mixed in some other grapes with the prized vintages. The mistake was caught, the manager was dismissed, and none of the adulterated wine was ever sold to consumers. Mike Bender did not accept Boris Thomson's explanation and refused to accept any of the wine he originally ordered.

The contract that Boris signed has a mandatory arbitration clause, but does not have a choice-of-law clause. Both Alimentia and Napania have ratified the United Nations Convention on Contracts for the International Sale of Goods (CISG). Each country has adopted a national law based on the U.N. Model Law on Electronic Commerce (MLEC).

In their chosen arbitration forum, BT Vineyards has made a claim for US$600,000 for the unpaid contract price for the wine ordered, with interest at the prevailing market rate from the date of breach to the date of payment, $2,500 for storage costs, and all costs of arbitration, including costs incurred by the parties. BT Vineyards argues that Avanti's offer was irrevocable under CISG Article 16, until Boris Thomson had a reasonable time to accept it. BT Vineyards argues that it accepted the contract offer by sending the signed contract to Avanti on 10 June, and that Avanti's refusal to accept the wine is in violation of CISG Article 53.

Avanti Stores denies that its offer to BT Vineyards was irrevocable. It argues that the exchange of e-mails between BT Vineyards' secretary and Mike Bender could not make the offer irrevocable under the rule of CISG Article 16(2)(a). Avanti argues that no contract was formed between it and BT Vineyards. If the arbitrators find that a contract was formed, Avanti argues that, under CISG Article 35(2)(b), the goods "do not conform with the contract" because they are not fit for the "particular purpose expressly or impliedly made known to the seller at the time of the conclusion of the contract", which was to promote the Red Sunset wine for its Autumn sales campaign. Avanti requests the arbitrators to dismiss BT Vineyards' claims, and to order it to pay all costs of the arbitration, including Avanti's legal costs.

BT Vineyards argues that Avanti's offer was irrevocable until 12 June, because Avanti stated a "fixed time for acceptance" under CISG Article 16(2)(a) of 12 June 2011. BT also argues that, under CISG Article 16(2)(b), "it was reasonable for [BT] to rely on the offer as being irrevocable [until 12 June] and [BT] acted in reliance" on such irrevocability, because Mike Bender told BT's secretary by e-mail to have the offer signed and returned immediately upon Boris Thomson's return and before 12 June.

BT Vineyards argues that, under CISG Article 16, it "dispatched an acceptance" before Avanti's email revocation reached BT, making the attempted revocation ineffective. [See Part B, Chapter 5 and Part C, Section I, Chapter 3, f) and Chapter 5, d) on "mailbox rules".] Additionally, it argues that Avanti's single e-mail attempting a revocation was insufficient for this purpose, given that the parties had established a previous "course of dealing" that required a printed offer, acceptance or revocation to be couriered to the other party in order either to form a binding contract, or to revoke an offer. [See Part A, Chapter 5, a), Part B, Chapter 9, i), and Part C, Section II, Chapter 1, b), i) on course of dealing.]

Although the e-mail revocation entered BT's computer system before the acceptance was dispatched, BT Vineyards argues that it was not "received" under the Model Law on Electronic Commerce (MLEC) Article 15(2) underlying principle that an electronic communication is received when it is capable of being retrieved by the recipient. The MLEC Guide to Enactment states, regarding this rule, that "the addressee should not be placed under the burdensome obligation to maintain its information system functioning at all times". [See Part C, Section II, Chapter 2, b), iii) on Electronic Contracts Convention "capable of being retrieved by the addressee" rule.] In addition, BT Vineyards argues that CISG Article 24's definition of "reaches", for purposes of contract formation, implies a requirement of ability to perceive the sent communication, by referring to communications "made orally or delivered... personally".

Avanti argues that, under the contract formation rule of CISG Article 24, its offer revocation "reached" BT Vineyards before BT dispatched its acceptance, because the revocation was delivered to Boris Thomson's personal e- mail address at the computer server at his place of business on the day before Thomson dispatched his acceptance. Avanti argues that its contract offer was revocable at that time, because neither the offer itself, nor Mike Bender's e-mail response to the BT secretary's e-mail concerning Thomson's business trip, stated that the offer was irrevocable until 12 June. Without this type of clear statement of irrevocability, neither CISG Article 16(2)(a)'s rule of irrevocability by indication of irrevocability, nor CISG Article 16(2)(b)'s rule of irrevocability by a reasonable reliance on the irrevocable nature of the offer, applies. The mention of the 12 June deadline in the offer and the e-mail to BT's secretary were only for the purposes of indicating the time limit after which the offer would lapse. [See Part A, Chapter 4, b), i) and Part C, Section I, Chapter 3, e) on irrevocable offers.]

Avanti argues that, contrary to BT's argument regarding the underlying principles of MLEC Article 15(2), the actual text of this article only defines the time of receipt of a "data message" as "the time when the data message enters the designated information system". This does not put the risk of a malfunction of the designated system on the sender of the data message. The offeree's responsibility for the risk that its system might malfunction is confirmed by the CISG Advisory Council Opinion No. 1 that opines that "'reaches' corresponds to the point in time when an electronic communication has entered the addressee's server, if the addressee expressly or impliedly has consented to receiving electronic communications of that type, in that format, and to that address." [See Part C, Section II, Chapter 1, a), ii) on time of sending and receipt of electronic communications under CISG.]

5. Unexpected Changes to a Printed Home Repair Contract

Many of the more expensive contracts that consumers make with businesses are printed. Although they could be in electronic form, they are likely to remain printed, because the familiarity and reliability of a printed form contract (perhaps with "carbon" copies) justifies any extra cost it might have compared to the expense of the subject of the contract. Automobile purchases, home purchases, and home repair contracts are some examples.

Hannah had water on her basement floor after a hard rainstorm. She had never seen water on her floor before, and she became concerned. After several similar experiences, she called a waterproofing company whose advertisements she had heard on the radio.

The company salesman looked at her house's exterior and

interior. He asked her some questions about her experience with water on her basement floor. Then, he made a prepared presentation to her about his company and the work they had done in the city, and in her neighborhood, of placing sump pumps in basements to draw away excess water. The salesman's remarks about a "staircase crack" in her exterior brickwork alarmed Hannah, because the salesman said that it could lead to a catastrophic collapse of the exterior wall at the corner of her house.

Hannah signed a contract with the company to have them place a sump pump in her basement. Because one of her neighbors had a sump pump in his basement, Hannah knew that the location of the pipe to take the water from the pump was important. She negotiated with the salesman to get him to agree that the pipe would extend beyond her backyard to the alley behind her house, where it would empty water away from her yard. Hannah wrote a check for a deposit of 10% of the amount of the price for the work.

When the work crew arrived to excavate her basement for the sump pump, the crew supervisor told Hannah that the location of the drain pipe agreed to in her contract was unworkable, because the distance was too far from the pump to effectively empty water. The supervisor proposed that the drain pipe be relocated to empty into the street at the front of her house. Hannah agreed.

During the following three weeks, Hannah called the company to see what progress they were making in getting the city to agree to allow the drain pipe to empty into the street. After three weeks, the company told her that the city would not allow the drain pipe to empty directly into the street, but would allow the pipe to connect to the sewer pipe under her house, which connected to the city sewer.

While Hannah was waiting for the company to tell her about the city's approval, she had talked with a home inspector. The home inspector told her that she did not need a sump pump at all. He told her that Hannah needed to fix the gaps in some bricks on her exterior porch wall. She needed to grade the concrete sidewalk so that it sloped away from her house. She needed to take the old paneling off her basement walls to see if there were any specific leaks in her basement walls that required plugging. All of that work could be done for much less than the cost of a sump pump, which would not even address the actual causes of the water leaks.

Hannah called the company and cancelled any future work. She asked the company to return her deposit, because the work they originally agreed to do (in locating the drain pipe) had been changed by the company. The first person whom Hannah spoke to said that she did not have authority to return her deposit. She was referred to a supervisor. The supervisor told Hannah that if she wanted to get her deposit back she should have cancelled the contract within three days of signing it, according to local consumer purchase laws. Hannah reminded the supervisor that the contract had been changed by the company after that deadline had passed. She said that if the company did not want to return her deposit, she would take them to small claims court. The supervisor hung up the telephone on Hannah.

Three weeks later, another salesperson from the company called Hannah to tell her that the company was offering a discount on the price of their basement waterproofing service. Hannah told the salesperson that she had already signed a contract with the company, that the company had not done the work that they and she had agreed to, and that a company supervisor had hung up on Hannah when she tried to get her deposit returned. The salesperson said she would try to resolve Hannah's problem.

Two weeks later, Hannah received a check in the mail in the amount of her 10% deposit. No explanation was included with the check.

What are the lessons of this story?

1. Unless the contract gives them the right to change terms, one party cannot change the terms of contract without the other party's permission.

[See Part A, Chapter 7, g) on contract modifications.]

2. The three-day period, included in many consumer protection laws, within which a consumer may rescind a contract for the purchase of goods or services, only limits a consumer's right to rescind without a specific reason. It does not limit a consumer's right to rescind if the business has breached the contract by not performing it as agreed, or by telling the consumer that it will not perform it as previously agreed. [See Part A, Chapter 6, b) on total, partial and material breach, and c) on anticipatory repudiation.]

3. Take your time before committing yourself to an expensive contract. Consult, if you can, with a party who does not have anything to sell you except good advice. It can be worth the price of the advice.

4. Practice patience and politeness with business people on the telephone, even if (especially if) it is not always reciprocated. You never know who might help you to resolve an expensive problem.

GLOSSARY

Arbitration – A private procedure for the resolution of a legal dispute, often pursuant to a contract choice-of-forum clause.

Assignment – A transfer of a legal right (such as a contract right) from one person to another person or entity.

Breach – A failure to perform a duty required by a contract, either when it is due to be performed, or by a repudiation of the duty before it is due (anticipatory repudiation).

Class Action – A lawsuit brought on behalf of multiple plaintiffs, with similar interests, to redress similar harm to each of them caused by the same defendant.

Consideration – A requirement of most U.S. state contract law for the legal enforcement of a promise. If required, it must be exchanged by a party in return for a promise that is to be enforced. The nature of the consideration is usually a benefit to the party whose promise is to be enforced. It can also be a detriment to the party receiving the promise that is to be enforced. Consideration can be in the form of a return promise, an act, or a voluntary failure to act. Courts will not usually measure the value of the consideration.

Convention – A treaty enacted/ratified by multiple nations.

Damages – An award, by a judge or jury, to a plaintiff in a lawsuit (or a claim for such an award) that requires the defendant to pay money for harm caused to the plaintiff.

Delegation – An arrangement for the performance of a contract duty of a party by another person or entity.

Diversity Jurisdiction – The subject matter jurisdiction of a federal trial court over a lawsuit between parties who are citizens of different U.S. states, or between a party who is a citizen of a U.S. state and a party who is a foreign citizen. The "amount in controversy" in the lawsuit must meet a federal statutory threshold.

Equity – 1. The power of a court under U.S. common law, and the rules regarding use of that power, to require a lawsuit party to perform an action, or to refrain from performing an action. 2. The rules and principles of U.S. common law that may supplement or supersede statutory law.

Estoppel – 1. The rule of U.S. common law that a party to a lawsuit cannot benefit by taking a position, or by making an argument or statement, that is contrary to a position it has previously taken, or that is contrary to an argument or statement it has previously made, if this would result in harm to another party. Also, the rule that a party cannot deny a fact that has been legally proved to be true. 2. Promissory Estoppel is a substitute for the requirement of consideration for a contract. It requires a promise that foreseeably and reasonably causes detrimental reliance by the promisee, which detriment can only be remedied by enforcing the promise, as justice requires.

Force Majeure (Act of God) – A type of contract term, or clause, which releases a party from its obligation to perform a contract duty if, and so long as, a condition that is beyond the party's control (such as weather events, labor strikes, and wars) prevents it from performing its duty. These specific events must be unforeseeable at the time of the making of the contract.

Injunction – An order by a judge of a trial court preventing a person or entity from performing an action. A temporary restraining order is an injunction that is in effect until an application for a preliminary or permanent injunction can be decided. A preliminary injunction may be issued during a lawsuit, while a permanent injunction is issued at the end of a lawsuit.

Judgment – A final decision by a trial court judge on the rights and obligations of the parties to a lawsuit, such as their liability or non-liability for damages.

Minority (Age of) – The age, under contract law, below which a person is legally incapable of making an enforceable contract. The age of majority is the age at which a person becomes legally capable of making an enforceable contract. A minor's legal incapacity to make a contract is a defense to its enforcement.

Motion – A formal request made orally, or in writing, by a lawyer to a trial judge for the judge to apply a rule of procedure. Examples include a motion to exclude offered evidence, or to end a trial through a motion for a judgment on the pleadings (legal documents that begin a lawsuit), or a summary judgment or a directed verdict. A motion might also be made for a judgment notwithstanding a contrary verdict, or for a new trial, or for an appeal.

Offer – A promise to perform a contract duty in return for an acceptance, either by a return promise of consideration by the promisee (bilateral contract), or by the performance of a requested action by the promisee (unilateral contract).

Restitution – 1. The subject of U.S. common law (also called unjust enrichment) covering legally required compensation by a person or entity for a benefit provided to them, in circumstances in which it would be unjust for them to not compensate the person or entity providing the benefit. Unlike contract law, the law of restitution does not require the existence of a promise to perform a contract duty. 2. The contract law remedy provided by a trial judge that requires one party to return to another party the value of a benefit provided to them by that other party.

Summary Judgment – A judgment by a trial judge that ends a lawsuit before the trial phase begins, based on the pre- trial pleadings and motions of the parties (complaint, answer, and other legal documents that begin a lawsuit), and made pursuant to the rules of civil procedure requiring that there be no genuine issue of material fact, and that the established facts and relevant law require a judgment in favor of the party requesting the judgment.

Terms – The parts of a contract that describe, among other things, the duties of the parties, the consideration for their promises, representations and warranties of the parties, circumstances of breach, remedies for breach, the parties' choice of law, their choice of forum and whether any terms of the contract exist outside of its written form. Most of a contract is usually made up of terms. Terms might be preceded by a description of the contract purposes ("whereas clauses"), and are usually followed by party signatures, addresses and other information. Contract duties are created by contract terms. U.S. common law and statutory law also imply into contracts certain unwritten (or unspoken) terms, such as duties to perform and to enforce contract duties "in good faith".

Unconscionability – The defense to enforcement of a contract, under U.S. common law and statutory law, based on procedures in contract formation, and/or the substance of contract terms, which are extremely unfair or deceptive.

Unjust Enrichment – See Restitution.

Verdict – The decision by a jury on the facts of a lawsuit, based on the instructions to it by a trial judge of the applicable law. A directed verdict is a judgment by a trial judge that precludes a jury verdict, because the judge determines that the evidence presented at trial can reasonably result in a verdict for only one party.

Versus – Latin for "against"; abbreviated as "v." in the title of lawsuits, such as "Smith v. Jones".

Warranty – 1. A statement by a party in a contract (usually in a "representations and warranties" paragraph) that a particular fact (such as the authority of the party to enter the contract) is true. 2. A statement in a contract for the sale of goods that the goods will have a specific quality, that the goods will perform in a certain way, and that if the goods do not have the guaranteed quality, or perform as promised, a specific remedy will be provided by the seller. 3. A guarantee, implied by law under Article 2 of the Uniform Commercial Code, in a contract for the sale of goods that a) a description, or sample, of the goods is accurate, b) the goods are fit for the ordinary purpose of goods of that type, or c) the goods are fit for the particular purpose of the buyer of the goods.

INTERNET LINKS TO FREE RESOURCES

Consumer Complaints

http://www.consumer.ftc.gov/articles/0228-solving-consumer-problems

This U.S. Federal Trade Commission web page describes various methods for solving consumer problems.

http://www.consumer.ftc.gov/articles/0296-sample-consumer-complaint-letter

This Federal Trade Commission web page provides an example of a consumer complaint letter.

http://www.consumer.ftc.gov/articles/0219-disputing-credit-card-charges

This FTC web page covers how to make a Fair Credit Billing Act complaint.

http://www.consumer.ftc.gov/articles/0176-protections-home-purchases-cooling-rule

This FTC web page describes the FTC rule that gives consumers the right to return certain merchandise within three days of purchase.

http://www.consumer.ftc.gov/articles/0332-credit-debit-and-charge-cards

This FTC web page describes the differences between credit, debit and charge cards, and compares their basic features.

http://www.consumer.ftc.gov/articles/0076-phone-scams

This FTC web page outlines the signs of a telemarketing scam, and the actions consumers should take to protect themselves, including the National Do Not Call Registry.

http://business.ftc.gov/advertising-and-marketing/online-advertising-and-marketing

This web site provides guidance for businesses on how to make clear and conspicuous online information disclosures to avoid unfair or deceptive advertising. It includes the 2013 .com Disclosures Guide described in Part B, Chapter 9, a), the FTC Mail or Telephone Order Merchandise Rule, the CAN-SPAM Act Compliance Guide, and a Selling Internationally (Online) Guide for Businesses. Consumers (and businesses) may want to look at this guidance if they think unfair or deceptive online advertising caused a problem with a purchase.

www.bbb.org

This is the web site of the Better Business Bureau of the United States and Canada. This organization collects and forwards complaints to its member business organizations. It also follows the complaints to see if, and how, they are resolved, and it discloses general information about the number of complaints against its business members and their resolution.

http://www.consumerfinance.gov

This U.S. Consumer Financial Protection Bureau web site allows consumers to file complaints about consumer finance products (like mortgages or student loans) that are forwarded to the product provider and followed.

Online Legal Resources

www.lexisnexis.com and www.lexisweb.com and www.westlaw.com

The Lexis and Westlaw legal research systems are paid subscription online services. They are sometimes available without charge to the public in the law libraries of state courts. Check with your local courts. Lexis and Westlaw are very accurate and up-to-date online libraries of U.S. state and federal judicial decisions/opinions, court records, party briefs (written arguments) and filings, verdicts and settlements, statutes, rules, regulations and pending legislation. These services also include surveys of federal, state, and international law, and secondary source (treatise, digest and encyclopedia) analyses of subject areas of the law. Lexis has also recently launched a free legal search engine called LexisWeb.

www.wirelawyer.com

This is a new Lexis free web search engine for contracts with (it says) access to millions of contracts and forms for use as models.

www.findlaw.com and http://lp.findlaw.com

Findlaw.com is a free online service. Its general web site provides consumer-oriented legal information. Its Findlaw for Professionals web site permits searches by party name for judicial decisions/opinions.

www.plol.org

The Public Library of Law (PLOL) is a free legal research web site sponsored by Fastcase, a paid subscription online legal research service. PLOL allows readers to search for federal and state judicial decisions/opinions, statutes, regulations, court rules, and constitutions.

www.scholar.google.com

Google Scholar allows searches for federal and state judicial decisions/opinions. It also allows searches for articles about law.

www.law.cornell.edu

The Cornell University Law School Legal Information Institute web site allows searches for federal and state statutes and regulations. It also provides a legal dictionary and encyclopedia.

www.law.gov

The web site of the Law Library of Congress has information about federal, state, foreign, and international law and legal information resources.

www.glin.gov

The Global Legal Information Network of the Library of Congress has information about foreign and international law.

www.gpo.gov/fdsys

The U.S. Government Printing Office Federal Digital System Web Site provides links to information about federal statutes, regulations, legislation, and the U.S. Constitution.

www.HG.org

This advertiser-sponsored web site provides information on various areas of the law, law firms and links to legal resources.

www.justia.com

This advertiser-sponsored web site provides general legal information and links to other legal resources.

HOW TO READ A JUDICIAL OPINION

The judicial opinions described in this book have been summarized for the sake of brevity. You might, however, actually read these opinions, or other opinions produced by your research using the online resources previously described. If you do read opinions, here are some ways to read them that might be helpful.

The final judgment by a trial judge is not usually accompanied by an opinion. Some trial judges do write opinions, however, to support their final judgments, or to explain the reasons for their decision on a motion, such as a motion for summary judgment. If a trial judge writes an opinion, an appellate judge might review this written explanation for the trial judge's decision, and, if the decision is a final judgment, the written record/transcript of the trial. Most opinions are written by appellate judges, who are responsible for determining (and explaining) the law applicable in trials. Trial judges (or juries) determine the facts of a lawsuit, pursuant to the rules of evidence, and apply the applicable law to those facts.

U.S. law students learn to read and to understand a judicial opinion by "briefing a case". A case is another term for a lawsuit with a judicial opinion. Students apply an acronym formula called "IRAC", which stands for Issue, Rule, Analysis, Conclusion.

The first thing you will see when you retrieve an opinion is the title of the case (usually the party names), and its citation. A citation is an abbreviation of numbers and letters referring to the location of the opinion in a printed or online volume of a series of case reports, and at a page in that volume. A volume is one book of a series of an official government printed "reporter" of opinions from a specific U.S. state or region or federal circuit, or of an unofficial printed reporter published by a private publisher. The names of the lawyers for the parties and of the judge(s) will often follow the case name and citation.

You might also see a summary of the case presented in short, numbered paragraphs. These "headnotes" were not written by the judge who wrote the opinion that follows, and they are not a part of the official opinion. They are the publisher's attempt to summarize the important parts of the opinion. Some private publishers also use them as a method of cross-referencing, among their various other legal publications, the subjects discussed in them. If the opinion is important to you, however, you should not rely on the publisher's summary. You should analyze the opinion yourself, using the IRAC formula.

Briefing a case means writing down a brief summary of the parts of the opinion that correspond to the parts of the IRAC formula. Where you write it depends on how much detail you want in your "brief". If you want significant detail, you might write it on a separate piece of paper. If only a bare outline of detail is enough, you might write it in the margins of your copy of the opinion. The brief should always be shorter than the actual opinion.

Your brief should begin with a quick summary of the facts of the case that are relevant to the legal issues that are of interest to you. The Issue is the legal issue that the judge addresses in her opinion. There might be multiple issues. It helps to phrase the issue as a question requiring a yes or no answer, such as "Can a state law unconscionability defense deny a consumer contract choice of arbitration, as a mandatory dispute forum, because that choice denies the consumer a right to bring a class arbitration?" This was the issue before the U.S. Supreme Court in *AT&T Mobility LLC v. Concepcion* (described in Part A, Chapter 7, d).

The Rule is the rule of law, existing at time of the opinion, which is relevant to the stated issue. There might be multiple rules. In *Concepcion*, there were two relevant rules. First, California contract law permits (at the time of the decision) a defense of unconscionability to enforcement of a contract, which requires arbitration, but denies class arbitration, if a group of consumer claims are for individual small amounts, and they all claim fraud by the defendant. Second, the Federal Arbitration Act (FAA) authorizes and promotes arbitration as a method of dispute resolution that is faster, cheaper and more informal than court litigation.

The Analysis is the most important part of the brief. It states the judge's reasons for her conclusion, which is her answer to the issue question. There might be multiple reasons. In *Concepcion*, the most important reasons given by the Supreme Court majority for their conclusion were first, that the California contract law interfered with the FAA goals of informality, speed and lower cost. Second, the California contract law created an unacceptable risk that an erroneous decision would occur in a class arbitration, which would not be reviewable by a court, because, unlike court trials, arbitrations are not generally reviewable for errors.

The Conclusion is the brief answer to the Issue question. The Conclusion should briefly state the essence of the opinion, but be specific enough to state what was decided and why. When the conclusion is later compared with other opinion conclusions, it should tell the reader enough to know if those conclusions are consistent with each other. Further details can be retrieved from the actual opinion.

In *Concepcion*, the Conclusion could be stated as "No. A state unconscionability defense cannot prevent enforcement of a contract choice of arbitration that prohibits class arbitration for small claims of fraud, because this defense would conflict with the purposes of the Federal Arbitration Act."

TABLE OF CASES

TABLE OF STATUTES AND TREATIES

TABLE OF OTHER AUTHORITIES

INDEX

NOTES

1. See Kirtsaeng v. John Wiley & Sons, Inc., No. 11-697, 568 U.S. ___ (2013), available at http://www.supremecourt.gov/opinions/12pdf/11- 697_d102.pdf.

2 See Vernor v. Autodesk, Inc., No. 09-35969, (9th Cir. Ct. of Appeals) available at http://cdn.ca9.uscourts.gov/datastore/opinions/2010/09/1 0/09-35969.pdf.

3 See Vernor v. Autodesk, Inc., No. 10-1421, petition for certiorari denied on October 3, 2011.

4 The manner of exercise of an e-book seller's "digital rights management" has sometimes been controversial, such as Amazon.com's deletion of unauthorized copies of George Orwell's books 1984 and Animal Farm from e-book readers without prior notice to its customers. See "Amazon Erases Orwell Books From Kindle" by Brad Stone, New York Times, July 17, 2009.

PART A – GENERAL CONTRACT LAW IN THE UNITED STATES

CHAPTER 1 - What is a Contract?

5 Pre-revolutionary France had a system of law, based on the decisions of *parlements* courts following custom and precedent, which was similar to English common law. This French common law was replaced by the Napoleonic Code. See The Black Count, Glory, Revolution, Betrayal, and the Real Count of Monte Cristo by Tom Reiss (Crown Publishers/Random House, 2012) p. 60 (discussing successful lawsuits for their freedom in these courts by slaves brought to France).

6 Uniform Commercial Code (UCC) §2-205, Firm Offers.

7 UCC §2-209(1), Modification, Rescission and Waiver.

8 UCC §2-209, Official Comment 2.

CHAPTER 2 - Laws Governing Contracts – Common Law and Commercial Code Law of U.S. States; Federal Diversity Jurisdiction Applicable Law; Federal Law on Contracts for the International Sale of Goods

9 Article III, Section 2 of the U.S. Constitution provides that "The judicial Power [of the United States] shall extend...to Controversies...between Citizens of different States...".

10 Title 28 U.S. Code §1332(a) provides that "The district courts shall have original jurisdiction of all civil actions where the matter in controversy exceeds the sum or value of $75,000, exclusive of interest and costs, and is between -
(1) citizens of different States...".

11 See Erie Railroad v. Tompkins, 304 U.S. 64 (Supreme Court 1938).

12 See http://www.uncitral.org/uncitral/uncitral_texts/ sale_goods/ 1980CISG.html.

13 See U.S. Constitution Article VI.

CHAPTER 3 - Legal Rights Similar to Contracts – Restitution (Unjust Enrichment) and Equity

14 See Restatement Third, Restitution and Unjust Enrichment, § 20, Protection of Another's Life or Health.

15 See, for example, Irving H. Picard v. Peter B. Madoff, Adv. Pro. No. 09-1503 (BRL)(05/04/12 complaint, in United States Bankruptcy Court-Southern District of New York, by bankruptcy trustee against daughters-in-law of Ponzi schemer Bernie Madoff for unjust enrichment by use of securities firm as "family piggy bank").

16 See Restatement (Second) of Contracts §24, Offer

Defined.

CHAPTER 4 - Requirements, Formalities and Parties

17 See Restatement (Second) of Contracts §33, Certainty.

18 See Restatement (Second) of Contracts §33, Certainty (reasonable certainty of terms of contract, providing a basis to determine a breach and a remedy, is required for an offer/promise).

19 See Restatement (Second) of Contracts §17, Requirement of a Bargain; §21, Intention to Be Legally Bound.

20 See Restatement (Second) of Contracts §26, Preliminary Negotiations, comment b.

21 See Restatement (Second) of Contracts §36(c), Methods of Termination of the Power of Acceptance.

22 See Restatement (Second) of Contracts §87(1)(a), Option Contract (signed writing reciting exchanged value creates option contract for a reasonable time—majority of states require actual exchanged consideration, while minority require only purported consideration).

23 2011 Florida Statutes, Title XXXIX, Chapter 672, Section 205, Firm Offers.

24 See Restatement (Second) of Contracts §50, Acceptance of Offer Defined.

25 Compare Hamer v. Sidway, 124 N.Y. 538, 27 N.E. 256 (New York Ct. of Appeals, 1891)(consideration requires either detriment to promisor or benefit to promisee, and was satisfied by nephew's promise to refrain from legal drinking, smoking, swearing and playing billiards or cards for money until 21 years old – made in exchange for uncle's promise of $5,000).

26 See Restatement (Second) of Contracts §71, Requirement

of Exchange; Types of Exchange.

27 See Restatement (Second) of Contracts §73, Performance of a Legal Duty.

28 See, for example, Cannon v. Cannon, 384 Md. 537, 865 A. 2d 563 (Md. Ct. of Appeals, 2005) ("Although perhaps based in part on legal fiction and part societal norm, we have stated that the consummation of the marriage is itself sufficient consideration for the antenuptial agreement (but not because it constitutes partial performance).")

29 See UNIDROIT Principles of International Commercial Contracts Article 2.1.1, Manner of Formation; United Nations Convention on Contracts for the International Sale of Goods Article 23.

30 See Petterson v. Pattberg, 248 N.Y. 86, 161 N.E. 428 (New York Ct. of Appeals, 1928).

31 See Restatement (Second) of Contracts §45, Option Contract Created by Part Performance or Tender.

32 See Restatement (Second) of Contracts §90(1), Promise Reasonably Inducing Action or Forbearance.

33 See Charles L. Knapp, Rescuing Reliance: The Perils of Promissory Estoppel, 49 Hastings Law Journal 1191 (1998).

34 See The Trial of Socrates, by I.F. Stone p.181

35 See, for example, State of Florida Constitution §22 (Trial by jury.—The right of trial by jury shall be secure to all and remain inviolate. The qualifications and the number of jurors, not fewer than six, shall be fixed by law.)

36 Other types of contracts covered by a writing and signature requirement may include a contract of an executor or administrator to answer for the duty of his decedent, and contracts made upon consideration of marriage. See Restatement (Second) of Contracts §110(1)(a) and (c), Statute

of Frauds – Classes of Contracts Covered.

37 See Uniform Commercial Code §2-201(1), Formal Requirements; Statute of Frauds.

38 See Uniform Commercial Code §1-206, Statute of Frauds for Kinds of Personal Property Not Otherwise Covered.

39 See Uniform Commercial Code §9-203(b)(3)(A), Attachment and Enforceability of Security Interest; Proceeds; Supporting Obligations; Formal Requisites, and Official Comment 3.

40 See Restatement (Second) of Contracts §130, Contract Not to Be Performed Within a Year.

41 See Restatement (Second) of Contracts §131, General Requisites of a Memorandum.

42 See Restatement (Second) of Contracts §131.

43 See Restatement (Second) of Contracts §132, Several Writings (several writings may together constitute sufficient writing) and §133, Memorandum Not Made as Such (sufficient writing may not have been intended as part of contract).

44 See Restatement (Second) of Contracts §317(2)(a), Assignment of a Right.

45 See Restatement (Second) of Contracts §322, Contractual Prohibition of Assignment.

46 Compare Herzog v. Irace, 594 A. 2d 1106 (Maine Supreme Court, 1991).

47 See Restatement (Second) of Contracts §317(2)(a).

48 See Restatement (Second) of Contracts §317(2)(a) and §322.

49 See Restatement (Second) of Contracts §318, Delegation of Performance of Duty.

50 See Restatement (Second) of Contracts §318.

51 Compare Vogan v. Hayes Appraisal Associates, Inc., 588 N.W.2d 420 (Supreme Court of Iowa, 1999).

52 See Restatement (Second) of Contracts §309, Defenses Against the Beneficiary and §311, Variation of a Duty to a Beneficiary.

CHAPTER 5 - What Are The Terms of a Contract?

53 See, for example, Restatement (Second) of Contracts §20, Effect of Misunderstanding, comment b ("The meaning given to words or other conduct depends to a varying extent on the context and on the prior experience of the parties.")

54 See, for example, Restatement (Second) of Contracts §19(2), Conduct as Manifestation of Assent, and comment b (party bound by own conduct that allows "person of ordinary intelligence" to infer assent to contract from conduct).

55 See Restatement (Second) of Contracts §202(1), Rules in Aid of Interpretation.

56 See Restatement (Second) of Contracts §202(2).

57 See Restatement (Second) of Contracts §202(3)(a).

58 See Restatement (Second) of Contracts §202(3)(b).

59 See Restatement (Second) of Contracts §202(5) and Uniform Commercial Code §1-205, Firm Offers.

60 See Restatement (Second) of Contracts §203(b), Standards of Preference in Interpretation, and Uniform Commercial Code §2-208, Course of Performance or Practical Construction.

61 See Restatement (Second) of Contracts §203(b), Standards

of Preference in Interpretation, and Uniform Commercial Code §1-205, Firm Offers.

62 See Restatement (Second) of Contracts §213, Effect of Integrated Agreement on Prior Agreements (Parol Evidence Rule) and Uniform Commercial Code §2-202, Final Written Expression: Parol or Extrinsic Evidence.

63 See Wood v. Lucy, Lady Duff-Gordon, 118 N.E. 214 (N.Y. Ct. of Appeals, 1917), Restatement (Second) of Contracts §205, Duty of Good Faith and Fair Dealing, and Uniform Commercial Code §1-203, Obligation of Good Faith, §1-201(19) and §2-103(b) (good faith definitions).

64 See Uniform Commercial Code §2-306(1), Output, Requirements and Exclusive Dealings.

65 See Uniform Commercial Code §2-504, Shipment by Seller.

66 See Uniform Commercial Code §2-507, Effect of Seller's Tender; Delivery on Condition.

67 See Uniform Commercial Code §2-509, Risk of Loss in the Absence of Breach, and Uniform Commercial Code §2-510, Effect of Breach on Risk of Loss.

68 See Uniform Commercial Code §2-513, Buyer's Right to Inspection of Goods.

69 2011 Florida Statutes, Title XXXIX, Chapter 671, §102(2), Purposes; Rules of Construction; Variation by Agreement.

70 See Uniform Commercial Code §1-102(3), Purposes; Rules of Construction; Variation by Agreement (obligations of good faith, diligence, reasonableness and care prescribed by UCC may not be eliminated by agreement).

71 See Uniform Commercial Code §1-203, Obligation of Good Faith.

72 See Restatement (Second) of Contracts §205, Duty of Good Faith and Fair Dealing.

73 See Uniform Commercial Code §1-201(19), General Definitions.

74 See Uniform Commercial Code §2-103(1)(b), Definitions and Index of Definitions.

75 See Uniform Commercial Code §2-313, Express Warranties by Affirmation, Promise, Description, Sample.

76 See Uniform Commercial Code §2-313, Official Comment 8.

77 See Uniform Commercial Code §2-314, Implied Warranty: Merchantability; Usage of Trade.

78 See Uniform Commercial Code §2-316, Exclusion or Modification of Warranties.

79 See Uniform Commercial Code §2-316(3)(a).

80 See Uniform Commercial Code §2-316(3)(b).

81 See Uniform Commercial Code §2-316(3)(c).

82 See Uniform Commercial Code §2-315, Implied Warranty: Fitness for Particular Purpose.

CHAPTER 6 - How Are Contracts Broken/Breached?

83 See Uniform Commercial Code §2-316(2) and (4).

84 See Restatement (Second) of Contracts §235(2), Effect of Performance as Discharge and of Non-Performance as Breach.

85 See Restatement (Second) of Contracts §235, Official Comment b.

86 See Restatement (Second) of Contracts §245, Effect of a Breach by Non-Performance as Excusing the Non-Occurrence of a Condition.

87 See Restatement (Second) of Contracts §205, Duty of Good Faith and Fair Dealing.

88 Compare Jacob & Youngs, Inc. v. Kent, 129 N.E. 889 (N.Y. Ct. of Appeals, 1921).

89 See Restatement (Second) of Contracts §243(1), Effect of a Breach by Non-Performance as Giving Rise to a Claim for Damages for Total Breach.

90 See Restatement (Second) of Contracts §242(a), Circumstances Significant in Determining When Remaining Duties Are Discharged.

91 See Restatement (Second) of Contracts §241, Circumstances Significant in Determining Whether a Failure is Material.

92 See Restatement (Second) of Contracts §242, Circumstances Significant in Determining When Remaining Duties Are Discharged.

93 Compare Sackett v. Spindler, 56 Cal. Rptr. 435 (Calif. Ct. of Appeals, 1967).

94 See Restatement (Second) of Contracts §250, When a Statement or Act Is a Repudiation, and Uniform Commercial Code §2-610, Anticipatory Repudiation (must "substantially impair the value of the contract").

95 See Uniform Commercial Code §2-610, Official Comment 2.

96 See Uniform Commercial Code §2-611(1) and Restatement (Second) of Contracts §256(1).

97 See Uniform Commercial Code §2-609(1), Right to Adequate Assurance of Performance; Compare Restatement (Second) of Contracts §251(1), When a Failure to Give Assurance May Be Treated as a Repudiation.

98 See Restatement (Second) of Contracts §251(2).

99 See Uniform Commercial Code §2-609(4).

100 See Uniform Commercial Code §2-609(4) and Restatement (Second) of Contracts §251(2).

CHAPTER 7 - What Defenses Are Possible Against a Claim of Breach?

101 See Restatement (Second) of Contracts §14, Infants.

102 See Restatement (Second) of Contracts §12, Capacity to Contract, Official Comment f.

103 See Restatement (Second) of Contracts §15(1), Mental Illness or Defect.

104 See Restatement (Second) of Contracts §15(2).

105 See Restatement (Second) of Contracts §174, When Duress by Physical Compulsion Prevents Formation of a Contract.

106 See Restatement (Second) of Contracts §175, When Duress by Threat Makes a Contract Voidable, and §176, When a Threat is Improper.

107 Compare Totem Marine Tug & Barge, Inc. v. Alyeska Pipeline Service Co., 584 P. 2d 15 (Supreme Court of Alaska, 1978).

108 See Restatement (Second) of Contracts §173, When Abuse of a Fiduciary Relation Makes a Contract Voidable.

109 See Restatement (Second) of Contracts §177, When Undue Influence Makes a Contract Voidable.

110 Compare Odorizzi v. Bloomfield School District, 54 Cal Rptr. 533 (Calif. Ct. of Appeals, 1966).

111 See Restatement (Second) of Contracts §164, When a Misrepresentation Makes a Contract Voidable (fraudulent or material misrepresentation makes contract voidable if recipient is justified in relying on it).

112 See Restatement (Second) of Contracts §162(2), When a Misrepresentation is Fraudulent or Material.

113 See Restatement (Second) of Contracts §164(1).

114 See Restatement (Second) of Contracts §162(1).

115 See Restatement (Second) of Contracts §161(a), When Non-Disclosure Is Equivalent to an Assertion.

116 Such a "merger" or "integration" clause typically states something like "Neither party shall be bound by any understanding, agreement, promise, or representation, expressed or implied, and not specified herein".

117 See Restatement (Second) of Contracts §161(d) and §173, When Abuse of a Fiduciary Relation Makes a Contract Voidable. See also Restatement (Second) of Contracts §153, When Mistake of One Party Makes a Contract Voidable.

118 Although Llewellyn was American, after his graduation at 16 years of age from Boys High School in Brooklyn in 1909, he studied in Germany and Switzerland. Later, as a Yale undergraduate, he was studying at the Sorbonne in Paris, when World War I began. He sympathized with his German schoolmates, fought surreptitiously with the Prussian Army at the Battle of Ypres, where he was wounded, and was awarded

the Iron Cross (second class). He was later refused as a volunteer in the U.S. Army, because of this "adventure". See Karl Llewellyn and the Realist Movement by William Twining (2d edition, 2012).

119 See Uniform Commercial Code §2-302, Unconscionable Contract or Clause, Official Comment 1.

120 See Restatement (Second) of Contracts §208, Unconscionable Contract or Term.

121 No. 09-893 (2011), available at http://www.supremecourt.gov/opinions/10pdf/09-893.pdf.

122 9 U.S. Code §2, Validity, Irrevocability and Enforcement of Agreements to Arbitrate.

123 Discover Bank v. Superior Court, 113 P. 3d 1100 (Cal. Supreme Ct., 2005).

124 No. 10-948 (2012), available at http://www.supremecourt.gov/opinions/11pdf/10-948.pdf.

125 15 U.S. Code §1679c(a).

126 Dodd-Frank Wall Street Reform and Consumer Protection Act ("Dodd-Frank Act"), available at http://www.gpo.gov/fdsys/pkg/PLAW-111publ203/pdf/PLAW-111publ203.pdf.

127 Dodd-Frank Act §1028(a), Authority to Restrict Mandatory Pre-dispute Arbitration.

128 Dodd-Frank Act §1028(b).

129 See Restatement (Second) of Contracts §187, Non-Ancillary Restraints on Competition.

130 See Restatement (Second) of Contracts §88, Ancillary Restraints on Competition.

131 See Restatement (Second) of Contracts §152, When

Mistake of Both Parties Makes a Contract Voidable, and §154, When a Party Bears the Risk of a Mistake.

132 See Restatement (Second) of Contracts §154(c).

133 Compare Lenawee County Board of Health v. Messerly, 331 N.W. 2d 203 (Mich. Supreme Ct., 1982).

134 See Restatement (Second) of Contracts §153, When Mistake of One Party Makes a Contract Voidable.

135 Compare Wil-Fred's Inc. v. Metropolitan Sanitary District, 372 N.E. 2d 946 (Ill. App. Ct., 1978).

136 See Restatement (Second) of Contracts, §261, Discharge by Supervening Impracticability, §262, Death or Incapacity of Person Necessary for Performance, §263, Destruction, Deterioration or Failure to Come into Existence of Thing Necessary for Performance, §264, Prevention by Governmental Regulation or Order; Uniform Commercial Code §2-613, Casualty to Identified Goods, and §2-615, Excuse by Failure of Presupposed Conditions. See also Restatement (Second) of Contracts §269, Temporary Impracticability or Frustration.

137 See Restatement (Second) of Contracts §272, Relief Including Restitution.

138 Compare Taylor v. Caldwell, 122 Eng. Rep. 309 (K.B. 1863).

139 See Restatement (Second) of Contracts §265, Discharge by Supervening Frustration.

140 Compare Krell v. Henry, 2 K.B. 740 (C.A. 1903).

141 See Restatement (Second) of Contracts §271, Impracticability as Excuse for Non-Occurrence of a Condition.

142 See Restatement (Second) of Contracts §279, Substituted Contract. See also Restatement (Second) of Contracts §280, Novation (substitution of a new party to the original contract).

143 Compare Alaska Packers' Association v. Domenico, 117 F. 99 (9th Fed. Cir., 1902).

144 See Restatement (Second) of Contracts §89(c), Modification of Executory Contract.

145 See Restatement (Second) of Contracts §89(a).

146 See Uniform Commercial Code §2-209(1), Modification, Rescission, and Waiver.

147 See Uniform Commercial Code §2-209(2).

148 See Restatement (Second) of Contracts §281, Accord and Satisfaction.

149 See Uniform Commercial Code §1-207(2), Performance or Acceptance Under Reservation of Rights. See also Uniform Commercial Code §2-209, Official Comment 2 (modifications must be negotiated in good faith).

CHAPTER 8 - How Are Contracts Enforced, or How Is Compensation Made for a Contract Breach?

150 See Lon L. Fuller & William R. Perdue, Jr., The Reliance Interest in Contract Damages, 46 Yale Law Journal 52 (1936), and Restatement (Second) of Contracts §344 Purpose of Remedies.

151 See Restatement (Second) of Contracts §347, Measure of Damages in General.

152 See Restatement (Second) of Contracts §351, Unforeseeability and Related Limitations on Damages, and §352, Uncertainty as a Limitation on Damages. See also Uniform Commercial Code §2-715, Buyer's Incidental and Consequential Damages.

153 See Restatement (Second) of Contracts §350, Avoidability as a Limitation on Damages.

154 Compare Walser v. Toyota Motor Sales, U.S.A., Inc., 43 F. 3d 396 (8th Fed. Cir., 1994).

155 Compare Walser v. Toyota Motor Sales, U.S.A., Inc., 43 F. 3d 396 (8th Fed. Cir., 1994).

156 See Restatement (Second) of Contracts §90(1), Promise Reasonably Inducing Action or Forbearance.

157 See Restatement (Second) of Contracts §349, Damages Based on Reliance Interest.

158 See Restatement (Second) of Contracts §349.

159 Compare Handicapped Children's Education Board v. Lukaszewski, 332 N.W. 2d 774 (Wisc. Supreme Ct., 1983).

160 See Restatement (Second) of Contracts §348, Alternatives to Loss in Value of Performance.

161 Compare Rockingham County v. Luten Bridge Co., 35 F. 2d 301 (4th Fed. Cir., 1929).

162 See Restatement (Second) of Contracts §351(1) and (2), Unforeseeability and Related Limitations on Damages. See also Uniform Commercial Code §2-715, Buyer's Incidental and Consequential Damages.

163 See Hadley v. Baxendale, 156 Eng. Rep. 145 (Ct. of Exchequer 1854).

164 See Restatement (Second) of Contracts §353, Loss Due to Emotional Disturbance.

165 See Restatement (Second) of Contracts §355, Punitive Damages.

166 See Uniform Commercial Code §2-711, Buyer's Remedies in General; Buyer's Security Interest in Rejected Goods.

167 See Uniform Commercial Code §2-712, "Cover"; Buyer's Procurement of Substitute Goods.

168 See Uniform Commercial Code §2-715, Buyer's Incidental and Consequential Damages (Consequential damages must be mitigated).

169 See Uniform Commercial Code §2-713, Buyer's Damages for Non-Delivery or Repudiation.

170 See Uniform Commercial Code §2-714, Buyer's Damages for Breach in Regard to Accepted Goods.

171 See Uniform Commercial Code §2-716, Buyer's Right to Specific Performance or Replevin.

172 See Uniform Commercial Code §2-607, Effect of Acceptance; Notice of Breach; Burden of Establishing Breach After Acceptance; Notice of Claim or Litigation to Person Answerable Over (notice of breach after tendered goods accepted by buyer).

173 See Uniform Commercial Code §2-715, Buyer's Incidental and Consequential Damages.

174 See Uniform Commercial Code §2-715(2)(a).

175 See Uniform Commercial Code §2-715(2)(b).

176 See Uniform Commercial Code §2-709, Action for the Price.

177 See Uniform Commercial Code §2-706, Seller's Resale Including Contract for Resale.

178 See Uniform Commercial Code §2-708, Seller's Damages for Non-acceptance or Repudiation.

179 See Uniform Commercial Code §2-710, Seller's Incidental Damages.

180 See Uniform Commercial Code §1-103, Supplementary General Principles of Law Applicable.

181 See Restatement (Second) of Contracts §370, Requirement That Benefit Be Conferred.

182 See, for example, United States ex. rel. Coastal Steel Erectors, Inc. v. Algernon Blair, Inc., 479 F. 2d 638 (4th Fed. Cir., 1973).

183 See Restatement (Second) of Contracts §373(2), Restitution When Other Party Is in Breach.

184 See Restatement (Second) of Contracts §374, Restitution in Favor of Party in Breach, and Uniform Commercial Code §2-718(2), Liquidation or Limitation of Damages; Deposits. See, for example, Lancellotti v. Thomas, 491 A. 2d 117 (Superior Ct. of Pa., 1985).

185 See Restatement (Second) of Contracts §374(2).

186 See Restatement (Second) of Contracts §374, Official Comment b. Compare "substantial performance" damages described in Chapter 6.

187 See Restatement (Second) of Contracts §375, Restitution When Contract Is Within Statute of Frauds, and §376, Restitution When Contract Is Voidable.

188 See Restatement (Second) of Contracts §377, Restitution in Cases of Impracticability, Frustration, Non-Occurrence of Condition or Disclaimer by Beneficiary.

189 See Restatement (Second) of Contracts §359, Effect of Adequacy of Damages. See also Uniform Commercial Code §2-716(1), Buyer's Right to Specific Performance or Replevin.

190 See Restatement (Second) of Contracts §360, Factors Affecting Adequacy of Damages.

191 See Restatement (Second) of Contracts §362, Effect of Uncertainty of Terms.

192 See Restatement (Second) of Contracts §364, Effect of Unfairness.

193 See Restatement (Second) of Contracts §365, Effect of Public Policy.

194 See Restatement (Second) of Contracts §366, Effect of Difficulty in Enforcement or Supervision.

195 See Restatement (Second) of Contracts §367, Contracts for Personal Service or Supervision.

196 See, for example, Reier Broadcasting Company, Inc. v. Kramer (Supreme Ct. of Montana, 2003) (injunction against working for competitor denied because of state statute).

197 See Restatement (Second) of Contracts §356, Liquidated Damages and Penalties. See also Uniform Commercial Code §2-718.

PART B - ELECTRONIC CONTRACTS

CHAPTER 1 - What is an Electronic Contract?

198 See NFL Players Association announces deal with DocuSign, at www.nfl.com/news (April 23, 2013).

199 The Class Action Fairness Act of 2005, 28 U.S. Code §1332(d), grants to federal district courts jurisdiction over class actions between any parties who are citizens of different states, where the aggregate amount in controversy exceeds $5

million. This statute was enacted to permit defendants to avoid class action plaintiff-friendly state courts and juries, in specified circumstances, by removing to federal trial courts class actions filed in state courts. The U.S. Supreme Court ruled in March, 2013 that a class plaintiff's lawyer cannot avoid federal court by making a non-binding stipulation, before the class is certified/approved by a court, that its total damages will be less than $5 million. See The Standard Fire Insurance Company v. Knowles, No. 11-1450, available at http://www.supremecourt.gov/opinions/12pdf/11-1450_9olb.pdf.

200 See U.S. Census Bureau News, February 15, 2013.

CHAPTER 2 - Laws Governing Electronic Contracts

201 U.N. Commission on International Trade Law, Model Law on Electronic Commerce Adopted by the United Nations Commission on International Trade Law, General Assembly Resolution 51/162, U.N. Doc. A/51/162 (Jan. 30, 1997).

202 15 United States Code §7001, General Rule of Validity, available at http://www.gpo.gov/fdsys/pkg/USCODE-2011-title15/pdf/USCODE-2011- title15-chap96.pdf.

203 15 United States Code §7001(a), General Rule of Validity—In General.

204 15 United States Code §7001(c)(1), General Rule of Validity--Consumer Disclosures, Consent to Electronic Records.

205 15 United States Code §7003(a) and (b), Specific Exceptions, Additional Exceptions.

206 15 United States Code §7021, Transferable Records.

207 No. 10-21418-CIV-Moore/Simonton, 2011 U.S. Dist. LEXIS 17517 (S.D. Florida, 2011).

208 17 United States Code §204, Execution of Transfers of Copyright Ownership.

209 No. 12-cv-00954, 2012 U.S. Dist. LEXIS 162111 (D. Md., 2012).

210 See 17 United States Code §204, Execution of Transfers of Copyright Ownership.

211 15 United States Code §7002, Exemption to Preemption.

212 See www.uniformlaws.org (web site of the National Conference of Commissioners on Uniform State Laws).

213 See Uniform Electronic Transactions Act §14, Automated Transaction.

214 See Uniform Electronic Transactions Act §7, Legal Recognition of Electronic Records, Electronic Signatures, and Electronic Contracts.

215 See Uniform Electronic Transactions Act §10, Effect of Change or Error.

216 See Uniform Electronic Transactions Act §15, Time and Place of Sending and Receipt.

217 15 United States Code §7001(b)(2), General Rule of Validity--Preservation of Rights and Obligations, and Uniform Electronic Transactions Act §5, Use of Electronic Records and Electronic Signatures; Variation by Agreement. Compare DWP Pain Free Medical P.C. v. Progressive Northeastern Insurance Co., 14 Misc. 3d 800 (N.Y. Dist. Ct., 2006) (Neither E-SIGN nor UETA requires use of electronic signatures or writings by private parties where agreement stated "electronic signatures are not acceptable".) with Seagate v. CIGNA, No. C 05-4272 PVT, 2006 WL1071881 (Northern Dist. of California April 21, 2006)(Requirement of "written notice" to change insurance beneficiary could be satisfied by electronic communication, if contract parties so intended.)

CHAPTER 3 -Examples – "Shrink-wrap", "Browse-wrap", "Click-wrap" and Other Electronic Contracts

218 See Uniform Commercial Code §2-102, Scope; Certain Security and Other Transactions Excluded from this Article.

219 See Uniform Commercial Code §2-105, Definitions: Transferability; "Goods"; "Future" Goods; "Lot"; "Commercial Unit".

220 See Advent Systems Limited v. Unisys Corp., 925 F. 2d 670 (3d Fed. Circuit Ct. of Appeals, 1991).

221 See Brower v. Gateway 2000, Inc., 676 N.Y.S. 2d 569 (N.Y. Sup. Ct., App. Div., 1998).

222 See Klocek v. Gateway, Inc., 104 F. Supp. 2d 1332 (District of Kansas, 2000).

223 See Register.com, Inc. v. Verio, Inc., 356 F. 3d 393 (2d Fed. Circuit Ct. of Appeals, 2004).

224 See Restatement (Second) of Contracts §69, Acceptance by Silence or Exercise of Dominion.

225 See Browse-wrap Agreements: Validity of Implied Assent in Electronic Form Agreements by C. Kunz, J. Ottaviani, E. Ziff, J. Moringiello, K. Porter and J. Debrow, 59 Business Lawyer 279 (Nov. 2003), and Ticketmaster Corp. v. Tickets.com, Inc., No. CV997654HLHVBKX, 2003 WL 21406289 (Central Dist. Cal. Mar. 7, 2003)(Offeror may specify that taking certain action is acceptance of offer—as with transport tickets, parking lot tickets, claim checks, and shrink-wrap licenses.)

226 See Marso v. United Parcel Service, Inc., No. COA11-201 (N. Carolina Ct. of Appeals Sept. 20, 2011).

227 See Hotels.com L.P. v. Canales, 195 S.W. 3d 147 (Tex. Ct. App., 2006), Salco Distributors, LLC v. iCode, Inc. No. 8:05-CV-642-T-27TGW, (Middle District of Florida, 2006),

and Hubbert v. Dell Corp., 835 N.E. 2d 113 (Ill. Ct. App., 2005), appeal denied, 844 N.E. 2d 965 (Ill. 2006)--each case discussed in Survey of the Law of Cyberspace: Electronic Contracting Cases 2005-2006, by J. M. Moringiello and W.L. Reynolds, 62 Business Lawyer 195 (Nov. 2006).

228 See Cloud Corporation v. Hasbro Inc., No. 02-1486 (7th Cir. Fed. Ct. of Appeals, 2002)(For pre-E-SIGN contract, e-mail was sufficient writing under UCC §2-201(1), and sender's name on an e-mail satisfies the signature requirement of the Statute of Frauds.)

CHAPTER 4 -Formalities for an Electronic Contract?

229 United Nations Model Law on Electronic Commerce with Guide to Enactment 1996 with additional article 5 bis as adopted in 1998, available at http://www.uncitral.org/pdf/english/texts/electcom/05-89450_Ebook.pdf.

230 See Uniform Electronic Transactions Act §8, Provision of Information in Writing; Presentation of Records.

231 15 United States Code §7001(e), General Rule of Validity--Accuracy and Ability to Retain Contracts and Other Records.

232 See Uniform Electronic Transactions Act §8(a).

233 See Uniform Electronic Transactions Act §8(c).

234 See Uniform Electronic Transactions Act §9(a), Attribution and Effect of Electronic Record and Electronic Signature.

235 See Uniform Electronic Transactions Act §9(b).

236 15 United States Code §7006(5), Definitions.

237 UETA §11, Notarization and Acknowledgement; 15 United States Code §7001(g), General Rule of Validity—

Notarization and Acknowledgement.

238 Directive 1999/93/EC of the European Parliament and of the Council of 13 December 1999 on a Community framework for electronic signatures.

239 Model Law on Electronic Signatures of the United Nations Commission on International Trade Law, G.A. Res. 56/80, U.N. Doc. A/Res/56/80 (Jan. 24, 2002).

240 No. 299025, Marquette Circuit Court, LC No. 09-047293-CZ, June 12, 2012, available at http://www.michbar.org/opinions/appeals/2012/061212/5 1855.pdf.

241 MCL 450.839, Attribution and Effect of Electronic Record and Electronic Signature.

242 See Title 28 United States Code, Appendix --Federal Rules of Evidence, Art. X, Rules 1001-1005 (as amended by the United States Congress and the United States Supreme Court, December 1, 2010).

243 15 United States Code §7001(d)(1)-(3), General Rule of Validity—Retention of Contracts and Records.

244 2011 Florida Statutes, Title XXXIX, Chapter 668, Section 50(12)(a) and (d).

245 See From Mount Sinai to Cyberspace: Making Good E-Business Records by R.A. Kahn and D.J. Silverberg, 57 Business Lawyer 431, November 2001.

246 See 15 United States Code §7001(d)(2) and Uniform Electronic Transactions Act §12(b).

CHAPTER 5 - Was a Contract Created, and When? (Time and Place of Sending and Receipt)

247 See Restatement (Second) of Contracts §60, Acceptance of Offer Which States Place, Time, or Manner of Acceptance

(If method of acceptance only suggested, another method is not precluded.)

248 See Restatement (Second) of Contracts §63(a), Time When Acceptance Takes Effect.

249 2011 Florida Statutes, Title XXXIX, Chapter 668, Section 50(15)(a) and (b).

250 See International Shoe Co. v. Washington, 326 U.S. 310 (1945).

251 2011 Florida Statutes, Title XXXIX, Chapter 668, Section 50(15)(d).

252 See, for example, 2011 Florida Statutes, Title XXXIX, Chapter 668, Section 50(15)(c), (e), (f) and (g).

CHAPTER 6 - What Are the Terms of an Electronic Contract? (Mistake and error)

253 See Restatement (Second) of Contracts §152, When Mistake of Both Parties Makes a Contract Voidable.

254 See Restatement (Second) of Contracts §153, When Mistake of One Party Makes a Contract Voidable.

255 See Uniform Electronic Transactions Act §10(1), Effect of Change or Error.

256 2011 Florida Statutes, Title XXXIX, Chapter 668, Section 50(10)(b).

257 See Uniform Electronic Transactions Act §10(3) and (4).

CHAPTER 7 - Who Can Act for the Parties to An Electronic Contract? (Automated Transactions and Electronic Agents)

258 15 United States Code §7001(h), Electronic Agents.

259 2011 Florida Statutes, Title XXXIX, Chapter 668, Section 50(14), Automated Transactions.

CHAPTER 8 - How Are Electronic Contracts Broken/Breached?

260 676 N.Y.S. 2d 569 (New York Supreme Court, Appellate Division, 1998).

261 2005 ME 37, 870 A.2d 133 (Maine Supreme Judicial Court, 2005).

262 Appeal No. 2004-137, 984 A. 2d 1061 (R.I. Supreme Ct., 2009).

263 Docket No. 00-9596, 356 F.3d 393 (2d Cir. Fed. Ct. of Appeals, 2004).

264 See Restatement (Second) of Contracts §69(1)(a), Acceptance by Silence or Exercise of Dominion.

265 306 F. 3d 17 (2d Fed. Cir. 2002).

266 Appeal No. 2004-137, 984 A. 2d 1061 (R.I. Supreme Ct., 2009).

267 No. 3-06-CV-0891-B (Northern District of Texas, 2007).

268 508 F. Supp. 2d 228 (Southern District of New York, 2007).

269 100 F. Supp. 2d 1058 (Northern District of Calif., 2000).

270 551 F. 3d 412, 2008 FED App. 0462P (6th Cir. Fed. Ct. of Appeals, 2008).

271 No. 04-1828, 407 F. 3d 546 (1st Cir. Fed. Ct. of Appeals, 2005).

272 No. 95,102, 144 P. 3d 747 (Kansas Supreme Ct., 2006)

273 No. 05 C 6923 (N. Dist. Ill., 2006).

274 No. 06-10749 (Eastern Dist. of Michigan, 2007), affirmed on other grounds (waiver of right to arbitration through

delay) in No. 07-2300 (6th Cir. Fed. Ct. of Appeals, 2009).

275 No. H-07-2543 (Southern Dist. of Texas, 2007).

276 No. 06-2540, 513 F.Supp. 2d 229 (Eastern Dist. of Pa., 2007).

277 CV 9905 (KMW) (Southern Dist. of N.Y., 2006).

278 No. 11 CIV 918 (RJH) (Southern Dist. of N.Y., 2012).

279 See Carnival Cruise Lines, Inc. v. Shute, 499 U.S. 585, 587 (1991).

280 No. 11 C 5857, 2012 U.S. Dist. LEXIS 40394 (Northern Dist. Illinois, Eastern Div.).

281 Nos. 05-3743, 05-3986, 474 F. 3d 379 (7th Cir. Fed. Ct. of Appeals, 2007).

282 No. 06 Civ 2490 (BHD) (Southern Dist. of N.Y., 2008).

283 No. 09 CVS 2582 (Ct. of Appeals of North Carolina, 2011).

284 No. 04-CIV-0030E(Sr) (Western Dist. of N.Y., 2007), affirmed in No. 07-2656-cv, 310 Fed. Appx. 447 (2d Cir. Fed. Ct. of Appeals, 2009).

285 No. 06 C 4467 (N. Dist. Illinois, 2007).

286 No. 3:03-CV-271 1-B, 425 F. Supp. 2d 756 (N. Dist. Texas, 2006).

287 2011 Florida Statutes, Title XXXIX, Chapter 671, Section 671.201(10), General Definitions.

288 No. 09-1110, (Central Dist. Ill., 2009).

CHAPTER 9 - What Defenses Are Possible Against a Claim of Breach?

289 See http://www.ftc.gov/os/2013/03/ 130312dotcomdisclosures. pdf. (2013 .com Disclosures)

290 See http://business.ftc.gov/documents/bus41-dot-com-disclosures-information-about-online-advertising. (2000 Dot Com Disclosures)

291 2013 .com Disclosures at 1.

292 15 United States Code §45.

293 2013 .com Disclosures at 6.

294 2013 .com Disclosures at ii.

295 2013 .com Disclosures at 6.

296 2000 Dot Com Disclosures at 2.

297 15 United States Code §8401.

298 15 United States Code §8402(a).

299 15 United States Code §8402(b).

300 15 United States Code §8403.

301 16 Code of Federal Regulations §310.2(u). See http://ecfr.gpoaccess.gov.

302 See http://www.ftc.gov/os/2009/02/ P064202negativeoptionreport.pdf.

303 15 United States Code §8404.

304 15 United States Code §8405.

305 California Business and Professions Code §§17600-17606.

306 California Business and Professions Code §17601.

307 California Business and Professions Code §17602(a)(3).

308 California Business and Professions Code §17602(b).

309 California Business and Professions Code §17604(b).

310 California Business and Professions Code §17603.

311 California Business and Professions Code §17605.

312 18 U.S. Code §2510.

313 See Ticketmaster Corp. v. Tickets.com, No. CV99-7654 (Central Dist. of California, March 27, 2000).

314 No. CV 99-7654, August 10, 2000.

315 No. CV 99-7654, March 6, 2003.

316 Nos. 01-7860, 01-7870, 01-7872, 306 F. 3d 17 (2d Fed. Cir. Ct. of Appeals, 2002).

317 18 U.S. Code §2510.

318 18 U.S. Code §1030.

319 No. 00-0962, (Mass. Superior Court, 2001).

320 See http://www.ag.ny.gov/press-release/comp-usa-settlement-requires-disclosure-internet-sales.

321 544 F.Supp. 2d 473 (Eastern Dist. of Va., 2008), affirmed in part and reversed in part and remanded in 562 F. 3d 630 (4th Fed. Cir. Ct. of Appeals, 2009).

322 495 F. 3d 1062 (9th Fed. Cir. Ct. of Appeals, 2007).

323 No. 09-4201-cv, 380 Fed. Appx. 22 (2d Fed. Cir. Ct. of Appeals, 2010).

324 No. 8:12-cv-0812-JST (RNBx), (Central Dist. Calif.,

August 28, 2012).

325 No. A-5022-09T3, 419 N.J. Super. 596, 18 A. 3d 210, 2011 N.J. Super LEXIS 91 (Superior Ct. N.J., App. Div., 2011).

326 No. 5:09-CV-1547, 2010 U.S. Dist. LEXIS 81502 (N. Dist. Ohio, 2010).

327 (Multidistrict Litigation), 2012 U.S. Dist. LEXIS 141803 (D. Nevada, 2012).

328 Hines v. Overstock.com, 668 F. Supp. 2d 362, at 367.

329 No. 10 C 2675, 795 F. Supp. 2d 770, 2011 U.S. Dist. LEXIS 72088 (N. Dist. Ill, Eastern Div., 2011)

330 795 F. Supp. 2d at 792.

331 795 F. Supp. 2d at 793.

332 2012 N.Y. Misc. LEXIS 1224 (Dist. Ct. of N.Y., 1st Dist, Nassau Cty.).

333 No. PC 97-0331, (R.I. Superior Ct., 1998).

334 No. A-2182-97T5, 323 N.J. Super. 118, 732 A. 2d 528 (N.J. Superior Ct., Appellate Division, 1999).

335 No. 97-CT-046534-CP, Ontario Superior Court of Justice, 1999.

336 No. CV 02-5164(DRH)(WDW), 309 F. Supp. 2d 446 (Eastern Dist. of N.Y., 2004).

337 No. 00 C 1366, (N. Dist. Illinois, 2000).

338 9 U.S. Code §4.

339 15 U.S. Code §7001(c) and (e).

340 No. 401325/06, NY Slip Opinion 50845(U) (N.Y. Sup. Ct., 2008).

341 544 F. Supp. 2d 473 (Eastern Dist. of Va., 2008), affirmed in part and reversed in part and remanded in 562 F. 3d 630 (4th Fed. Cir. Ct. of Appeals, 2009).

342 No. 4:08-CV-301, (E. Dist. Tex., 2009).

343 No. 09-cv-1557(JFB)(ARL), 684 F. Supp. 2d 313 (E. Dist. N.Y., 2010).

344 No. 3466, 282 A.D. 2d 180, 726 N.Y.S. 2d 60 (Supreme Ct. of N.Y., Appellate Division, 2001).

345 No. 04 CIV 2121 (SCR), 346 F. Supp. 2d 563 (S. Dist. N.Y., 2004).

346 No. 03-2582-GTV-DJW, (Dist. Kansas, 2004).

347 No. 401325/06, NY Slip Opinion 50845(U) (N.Y. Sup. Ct., 2008).

348 551 F. 3d 412, 2008 FED App. 0462P (6th Fed. Cir. Court of Appeals, 2008).

349 2011 Florida Statutes, Title XXXIX, Chapter 668, Section 50(2)(h).

350 2011 Florida Statutes, Title XXXIX, Chapter 668, Section 50(9)(a) and (b).

351 Civil No. 05-5093 (Western Dist. of Arkansas, 2006)

352 Compare 2011 Florida Statutes, Title XXXIX, Chapter 668, Section 50(5)(b): This section applies only to transactions between parties each of which has agreed to conduct transactions by electronic means. Whether the parties agree to conduct a transaction by electronic means is determined from the context and surrounding circumstances, including the parties' conduct.

353 No. 04-12293-WGY, 415 F. Supp. 2d 6 (Dist. Mass., 2006).

354 No. 07-2604-KHV (Dist. Kansas, 2009).

355 No. 07-C-589, 570 F. Supp. 2d 1061 (E. Dist. Wisc., 2008).

356 Wis. Stat. §402.204(1).

357 Wis. Stat. §§137.11-137.26.

358 Wis. Stat. §137.13(2).

359 No. A124262 (Cal. App., 2010).

360 No. CV 09-2373 AHM (RZx) (C. Dist. Cal., 2009).

361 No. 1517, 196 Md. App. 318, 9 A. 3d 508 (Md. Ct. Spec. App., 2010).

362 704 F. Supp. 2d 499 (Dist. Md., 2010).

363 No. 11-1311-CV, 2012 U.S. App. LEXIS 18875 (2d Fed. Cir. Ct. of Appeals, 2012)

364 No. 11-1311-CV, 2012 U.S. App. LEXIS 18875 at footnote 14.

365 No. 11-1311-CV, 2012 U.S. App. LEXIS 18875 at page 48.

366 No. 11-1311-CV, 2012 U.S. App. LEXIS 18875 at footnote 18.

367 No. CO9-1392JLR, 2011 U.S. Dist. LEXIS 150145 (Western Dist. Wash., 2012)

368 No. CO9-1392JLR, 2011 U.S. Dist. LEXIS 150145 at page 27.

369 No. 4D05-1193, 920 So. 2d 1286 (Fla. Ct. of Appeal,

2006).

370 No. 2:04-CV-592 TC (Dist. Utah, 2005).

371 No. 08-13234, 2009 U.S. Dist. LEXIS 13662 (E.Dist. Mich., 2009).

372 No. C06-1325Z (W. Dist. Wash., 2006).

373 Civil Action No. 06-4925, 487 F. Supp. 2d 593 (E. Dist. Pa, 2007).

374 No. C-07-01700 RMW (N. Dist. Cal., 2007).

375 No. C 07-03967 (N. Dist. Cal., 2008).

376 No. 4:09-cv-0089-SEB-WGH (S. Dist. Indiana, 2009).

377 No. 09-cv-01840-RBJ-CBS, 857 F. Supp. 2d 1135, 2012 U.S. Dist. LEXIS 31076 (Dist. Colo. 2012).

378 857 F. Supp. 2d at 1143.

379 857 F. Supp. 2d at 1151.

380 No. C-09-5443 EDL, 805 F. Supp. 2d 904, 2011 U.S. Dist. LEXIS 85983 (N. Dist. Calif., 2011).

381 No. 2:07-CV-916-TC (Dist. Utah, 2008).

382 No. 3:09-cv-217-M, 622 F. Supp. 2d 396 (N. Dist. Texas, 2009).

383 18 U.S. Code §2710.

384 No. RWT 07cv1203, 575 F. Supp. 2d 696 (Dist. Md., 2008).

385 No. 08 CIV 8980 (PKC) (S. Dist. N.Y., 2009).

386 No. 82S04-0806-CV-00309, 906 N.E. 2d 805 (Supreme Ct. of Indiana, 2009).

387 No. 08-3194, 345 Fed. Appx. 74 (6th Fed. Cir. Ct. of Appeals, 2009).

388 No. 09-62020-CIV-Altonaga/Brown, 2011 U.S. Dist. LEXIS 29999 (S. Dist. Fla. 2011).

389 See Restatement Second of Contracts §89(c), Modification of Executory Contract (promissory estoppel basis for enforcement) and compare §150, Reliance on Oral Modification (promissory estoppel basis for enforcement of subsequent oral modification not satisfying a Statute of Frauds).

390 Nos. 10-11209 and 10-11251, 424 Fed. Appx. 862 (11th Fed. Cir. Ct. of Appeals, 2011).

391 See 2011 Florida Statutes, Title XXXIX, Chapter 672, Section 609(4).

392 No. 06-6147, 741 F. Supp. 2d 651 (Dist. N.J., 2010).

CHAPTER 10 - How Are Electronic Contracts Enforced, or How is Compensation Made for a Contract Breach?

393 Council Directive 93/13/EEC of April 5, 1993 on unfair terms in consumer contracts. See http://eur-lex.europa.eu/LexUriServ/LexUriServ.do?uri=CELEX:3199 3L0013:EN:NOT.

394 Directive 97/7/EC of the European Parliament and of the Council of 20 May 1997 on the protection of consumers in respect of distance contracts. See http://eur-lex.europa.eu/LexUriServ/LexUriServ.do?uri=CELEX:3199 7L0007:EN:HTML.

395 Directive 1999/44/EC of the European Parliament and

of the Council of 25 May 1999 on certain aspects of the sale of consumer goods and associated guarantees. See http://eur-lex.europa.eu/LexUriServ/LexUriServ.do?uri=CELEX:3199 9L0044:EN:HTML.

396 Directive 2005/29/EC of the European Parliament and of the Council of 11 May 2005 concerning unfair business-to-consumer commercial practices in the internal market. See http://eur-lex.europa.eu/LexUriServ/LexUriServ.do?uri=OJ:L:2005:149 :0022:01:EN:HTML.

397 Directive 2011/83/EU of the European Parliament and of the Council of 25 October 2011 on consumer rights. See http://eur-lex.europa.eu/LexUriServ/LexUriServ.do?uri=OJ:L:2011:304 :0064:0088:EN:PDF.

398 OFT 311 Unfair Contract Terms Guidance, Guidance for the Unfair Terms in Consumer Contracts, Regulations 1999, September 2008. See http://www.oft.gov.uk/ shared_oft/reports/unfair_contract_ terms/oft311.pdf.

399 See The Impact of EU Unfair Contract Terms Law on U.S. Business-to-Consumer Internet Merchants, The Business Lawyer, Volume 62, Number 1, November 2006, Section of Business Law, American Bar Association, pages 209, 211.

400 15 United States Code §7006(1).

401 Council Directive 93/13/EEC of April 5, 1993 on unfair terms in consumer contracts, Article 2(b).

402 See The Impact of EU Unfair Contract Terms Law on U.S. Business-to-Consumer Internet Merchants, The Business Lawyer, Volume 62, Number 1, November 2006, Section of Business Law, American Bar Association, pages 209, 215.

CHAPTER 11 – European Union Consumer Contract Law

403 Council Directive 93/13/EEC of April 5, 1993 on unfair terms in consumer contracts, Article 3.1.

404 See http://www.eu-consumer-law.org/caselaw_en.cfm.

405 BGH (DE) 09. Dec. 2009 VIII ZR 219/08.

406 See http://www.clauses-abusives.fr/recom/03r01.htm.

407 See www.quechoisir.org.

408 See The Impact of EU Unfair Contract Terms Law on U.S. Business-to-Consumer Internet Merchants, The Business Lawyer, Volume 62, Number 1, November 2006, Section of Business Law, American Bar Association, pages 209, 224.

409 Unfair Terms in Consumer Contracts Regulations 1999, No. 2083, Provision 8 (U.K.). See http://www.legislation.gov.uk/uksi/1999/2083/contents/made.

410 Unfair Terms in Consumer Contracts Regulations 1999, No. 2083, Provision 12 (U.K.). See http://www.legislation.gov.uk/uksi/1999/2083/contents/made.

411 See OFT Press Release, July 6, 2006 available at http://www.oft.gov.uk/news-and-updates/press/2006/111-06.

412 See The Impact of EU Unfair Contract Terms Law on U.S. Business-to-Consumer Internet Merchants, The Business Lawyer, Volume 62, Number 1, November 2006, Section of Business Law, American Bar Association, pages 209, 225.

413 Council Directive 93/13/EEC of April 5, 1993 on unfair terms in consumer contracts, Article 5.

414 Directive 97/7/EC of the European Parliament and of the Council of 20 May 1997 on the protection of consumers in respect of distance contracts, Annex I.

415 Distance Selling Directive Articles 4, 6.1 and 7.1.

416 Sales Guarantees Directive Article 2(a). Compare Uniform Commercial Code §2-313.

417 Sales Guarantees Directive Article 2(c). Compare Uniform Commercial Code §2-314.

418 Sales Guarantees Directive Article 2(b). Compare Uniform Commercial Code §2-315.

419 Sales Guarantees Directive Articles 3, 4 and 5.

420 Sales Guarantees Directive Articles 6 and 7. Compare Magnuson-Moss Warranty Act, 15 U.S. Code §§2301-2312.

421 Directive 2000/31/EC of the European Parliament and of the Council of 8 June 2000 on certain legal aspects of information society services, in particular electronic commerce, in the Internal Market (Directive on electronic commerce). See http://eur-lex.europa.eu/LexUriServ/LexUriServ.do?uri=CELEX:32000L0031:EN:HTML.

422 Directive on Electronic Commerce Articles 6 and 7.

423 Directive on Electronic Commerce Article 9.

424 Directive on Electronic Commerce Articles 10 and 11.

425 Directive on Electronic Commerce Article 12.

426 Directive 2005/29/EC of the European Parliament and of the Council of 11 May 2005 concerning unfair business-to-consumer commercial practices in the internal market. See

http://eur-lex.europa.eu/LexUriServ/
LexUriServ.do?uri=OJ:L:2005:149 :0022:01:EN:HTML.

427 Directive on Unfair Business-to-Consumer Commercial Practices Article 5.

428 Directive on Unfair Business-to-Consumer Commercial Practices Article 2(h).

429 2011 Florida Statutes §671.203, Obligation of Good Faith.

430 Directive on Unfair Business-to-Consumer Commercial Practices Article 5, paragraph 3.

431 Directive on Unfair Business-to-Consumer Commercial Practices Article 8.

432 Directive on Unfair Business-to-Consumer Commercial Practices Article 2(j).

433 Directive on Unfair Business-to-Consumer Commercial Practices Article 9(b) and (e).

434 Directive on Unfair Business-to-Consumer Commercial Practices, Annex I, paragraph 14.

435 Directive on Unfair Business-to-Consumer Commercial Practices, Annex I, paragraph 11.

436 Directive on Unfair Business-to-Consumer Commercial Practices, Annex I, paragraph 26.

437 Directive on Unfair Business-to-Consumer Commercial Practices, Annex I, paragraph 28.

438 Directive 2011/83/EU of the European Parliament and of the Council of 25 October 2011 on consumer rights, Article 31. See http://eur-lex.europa.eu/LexUriServ/
LexUriServ.do?uri=OJ:L:2011:304

:0064:0088:EN:PDF.

439 Consumer Rights Directive Article 5, paragraph 3.

440 Consumer Rights Directive Article 5, paragraph 1.

441 Consumer Rights Directive Article 6, paragraph 1.

442 Consumer Rights Directive Article 8, paragraph 2.

443 Consumer Rights Directive Article 8, paragraph 3-7.

444 Consumer Rights Directive Article 9, paragraph 1.

445 Consumer Rights Directive Article 9, paragraph 2.

446 Consumer Rights Directive Article 13.

447 Consumer Rights Directive Article 14, paragraph 1.

448 Consumer Rights Directive Article 16.

449 Consumer Rights Directive Article 19.

450 Consumer Rights Directive Article 20.

451 Consumer Rights Directive Article 21.

452 Consumer Rights Directive Article 27.

PART C - INTERNATIONAL CONTRACTS

SECTION I. COMMERCIAL CONTRACTS

CHAPTER 1 - Choice-of-Forum and Choice-of-Law Clauses

453 See, for example, New York State General Obligations Law §5-1402, which provides that:

Choice of forum. 1. ...[A]ny person may maintain an action or proceeding against a foreign corporation, non-resident, or foreign state where the action or proceeding arises out of or relates to any contract, agreement or undertaking for which a choice of New York law has been made in whole or in part pursuant to section 5-1401 and which (a) is a contract, agreement or undertaking, contingent or otherwise, in consideration of, or relating to any obligation arising out of a transaction covering in the aggregate, not less than one million dollars, and (b) which contains a provision or provisions whereby such foreign corporation or non-resident agrees to submit to the jurisdiction of the courts of this state.

2. Nothing contained in this section shall be construed to affect the enforcement of any provision respecting choice of forum in any other contract, agreement or undertaking.

454 See, for example, Piper Aircraft Co. v. Reyno, 454 U.S. 235 (1981) explaining U.S. federal court rules on *forum non conveniens*, including the lesser legal presumption in favor of a U.S. forum choice by a non-U.S. plaintiff.

455 See, for example, New York State General Obligations Law §5-1401, which provides:

Choice of law. 1. The parties to any contract, agreement or undertaking, contingent or otherwise, in consideration of, or relating to any obligation arising out of a transaction covering in the aggregate not less than two hundred fifty thousand dollars, including a transaction otherwise covered by subsection one of section 1-105 of the uniform commercial code, may agree that the law of this state shall govern their rights and duties in whole or in part, whether or not such contract, agreement or undertaking bears a reasonable relation to this state. This section shall not apply to any contract, agreement or undertaking (a) for labor or personal services, (b) relating to any transaction for personal, family or household services, or (c) to the extent provided to the contrary in subsection two of section 1-105 of the uniform commercial code.

2. Nothing contained in this section shall be construed to limit or deny the enforcement of any provision respecting choice of law in any other contract, agreement or

undertaking.

IRB-Brasil Resseguros, S.A. v. Inepar Investments, S.A., Inepar S.A. Industria e Construcoes (New York Ct. of Appeals, Dec. 18, 2012) considered whether, despite a choice of New York state law, and a choice of a New York state court forum, in contracts for loans (negotiable promissory notes) to a Brazilian-Uruguayan company, application of New York conflict of laws rules was necessary to determine whether or not Brazilian contract law applied in litigation by a Brazilian buyer of the defaulted loans. The court decided that the purpose of the New York State General Obligations Law §5-1401 and §5-1402 was to avoid a conflict of laws analysis where a contract choice of law and forum met these statutory requirements. The purposes of the laws was "to allow parties without New York contacts to choose New York law to govern their contracts", "to encourage the parties of significant commercial, mercantile or financial contracts to choose New York law", and "to permit the parties to choose New York's well-developed system of commercial jurisprudence". The court ruled that express contract language excluding New York conflict of laws principles was unnecessary.

456 2011 Florida Statutes §671.105(1), Territorial application of the code; parties' power to choose applicable law.

457 2011 Florida Statutes §671.105(2).

458 See Graves, Jack M. (2006) "Party Autonomy in Choice of Commercial Law: The Failure of Revised U.C.C. § 1-301 and a Proposal for Broader Reform," Seton Hall Law Review: Vol. 36: Iss. 1, Article 3. Available at: http://erepository.law.shu.edu/shlr/vol36/iss1/3.

459 Convention of 30 June 2005 on Choice of Court Agreements. See http://www.hcch.net/index_en.php?act=conventions.text&c id=98.

460 See http://www.hcch.net/index_en.php?act= conventions.status &cid=98.

461 June 10, 1958, 21 U.S.T. 2517, T.I.A.S. No. 6997, 330 U.N.T.S. 38.

462 See, for example, District of Columbia Statutes §15-364, Standards for recognition of foreign-country judgment, in "Uniform Foreign-Country Money Judgments Recognition Act of 2011". See also U.S. Supreme Court decisions in The Bremen v. Zapata Off-Shore Co., 407 U.S. 1 (1972) (Negotiated choice-of-forum clause in international transaction is valid, unless proved unreasonable and unjust, or invalid for such reasons as fraud or overreaching), and Scherk v. Alberto-Culver Co., 417 U.S. 506 (1974) (Negotiated choice of arbitration forum in Paris, France in international business sale is valid, unless proved invalid under Bremen grounds.)

CHAPTER 2 - The Convention on Contracts for the International Sale of Goods

463 General Assembly Resolution 51/162 of 16 December 1996, UNCITRAL Model Law on Electronic Commerce with Guide to Enactment 1996, with additional article 5 bis as adopted in 1998. See http://www.uncitral.org/uncitral/en/ uncitral_texts/electroni c_commerce/1996Model.html.

464 June 10, 1958, 21 U.S.T. 2517, T.I.A.S. No. 6997, 330 U.N.T.S. 38. See http://www.uncitral.org/uncitral/en/ uncitral_texts/arbitrati on/NYConvention.html.

465 April 11, 1980, 1489 U.N.T.S. 3. See http://www.uncitral.org/uncitral/en/uncitral_texts/sale_goo ds/1980CISG.html.

466 See CISG Article 2(a).

467 UCC §1-102(3) similarly permits contract parties to change by their agreement the rules of the UCC as they apply to their contract "except as otherwise provided in [the UCC]".

468 See, for example, Asante Technologies v. PMC-Sierra, Inc., 164 F. Supp. 2d 1142 (N. Dist. Cal., 2001). See also The International Contract: Knowing When, Why, and How To "Opt Out" of the United Nations Convention on Contracts for the International Sale of Goods by Allison E. Butler, 76 Fla. Bar J. 24, May 2002.

469 CISG penultimate sentence.

CHAPTER 3 - The CISG Compared to the UCC

470 For a section-by-section comparison of the CISG, UCC Article 2, and the Principles of International Commercial Contracts, see Contracts for the Sale of Goods: a comparison of U.S. and international law, by Henry D. Gabriel (Oxford Univ. Press, 2d ed. 2009)

471 2011 Florida Statutes §671.103, Supplementary General Principles of Law Applicable.

472 CISG Article 4.

473 See, for example, 2011 Florida Statutes §95.11(2)(b) establishing a five year period for "A legal or equitable action on a contract, obligation or liability founded on a written instrument…", §95.11(3)(k) establishing a four year period for "A legal or equitable action on a contract, obligation or liability not founded on a written instrument, including an action for the sale and delivery of goods, wares, and merchandise, and on store accounts", §95.11(3)(l) establishing a four year period for "An action to rescind a contract," and §95.11(5)(a) establishing a one year period for "An action for specific performance of a contract."

474 1974 Convention on the Limitation Period in the International Sale of Goods, as amended by the 1980

Protocol Amending the Convention on the Limitation Period in the International Sale of Goods, Article 8. See http://www.uncitral.org/pdf/english/texts/sales/limit/limit _conv_E_Ebook.pdf.

475 CLPISG Article 4.

476 CLPISG Article 5(a).

477 CLPISG Article 1(3)(a).

478 CLPISG Article 3(2).

479 CLPISG Articles 22(2) and 23.

480 CISG Article 39(2).

481 2011 Florida Statutes §672.607(3)(a).

482 CISG Article 11: "A contract of sale need not be concluded in or evidenced by writing and is not subject to any other requirement as to form. It may be proved by any means, including witnesses."

483 MCC-Marble Ceramic Center v. Ceramica Nuova d'Agostino, 144 F. 3d 1384 (11th Fed. Cir. Ct. of Appeals, 1998).

484 See MCC-Marble Ceramic Center v. Ceramica Nuova d'Agostino.

485 2011 Florida Statutes §672.204(3).

486 2011 Florida Statutes §672.305(1).

487 See, for example, 2011 Florida Statutes §672.205.

488 See Teaching the CISG in Contracts by William S. Dodge, 50 Journal of Legal Education 72, 79 (March 2000).

489 2011 Florida Statutes §672.207(1).

490 2011 Florida Statutes §672.207(2).

491 2011 Florida Statutes §672.207(3).

492 CISG Article 19(3) states "Additional or different terms, relating, among other things, to the price, payment, quality and quantity of the goods, place and time of delivery, extent of one party's liability to the other or the settlement of disputes are considered to alter the terms of the offer materially."

493 2011 Florida Statutes §672.316(3)(b).

494 2011 Florida Statutes §672.715(2)(b).

495 2011 Florida Statutes §672.609(1).

496 2011 Florida Statutes §672.609(2).

497 2011 Florida Statutes §672.609(4).

498 2011 Florida Statutes §672.601.

499 2011 Florida Statutes §672.508(1).

500 2011 Florida Statutes §672.715(2)(a).

501 See 2011 Florida Statutes §671.103, Supplementary General Principles of Law Applicable.

502 2011 Florida Statutes §672.613.

503 2011 Florida Statutes §672.615(1).

504 See The Unidroit Principles 2010: An International Restatement of Contract Law by Michael Joachim Bonell ("Bonell"), Georgetown University Law Center, Center for Transnational Business and the Law, Symposium on the 2010 UNIDROIT Principles of International Commercial Contracts: Towards A "Global" Contract Law ("2011 PICC Symposium"), available at http://www.law.georgetown.edu/cle/materials/UNIDROIT/2011.pdf.

CHAPTER 4 - The Principles of International Commercial Contracts

505 See http://unidroit.org.

506 See http://www.unidroit.org/english/principles/contracts/main. htm.

507 See Bonell at 3.

508 PICC Preamble (Purposes of the Principles).

509 These concerns might be alleviated by parties appending the text of the PICC to their contracts and incorporating its rules into their contracts by reference, if they wish to have them applied by U.S. judges. Professor Henry D. Gabriel, Elon University School of Law and Eckart Brödermann of Brödermann & Jahn, Hamburg, made this suggestion at the 2011 PICC Symposium at Georgetown Law School.

510 See The UNIDROIT Principles of International Commercial Law, An American Perspective on the Principles and Their Use by Henry D. Gabriel ("Gabriel") Georgetown University Law Center, Center for Transnational Business and the Law, Symposium on the 2010 UNIDROIT Principles of International Commercial Contracts: Towards A "Global" Contract Law ("2011 PICC Symposium"), available at http://www.law.georgetown.edu/cle/materials/UNIDROIT/2011.pdf.

511 The Ministry of Defense and Support for the Armed Forces of the Islamic Republic of Iran v. Cubic Defense Systems, Inc., Civ. Case No. 98-1165-B, 29 F. Supp. 2d 1168 (S.D. Cal., 1998).

512 See Krstic v. Princess Cruise Lines, No. 09-23846-CIV-GOLD/MCALILEY, 706 F. Supp. 2d 1271 (S.D. Fla., 2010).

513 Gabriel at 17.

514 PICC Article 1.1, Freedom of Contract.

515 PICC Article 1.7, Good Faith and Fair Dealing.

516 PICC Article 1.8, Inconsistent Behaviour.

517 PICC Article 1.9, Usages and Practices.

518 See The UN Sales Convention, The UNIDROIT Contract Principles and The Way Beyond, 25 Journal of Law & Commerce 451, 455 (2005) by Herbert Kronke.

519 Bonell at 21.

520 Bonell at 21.

CHAPTER 5 - The PICC Compared to the Restatement 2d of Contracts and UCC

521 PICC Article 1.2, No Form Required.

522 PICC Article 1.4, Mandatory Rules.

523 PICC Article 2.1.17, Merger Clauses.

524 Restatement (Second) of Contracts §205.

525 2011 Florida Statutes §671.203, Obligation of Good Faith.

526 2011 Florida Statutes §671.102(2)(b), Purposes; rules of construction; variation by agreement.

527 2011 Florida Statutes §671.201(20), General definitions.

528 2011 Florida Statutes §672.103(1)(b), Definitions and index of definitions.

529 PICC Article 1.7, Good Faith and Fair Dealing.

530 PICC Article 2.1.15, Negotiations in Bad Faith.

531 PICC Article 2.1.16, Duty of Confidentiality.

532 See Friedrich Kessler & Edith Fine, Culpa in Contrahendo, Bargaining in Good Faith and Freedom of Contract: A Comparative Study, 77 Harvard Law Review 401 (1964).

533 See Contracts, 4th Edition by E. Allen Farnsworth, §3.26, Precontractual Liability ("Farnsworth") (discussing cases).

534 See Farnsworth, §3.26 (discussing cases).

535 See Farnsworth, §3.26 (discussing practical reasons for reluctance to impose pre-contractual liability; also discussing trend in favor of enforcement of agreements to negotiate, such as letters of intent).

536 See Restatement (Second) of Contracts, §226, How an Event May Be Made a Condition.

537 PICC Article 5.3.1, Types of Condition.

538 Gabriel at 28.

539 PICC Article 2.1.6, Mode of Acceptance.

540 PICC Article 2.1.9, Late Acceptance. Delay in Transmission.

541 PICC Article 2.1.4, Revocation of Offer.

542 See Restatement (Second) of Contracts §45, Option Contract Created by Part Performance or Tender, and §87, Option Contract.

543 PICC Article 2.1.22, Battle of Forms.

544 PICC Article 3.2, Validity of Mere Agreement.

545 See PICC Article 7.1.7, Force Majeure.

546 Restatement (Second) of Contracts §359(1), Effect of

Adequacy of Damages.

547 2011 Florida Statutes §672.709, Action for the Price.

548 2011 Florida Statutes §672.502, Buyer's Right to Goods on Seller's Repudiation, Failure to Deliver, or Insolvency.

549 2011 Florida Statutes §672.716, Buyer's Right to Specific Performance or Replevin.

550 PICC Article 7.2.2, Performance of Non-Monetary Obligation.

551 PICC Article 7.2.4, Judicial Penalty.

552 PICC Article 7.3.1, Right to Terminate the Contract.

553 See Restatement (Second) of Contracts §241, Circumstances Significant in Determining Whether a Failure Is Material, §242, Circumstances Significant in Determining When Remaining Duties Are Discharged, §243, Effect of a Breach by Non-Performance as Giving Rise to a Claim for Damages for Total Breach.

554 PICC Article 7.3.2(1), Notice of Termination.

555 PICC Article 7.1.4, Cure by Non-Performing Party.

556 Restatement (Second) of Contracts §317(2)(a), Assignment of a Right.

557 Restatement (Second) of Contracts §317(2)(b).

558 See Restatement (Second) of Contracts §317(2)(c) and §322, Contractual Prohibition of Assignment.

559 PICC Article 1.4, Mandatory Rules.

560 PICC Article 9.1.9(2), Non-Assignment Clauses.

561 See PICC Chapter 11, Plurality of Obligors and of Obligees.

562 PICC Article 10.2 (1) and (2), Limitation Periods.

563 PICC Article 10.3, Modification of Limitation Periods by the Parties.

564 PICC Article 10.9, The Effects of Expiration of Limitation Period.

565 PICC Article 1.4, Mandatory Rules.

566 See Gabriel at 29.

SECTION II. INTERNATIONAL ELECTRONIC CONTRACTS AND ONLINE DISPUTE RESOLUTION PROPOSALS

CHAPTER 1 - Electronic Contracts Under Pre-CUECIC Law

567 See CUECIC Status at http://www.uncitral.org/uncitral/en/uncitral_texts/electronic_commerce/2005Convention_status.html.

568 CUECIC Article 23.1, Entry Into Force.

569 CISG Article 7(2).

570 CISG Article 11.

571 See Pace University Law School CISG Database, CISG-Advisory Council Opinion No. 1, Electronic Communications under CISG, Comment 11.1, available at http://www.cisg.law.pace.edu/cisg/CISG-AC-op1.html.

572 CISG-Advisory Council Opinion No. 1, Comment 13.1.

573 CISG-Advisory Council Opinion No. 1, Comment 13.2.

574 CISG-Advisory Council Opinion No. 1 on CISG Article 24.

575 CISG-Advisory Council Opinion No. 1 on CISG Article

20(1).

576 CISG-Advisory Council Opinion No. 1 on CISG Article 20(1), Comment 20.3.

577 CISG-Advisory Council Opinion No. 1 on CISG Article 20(1), Comment 20.4.

578 CISG-Advisory Council Opinion No. 1 on CISG Article 20(1), Comment 20.5.

579 CISG-Advisory Council Opinion No. 1 on CISG Article 21(2).

580 CISG-Advisory Council Opinion No. 1 on CISG Article 21(2), paragraphs 21.3-21.6.

581 CISG-Advisory Council Opinion No. 1 on CISG Article 65.

582 CISG-Advisory Council Opinion No. 1 on CISG Article 19(2).

583 Statute of the International Court of Justice, June 26, 1945, 59 Stat. 1055, Treaty Series No. 993, 3 Bevans 1179.

584 2011 Florida Statutes §671.102, Purposes; rules of construction; variation by agreement.

585 2011 Florida Statutes §671.205, Course of performance; course of dealing; usage of trade.

586 UCC §1-205 Official Comment 4.

587 UCC §1-205 Official Comment 5.

588 UCC §1-205 Official Comment 6.

589 UCC §1-205 Official Comment 4.

590 UCC §1-205 Official Comment 9.

591 Directive 2000/31/EC of the European Parliament and of the Council of 8 June 2000 on certain legal aspects of information society services, in particular electronic commerce, in the Internal Market (Directive on electronic commerce), Articles 10 and 11. See http://eur-lex.europa.eu/LexUriServ/LexUriServ.do?uri=CELEX:3200 0L0031:EN:HTML.

592 See http://business.ftc.gov/documents/bus41-dot-com-disclosures-information-about-online-advertising.

593 See Przemyslaw P. Polanski, Customary Law of the Internet (2007) at 333-337.

594 United Nations Model Law on Electronic Commerce with Guide to Enactment 1996 with additional article 5 bis as adopted in 1998, available at http://www.uncitral.org/pdf/english/texts/electcom/05-89450_Ebook.pdf.

595 15 U.S. Code §7001-7007.

596 See, for example, 2011 Florida Statutes §668.50, Uniform Electronic Transaction Act.

597 MLEC Guide to Enactment, paragraph 5.

598 See 2011 Florida Statutes §671.102(1)(b) (UCC purpose to permit the continued expansion of commercial practices through custom, usage and agreement of the parties).

CHAPTER 2 - The United Nations Convention on the Use of Electronic Communications in International Contracts (CUECIC, the Electronic Contracts Convention, or the ECC)

599 See UNCITRAL Working Group on Electronic Commerce, Note by the Secretariat, Proposal by the United States of America, U.N. Doc. A/CN.9/WG.IV/WP.77 (May 25, 1998) available at www.uncitral.org/pdf/english/workinggroups/wg_ec/wp-77.pdf; see also E-SIGN, 15 U.S.C. §7031(a)(1) (The Secretary of Commerce shall promote international acceptance and use of electronic signatures based on Model Law on Electronic Commerce principles, including technological and national neutrality.)

600 15 U.S.C. §7031(a)(2).

601 See UNCITRAL CUECIC web page on "Why is it Relevant?"available at http://www.uncitral.org/uncitral/en/uncitral_texts/electronic_commerce/2005Convention.html.

602 See Press Release, General Assembly, General Assembly Adopts New Convention on Use of Electronic Communications in International Contracting, U.N. Doc. GA/10424 (Nov. 23, 2005) available at http://www.un.org/News/Press/docs/2005/ga10424.doc.htm.

603 See http://www.uncitral.org/uncitral/en/uncitral_texts/electroni c_commerce/2005Convention_status.html.

604 CUECIC Article 23.1, Entry into force.

605 See Resolution 303 of the American Bar Association House of Delegates 2006 A.B.A. Section of Science & Technology Law, A.B.A. Section of International Law Resolution 303, at note 2 (2006) available at http://apps.americanbar.org/intlaw/policy/investment/unel ectroniccomm0806.pdf.

606 Report on Implementing the United Nations Convention on the Use of Electronic Communications in International Contracts, International Issues Working Group, Cyberspace

Committee, Section of Business Law, April 2010.

607 Case No. 06-984, decided March 25, 2008, available at http://www.supremecourt.gov/opinions/07pdf/06-984.pdf.

608 April 24, 1963, 21 U.S.T. 77, T.I.A.S. No. 6820, 596 U.N.T.S. 261.

609 U.S. Constitution Article VI.

610 Report on Implementing the United Nations Convention on the Use of Electronic Communications in International Contracts, International Issues Working Group, Cyberspace Committee, Section of Business Law, April 2010.

611 See Charles H. Martin, The UNCITRAL Electronic Contracts Convention: Will It Be Used or Avoided? Volume XVII Pace International Law Review 261 (Fall 2005) in footnote 112, available at http://papers.ssrn.com/sol3/cf_dev/AbsByAuth.cfm?per_id =490498.

612 See Uniform Law Commission Guidelines For Uniform Law Commission Participation In The Negotiation And Implementation Of Private International Law Conventions at http://www.uniformlaws.org/shared/docs/IntlLegalDev/Co nvention%20Implementation%20Guidelines_Jan12.pdf.

613 See CUECIC Article 19.2, Declarations on the Scope of Application ("Any Contracting State may exclude from the scope of application of this Convention the matters it specifies in a declaration…".)

614 CUECIC Article 20(1), Communications Exchanged Under Other International Conventions.

615 CUECIC Article 1.1, Scope of Application.

616 See Asante Technologies v. PMC-Sierra, Inc., 164 F. Supp. 2d 1142 (N. Dist. Cal., 2001), and the discussion of the required CISG opt-out contract language in Part C, Section I,

Chapter 2.

617 CUECIC Preamble.

618 See Charles H. Martin, The UNCITRAL Electronic Contracts Convention: Will It Be Used or Avoided? Volume XVII Pace International Law Review 261 (Fall 2005) available at http://papers.ssrn.com/sol3/cf_dev/AbsByAuth.cfm?per_id =490498.

619 CUECIC Article 1.1, Scope of Application.

620 CUECIC Article 4(h), Definitions.

621 CISG Article 1(a) (U.S. version excludes applicability of CISG by conflict-of-laws/private international law rules under Article 1(b).)

622 CUECIC Article 1.1, Scope of Application, and Explanatory Note, paragraph 60, available at http://www.uncitral.org/uncitral/en/uncitral_texts/electroni c_commerce/2005Convention.html.

623 CUECIC Article 2, Exclusions.

624 CUECIC Article 2, Exclusions.

625 CISG Article 6.

626 CUECIC Article 3, Party Autonomy.

627 CISG Article 7(1).

628 CUECIC Article 5.1, Interpretation.

629 CISG Article 7(2).

630 CUECIC Article 5.2, Interpretation.

631 CUECIC Article 20.1, Communications exchanged under other international conventions.

632 CUECIC Article 4, Definitions.

633 CUECIC Article 8.1, Legal recognition of electronic communications.

634 CUECIC Article 9.1, Form Requirements.

635 CUECIC Article 6, Location of the parties. This article provides rules for determining the "place of business" of a party. These rules depend on the location indicated by a party, proof of location by the other party, the place of business with the closest relationship to the contract, and a natural person's habitual residence.

636 CUECIC Article 10, Time and place of dispatch and receipt of electronic communications.

637 CUECIC Article 11, Invitations to make offers.

638 CUECIC Article 12, Use of automated message systems for contract formation.

639 CUECIC Article 14, Error in electronic communications.

CHAPTER 3 - Major Differences Between Pre-CUECIC and CUECIC Rules

640 CISG-Advisory Council Opinion No. 1 on CISG Article 13.

641 CUECIC Article 9.3, Form requirements.

642 CUECIC Article 10.

643 CISG-Advisory Council Opinion No. 1 on CISG Article 15.

644 CUECIC Explanatory Note, paragraph 99, available at http://www.uncitral.org/pdf/english/texts/electcom/06-57452_Ebook.pdf.

645 CUECIC Article 12, Use of automated message systems for contract formation.

646 See Charles H. Martin, The Electronic Contracts Convention, The CISG, and New Sources of E-Commerce Law, 16 Tulane Journal of International and Comparative Law 467 (Spring 2008) at 492 regarding artificial intelligence-programmed electronic agents.

647 CUECIC Article 9.4.

648 CUECIC Article 9.5(b).

649 CUECIC Article 6, Location of the parties.

650 CISG Article 10.

651 CUECIC Article 14, Error in electronic communications.

652 CISG Article 27.

653 2011 Florida Statutes §668.50(10), Effect of Change or Error.

654 Statute of the International Court of Justice, June 26, 1945, 59 Stat. 1055, Treaty Series No. 993, 3 Bevans 1179.

655 MLEC Guide to Enactment, paragraph 5, available at http://www.uncitral.org/pdf/english/texts/electcom/05-89450_Ebook.pdf.

656 MLEC Article 8, Original.

657 CUECIC Article 9.4, Form Requirements.

658 See, for example, 2011 Florida Statutes §668.50(12)(d), Retention of Electronic Records; Originals.

659 MLEC Article 15, Time and place of dispatch and receipt of data messages.

660 MLEC Article 15.

661 MLEC Article 13, Attribution of data messages.

662 15 U.S. Code §§7001-7007.

663 15 U.S. Code §7001(a), General Rule of Validity, In General.

664 15 U.S. Code §7002, Exemption to Preemption.

665 See, for example, 2011 Florida Statutes §668.50.

666 CUECIC Article 2.1(a), Exclusions.

667 CUECIC Article 2.1(b).

668 CUECIC Article 2.2.

669 15 U.S. Code §7003, Specific Exceptions.

670 See, for example, 2011 Florida Statutes §668.50(3), Scope.

671 CUECIC Article 3, Party Autonomy.

672 See, for example, 2011 Florida Statutes §668.50(5), Use of Electronic Records and Electronic Signatures; Variation by Agreement, and §668.50(8) (d) (Electronic record equivalence with required writing rule cannot be varied by agreement, except to extent writing requirement of other law permits.)

673 CUECIC Article 3, Party Autonomy.

674 See, for example, 2011 Florida Statutes §668.50(5)(b).

675 15 U.S. Code §7002(a), Exemption to Preemption, In General.

676 15 U.S. Code §7001(a), General Rule of Validity, In General, and 15 U.S. Code §7002(a), Exemption to Preemption, In General.

677 15 U.S. Code §7001(c), Consumer Disclosures.

678 See, for example, 2011 Florida Statutes §668.50(8), Provision of Information in Writing; Presentation of Records, and §668.50(11), Notarization and Acknowledgement.

679 CUECIC Article 2.1, Exclusions, and Article 7, Information Requirements.

680 CUECIC Article 9.2, Form Requirements.

681 2011 Florida Statutes §668.50(9)(a), Attribution and Effect of Electronic Record and Electronic Signature.

682 15 U.S. Code §7001(d)(1) Retention of contracts and records--Accuracy and accessibility, and (2) Exception. 2011 Florida Statutes §668.50(12)(a)- (c) Retention of Electronic Records; Originals.

683 15 U.S. Code §7001(d)(3), Retention of contracts and records—Originals. 2011 Florida Statutes §668.50(12)(d) Retention of Electronic Records; Originals.

684 15 U.S. Code §7001(d)(4), Retention of contracts and records—Checks. 2011 Florida Statutes §668.50(12)(e) Retention of Electronic Records; Originals.

685 CUECIC Article 10, Time and place of dispatch and receipt of electronic communications.

686 See, for example, 2011 Florida Statutes §668.50(15), Time and Place of Sending and Receiving.

687 CUECIC Article 11, Invitations to make offers.

688 CUECIC Article 14, Error in electronic communications.

689 See, for example, 2011 Florida Statutes §668.50(10), Effect of Change or Error.

CHAPTER 4 – A Short History of Alternative Dispute Resolution (ADR)

690 See, for example, 14 Penn Plaza LLC v. Pyett, No. 07-581, U.S. Supreme Court (2009) (labor agreement requiring arbitration of age discrimination claims enforceable).

691 See, for example, District of Columbia Code §11-13-1321, Exclusive jurisdiction of small claims ($5,000 ceiling on Small Claims and Conciliation Branch jurisdiction, exclusive of interest, attorneys' fees, protest fees and costs, and excluding real property claims).

CHAPTER 5 - Organization of American States Proposals for Consumer Dispute Resolution

692 June 10, 1958, 21 U.S.T. 2517, T.I.A.S. No. 6997, 330 U.N. Treaty Series 38 (entered into force in the United States on 12/29/70.)

693 New York Convention, Article I.3.

694 See http://www.oas.org/en/default.asp.

695 See http://www.oas.org/dil/CIDIP-VII_consumer_protection_brazil_joint_proposal.htm.

696 See United States Response to Proposals for a Convention and Model Law on Jurisdiction and Applicable Law, April 16, 2010, available at http://www.oas.org/dil/CIDIP-VII_consumer_protection_brazil_joint_proposal_Comments _United_States.pdf.

697 See Legislative Guidelines for Inter-American Law on Availability of Consumer Dispute Resolution and Redress for Consumers ("Legislative Guidelines") submitted by the United States of America for CIDIP VII, available at http://www.oas.org/dil/Legislative_Guidelines_for_Inter-American_Law_on_Availability_of_Consumer_Dispute_Res olution_United_States.pdf.

698 See Annex A to Legislative Guidelines, available at http://www.oas.org/dil/esp/CIDIPVII_proteccion_al_cons umidor_united_states_guia_legislativa_anexo_A.pdf.

699 See Annex B to Legislative Guidelines, available at http://www.oas.org/dil/esp/CIDIPVII_proteccion_al_cons umidor_united_states_guia_legislativa_anexo_B.pdf.

700 See Annex C to Legislative Guidelines, available at http://www.oas.org/dil/esp/CIDIPVII_proteccion_al_cons umidor_united_states_guia_legislativa_anexo_C.pdf.

701 See Annex D to Legislative Guidelines, available at http://www.oas.org/dil/esp/CIDIPVII_proteccion_al_cons umidor_united_states_guia_legislativa_anexo_D.pdf.

702 See "Building a Practical Framework for Consumer Protection" (U.S. Presentation on Legislative Guidelines), page 26, available at http://www.oas.org/dil/CIDIP-VII_consumer_protection_united_states_presentation.pdf.

703 See Legislative Guidelines, Section 2.3, Scope and General Application.

704 See U.S. Presentation on Legislative Guidelines, page 46, and "Consumer Dispute Resolution and Redress in the Global Marketplace", Organization for Economic Cooperation and Development (2006), available at http://www.oecd.org/dataoecd/26/61/36456184.pdf.

705 Annex B to Legislative Guidelines, Section 2.2., "Consumer Credit Card Claim" definition.

706 Annex B to Legislative Guidelines, Section 2.6, "Consumer Payment Card Claim Notice" definition.

707 Annex B to Legislative Guidelines, Section 4, Right of credit cardholder to assert claims or defenses against card issuer.

708 See Annex A to Legislative Guidelines, Section 1,

Purpose - Comment.

709 See Annex A to Legislative Guidelines, Addendum I, Draft Model Rules for Electronic Resolution of Cross-Border E-Commerce Consumer Disputes, Section 9, Cost of ODR.

710 See Annex A to Legislative Guidelines, Section 9.3, Enforcement of Arbitration Awards and Agreements.

711 See Annex A to Legislative Guidelines, Section 7, Confidentiality and Reporting Requirements.

712 See Annex D to Legislative Guidelines, Section 5, Cross-Border Cooperation, and Section 6, Recognition of Foreign Civil Judgments for Consumer Redress.

713 See Annex D to Legislative Guidelines, footnote 6 citing Pub. L. No. 109-455 (2006).

714 See U.S. Presentation on Legislative Guidelines, page 49.

715 See U.S. Presentation on Legislative Guidelines, page 50, and Regulation of the European Parliament and of the Council No. EC 861/2007, May 22, 2007, available at http://register.consilium.europa.eu/pdf/en/07/st03/st03604.en07.pdf.

716 Annex C to Legislative Guidelines, Section 3, Scope of Claims.

717 Annex C to Legislative Guidelines, Section 7.4, Judgment and Collection.

718 Annex C to Legislative Guidelines, Section 8.2, Appeals.

719 See Legislative Guidelines, Section 4, Collective and/or Representational Dispute Resolution and Redress for Common Injuries to Consumers.

720 See Legislative Guidelines, Section 4.11.

721 15 U.S. Code §1666-1666j, available at http://www.gpo.gov/fdsys/pkg/USCODE-2011-title15/pdf/USCODE-2011-title15-chap41-subchapI-partD.pdf.

722 15 U.S. Code §1666(b), Correction of Billing Errors.

723 15 U.S. Code §1666(a).

724 15 U.S. Code §1666(e).

725 15 U.S. Code §1666i, Assertion by cardholder against issuer of claims and defenses arising out of credit card transaction; prerequisites; limitation on amount of claims or defenses.

726 15 U.S. Code §1607, Administrative enforcement.

727 15 U.S. Code §1693-1693r, available at http://www.gpo.gov/fdsys/pkg/USCODE-2011-title15/pdf/USCODE-2011-title15-chap41-subchapVI.pdf.

728 See Electronic Code of Federal Regulations (e-CFR), Title 12, Banks and Banking, Chapter II, Federal Reserve System, Subchapter A, Board of Governors of the Federal Reserve System, Part 205 – Electronic Fund Transfers (Regulation E), available at http://ecfr.gpoaccess.gov/cgi/t/text/text-idx?c=ecfr&tpl=/ecfrbrowse/Title12/12cfr205_main_02.tpl.

729 15 U.S. Code §1693f, Error resolution-- (f), Acts constituting error.

730 15 U.S. Code §1693f, Error resolution-- (c), Provisional recredit of consumer's account.

731 15 U.S. Code §1693f, Error resolution-- (e) Treble damages.

732 15 U.S. Code §1693m, Civil liability.

CHAPTER 6 – European Union Proposals for Consumer Online Dispute Resolution

733 2011/0374 (COD) Proposal for a Regulation of the European Parliament and of the Council on online dispute resolution for consumer disputes (Regulation on consumer ODR), available at http://ec.europa.eu/consumers/redress_cons/docs/odr_reg ulation_en.pdf.

734 2011/0373 (COD) Proposal for a Directive of the European Parliament and of the Council on alternative dispute resolution for consumer disputes and amending Regulation (EC) No 2006/2004 and Directive 2009/22/EC (Directive on consumer ADR), available at http://ec.europa.eu/consumers/redress_cons/docs/directive _adr_en.pdf.

735 See Position of the European Parliament…on online dispute resolution for consumer disputes (EP-PE_TC1-COD(2011)0374), Text No. A7-026/2012 available at http://www.europarl.europa.eu/plenary/en/texts-adopted.html#sidesForm.

736 See Consumer ODR Regulation, Article 9.3(a).

737 See Consumer ODR Regulation, Article 9.5(e).

CHAPTER 7 - United Nations Proposals for Consumer Online Dispute Resolution

738 Report of Working Group III (Online Dispute Resolution) on the work of its twenty-fifth session (New York, 21-25 May 2012) A/CN.9/744, 7 June 2012, paragraph 15 http://daccess-dds-ny.un.org/doc/UNDOC/GEN/ V12/540/19/PDF/V1254019.pdf?OpenElement.

739 Report of Working Group III, paragraph 118.

740 CUECIC Article 20, Communications exchanged under

other international conventions.

741 See Online dispute resolution for cross-border electronic commerce transactions: issues for consideration in the conception of a global ODR framework, Note by the Secretariat, A/CN.9/WG.III/WP.110, 28 September 2011, paragraphs 25-27.

742 See Note by the Secretariat, A/CN.9/WG.III/WP.110, paragraph 43.

743 See Note by the Secretariat, A/CN.9/WG.III/WP.110, paragraphs 48-49.

744 See Note by the Secretariat, A/CN.9/WG.III/WP.110, paragraph 50.

745 I first heard this term used by Judge Goodwin Liu of the U.S. Court of Appeals for the Ninth Circuit. It might have been used previously by others.

746 15 U.S.C. §§1693-1693r, available at http://www.federalreserve.gov/boarddocs/caletters/2008/0807/08-07_attachment.pdf.

747 This case is based partly on the 15th Annual Willem C. Vis International Commercial Moot Problem (2007-2008), available at
http://www.cisg.law.pace.edu/cisg/moot/moot15.pdf.

www.ingramcontent.com/pod-product-compliance
Lightning Source LLC
Chambersburg PA
CBHW061229220326
41599CB00028B/5376